OLD SCHOOLS

Sara Guyer and Brian McGrath, series editors

Lit Z embraces models of criticism uncontained by conventional notions of history, periodicity, and culture and committed to the work of reading. Books in the series may seem untimely, anachronistic, or out of touch with contemporary trends because they have arrived too early or too late. Lit Z creates a space for books that exceed and challenge the tendencies of our field and in doing so reflect on the concerns of literary studies here and abroad.

At least since Friedrich Schlegel, thinking that affirms literature's own untimeliness has been named "Romanticism." Recalling this history, Lit Z exemplifies the survival of Romanticism as a mode of contemporary criticism as well as forms of contemporary criticism that demonstrate the unfulfilled possibilities of Romanticism. Whether or not they focus on the Romantic period, books in this series epitomize Romanticism as a way of thinking that compels another relation to the present. Lit Z is the first book series to take seriously this capacious sense of Romanticism.

In 1977, Paul de Man and Geoffrey Hartman, two scholars of Romanticism, team-taught a course called "Literature Z" that aimed to make an intervention into the fundamentals of literary study. Hartman and de Man invited students to read a series of increasingly difficult texts and through attention to language and rhetoric compelled them to encounter "the bewildering variety of ways such texts could be read." The series' conceptual resonances with that class register the importance of recollection, reinvention, and reading to contemporary criticism. Its books explore the creative potential of reading's untimeliness and history's enigmatic force.

OLD SCHOOLS

Modernism, Education, and the Critique of Progress

Ramsey McGlazer

Fordham University Press
New York 2020

Copyright © 2020 Fordham University Press

All rights reserved. No part of this publication may be reproduced, stored in a retrieval system, or transmitted in any form or by any means—electronic, mechanical, photocopy, recording, or any other—except for brief quotations in printed reviews, without the prior permission of the publisher.

Fordham University Press has no responsibility for the persistence or accuracy of URLs for external or third-party Internet websites referred to in this publication and does not guarantee that any content on such websites is, or will remain, accurate or appropriate.

Fordham University Press also publishes its books in a variety of electronic formats. Some content that appears in print may not be available in electronic books.

Visit us online at www.fordhampress.com.

Library of Congress Cataloging-in-Publication Data available online at https://catalog.loc.gov.

Printed in the United States of America

22 21 20   5 4 3 2 1

First edition

for Bob Glazer, Martricia McLaughlin,
and Ryan and Mariele McGlazer

Contents

	Introduction: On Counter-Progressive Pedagogy	1
1.	Surviving *Marius*: Pater's Mechanical Exercise	25
2.	Among *Fanciulli*: Poetry, Pedantry, and Pascoli's *Paedagogium*	59
3.	"Copied Out Big": Instruction in Joyce's *Ulysses*	89
4.	*Salò* and the School of Abuse	114
5.	Schooling in Ruins: Glauber Rocha's Rome	137
	Acknowledgments	161
	Notes	165
	Index	219

OLD SCHOOLS

Introduction:
On Counter-Progressive Pedagogy

> She followed not all, a part of the whole, gave attention with interest, comprehended with surprise, with care repeated, with greater difficulty remembered, forgot with ease, with misgiving reremembered, rerepeated with error.
> —James Joyce, *Ulysses*

With these phrases, the narrator of Joyce's "Ithaca" renders Molly Bloom's experience of "direct instruction."[1] From the perspective of her teacher, who is interested in outcomes, this experience is not a success. Molly's insouciance and inconsistency, as recorded in the sentence above, lead the self-appointed pedagogue Leopold Bloom to adopt a "more effective" and modern approach: "indirect suggestion implicating selfinterest" (*U* 17.703–4). Joyce's language suggests here, however, that the "direct" method proves surprisingly enabling—more so, in fact, than the updated, "implicating" alternative. The latter leads, in "Ithaca," to an ultimately straightforward if initially perplexing consumer equation: "She disliked umbrella with rain, he liked woman with umbrella, she disliked new hat with rain, he liked woman with new hat, he bought new hat with rain, she carried umbrella with new hat" (*U* 17.706–8). Note the relative predictability of the sentence, its directness, even, "indirect suggestion" notwithstanding. It's as if "indirect suggestion implicating selfinterest" could yield only this parade of pros, cons, and commodities, this regular succession of dislikes and likes.

By contrast, as my epigraph suggests, "direct instruction" produces rich and strange results, both conceptual and syntactic. Such instruction, which might at first seem to demand full concentration by definition, in fact allows the student to follow "not at all" or only in part. Like *Ulysses* itself, "direct instruction" affords a range of possibilities for comprehension and repetition, remembering and forgetting, reremembering and rerepeating. And the variation in the narrator's formulations belies their obvious and joking repetitiousness. Joyce's verbs and adverbial phrases, for instance, only belatedly and uneasily settle into the chiastic alternation toward which they tend all along, and we are invited to notice that to rerepeat is already to repeat "with error." Here, then, the "Ithaca" episode, structured like a catechism, shows the convergence of repetition and difference that instruction makes possible, the coexistence of past and present, memory and forgetting, recall and imagination, that it sustains.

Readers may be surprised to find such an apology for "direct instruction" in a text like *Ulysses*, a novel committed to radical formal innovation, written by an author who, as a young man, had forsworn instruction precisely.[2] Surely, we might think, nothing could be further from the flagrantly rule-breaking Joycean text than the rule-bound method that the narrator names "direct instruction"? Surely one main aim of "Ithaca" is to highlight the contrast between the novel's enlivening capaciousness, on the one hand, and the deadening constraints of the old-school catechism, on the other? Surely Joyce, like his character Bloom, abandons instruction in favor of a novel approach to the novel, one that lets us draw our own connections, revel in our own associations, and, above all, think for ourselves?

Before we can answer these questions—or rethink our first, reflexive answers to them—we need to ask another, simpler one: what is "instruction"? In 1919, just before Joyce returned to Trieste from Zurich, the idealist philosopher and educational reformer Giovanni Gentile, later made minister of education under Mussolini, presented a series of lectures to Triestine schoolteachers that undertook to offer rigorous definitions of key concepts in pedagogy, including instruction. Gentile's lectures, published during Joyce's brief 1920 stay in Trieste as *La riforma dell'educazione: Discorsi ai maestri di Trieste* [*The Reform of Education: Addresses to the Teachers of Trieste*], took pains to distinguish true education from mere "instruction," which, for Gentile and his followers, named a specific set of outmoded educational practices long associated with Latin class. These practices were, Gentile argued, "narrow, formal, and sterile"; they were alienating rather than absorbing, deadening rather than enlivening, merely repetitive rather than allowing for innovation of any kind.[3] Indeed, they were queer, if, in Penelope Deutscher's paraphrase of Lee Edelman, "to be queer is to have the death drive projected onto you."[4] Education was a matter of what Edelman calls "compulsory reproduction," and instruction posed a queer threat to this undertaking, which it thwarted. Hence the charge of sterility.[5] The prevalence of instructional practices led, Gentile argued, to the creation and persistence of a stagnant culture: "Intruding with violence into the life of the spirit, instruction generates the monstrous culture that we call material, mechanical, and spiritually worthless."[6] Such a culture could not but be "fragmentary and inorganic," and yet it could grow, Gentile continued: "It can grow to infinity without transforming students' minds or merging with the process of the personality, to which it adheres extrinsically."[7] Such outward adherence, like Joycean "direct instruction," could only be partial—in the words of the narrator in "Ithaca," "a part of the whole." It could forge neither whole selves nor whole nations.

Gentile therefore devised an approach to education that was inward as well as integrative. This approach was also—counterintuitively, given Gentile's political leanings—progressive.[8] It followed from the philosopher's discovery of the "secret" of effective education, as disclosed in his lectures in Trieste: "that the book that is read, or the word of the teacher that is heard, must set our mind in motion and be transformed into our inner life, ceasing to be a thing ... and being transfused [trasferendosi] into our personality."[9] Unlike Joyce's narrator, Gentile does not use the language of self-interest here, and his goals are spiritual rather than material. Reformed education, according to Gentile, forms personalities and minds; it does not traffic with things. In fact, Gentile finds fault with "instruction" for such traffic precisely. We would thus seem to be far from the Blooms' umbrellas and new hats. Clearly, though, the new method that Gentile advocates is, in theory if not in practice, nothing if not "implicating"; it shares with Joyce's "indirect suggestion implicating self-interest" an investment in the student's "inner life." Whereas instruction centers on memorization and compels repetition, Gentile's education and Joyce's indirect suggestion alike seek transformation.

But "Ithaca" teaches us to ask: transformation to what end? And what's lost when "direct instruction" is replaced by other, kinder and gentler, more efficient and more implicating educational techniques? *Old Schools* proceeds from these questions and considers the striking answers given in works by Walter Pater, Giovanni Pascoli, Joyce, Pier Paolo Pasolini, and Glauber Rocha. Reading across Italian- and English-language contexts and across genres and media, I trace a modernist countertradition's surprising affinities with the very instructional methods that Gentile decried. I argue that instruction's outward and outmoded forms become key resources for the kind of radical aesthetic project that they might appear to rule out, or at least to impede. I thus challenge a still-abiding tendency to locate modernism's critical potential in its attempt to break with the past or make it new. This tendency, I show, is continuous with both the ethos of the avant-gardes, with their Marinettian "love of progress,"[10] and the discourse of progressive pedagogy, with its roots in Jean-Jacques Rousseau and its twentieth-century culmination in the work of John Dewey.[11] Gentile's *La riforma* exemplifies the latter discourse, which takes rightist as well as radically democratic forms, and which remains influential in educational theory and practice today. Joyce's "direct instruction," by contrast, instantiates the pedagogy that I call "counter-progressive."

By claiming that *La riforma* and *Ulysses* bear rereading alongside one another, I do not mean to suggest that Joyce drew direct inspiration—or, indeed, direct instruction—from Gentile's lectures. Clearly, though, the Irish author and language teacher, residing in Italy, would have been aware of the debates that both preceded and followed the influential *Discorsi*.[12] These debates pitted old-school instructors—a whole old, degraded institution called "instruction"—against progressive educators equipped to usher students into modernity, to sponsor both collective innovation and individual self-realization. If at first it seems obvious that Joyce would side with the latter camp—that he would be among the moderns, not the ancients; the educators, not the instructors; the advocates of the mind in motion, not the defenders of mechanical exercise—*Ulysses* suggests otherwise. In "Ithaca" and elsewhere in the novel, Joyce recasts the old school's forms as unlikely resources for both creativity and critique. Joyce wagers, then, with the Ithacan narrator and against Gentile, that "direct instruction" is strangely more enabling than the "more effective," modernized and modernizing teaching that takes its place. With its enforced repetitions and formative wastes of time, instruction becomes the model for the counter-progressive text itself.

The Problem of the School

A later moment in Gentile's reception provides another key context for understanding the engagements with instruction that I will investigate—backward engagements that, I will argue, are motivated neither by nostalgia nor by a merely reactionary impulse. In the twelfth of his *Prison Notebooks*, Antonio Gramsci refuses the distinction between instruction and education, on which so much of Gentile's pedagogical philosophy rests. For, Gramsci argues, education is also instruction; the former cannot do away with the latter. And this implies—again, perhaps scandalously to today's teaching sensibilities—that education cannot do without a degree of compulsion, or what Gramsci memorably calls "coercizione meccanica," "mechanical coercion."[13] This may be the inverse of the more familiar, affirmative, and humanist Gramscian claim that "in any physical work, even the most mechanical and degraded, there exists a minimum of technical qualification, that is, a minimum of creative intellectual activity" (*QC* 1516; *PN* 8, trans. modified). In no sense do Gramsci's reflections on instruction cancel out this celebrated account of the universality of intellectual capacities.[14] Still, his pedagogical reflections remain startling for the force and thoroughness of their dismantling of "libertarian ideologies" and progressive fictions (*QC* 1537; *PN* 32). These fictions, on which Gentile's idealist pedagogy depends and which this pedagogy perpetuates, insist on the child's wholeness, his active nature, his propensity for play, his spontaneity. Gramsci's sobering corrective instead makes education a matter of work or labor (*lavoro*) first and foremost (*QC* 1542; *PN* 35): labor driven by a contradiction or "coercion" that knows itself, rather than masquerading as freedom, as in the mystifications of Gentile's progressive pedagogy. Whereas Gentile sought, in his own phrase, "the liberation of the school from mechanism,"[15] Gramsci deemed such liberation impossible. His acknowledgment that all education is also instruction implies an acceptance of repetition, discipline, and even deadness—of negotiation not only with the "things" that Gentile would conjure away in his effort to spiritualize (where "the book that is read or the word of the teacher that is heard" must, he insists, "ceas[e] to be a thing and b[e] transfused into our personality"),[16] but more specifically with "dead things." For without such things, Gramsci claims arrestingly, there can be no real study among children: "all analyses made by children cannot but be of dead things" (*QC* 1544; *PN* 38).

The dead things that Gramsci has in mind are words in a dead language, specifically Latin words. And Latin's privileged place in his notes on instruction registers its status as a target of the reformers' polemics. Just as traditional education centered on "the learning by heart of Latin grammar," that is, Latin came to stand for this education's inefficiency, its obsolescence.[17] Instruction, in the discourse of reformers, was a relic from the premodern past. Hence the need that Gentile and others perceived: to update instruction so thoroughly as to clear it away. Yet this clearing was always meant to be differential, not indiscriminate. Gentile objected, in other words, not to Latin as such but rather to its function as what Gramsci calls the "fulcrum" in all public schools (*QC* 1546; *PN* 39). In the policies known as the Riforma Gentile, implemented by Gentile in his capacity as minister of education under Mussolini in 1923, Latin retained a key place in the education of the ruling class. But for other students—for most students—in the new, tiered school system, which now included vocational tracks, Latin was no longer compulsory.

These reforms, realized by a fascist regime but underwritten by progressive educational theories, form the backdrop of Gramsci's reflections, and they help to account for the paradox of the Marxist's "apparently 'conservative' eulogy for the old curriculum."[18] Though nominally democratic, the Riforma Gentile in fact entrenched class hierarchies, Gramsci observes, to the point of tending to "eternare," to render them eternal (*QC* 1547). The new policies deprived all but the most elite students of the training in patience and comparison and the practice for critical reflection that, according to Gramsci, alone sustain democracy. Latin had long since marked the place of this training and practice, and the *Notebooks* locate the dead language's pedagogical—and indeed political—value not ultimately in its substance or the civilizational "myth" that attaches to it (QC 1544–45; PN 38). To be sure, Gramsci sees value in this myth as well, even while he opposes the Fascist iteration of it.[19] But above all, in his view, instruction in Latin offers *forms* of discipline and disinterest (QC 1531, 1543; PN 27, 37), where the latter already implies an association with the aesthetic, as if what instruction made available to students were a version of Kantian aesthetic experience.[20] The Latin class is a repository of these forms, the site of "a cultural-scholastic tradition" (QC 1545; PN 38, trans. modified) and an intellectual "itinerary" (QC 1546; PN 39). It is an experience, often though not always an ordeal, that is undergone, rather than primarily a means of imparting knowledge or instilling belief, let alone shoring up (national or imperial) identity.

Gramsci's views on Latin should thus be sharply distinguished not only from Gentile's, but also from T. S. Eliot's more familiar modernist classicism. For Eliot, famously, "the Roman Empire and the Latin language were not any empire and any language, but an empire and a language with a unique destiny in relation to ourselves."[21] To learn Latin was to participate in this singular destiny—indeed, "to come into our inheritance."[22] Eliot's is thus almost literally a "banking concept" of education, or of instruction: to learn Latin is to acquire cultural capital, however laboriously; it is to be enriched by contact with "our parentage."[23] For his part, Gramsci thinks of Latin as a kind of "'baggage' or 'equipment'" (QC 1542; PN 36). Far from being a treasury or trust fund, as in Eliot's formulations, the dead language is, for Gramsci, a weight to be borne or a set of tools to be wielded. These figures are in keeping with Gramsci's insistence that, first and foremost, instruction forms habits and develops critical capacities. Although he stops short of suggesting that Latin could be "any language" whatsoever, Gramsci does go so far as to claim that "one does not study Latin in order to learn the language" (QC 1545; PN 38). For this very reason, though—that is, by virtue of its privileging of forms and processes over contents—the Latin class becomes a truly democratic training camp. Much more than the ostensibly open technical schools peddled by Gentile and the Fascist regime, it seeks to prepare everyone, including every child of the subaltern classes, to govern (QC 1547; PN 40). "Mechanical coercion" in the Latin class—its very compulsoriness, what Gentile would call its violent intrusion into the life of the spirit—can in this way represent a traditional, even a retrograde means to a radical end.

For Gramsci, the co-optation of progressive pedagogy by the Fascist regime revealed this pedagogy's inherent limitations, its capacity to sustain a false promise of liberation. Though potentially broadly enabling, progressive education could also serve as an alibi for a narrowing of interest and foreclosure of collective possibility. This, at least, would be one way to translate Gramsci's lesson on Latin, which would thus prompt us to interrogate the progressive pedagogy that many of us still tend to treat as an unqualified good.

To this end, we might begin by rereading *Émile*. Indeed, like Molly Bloom, we might "reremember" that text "with misgiving." For Rousseau, who stipulates that his model pupil "will never learn anything by heart," the kind of education that centered on repetition and recall—and the curriculum that centered on the Latin class—led to broad collective stagnation and stunted growth.[24] The old school stood in the way of progress, impeding both individual and social advancement: "All our practices are only subjection, impediment, and constraint," Rousseau complains of actually existing schools.[25] Reforming these schools would therefore not only mean liberating students from the needless chores that made for "sad and sterile childhoods."[26] It would also put an end to the dependency, at once intellectual and political, that continued into adulthood. Such reformed education, in short, would finally fashion citizens rather than subjects, free men rather than mere trained animals.[27]

To be sure, many of the reforms inspired by Rousseau's critique of the old school have been enabling. Neither *Old Schools* nor the works that it considers suggest that we should dispense with or could do without the progressive tradition that *Émile* inaugurates. Instead, drawing on a tradition of immanent critique, I argue that what Rousseau and those who follow him—including Gentile—call the student's "freedom" is not, in fact, the absence of constraint but its occlusion or mystification.[28] In influential strands of progressive educational theory, unavoidable and unavoidably formative intergenerational contradiction is disguised as play, just as the inescapable imposition of language masquerades as the child's spontaneous self-expression. In the old school, by contrast, contradiction and imposition know themselves, and the student knows them, too, undeniably. But this very knowledge, this acknowledgment, can prevent the student from *internalizing* the teacher's demand, confusing it with her own interest or what Gentile would call her "inner life." Instruction's very outwardness, its avowal of the compulsory, would thus preserve the distance that makes it possible for the student to do something other than what's imposed, simultaneously: to daydream, to drift and deviate, to cultivate her resources for resistance and refusal.

Admittedly, this last possibility is only latent in Gramsci. The *Prison Notebooks* attend mainly to the transposability of scholastic discipline—its implications for the production of intellectuals and for the creation of democracy—rather than to the dialectical *reversal* of this discipline that Joyce lets us locate in the scene of "direct instruction," and that will become increasingly important as the following chapters proceed, finding its most vivid realization in Rocha.[29] But Gramsci does explicitly suggest that the old school is worth revisiting because it encourages the avowal of what progressive education—or modernizing reform as represented by the Riforma Gentile—disavows.

There can be no denying that his defense of the old school sounds "old-fashioned," as Gayatri Chakravorty Spivak has conceded.[30] Yet Spivak also points to the urgency of returning to Gramsci's work in the context of new educational crises, different from but not altogether unrelated to those that Gramsci faced. Without emphasizing Latin or engaging specifically with the Riforma Gentile, Spivak valorizes the "tough effortfulness" of education in Gramsci's writings and argues for their relevance to the joint project of defending and rethinking "humanist education" today.[31] Noting that the Italian theorist made such education central to his version of Marxism, Spivak also adduces Gramsci to identify another set of disavowals. Citing Gramsci, that is, Spivak counters "both 'the position assumed by the social complex of intellectuals [whose philosophy] can be defined as the expression of that social utopia by which intellectuals think of themselves as "independent," autonomous, endowed with a character of their own, etc.' and those who have forgotten that 'school is the instrument through which intellectuals of various levels are elaborated.'"[32] Spivak's arrangement of these Gramscian citations lets us see that the school's occlusion both follows from and furthers the effort to shore up intellectual autonomy—where "autonomy" is defined not in the sense of Theodor Adorno's "education for autonomy," which is "really an education for contradiction and resistance,"[33] but as a fantasy according to which intellectuals are effectively self-taught.

Indeed, a forgetting of the school has marked recent studies of modernism.[34] This is less obviously true in the Italian case than in the English-language one. It has become something of a commonplace to note Pasolini's pedagogical commitments, for instance, and Pascoli's have likewise been impossible to ignore.[35] Still, even studies of these authors have stopped short of the theorization that I undertake here as I seek to recover the aesthetic and political potentials of the countertradition that I identify. This means working against still-prevalent liberal and progressive assumptions, "oriented to freedom [defined as noncoercion] and autonomous agency against the background of a modern social imaginary," where the modernity of this imaginary is thought to entail a refusal of convention and constraint.[36]

Inasmuch as what Gramsci calls "the old school" names the place of this convention and constraint, it stands to reason that progressive criticism has sought to leave it behind. But Gramsci's *Notebooks* suggest that the attempt to abandon instruction may constitute a betrayal of education as such. It may entail consequences that are significantly less liberating than the release from scholastic strictures would seem. The works that I study in what follows all indicate why this is the case. And they share in Gramsci's vision of instruction, whether anticipating it, as do Pater, Pascoli, and Joyce, or inheriting it, as do Pasolini and Rocha. With his reassessment of the old school in the wake of its eclipse, Gramsci establishes a template for the texts treated in this book's chapters, even if his version of the old school is philosophical, whereas the authors and directors I consider set instruction to work aesthetically. I call their aesthetic efforts counter-, and not anti-, progressive because, like the Gramscian account, written after the Riforma Gentile, they look to the old school for means of resisting the "progress" that levels while pretending to liberate, and this resistance constitutes a response, not a denial.

Teaching Styles

The texts and films that I address thus all refuse to leave the past behind. I mean this in a double sense: they refuse to abandon, or to graduate from, the past in order to attend to the concerns of the present on its "own" terms, as progressive ideologies would dictate; but they also studiously avoid leaving *themselves* behind as appropriable pasts, as lessons easily learned. Instead, these texts and films foreground—and compound—the conditions that thwart transmission even while they insist, like Gramsci, on transmission's crucial importance and radical potential. It is as if only a prolonged dwelling in and on obstruction could lead to this blockage's giving way to something else.

Each of this book's chapters considers a late style, then. And in each case lateness implies both untimeliness and programmatic difficulty. "Late style is *in*, but oddly *apart* from the present," according to Edward Said,[37] whose definition recalls the distinction that I just have made between anti- and counter-progressive tendencies. For to be in and apart is not to deny, but rather to respond to—even to "militat[e] ferociously against"—the present.[38] It is actively to counter, rather than to conjure away, the modernity from which one takes distance through a "regression from *now* to *back then*."[39] Indeed, anachronism inheres in late-career regressions or "retreats" as dissimilar as Pater's and Pasolini's. "Lateness" in their works, as in those Said discusses, becomes "a kind of self-imposed exile from what is generally acceptable, coming after it, and surviving beyond it."[40] But Pater's late lectures and Pasolini's last essays also share other key qualities of the late style that Said identifies: "sustained tension, unaccommodated stubbornness," "*negativity*," and obscurity.[41] These qualities pervade the works that I discuss even when, like Pater's *Marius* or Pascoli's *Paedagogium*, they might seem to reach for resolution, or when negativity is leavened by humor, as in Joyce or Rocha. All of the texts that I treat derive their "negative power," to repeat Said's paraphrase of Adorno, from their "dissonant relationship with the affirmative developmental thrust" of progressive discourse, often also the thrust of the same authors' earlier works.⁴²

I thus look to moments in authors' careers that some readers might reflexively dismiss as reactionary. In this sense, I follow the lead of the works that I analyze. My approach, too, is counter-progressive, in other words—not because it privileges earlier texts over later ones, but rather inasmuch as it valorizes backward- rather than forward-looking works. Let me explain. Every right-thinking reader knows how to love—and has been trained to affirm—the Pater of the liberating "Conclusion" to his *Studies in the History of the Renaissance*; the Pascoli whose lyrics entered Italian public schools; the Joyce of *Dubliners* and *A Portrait of the Artist as a Young Man*; and the Pasolini of the exuberant *Trilogy of Life* (1971–74). The same might even be said of Rocha, whose work I consider in Chapter 5: the early films of his Cinema Novo present serious challenges, but their youthful energy remains irresistible. In each case, we affirm these works because they conform to our faith in the new, which we know to be good. Pater bravely casts off the strictures of convention in his "Conclusion," just as, at the end of *A Portrait*, Joyce's Stephen Dedalus leaves behind an imprisoning familial past and a parochial Irish scene. Pascoli the vernacular lyricist and author of *Il fanciullino* keeps renewing his commitment to youth in verse and prose, just as Pasolini addresses "la meglio gioventù," "the best of youth," time and again. Even when this youth seemed to be disappearing, Pasolini sought to salvage something of it, to sing it back into existence, however impossibly. Hence the title of his late collection *La nuova gioventù*; for all its disaffection, this late verse still unfolds under the sign of the new.

Something different happens, though, in *Salò o le 120 giornate di Sodoma* [*Salò or the 120 Days of Sodom*] (1975) and the writings that surround it, works that are at the center of Chapter 4. Here Pasolini "abjure[s] the *Trilogy of Life*" and takes distance from all that it celebrates: youth and sexual freedom, rebellious bodies and their lovable vitality.⁴³ *Salò* instead illustrates the persistence of old regimes, of forces of constraint and coercion that no amount of youthful energy can vanquish. The film undertakes this demonstration, according to Pasolini, for reasons related to "legibility."⁴⁴ But this legibility turns out to give rise not to vernacular ease or viewer-friendliness, but rather to lessons reminiscent of, if not modeled on or "after," as in this book's former working title, "After School," the old-school Latin class. *Salò* returns to, even while it reimagines, this class and its ritual function. Like the techniques of instruction, Pasolini's punishing insistence on the survival of outmoded powers compels viewers to reckon with a past that they would abandon and thus deny. In this way, *Salò* distills even while it radicalizes the broader tendency—the late turn or return—that *Old Schools* sets out to analyze. Various though they are, all of the works I treat share a determination to register the past's persistence, enlisting outmoded scholastic forms in the service of a critique of the ideology of progress. Although the definition and political inflections of progress differ in each case, a narrative or conceit of progress that privileges the new and posits a liberating break with the old remains consistently the target of my authors' polemics, whether the latter are overt or, as in the case of Joyce, mediated by fiction.

This counterintuitive transvaluation of the old school—its return and radical recasting in modernist literature and cinema—has analogs in other contexts. The processes that I examine represent only one set of attempts to redeploy what Raymond Williams calls "the residual" in response to a consolidation of the cultural "dominant."[45] Other instances could of course be identified. To take just two examples from earlier moments in European modernity: Massimiliano Biscuso and Franco Gallo argue compellingly that in the context of an ascendant bourgeois culture in Italy, the "aristocratic" thought of Giacomo Leopardi becomes a potentially revolutionary resource.[46] Anne-Lise François comparably reassesses an "aristocratic ethos" found in certain strains of Romanticism.[47] Though mediated by pastoral forms that might appear retrograde, this ethos, for François, offers alternatives to "the modern ideology of improvement"; "this ethos," François further contends, "far from negating, keeps alive the possibility of imaginative exercise" and counters the foreclosures of capitalism, so often falsely presented as sources of openness.[48]

Scholars of modernism have also highlighted how the reinvention of old forms often marked attempts to forge the new. Recently, Barry McCrea has drawn attention to the role of "the vanishing vernaculars of the European peasant world" in the modernist effort "to find or invent new linguistic forms."[49] Benjamin Baer has similarly repositioned "the peasant and the autochthon" in modernist writing: far from lagging behind the metropolitan authors who looked to them repeatedly, these figures, Baer shows, came to occupy modernity's "cutting edge."[50] Decades ago, Jean Franco already analyzed a related phenomenon in the work of the Peruvian modernist César Vallejo. In Franco's account, Vallejo comes to imagine himself as "a poet-prophet who is not avant-garde or 'vanguard' but, as it were, bringing up the rear," following rather than leading the workers his late poems intermittently address.[51]

All of these critical approaches have informed my own.[52] But I consider a different site of the residual, one that, to my knowledge, has not recently been seen to shelter radical potential. On the contrary, the old school and the Latin class in particular have seemed beyond saving. They have looked to us—as they looked to their nineteenth- and twentieth-century detractors, including Gentile—like sites of stagnation that allowed for nothing more than the rote repetition of the same. In arguing that there is a critical rather than merely antiquarian, revivalist, nostalgic, or reactionary use of instruction in modernism, I am therefore closer to Biscuso, Gallo, and François—or to Robert Kaufman, who analyzes the persistence of Romantic lyric in the twentieth century—than to the scholars of modernism whom I have just mentioned.[53] Rather than bringing modernist projects into closer proximity with the rural poor or revolutionary workers as do McCrea, Baer, and Franco, I align it with an institution that had long since been claimed by and for an elite.[54] (Compare the Leopardian *letterato* discussed by Biscuso and Gallo; François's pastoral; Kaufman's lyric aura; or Said's late style.)[55] At the same time, though, following Gramsci, I work to show that this institution came to house other possibilities, irreducible to and even at odds with the "shoring . . . up" of "apparatuses of power."[56] These were, I argue, the possibilities that a modernist countertradition recognized and that it undertook to realize in an effort to counter the ideology of progress.

This claim may still seem to be merely perverse, suspiciously contrarian. But when read closely and with a willingness to suspend liberal and progressive certainties, the texts that I consider in what follows all bear out my counterintuitive claim, while attesting both to the recurrence and to the range of the aesthetic pedagogy that I call counter-progressive. These texts also compel us to rethink familiar accounts of education in modernity. Such accounts often stress the school's role as "ideological state apparatus,"[57] or as guarantor "of legitimation of the social order and of hereditary transmission of privileges."[58] Does the school not, after all, one such account asks, "contribute towards persuading each social subject to stay in the place which falls to him *by nature*, to know his place and hold to it"?[59] Does the school not function as a technology of domination or at least of hegemony?

Indeed, it does. There can be no denying the school's—and especially the old school's—deadening, mind-numbing, merely norm-consolidating potentials. But an abiding and nearly exclusive emphasis on these potentials, in our accounts of modernism in particular, has prevented us from attending to what Judith Butler calls, in another context, "the possibility of a counterdiscourse that emerges in the midst of breakdown, animating the remnants of a broken" and outmoded "ideological machine for critical purposes."[60] We might also call this, with Stefania Pandolfo, the possibility of an "other space of the institution" that the counter-progressive tradition makes visible.[61] I would argue that we have ignored this possibility at our peril, for it has become difficult to articulate defenses of endangered, sometimes already decimated, institutions, given our widely shared if often only ostensible anti-institutional bent, or to make the case for schools given our notional commitment to deschooling. It has become difficult, in other words, to defend teaching when we have complied, as Stefano Harney and Fred Moten suggest, with the demand to get beyond it, affirming instead, time and again, the value of being self-taught.[62]

An "other space of the institution" might allow, however, for the flourishing of resistances even in contexts of compulsory docility. It might provide a venue for the elaboration of forms not compliantly synced up with capitalist modernity. Such a space might, then, become a kind of refuge, letting students take distance from demands for individual self-realization and collective self-identity. Allowing for the interruption of these progressive demands, the teaching that happens in this "other space" might *not*, then, ultimately keep the pupil in place or emphasize what "falls to him *by nature*"; on the contrary, under certain conditions, and perhaps against all odds, it might denaturalize and in this way promote a certain kind of mobility, if only one exercised behind the institution's back or in its interstices.[63]

Importantly, the works that I study do not merely represent such an other space; they actively seek to produce it, by *administering* the instruction that they thematize. They interpellate readers and spectators as pupils, and in the process they programmatically solicit many of the resistances associated with the brick-and-mortar old school, even while they afford pleasures ranging from the comic (as in Joyce's "Oxen of the Sun") to the voyeuristic (as in Pasolini's *Salò*). Imitating while also reimagining the old school's techniques, works ranging from Pater's *Marius* to Rocha's *Claro* bore us with their didactic digressions. They block our narrative interest and impede our understanding. They cause us to chafe against the limitations they impose. But these very blockages, impediments, and frustrations become formative; these difficulties and the resistances to which they give rise constitute the means by which these authors make the case—the increasingly radical case, as I'll show—for the school that progressive reformers and liberal critics would leave behind.

Latin for Losers

Counter-progressive pedagogy thus names a mode rather than a mere theme. And the specificity of the works—the coherence of the countertradition—that I discuss derives in part from this distinction. A pair of contrastive examples can shed light on this specificity by indicating what counter-progressive pedagogy is not. It is not, to be clear, any and every representation of the old school still in session in modernity, or any and every instance of Latin still in use in a modern text. *Madame Bovary*, for instance, opens with a famously strange schoolroom scene. In this brief episode, to which I will return in Chapter 3, a teacher assigns two pensums, requiring both the slow, bullied Charles Bovary and the rest of the class repeatedly to copy out phrases as punishment. But Flaubert nowhere takes cues from this pedagogue; in no sense does his opening scene itself resemble the repetitive pensum its teacher assigns. Neither does Flaubert return to or redeploy this scholastic punishment later in his novel, although he did compare "the chore of writing *Madame Bovary*" to a pensum precisely.[64]

Anthony Asquith's film *The Browning Version* (1951) deals with traditional education at greater length and might therefore seem more likely to belong to the set of texts that *Old Schools* assembles. The film follows Mr. Crocker-Harris (Michael Redgrave), a prematurely aged classics teacher in an old-fashioned English public school (Figure 1). This master's class, "the soul-destroying lower fifth," is so regimented—and the master himself so uninspired and mechanical in his methods—that "the boys have been known to set their watches by his comings and goings," in one character's words (Figure 2). Crocker-Harris is pathetically pitted against a representative of "the modern psychological method," a fresh-faced and progressive younger instructor who will soon replace him. Far from siding with its protagonist, though, *The Browning Version* is, like this replacement teacher, both modern and psychological. There is nothing soul-destroying and very little that's regimented about Asquith's direction, even during the film's early schoolroom scenes. Protracted silences in these scenes register students' boredom, but these silences never last so long as to suspend the flow of the film's narrative, which requires that the old teacher recognize and renounce the anachronism that he has become.

Indeed, when this recognition finally takes place, the teacher admits to being already dead; he can produce nothing more, he says, than "the muscular twitchings of a corpse." But, his interlocutor in this scene insists, "a corpse can be revived!" The latter man speaks for the film, which remains committed to reanimation. So in keeping with a different regular schedule—that of progress, not the Latin class—Crocker-Harris returns to life. In order to be made fully human again, though, he must be brought down to the level of his students; he must become what Paulo Freire will call a "student among students."[65] This process is marked as complete in the film's final exchange, when a student tells Crocker-Harris that his translation in progress

Figure 1. Teaching as "Muscular Twitching." *The Browning Version* (1951).

Figure 2. "The Soul-Destroying Lower Fifth." *The Browning Version* (1951).

of Aeschylus is "worth finishing"—because "it's like a modern play." The student in this classically progressive scene schools his master; the child fathers the man. But well before this moment, the film has visually signaled—and trained us both to desire and to expect—the bad teacher's transformation into a good-enough one, the old school's effectively becoming the new. A dissolve shows Crocker-Harris's empty classroom, with the image of the teacher at his home desk superimposed onto the students' vacant seats. The old schoolmaster comes to occupy the place of those whom he instructs, and he must do so in order to be deemed worthy of them. Progressive pedagogue that he is, Crocker-Harris's replacement has taken his place among these students from the first. But the older Crocker-Harris must be schooled in the ways of the new generation. For their part, the students, like those whom Gentile imagined, must be liberated from mechanism, taught not by a corpse but by a living spirit. In Gentile's terms, they must be educated, not instructed.

In the end, *The Browning Version* thus affirms the values with which we approach it as progressive spectators. It confirms what we already know and congratulates us in our knowingness. A realist text—based on a "modern play" that is not a modernist one—Asquith's film takes distance from the figure at its center, and it builds toward the climactic conversion of this figure, both narratively and at the level of the image, as we have seen. The disciplinarian is himself disciplined, though by apparently uncoercive means, through lessons taught by a child. To be sure, these lessons entail plenty of shame and social humiliation for Crocker-Harris, but such hard knocks are nothing, the film suggests, compared to the soul-destruction that he has long overseen as master of the lower fifth. "Out with the old," Asquith's film thus says. And is this not the progressive—and democratizing—educational dictate par excellence?

Gramsci has already offered us ways to complicate our ingrained, automatic "yes." The chapters that follow continue the work that my discussion of Gramsci's response to the Riforma Gentile began: that of resisting the slippage between "progress," or modernization, on the one hand, and democratization, on the other. This slippage still characterizes our approaches to education when they center on innovation and individuation.[66] Indeed, in this sense, the Rousseauist and Deweyan—or the Gentilean—legacy lives. Consider this basic tenet of neoliberal educational reform, borrowed from earlier progressive pedagogical theories: that we should "personalize" education and see students "not as receivers of information, but as shapers of knowledge," as so many self-starters in the making.[67] Student-centered teaching, with its emphasis on play, self-guidance, and spontaneity and its eschewal of rote exercise, has long since become hegemonic, at least in theory, at least in the humanities.[68] In the Gramscian sense, such teaching constitutes our common sense. Alternatives to such student-centered approaches have been rendered marginal, residual. In particular, practices that privilege repetition rather than variation and constraint rather than "freedom" have become heretical for right-thinking humanities educators.[69]

But perhaps the very relegation of these methods to the trash heap of history suggests that they're worth returning to—if not salvaging wholesale, then at least reassessing, rereading. Imagine that, rather than being revived and modernized, Asquith's Crocker-Harris had remained "a corpse." Then imagine that this corpse's very deadness had something to teach us—that this deadness, this difference from the living present and distance from students' self-interest, this status as a cadaverous "thing" with which students would not identify, were a strength rather than a weakness, a resource rather than a deficiency. This is the wager shared by the authors I study here: that the old school's potentials remained unspent and that the Latin class, as the site of a long-dead language and defunct tradition, might yet shelter alternative possibilities, that it might put students in touch with still-available resources from the past and even in some cases show them ways out of a present impasse. Pascoli, the subject of Chapter 2, expresses this last hope most forcefully, even while his Latin poem *Paedagogium* takes formal cues from the old school's grammar drills. Pater similarly makes the "mechanical exercise" into an organizing formal principle in his late works. Against Pater's own early liberal assertions and a backdrop of broad progressive educational reform, these works affirm both the past's persistence and instruction's complicating influence.[70] Even more complicating is Joyce's use of the pensum, or the punitive copying out of text, to structure "Oxen of the Sun," a use that at once refers back to and outbids *Bovary*'s beginning, as I argue in Chapter 5. In my final chapters, I turn to the modernist cinema of Pasolini and Rocha in order to consider corporal punishment in *Salò* and repetitious lectures in Rocha's *Claro* (1975).[71]

Returns to Rome

These brief chapter summaries already indicate that although counter-progressive pedagogy depends on the setting to work of deadness and temporal difference, another ingredient is required. This is the avowal that the unchosen, unwanted, and compulsory are inescapable in education. Hence the "mechanical exercise" (in Pater), the grammar drill (in Pascoli), the pensum (in Joyce), the punishment (in Pasolini), and the long lecture (in

Rocha). These are all valuably resistance-prompting forms for registering and affirming what Gramsci, revising Gentile, calls the "instruction"—or, again, the "mechanical coercion"—that will always inhere in education.

We can find another echo of Gentile, one that is fainter but not for all that less significant for my argument, in Muriel Spark's *The Prime of Miss Jean Brodie*. Spark's novel can serve as a third and final contrastive example; both its narrative affinities with and its formal differences from the works that I treat in the following chapters help us to appreciate the specificity of counter-progressive pedagogy. If *The Browning Version* channels the common sense of progressive educational theory, Spark's *Prime*, from a decade later (1961), challenges this same common sense. Spark's best-known character, Miss Jean Brodie, appeals to etymology while outlining her often-quoted "principles of education" early in the novel: "The word 'education' comes from the root *e* from *ex*, out, and *duco*, I lead. It means a leading out. To me education is a leading out of what is already there in the pupil's soul," whereas to Miss Brodie's detractors, led by the school's headmistress, "it is a putting in of something that is not there, and that is not what I call education, *I call it intrusion* from the Latin root prefix *in* meaning in and the stem *trudo*, I thrust."[72] (Recall Gentile's characterization of traditional education as "*intruding* with violence into the life of the spirit.")[73] Miss Brodie will go on unsubtly to *educe* from one of her pupils the very definition that she has just put into her head, and critics have noted that Spark's teacher does not practice what she preaches. Instead, true to her famous Fascist sympathies, she wields nearly *duce*-worthy authority in her classroom; "she is ... extravagantly overbearing and tyrannical, shaping her pupils in her own image."[74]

But this is not the end of the story, and the teacher's charisma risks distracting us from just how patently derivative her "principles of education" are. These could be copied out from any critique of "cram," in fact, and this makes the "I" in Brodie's proud "I call it intrusion" almost every bit as empty, if not as emphatic, as the "I" in her "I thrust." In neither case, that is, does Miss Brodie speak for herself, in her own voice. If in defining Latin verbs she cites the dictionary, in refusing the education that is really intrusion, she cites another available discourse, one that we have already seen represented by Gentile: the discourse of countless educational reformers who had recast traditional education as mere mechanical "putting in" and had forsworn all such intrusive methods for the sake of students' self-realization. In *The Prime of Miss Jean Brodie*, reformed education becomes a matter of *quotation*.

That Miss Jean Brodie's statement of teaching philosophy is made up of commonplaces drawn from this reformist discourse means that the point, in the passage I have been reading, is not simply about character. Instead, I take the passage and Spark's novel as a whole to be making a much stronger set of suggestions: first, that, debatable etymology aside,[75] the claim that education is or ever could be "a leading-out of what is already there in the pupil's soul" is a mystification; and, second, that there is, in fact, no education without intrusion. (This is not to imply that any intrusion is entirely effective, or that there is nothing "in the pupil's soul" to resist it. On the contrary, Spark lays stress on such resistance precisely, even while she stops short of suggesting that it is necessarily prior to or "already there" before the intrusion that occasions it.) By now readers may well recognize that this lesson is deeply counter-progressive. But the way in which the lesson is taught is not.

The Prime of Miss Jean Brodie does not figure in the chapters that follow, then, because the novel does not look to the old school for alternatives to its title character's new school.[76] Famously focalized through its student-protagonists, so that Miss Jean Brodie is only seen through their eyes and heard through their young ears, *The Prime* does not chart these disciples' struggles with or resistances to "the authorised curriculum" that their teacher proudly abandons.[77] To be sure, Miss Brodie quotes Pater directly, and she everywhere deploys the kinds of "rememberable sayings" in which he specialized.[78] But these, for her, are sayings in the service of a pedagogical program that understands itself to be progressive, not at all in keeping with the traditions, rituals, or aims of "instruction." Sandy, the member of "the Brodie set" who most often mediates our experience of Miss Brodie's idiosyncratic teaching, will convert to Catholicism and choose to spend her adult life in a convent that can be seen as a version of the old school—as if she were engaged in a version of the "retreat" or return to Rome that figures from Pater to Rocha share. But Spark does not dwell on this return, let alone use it to structure her text. Thus if *The Prime of Miss Jean Brodie* arrives at an insight that can be called Gramscian as well as counter-progressive, if it teaches readers something about the surprising compatibility of Fascism and strands of progressive educational thought, its means of rendering this insight—its teaching style, which is light rather than arduous, or educational rather than instructional, to deploy Gentile's distinction once again—sets it apart from the texts and films that I analyze at length in *Old Schools*.

Each of the following chapters foregrounds a different instructional technique, although the works that I discuss often use several such techniques concurrently or in succession: recitation, memorization, copying out, corporal punishment, repetitious lecturing. Returns to Rome, the dead center of instruction, connect these disparate texts thematically. To be sure, though, these returns take various forms. Some are pilgrimages or field trips; others are forced migrations. Sometimes Rome provides a setting and set of explicit concerns; at other times, the city recedes, becoming a memory or an only implicit point of reference. I begin, with Pater and Pascoli, very much in Rome—the place of emperors and early Christians—and move outward from there, locating in the works of Joyce and Pasolini an ongoing if underground engagement with Latinity, only to return again to Rome with Rocha. Throughout what follows, then, "Rome" refers not simply to a place, but rather, as in Gramsci, to the site of a whole "cultural-scholastic-tradition." This tradition—which, again, for Gramsci, also constitutes an "itinerary"—crosses both spatial and temporal boundaries, calling for the kind of comparative approach that I adopt here.[79] In this approach, which importantly connects liberal and Fascist periods, both within Italian history and by considering that history's relations to other national and (neo-)colonial contexts ranging from Pater's England to Rocha's Brazil, comparison entails movement between languages. But it also entails attention to the means by which texts signal outside or elsewhere within their own historical moments.[80] Pascoli's Latin brings both types of comparison together, or rather demands both at once, since it effects a shift that is both linguistic and historical. But the comparative impulse to move beyond—by returning to a time before—the present motivates all of the authors whose works I treat here. Implying a critique of historicism as well as a critique of progress, these authors' works share an understanding of the present as anything but "homogeneous [and] empty"[81]—an understanding of the present as instead heterogeneous and shot through with "survivals" from the past. Though threatened by "progress," or modernization, the past remains available as a resource. Or minimally, as in Pasolini's "Abiura dalla *Trilogia della vita*," it remains in the form of a mechanical, muscular twitching.[82]

After Educations

I borrow the language of "survivals" both from the Victorian anthropology that I discuss in Chapter 1 and from Sigmund Freud, who takes up this anthropological discourse.[83] In what follows, I use "the doctrine of survivals" to make sense of the enabling temporal unevenness to which I have just referred. Already, though, my reference to Walter Benjamin's critique of progress, a critique to which I return in Chapter 2, will have indicated that I draw on other theoretical vocabularies as well. The heterogeneity of the fields and cultural objects that I analyze leads me to draw on a diverse range of theories. My methods are multiple, in other words, and they are responsive to the particular texts and contexts that I address. But patterns do emerge. All of my chapters rely on contrastively structured close readings, pairing counter-progressive with progressive texts and figures. In addition, all of the chapters that follow deploy psychoanalytic theory. In my discussion of Pater, I look to Jean Laplanche's work, and in Chapter 2, D.W. Winnicott's distinction between relating and use helps me to make sense of the divergent deployments of "dead language" in Pascoli's poetics and Gentile's pedagogy. My chapter on instruction in Joyce engages with psychoanalytically inflected queer theory, and in "*Salò* and the School of Abuse," I revisit Freud's early understanding of "survivals" while also drawing on more recent work by Leo Bersani. Finally, in "Schooling in Ruins," my chapter on Rocha, I return to Laplanche's account of "the priority of the other."[84]

Thus, although *Old Schools* is not systematic or orthodox in its engagements with psychoanalytic thought, it draws repeatedly on insights derived from Freudian psychoanalysis, itself a discourse "developed at the margins of European modernity, from the debris of minor or obliterated traditions, and in the form of a countermove."[85] In fact, psychoanalysis, defined by Freud as a "second," a belated, or an "after-education" (*Nacherziehung*), offers one model of counter-progressive pedagogy.[86] This is the case first because psychoanalysis privileges the experience of the transference—an experience of both repetition and difference—over the imparting of knowledge as content. At the same time, the analytic process requires that one of its participants provisionally occupy a place "over and above" the other, as Pater might say.[87] Recall the analyst's perpendicularity with respect to the analysand, implied in the phrase "under transference" and literalized in the clinical situation: an illustration or bodily registration of the fact that, for a time, the analyst must become what Laplanche calls an "adult" for the patient. This designation, for Laplanche, underscores the generational rather than familial nature of the analyst's authority, if it is authority.[88] This follows not from particular qualities or qualifications, but rather from the analyst's willingness to occupy a place and play a part in a situation, a limited relational field, one that, like the old school, becomes a frame for resistance.[89]

In a similar sense, the works that I examine all stage scenes of teaching and all privilege teaching's status as a scene over its imparting of knowledge.[90] These works treat pedagogy as a matter of process, practice, and ritual form. Bracketing students' "understanding" and teachers' "intelligence," they resemble Jacques Rancière's ignorant schoolmaster, although they use different means.[91] I follow Rancière in emphasizing "capabilities" that are not reducible to contents. "Pedagogy" as I define it therefore names a site of transmission and a type of relationship rather than a method for guaranteeing that predetermined contents will be delivered, that particular, substantive lessons will be learned and retained. This is what distinguishes counter-progressive pedagogy from the education of "cram," which I consider in Chapter 1: whereas critics of "cram" up to and including Miss Jean Brodie denounce this education's failure to deliver lasting content—its churning out generations of students who know nothing about Roman history, say—Pater, perhaps improbably like Gramsci long after him, foregrounds the form of education, the existence of instruction.

So, too, does clinical psychoanalysis, I have claimed. Psychoanalysis informs the pages that follow, then, because—like queer theory, on which I also draw—it provides, as alternatives to linear progress, eloquent and complex accounts of the persistence of the past in the present, of the abiding afterlives and posthumous consequences of what would appear to be dead and gone.[92] For Freud, the "succession" of stages in psychic life "also involves [their] co-existence."[93] Conversely, the psyche's "special capacity ... for regression" constitutes both the precondition for and the mechanism of analytic work.[94] This work requires—that is, both presupposes and prescribes—backward movement in order to advance.[95] Even while it uncovers our compulsion to repeat, psychoanalysis, instruction-like, compels us to repeat.

Not for nothing, then, does W. H. Auden claim that Freud "wasn't clever at all: he merely told / the unhappy Present to recite the Past / like a poetry lesson."[96] Pointedly setting aside the question of cleverness—the content of Freud's lessons—these lines remind readers that psychoanalysis constitutes a pedagogy in its own right. They also suggest, though, that Freud practiced a particular kind of teaching, one familiar to schoolchildren and that would seem to have nothing to do with unconscious depths or adult analyses. But for Auden, in the context of the psychoanalytic session *cum* "lesson," the recitation of the past, its recollection and rote repetition, opened onto insights in ways that no Gentilean transfusion or traffic with inner life could. To return to Joyce's terms in "Ithaca," the poetry lesson is a method of "direct instruction" and precisely *not* a means of "indirect suggestion implicating selfinterest." In Auden's lines, the analysand thus comes to resemble Molly Bloom—rerembering, rerepeating, and working-through, we might say.

For a kind of working-through, etymologically related to Gramsci's "elaboration," is what instruction enables and progressive education precludes when it compels students to leave the past behind or disavow it. "Progress is the pedagogical fiction built into the fiction of the society as a whole," Rancière writes—and I would specify, the *progressive* pedagogical fiction. Indeed, the counter-progressive tradition that I identify allows us to complicate and ultimately to refuse Rancière's totalizing claim that "all pedagogy is spontaneously progressive."[97] Rancière continues: "At the heart of the [progressive] pedagogical fiction is the representation of inequality as a *delay* in one's development: ... inferiority is only a lateness, a delay, that is posited so one can put oneself in the position of curing it."[98] This catching up is the cure—distinct from both Freudian working-through and Gramscian elaboration—that Gentile and other Italian reformers prescribe. And yet the Italian case is especially instructive because the shamed and shaming rhetoric of national belatedness in Italian politics and pedagogy is countered, though not conquered, by another way of relating to *arretratezza*, or belatedness, a way that Leopardi models as he ruins the dream of *"magnifiche sorti e progressive"* [*splendid and progressive destinies*].[99] In this ruin, Pascoli goes to school. And Pasolini follows with this reminder: "Remember that I, your teacher, do not believe in this history and this progress."[100]

In another context, Gramsci writes that Giambattista Vico's genius resided "in having conceived a vast world from a dead little corner of history [un angoletto morto della storia]."[101] This last phrase can serve as another name for the old school that emerges in the work of the authors I treat here, Italian or otherwise. Such a close, confined place, relegated to the past, nevertheless sustains the acceptance of belatedness—and the late style—that I have been describing. The "angoletto morto" indeed becomes the site of the setting-to-work of dead language and repetitive form that I analyze: for the Italian authors, the backward or politically belated space into which they are born, as Vico already was, according to Gramsci; for the non-Italians, Pater, Joyce, and Rocha, differently, the prison into which they doom themselves. Wordsworth thought that such a prison, entered through literary form, "no prison is."[102] For Gramsci, too, the "dead little corner" is worth preserving not as such but rather because it opens onto a vaster world. As the "angoletto morto" becomes more, not less, confining with time, this world likewise becomes more, not less, difficult to reach with the ostensible expansion of postwar global space. The foreclosures of progress—the mounting pressures of modernization and of capitalist presentism—call for ever more extreme measures and ever more demanding teaching styles, for ways out of the present that are at once more urgent and more immanent than those previously imagined.[103] For this reason, the chapters that follow, which move from good-enough to bad pasts, also trace a process of radicalization, a movement away from Pater's relative docility, his valorization of "reserve," to Rocha's dream of collective, counterimperial revolt. If, in a sense, then, all roads in this book lead to *Salò*, they do not end there, for the world of Rocha's *Claro*, extending beyond Europe, is importantly vaster than that of Pasolini's Sadean villa. *Claro* thus indicates the limitations of the counter-progressive project, its pedagogy of limitation. At the same time, though, Rocha's return to Rome—and to rote learning and "direct instruction"—attests to this pedagogy's persistence, the old school's remains.

1. Surviving *Marius*
Pater's Mechanical Exercise

> The sacraments were instituted for the sake of exercise.
> —Hugh of St. Victor, *De Sacramentis*

> Every school exercise ... is like a sacrament.
> —Simone Weil, "Reflections on the Right Use of School Studies with a View to the Love of God"

The Idol of Their School

To posterity, Walter Pater has handed down phrases. Today's readers tend to remember only one or two of these: "to burn always with a hard, gemlike flame"; "She is older than the rocks among which she sits"; "*All art constantly aspires to the condition of music*"; "Failure is to form habits"; "art for art's sake."[1] Pater lifted the last of these phrases from Théophile Gautier and Algernon Charles Swinburne and coined the rest himself. All but one of them appeared in the first edition of his *Studies in the History of the Renaissance*, first published in 1873.[2] Indeed, with this text Pater made his name, and he continues to be associated with the sound bites that *The Renaissance* contains.

These were effectively sound bites from the start, already verging on cliché when they were first circulated. This, at least, is what W. B. Yeats startlingly suggests in the Introduction to his edition of the *Oxford Book of Modern Verse*.[3] Here Yeats recalls that among Pater's earliest readers, habits were, despite Pater's own warnings against them, very quick to form; that the author's aphorisms were right away repeated *ad nauseam*; and that the flame imagined in the "Conclusion" to *The Renaissance* had no sooner been ignited than it had burned out, or at least led to collective burnout among Pater's many disciples and devotees.

In light of Yeats's claims, Pater's late reflections on lines learned by heart, phrases worshipped, and "short rememberable sayings" put into practice are especially striking.[4] These recur in the fiction, essays, and lectures—later texts that also return repeatedly to schools—that Pater wrote after *The Renaissance* and the controversy that it caused. Consider, to begin with, one such return, staged in an exemplary passage from the story "Emerald Uthwart" (1892):

> Horace!—he was, had been always, the idol of their school; to know him by heart, to translate him into effective English idiom, have an apt phrase of his instinctively on one's lips for every occasion. That boys should be made to spout him under penalties, would have seemed doubtless to that sensitive, vain, winsome poet, even more than to grim Juvenal, quite the sorriest of fates; might have seemed not so bad however, could he, from the "ashes" so persistently in his thoughts, have peeped on these English boys, row upon row, with black or golden heads, repeating him in the fresh morning, and observed how well for once the thing was done; how well he was understood by English James Stokes, feeling the old "fire" really "quick" still, under the influence which now in truth quickened, enlivened, everything around him.[5]

This is vintage Pater. From the opening self-correction—"was, had been always"—to the convergence of old and new in the scene of schoolboys reciting Horace "in the fresh morning"; from the single words in arch quotation marks to the archaizing epithets ("grim Juvenal," "English James Stokes"); from the repeated words and phrases ("row upon row"; "how well . . . how well") to the thoughts that circle back to qualify previous thoughts (so that Horace's turning over in his grave becomes his finding "quite the sorriest of fates" "not so bad"), the passage collects some of the author's most distinctive tics and tendencies.

These constitute Pater's own "effective English idiom," a language that might at first seem to rule out the reception that it here describes. Who, after all, even "under penalties," could learn such sinuous sentences by heart? Under what conditions could these sentences ever quicken or enliven readers, rather than trip them up or weigh them down? There is a heaviness to Pater's prose and a laboriousness to the reading of it, as the ode to Horace that I have quoted attests. At the same time, though, at every turn the passage on Horace aspires to the condition of the "apt phrase" it celebrates. By means of the hedges and hesitations that the passage features, Pater's sentences *decompose* themselves even while they compose scenes of schoolwide study and recitation. This was one charge leveled against Pater's prose during his lifetime: "The unity of the book," one critic complained, "is decomposed to give place to the independence of the page, . . . the page is decomposed to give place to the phrase, and the phrase to give place to the independence of the word."[6] Such a privileging of parts over wholes leads, by this account, to incoherence. But from another perspective the "independence" of the phrase makes it "remarkable," repeatable (*PP* 198). The sentence's decomposition makes it possible, in other words, "to know him by heart," if only partially and never quite as well as the gifted James Stokes knows Horace.

Pater's style thus "blends, or contrasts itself"—both blends and contrasts itself—with the scenes it renders in "Emerald Uthwart" (*MS* 215). And the content of these schoolroom scenes is as distinctive as Pater's style in rendering them. Most significantly, the repetition of Horace's verses is, for Pater's schoolboys, first a thing to be "done"; only secondarily is the Roman poet "understood." Learning by heart forms habits, and Pater delights in poetry's outward performance more than in its inward significance:

> One's day, then, began with [Horace], for all alike, Sundays of course excepted,—with an Ode, learned over-night by the prudent, who, observing how readily the words which send us to sleep cling to the brain and seem an inherent part of it next morning, kept him under their pillows. Prefects, without a book, heard the repetition of the Juniors, must be able to correct their blunders. Odes and Epodes, thus acquired, were a score of days and weeks; alcaic and sapphic verses like a bead-roll for counting off the time that intervened before the holidays. (*MS* 215–16)

"Odes and Epodes" saturate everyday scholastic life. And the "bead-roll" or rosary that measures passing time becomes the sign of a continuity between "Roman bricks" and "Gothic stones"; "pagan" and Christian worlds; "uninstructed" and instructed times; Horace himself and the "English James Stokes" (*MS* 215). But the shading of "alcaic and sapphic verses" into "a bead-roll for counting off the time" suggests something else as well: namely, that in Pater instruction is *ritual*, aligned with what *The Renaissance* already calls "the unprogressive, ritual element" in religious observance (*R* 100).

For Pater, then, as for Simone Weil, "every school exercise," in the old school of "Emerald Uthwart," "is like a sacrament." And "exercise" in Pater's later works names a crucial function of the sacraments themselves. These are not primarily, then, institutions that secure belief; they represent "something to be done, rather than something to be thought, or believed."[7] Doing can, of course, lead to thought and belief, just as James Stokes can truly understand the Horatian verses he repeats. But doing comes first, and its primacy matters. Indeed, it gives a critical—and a counter-progressive—edge to what might at first appear to be a merely nostalgic or reactionary project.

This chapter undertakes to show that Pater's prioritization of ritual over belief and of practice over understanding in education follows from his refusal of the liberal ideology of progress. Like their Enlightenment antecedents, Victorian versions of this ideology defined modernity as a liberating exit from convention and constraint, a means of achieving freedom from traditional bonds, outward forms, and various kinds of historical baggage. The weight of the past, of religion and superstition, of "illegitimate rulers, rigid traditions, and unreal fetishes," could be shed.[8]

So liberal reformers claimed, and in his "Conclusion" Pater concurred. A break with convention is what the youthful—the famous, the familiar, and, I am suggesting, the naïve—Pater sought to achieve. To be sure, the essays collected in *The Renaissance* had everywhere stressed the value of tradition, and some had even extolled "limitation" as a virtue (*R* 106). But the singularly influential "Conclusion" sounded another note altogether. In prose whose programmatic fetteredness escaped most readers' notice, eclipsed as it was by an epoch-making energy, Pater sided with the new: "What we have to do is be for ever curiously testing new opinions and courting new impressions, never acquiescing in a facile orthodoxy" (*R* 120). Nor should we be bound by convention, for "what is only conventional," Pater wrote, "has no real claim upon us" (*R* 120).

Proclamations like these contrast starkly with "Emerald Uthwart." Here "what is only conventional" is shown to be worthy of loving attention, even veneration: "The well-worn, perhaps conventional, beauties of their 'dead' Greek and Latin books . . . really shine . . . with their pristine freshness; seem more than to fulfill their claim upon the patience, the attention, of modern youth" (*MS* 213). The language of conventions and claims from the "Conclusion" returns here, but with a difference: "Emerald Uthwart" affirms what the "Conclusion" denies. The late text calls on "modern youth" to attend to—and, as the etymology of "patience" suggests, even to suffer from—the old, "well-worn" things and even the orthodoxies that the early Pater urged readers to outgrow. At the same time, the late "Emerald Uthwart" returns to the old school that had long been the target of progressive educators' polemics. Pater's late text thus not only revises his own earlier position; it also counters liberalism's tendency to devalue the traditions that it relegates to the past.

Pedagogy occupied a central place in the project of liberalism, and the old school's well-worn conventions were chief among the past practices that liberal reformers sought to leave behind.[9] In his *Autobiography*, John Stuart Mill lamented that most students "have their mental capacities not strengthened, but overlaid by" the "knowledge drilled into them" at school.[10] Such students learn merely to repeat "the opinions or phrases of other people, and these are accepted as a substitute for the power to form opinions of their own."[11] But here Mill himself repeated an opinion of Rousseau's: that children should be protected from exposure to facts and phrases they are not equipped to understand. Such phrases, for Rousseau, stunted students' growth and stood in the way of collective flourishing. The education that centered on such phrases—which was all traditional education, according to *Émile*—thus led to the creation of dependent subjects, rather than self-reliant citizens. Hence the founding stipulation that Émile should "never learn anything by heart."[12]

Pater never explicitly seconded this stipulation, of course. Still, the distance that separates his "Conclusion" from "Emerald Uthwart," and the early from late Pater, in this respect is remarkable. With its *Émile*-like emphasis on "Present interest,"[13] the "Conclusion" echoes liberal and progressive discourses—and this even if *The Renaissance* as a whole everywhere engages with the past. By the time of "Emerald Uthwart," though, things had changed: at the cost of any semblance of narrative momentum, Pater's late text refutes progressive educational theories in a series of asides that find "value" in the very "classical education" that Rousseau and Mill opposed (*MS* 218). For the late Pater, the techniques of this education—learning by heart, the use of "penalties," and even the inculcation of "Submissiveness"—teach first and foremost "the preponderating value of the manner of the doing it in the thing done": "Just at those points, scholarship attains something of a religious colour. And in that place"—in that school—"religion, religious system, its claim to overpower one, presented itself in a way of which even the least serious by nature could not be unaware" (*MS* 218). Here again, religion marks the place where "the manner of the doing" trumps "the thing done," and Pater affirms even what is apparently least liberating about "religious system." This passage makes critical characterizations of the late Pater as reactionary seem perfectly understandable. Indeed, we might well wonder who *but* a reactionary could write such an apology for "authority" (*MS* 218). I have already begun to argue, however, that moments like these in Pater's late works should be read otherwise in light of both Pater's own "Conclusion" and the educational discourses to which, late in his career, the author responds.

Pater's defenses of the old school, which abound in *Marius the Epicurean* and the texts written after it, represent retractions of his own youthful views and refutations of educational reformers' projects. These projects culminate in the widespread effort to liberate "the school from mechanism" that I considered in my Introduction.[14] Pater's late work, by contrast, affirms the mechanical methods of the old school precisely: unenlightened methods based on what Mill calls "the phrases of other people," on what Rousseau decries as mere imitation. For Pater, such practices become means by which to acknowledge the claims and the systems from which we are not free. These claims and systems are social, and they are old. The new school—in both Rousseau and Mill, a home school—centers, in theory if not always in practice, on the individual student and his "present interest." What Pater recognized in the old school, by contrast, was its ability to sustain another interest, one not perfectly aligned with but rather at a "diagonal" to the present (*MS* 205).

This becomes clear early in "Emerald Uthwart," when Pater's narrator makes the all but explicitly anti-Rousseauist case for teaching "modern boys the Classics" "amid the haunts, the traditions, and with something of the discipline, of monasticism":

> The French and others have swept their scholastic houses empty of it, with pedantic fidelity to their theories. English pedants may succeed in doing the like. But the result of our older method has had its value so far, at least, say! for the careful aesthetic observer. It is of such diagonal influences, through complication of influence, that expression comes, in life, in our culture, in the very faces of men and boys—of these boys. (*MS* 205)

The breathlessness of those last phrases registers, even while it risks obscuring, the force of Pater's polemic.[15] According to the logic of this polemic, to sweep away monasticism's residues is to leave "scholastic houses" "empty." It is to deprive students of resources that constitute "complication of influence." To be sure, such complication here is in the eye of the beholder; or rather, it benefits the "careful aesthetic observer." But the generalizing, interpellative phrases that follow, "in life" and "in our culture," indicate that such observers are by no means the only beneficiaries of the old school's "older method," in Pater's view. On the contrary, this method at least potentially offers *everyone* access to formative complications of influence. Indeed, the last sentence above implies that the men and boys gathered here, occasioning Pater's particular breathlessness, are only one "expression" of this general phenomenon.

Strikingly, for Pater, it is the enemies, not the advocates, of the old school who are pedants. Pascoli will make a similar claim, as will Joyce and Gramsci after him.[16] All three authors thus refuse the rousing image of a cleaned-up, swept-out, and pedant-free present enshrined in liberal discourses of progress. Such a present looks impoverished indeed when, as in "Emerald Uthwart," it is shown to be bereft of "complication of influence." This past influence, which "Emerald Uthwart" calls "diagonal," *Marius* more forcefully repositions "over and above" the present (*M* 178). In this way, Pater unexpectedly overturns one of the civilizational hierarchies that figures like Mill had naturalized: forms of life that liberalism takes to be lower come to reside on another plane, one that the present cannot rightly claim to have superseded, to have left behind.

In this chapter, I show that such a critique of progress inheres in Pater's pedagogy. Here as in this book's other chapters, I take "pedagogy" to name both a theme and a mode. I consider *scenes* of instruction in Pater while attending to his work's tendency to look to the old school for its *means* of expression. More specifically, I trace Pater's redeployment of one of the classical school's "older methods" in particular (*MS* 205): the "mechanical exercise" or task in memorization and recitation that Mill would have teachers forswear. I ask what "mechanical" might have meant for Pater and what led him to locate critical potential in rote and ritual tasks. Finally, I read Pater alongside Roland Barthes, who cultivated—indeed, "*overcultivated*"—another "clipped" and classicizing style.[17] If it has been easier for us to learn from the late Barthes's style than from the late Pater's, the latter is, I suggest, surprisingly the more instructive today inasmuch as its influence is complicating.

To Form Habits

The late Pater's lesson has proven difficult to learn because, from the perspective of progress, it has looked both pedantic and retrograde, because it has seemed both scholastic, in the disparaging sense, and like a betrayal of the principles enshrined in Pater's galvanizing "Conclusion." Here is how the usual critical narrative goes: after the scandal caused by *The Renaissance*, the once-liberated Pater "slouched back toward Anglo-Catholicism."[18] He returned to and remained within the institutional strictures from which the "Conclusion" had gotten free. In this narrative of retrenchment, youthful enthusiasms give way to soberer, not to say stilted, reflections. Pater's early "outcast fame" becomes his late "conservative reprobation."[19]

The mature Pater acquiesces, by this account, to the orthodoxy that the youthful Pater had refused.[20] Thus whereas the "Conclusion" builds toward the assertion that "what is only conventional, has no real claim upon us" (*R* 120), convention acquires another valence altogether—and makes all kinds of real claims—in and after *Marius the Epicurean: His Sensations and Ideas*, first published in 1885. Here Pater treats convention with reverence from the start, and the "liturgical" principle announced on the novel's first page remains operative—just as its "repetitions of ... consecrated form[s] of words" remain repetitive—until the end (*M* 37). With its *incipit*'s valorization of the ancient Roman "religion of usages and sentiment rather than of facts and belief" (*M* 37), moreover, *Marius* sets itself up to fail according to the younger Pater's lights, for the "Conclusion" claims, again, that "failure is to form habits," to rely on customs and repeat oneself in such reflexive reliance (*R* 100). It's not surprising that, from this perspective, generations of critics have agreed that Pater's novel does fail: to come to life or to an end; to make a difference and thus measure up to *The Renaissance*; and, especially, to deliver on the earlier text's liberal and liberating, its modern and modernizing, promises.[21]

Contesting these critical verdicts, some of Pater's more recent readers have reclaimed the author's works for a range of projects.[22] In the process, they have reconsidered the relationship between Pater's early texts and his late work, and they have shed new light on the "institutional and instructional contexts" in which Pater wrote and with which he engaged.[23] William Shuter, for instance, has shown that his responses to these contexts went beyond the denial of reality and the defensive, irresponsible, indulgent, and merely nostalgic escape from modernity that Pater's detractors found and still find in his works.[24] Pater's responses to his present were, in fact, according to Shuter, less retreats from than rejoinders to the public world that had either maligned or compulsively, perhaps all too easily, quoted the "Conclusion."

In this world, the ordinary business of educational reform continued apace. Shuter notes that Oxford was "decisively reformed, secularized, and, in effect, modernized" even while it was Hellenized during Pater's tenure there.[25] These processes prompted corresponding changes in Pater's teaching—and not only in his teaching, but also in his texts. Matthew Kaiser reads Pater's later work as attempting to correct by re-eroticizing "an Oxonian Platonism from which *eros* had been all but excised" by the very reformers who were busy modernizing the curriculum.[26] Insisting on eros, then, Pater would have undertaken to counter reform not from a conservative position, but rather out of a progressive and proto-gay allegiance to individual bodies and pleasures.[27]

In this way, we have learned to complicate the received portrait of the late Pater as a hidebound pedant. But I would argue that we have yet to reckon with how precisely Pater would have us learn. As my paraphrase of these critical arguments already suggests, in their efforts to recuperate the late Pater, revisions of the "retreat hypothesis" have tended to downplay the moments in Pater that *do* look a lot like retreats—retreats, that is, both from liberal modernity and from the individualism celebrated in the "Conclusion."[28] This tendency has obscured the specificity of Pater's late pedagogy and the force of his critique of progress.

Paradoxically, this critique depends on a teaching sytle that centers on uncritical imitation, on mechanical, rote, and ritual repetition. As we have seen, Pater extolls these techniques in "Emerald Uthwart," with its rows upon rows of boys repeating Horace. But the methods of the old school inform Pater's late work even when they are not treated directly. Yeats's reading of Pater gives sanction to this claim. Yeats implies that a pedagogical model is already operative in *The Renaissance*. He writes of the "uncritical admiration," verging on devotion, that "a single passage" in Pater's book elicited, prompting a generation of aestheticists to accept the author "for master."[29] Yeats thus invites us to imagine Pater's readers as so many schoolchildren, ranged "row upon row" and keeping *The Renaissance*, rather than the "Odes and Epodes," "under their pillows" (*MS* 215).

Mechanicity inheres, for Yeats, not only in the endless repetition of phrases from *The Renaissance* by Pater's self-appointed students, but also in the phrases themselves. "Pater was accustomed to give each sentence a separate page of manuscript, isolating and analysing its rhythm."[30] This process made it possible for "a poem to arise" in Pater's prose,[31] but Yeats suggests that Pater's piecemeal writing procedure also made the resulting sentences eminently repeatable. Counterintuitively, then, Yeats locates habit-forming potential in the very Paterian text that would have left habit behind, so that readers of *The Renaissance* become from the first repeaters of its claims. It is as though they were compelled by the text, as by a schoolteacher. But the old school remains latent in *The Renaissance*. Its "older methods" become manifest only in Pater's later texts (*MS* 205), his variations on mechanical exercise.

The Condition of Mechanicity

The school is central to many of these texts written after *The Renaissance*. *Marius the Epicurean* follows its protagonist's philosophical, religious, and "'aesthetic' education" (*M* 117), and the scholar figures prominently in Pater's essay on "Style." "Emerald Uthwart" weighs the advantages and disadvantages of the "English manner of education" (*MS* 209), and "Lacedaemon," one of Pater's lectures on *Plato and Platonism*, reconstructs Sparta, lavishing particular attention on the ancient city's methods of schooling. In each of these texts, Pater returns to the mechanical so as to redefine it. What begins as a disparaging charge—the charge of mechanicity—becomes an organizing principle in Pater's late work, which affirms the "mechanical exercise" that forward-thinking educators would disallow. This section tracks that process of redefinition and transvaluation.

Yeats was not alone, of course, in summoning the specter of mechanically phrase-repeating students. Nor was he the only reader to note Pater's penchant for the phrase or to relate this penchant to his way of working by isolating single sentences and even words on pages. For Pater's first biographers and critics, this method was "mechanical"—by which they meant artificial, bloodless, or pedantic. Their comments are often dismissive, to be sure. Still they index a response to something that really does inform Pater's texts: an aspiration to the condition of mechanicity.[32]

Two instances are particularly telling. First, in his biography, Thomas Wright observes the same compositional procedure that Yeats admires, but he arrives at a different assessment altogether. According to Wright, Pater "worked in the most mechanical way a man could work, with his squares of paper and his ceaseless turning of the leaves of his dictionary.... As a rule, his method of work was like that of Pope, only worse. 'If,' said one of Pater's most intimate friends ... , 'Pater found a word anywhere that pleased him, in that word would go—somewhere or other, whether it meant anything or not.'"[33] In his study of Pater, Edward Thomas also laments the author's habit of using learned words—plucked, presumably, from the dictionary to which Wright refers—that call much too much attention to themselves, "sticking out, like the raisins that will get burnt on an ill-made cake. It is clear," Thomas concludes of these words, which here go from being desiccated to belonging to a dead language, "that they have been carefully chosen as the right and effective words, but they stick out because the labour of composition has become so self-conscious and mechanical that cohesion and perfect consistency are impossible. The words have only an isolated value; they are labels; they are anything but living and social words."[34]

The staid writer pictured in passages like these is laughable rather than threatening. But this writer's slavish adherence to norms—his obsessive decorousness, his attachment to dictionaries, his "mechanical" method and arduous discipline—turns out to give rise to the opposite: an indulgence of the author's own whims that makes his language so idiosyncratic as to be "isolated." Pater gives offense by thus exempting himself from the "living and social." It is as if propriety taken to such an extreme could only result in impropriety, or at least in inconsistency: like so many burnt and badly blended-in raisins, labels in Pater's prose become detached from their referents. They become inoperative, or they come to operate only as indices of the baker's blunders. The problem, for Pater's biographers, then, is not such words' signifying nothing, but rather their signifying all too clearly that "the labour of composition has become ... self-conscious and mechanical."

This last phrase, which verges on oxymoron, is striking not least because in Pater's own prose "mechanical" means first and foremost unselfconscious. For Pater as for many others, mechanical activity is generally "routine, unthinking activity—thus action without consciousness."[35] When the narrator of "The Child in the House" notes, for example, that "accidents ... so mechanically determine" the feeling we have for home (*MS* 179), he locates this feeling outside the reach of conscious thought and willful intervention. We are powerless to resist such forces, for in our infancy "irresistibly, little shapes, voices, accidents ... become parts of the great chain wherewith we are bound" (*MS* 178). *Bildung* gives way to *Bindung* in "The Child in the House," where what happens mechanically is what happens early—what keeps us in touch with our formation in and by the material world, "in that process of brain-building by which we are, each one of us, what we are" (*MS* 173).

The "mechanical" returns near the very end of the slightly later *Marius*, where the word is used in a related but somewhat different sense. Here the agent of the mechanical process is human, and though the word still implies "unthinking," it does so paradoxically, since it is used to describe a movement of thought. With death fast approaching, Pater's protagonist calls to memory "all the persons he had loved in life," "like a child thinking over the toys it loves, one after another": "One after another, he suffered those faces and voices to come and go, as in some mechanical exercise, as he might have repeated all the verses he knew by heart, or like the telling of beads one by one" (*M* 296). That toys become faces and voices, which become verses, which become beads during this act of recollection, already indicates that in *Marius* the faculty of memory—or, more precisely, the practice of memorization—is closely and counterintuitively related to a potential for change.

The implications of this relation become clearer if we reread *Marius* alongside progressive theories of education from Rousseau to Mill. If, in a sense, as critics have maintained, hearing echoes of Rousseau throughout Pater's novel, Marius is meant to be "an Emile of the second century,"[36] then it's worth noting Pater's flagrant violation of Rousseau's stipulation that his pupil should "never learn anything by heart."[37] More pointedly, the ending of Pater's novel also suggests that the ailing protagonist reverts—mercifully—to the "mere exercises of memory" that the home-schooled Mill was spared.[38] Far from dead weight to be shed, such exercises become, for Marius, means of staying in touch with a past he has learned painstakingly not to leave behind: ways of summoning those "others, from whom he could not endure to break away" (*M* 178), those "souls ... whose faces averted from him, would be more than he could bear" (*M* 179). He *can* bear, by contrast, what Mill cannot: the thought of a past that makes a continuing claim on the present that would supersede it. In *Marius,* this claim takes the form of "observances, customs, usages" (*M* 178), and the mechanical exercise turns out to be one of these.

The moment of mechanical recollection late in *Marius* that I have been reading suggestively recalls another moment in Pater's work, one in his essay on "Winckelmann," included in his book on the Renaissance. Here Pater swerves away from his imaginary portrait of the art historian to consider the relationship between art and an archaic cultic practice that persists, Pater suggests, in later forms of religion that would appear to be based on inward belief rather than outward form: "Even the mysteries," Pater writes in "Winckelmann," "the centres of Greek religious life at a later period, were not a doctrine but a ritual; and one can imagine the Catholic church retaining its hold through the 'sad mechanic exercise' of its ritual, in spite of a diffused criticism or skepticism" (*R* 101).

The words quoted here are from early in Tennyson's *In Memoriam*:

> I sometimes hold it half a sin
>   To put in words the grief I feel;
>   For words, like Nature, half reveal
> And half conceal the Soul within.
>
> But, for the unquiet heart and brain,
>   A use in measured language lies;
>   The sad mechanic exercise,
> Like dull narcotics, numbing pain.[39]

In the context of his essay on Winckelmann, Pater's gesture toward these lines is striking and more than a little strange, since Tennyson's "sad mechanic exercise" refers not to the language of liturgy, but rather to the speaker's own rendering of grief despite his "hold[ing] it half a sin" to do so, given all words' tendency to deliver half-truths, to "half reveal / And half conceal the Soul." There are a lot of halves here, and in Tennyson language "measured" both rhythmically and by means of moderation splits the difference between print and privacy, while also making the speaker's mournful recourse to mere words feel less sinful, if not less "sad." But this recourse, for Tennyson, is not strictly recitation. *In Memoriam*'s "sad mechanic exercise" instead names the production of the poem itself, here recast as the result of a discipline that entails repeatedly trying and half-failing to give verbal form to "unquiet" inward states. The heart isn't fully in this process, and neither is the brain, since both are anaesthetized rather than enlivened by it.

Pater, too, at times associates liturgical practice, "mechanic exercise," with such anaesthetizing effects. Consider a claim he makes earlier in "Winckelmann" about the cult that forms "the base of all religions" and survives in them: "It is the anodyne which the religious principle ... has added to the law which makes life somber for the vast majority of mankind" (*R* 100). For Pater as for Tennyson a certain repetitive verbal practice thus administers opiates. Note, though, that Pater's citation of *In Memoriam* transposes an aesthetic problem into a religious register, reactivating the cultic senses of "exercise," which can mean "the practice and performance of rites and ceremonies" as well as "operation" and "habitual employment" more generally.[40] What purpose might this transposition serve? Clearly the citation says something—something that seems to be *retracted* by the moment in *Marius* that I have analyzed, when "mechanic exercise" reappears, without quotation marks, as "mechanical exercise" and with a very different valence. Before this retraction, the citation of Tennyson distills the claim that it's both possible and desirable to graduate from mechanical exercise and accede to fully organic and original, new and not-yet-recited speech.[41]

What I have called Pater's retraction of this claim at the very end of *Marius* could also be seen as his way of venturing the opposing wager that there is a mechanical exercise that is not "like dull narcotics," not numbing but rather invigorating, even indispensible. In *Marius*, to be sure, "mechanical exercise" eases the passage out of life and into death, defined as a state of obliviousness as anodyne as nightly sleep. In this sense, it might seem that in Pater's novel we have not traveled far from his reference to Tennyson's "mechanic exercise" in "Winckelmann," after all. But we have, I would argue,[42] because elsewhere in the novel such exercises work, and set the protagonist to work, differently, so that the reader is trained to hear "mechanical" as connoting something other than "sad." If the word sometimes designates, as in "The Child in the House," the shaping force of contingency, the object world defined as "a mechanical and material order" (*MS* 208), elsewhere in the novel it describes "pagan" aesthetic practices that are also touched with cultic significance: a performance in which dancers "contrived that their mechanical march-movement should fall out into a kind of highly expressive dramatic action" (*M* 291), or Homeric epic as "but the mechanical transcript of a time, naturally, intrinsically poetic" (*M* 91).

Such usages retain Tennyson's suggestion that poetic production is in some sense like manual labor, that the latter is at least sometimes constitutive of dramatic or poetic practice. Again, though, Pater tends actively to affirm—and not, like Tennyson, reluctantly to accept—mechanical work. It matters in this sense that *In Memoriam*'s speaker becomes mechanical while grieving alone, whereas *Marius* repeatedly if inconsistently associates mechanical exercise with collective phenomena, whether ensemble dances or whole historical periods. "Inconsistently" because the novel also includes moments like this summing-up of its protagonist's work routine: "'The morning for creation,' he would say; 'the afternoon for the perfecting labour of the file; the evening for reception—the reception of matter from without one, of other men's words and thoughts—matter for our own dreams, or the merely mechanic exercise of the brain, brooding thereon silently, in its dark chambers'" (*M* 252). Here the phrase from Tennyson appears for the first of two times in *Marius*, without quotation marks but a syllable short of its more modified form in the novel's conclusion. The phrase appears, in other words, as it did in "Winckelmann," in its original, Tennysonian scansion, and its association with *In Memoriam* is reinforced here by the "brain" said to do the exercising. But this in effect gives the phrase's second, modified appearance in *Marius*—again, in the novel's concluding deathbed scene—the force of a redoubled retraction. It is as if Pater must repeat his citation of Tennyson's poem not once but twice in order fully to take back the disparagement that it implies, to decouple sad, solipsistic individuality from "mechanic exercise."[43]

More obviously in keeping with *Marius*'s overall transvaluation of the mechanical are moments like these: among the Cyrenaics, Marius accepts "some curtailment of his liberty," and this acceptance prompts Pater's narrator to observe that "the authority they exercised was that of classic taste—an influence so subtle yet so real, as defining the loyalty of the scholar—or of some beautiful and venerable ritual, in which every observance is become spontaneous and almost mechanical" (*M* 188). "Classic taste" both defines the scholar and becomes interchangeable with ritual in the space of this single sentence, whose handling of categories is as telling as it is slippery. *Marius* brings the aesthetic, the scholastic, and the religious (persistently and polemically made synonymous with ritual) into inextricable relation, and here Pater implicitly makes the case that he will make explicit in "Lacedaemon": the case for a good-enough mechanical method of instruction, in which memory aids, rather than impedes, imagination: "Hard and practical as Lacedaemonians might seem, they lived nevertheless very much by imagination, and to train memory, to preoccupy their minds with the past, as in our own classic or historic culture of youth, was in reality to develop a vigorous imagination" (*PP* 223).

"As in our own": the phrase, reminiscent of the many proleptic moments in *Marius*, points to the "classic or historic culture of youth" in Pater's present. In this present, in his capacity as a practicing teacher, Pater criticized what was called the "education of cram":[44] with reforms at Oxford leading to increased emphasis on competitive examinations for undergraduates, Pater distanced himself and his own teaching from "the long, pedantic, mechanical discipline ... which is the necessary accompaniment of a system of examination."[45] Indeed, the author engaged in small acts of protest against this discipline, which he was under considerable administrative pressure to apply: asked to help with preparation for one such exam, Pater is reported to have told his grade-grubbing student to read all of Kant.[46] But the corrective to the reformed system that he imagined was an old-school rather than a progressive one.[47]

This correction never becomes a matter of valuing mechanical exercise for its own sake, because for Pater there are better and worse mechanical methods. There are the kinds of test-prep associated with "cram," again, but also the drills in the recitation of "rememberable sayings" through which philosophers were trained (*PP* 198). Likewise, there are the numbingly unthinking modes of participation in ritual ("sad mechanic exercises"), but then there are the quickening ways in which one can be mechanically affected by the world, or at least some of its places: "'Abide,' [the Platonist] says to youth, 'in these places, and the like of them, and mechanically, irresistibly, the soul of them will impregnate yours.... They will tell (despite, it may be, of unkindly nature at your first making) upon your very countenance, your walk and gestures, in the course and concatenation of your inmost thoughts'" (*PP* 279–80).

Yet Pater also suggests that it is impossible fully or finally to separate "sad, mechanic exercises" from other kinds—which is also to say that even the most enlivening exercises are still liturgical. The Spartans, after all, were, according to Pater, deeply religious, and their education was also a kind of ritual training. But Pater returns to this Sparta not simply to endorse the cultic practice and punishing pedagogical program that he sees there. He goes "to school again" in Sparta in order to locate the promise that what look like the most determined and determining, the most closed and conventional forms might shelter the possibility of the as yet undetermined (*PP* 213).[48] What seems to be, in the late Pater, an insistence on the repetition of the same therefore turns out to be a desire to preserve the conditions that make change possible.

Note, for instance, the parenthesis in the passage that I have just quoted: "(despite, it may be, of unkindly nature at your first making)." This is as close as Pater comes to faith in aesthetic education as *re*making, since the phrase "first making" invites us to regard Spartan schooling as a second making. What "The Child in the House" took to be fixed, "Lacedaemon" in this way makes malleable: "unkindly nature" or no, there is hope for the scholar who is late in his loyalty to Sparta. Announcing a reprieve from determination by "first making" and finding this reprieve in, of all things, a mechanical process, Pater retracts or at least revises the proposition about first formation that he made in "The Child in the House"; he replaces that text's "great chain" with another "concatenation."

This moment clarifies a more general tendency in Pater's late work: here the *repetition* of phrases or of lines learned by heart enables the *revision* (if not, again, the retraction) of past iterations of the same. This is why, of Dante's three *cantiche*, Pater prefers the *Purgatorio*.[49] It's not as if—in Purgatory, in Sparta, or on one's deathbed—one can fully rewrite the formula or verse. But one can reinflect it, or see how it already has been reinflected without one's willing, because the world's "accidents" have changed the context of its repetition, its remaking (*MS* 179). In either case, it is repetition that makes such reinflection possible and perceptible.

Recall that, in "The Child in the House," the world and its accidents "mechanically determine" "each one of us" with a force that we cannot hope to forestall (*MS* 179, 173). Given that the world already shapes and enchains us, according to Pater, it is good to be trained in a place where constraint knows itself, and education through memorization, recitation, and other forms of mechanical exercise molds a brain and an imagination that are "vigorous" but not for all that unchained. This suggestion may be troubling to critical sensibilities steeped in liberal and progressive educational traditions and used to associating Pater—at least the better Pater—with an expansion, rather than a limitation, of both perceptual and political possibilities.[50] But Pater undertook precisely to think expansion and limitation, freedom and constraint, imagination and memory, and inward and outward forms, together, as "woven through and through each another into one inextricable texture" (*MS* 173).[51] The author whom, according to Yeats, generations of writers "accepted . . . for master"[52] thus fittingly came to resemble one of his imaginary students in "Emerald Uthwart," reciting classical texts because he was all but compelled to do so: "Singular!—The words, because seemingly forced from him, had been worth hearing" (*MS* 225). My next section attends to some of the words seemingly forced from *Marius*.

The Mechanical *Marius*

None of the above is meant to suggest that Pater's preoccupation with the mechanical was unique. From Shakespeare to Swift and from Blake to Wordsworth—to say nothing of Pope, Tennyson, Yeats's mechanical bird, or the whole host of other modernist machines that arose during the decades following Pater's death—a wide range of mechanical bodies, spirits, and poets appear regularly in early and late modern English-language literary history, in works written before, during, and after the age of Marx's "mechanical monster."[53] They appear variously as well, so that the mechanical is sometimes devalued but at other times nearly value-neutral, and the word "mechanical" is "used sometimes descriptively, sometimes abusively."[54] The "Preface" to *Lyrical Ballads* (1802), for instance, includes both a famous refusal of the "mechanical device[s] of style," as opposed to "the very language of men," and the admission that, "however exalted a notion we would wish to cherish of the character of a Poet, it is obvious, that, while he describes and imitates passions, his situation is altogether slavish and mechanical."[55]

Likewise, if a certain still-prevalent critical common sense disparages "those works of art which mechanically perpetuate outmoded or depleted aesthetic formulas,"[56] deconstructive criticism has long since drawn readers' attention to the machine-like properties of language as such, properties that, in this account, animate even while they automate all literary texts.[57] The mechanical would therefore appear to be old news by now at the level of literary history as well as that of theory.

But if the mere fact of Pater's attention to the mechanical is unremarkable, his *inflection* of mechanicity sets his project apart even as it renders this project pedagogical. Beginning with *Marius*, Pater sought to privilege scholastic forms of "mechanical exercise," to disclose and valorize "the unprogressive, ritual element" in them (*R* 100). Pater distinctively affirms mechanical scholastic chores and sets them to work on account of their very mechanicity. This mechanicity becomes a strength rather than a weakness, and even a resource for critique.

In her reading of *Marius*, Linda Dowling argues that Pater took on and even turned to profit the charges leveled against a modern literature presumed to be in decline. Chief among these was the claim "that literary English is quite literally a dead or moribund language," and granting this claim meant undertaking "to establish a new mode of writing on [this language's] very morbidity, dissolving the antagonistic opposition [then prevalent] between philology and literature in a new vision of the writer as a sort of philologist or scholar of words."[58] Pater's privileging of this figure entailed

> the urging of written language—that is, language frozen in writing and divorced from living speech in the philological sense—as a literary medium. For to urge composing English "more as a learned language" is to conceive of the language as a written dialect, whose spoken form is insignificant or nonexistent. To recommend archaisms is to do the same, for the etymological weight . . . that Pater so prizes in such words, inheres in them only because of the lexicographical, which is to say, the written tradition.[59]

This reading is undeniably useful, but it gives short shrift precisely to use. In other words, Dowling risks understating Pater's acute sensitivity to language's deployment, its pragmatic or indexical as well as its semantic dimension. If the semantic is privileged in lexicography, then the latter remains importantly distinct from, because only part of, "the written tradition" as it is taken up and transmitted, say, in schools. Despite Dowling's conflation of the two ("the lexicographical, which is to say, the written tradition"), they are not strictly coextensive, since no dictionary can exhaust the possibilities of any language in use. Whether a language is dead or living, written or spoken, a boarding school subject or a lingua franca, its setting to work in use entails the eclipse of the dictionary, even when the latter proves indispensable.

Pater knows this. Thus if "living speech" falls away for him, as Dowling convincingly demonstrates, the ongoing use of language does not. On the contrary, adapting Tennyson's concession that "a *use* in measured language lies," I would argue that Pater privileges precisely the use of "dead or moribund" language. It was not simply the existence of "the written tradition" that mattered to Pater as he sought to render his English increasingly Latinate. Equally important were the means of transmission by which this tradition was activated, though not exactly enlivened, in the scholastic and religious settings that recur in Pater's late works. Far from lying dormant, then, in the discipline of philology or in the dictionaries over which he pored, the language whose deadness Pater accepts is one that he also deploys pedagogically.

"'One learns nothing from him . . . but one becomes something'" (R 90). So Pater quotes Goethe on reading Winckelmann. Here he also incidentally offers one way of defining pedagogy in this book's sense. Winckelmann, according to Goethe, abandons one kind of pedagogy, the knowledge-imparting kind that leads to learning, in favor of another: that which leads to one's becoming "something." I note that there is the slightest hint of diminution here in the reader's sliding toward the indeterminate and vaguely inanimate status of some*thing*. This sliding is idiomatic, of course, but it remains the case that one has not yet become some*one*.

Diminution and deanimation are also latent possibilities in Pater's recourse to the mechanical. Even while the author distances himself from the modern application of "long, pedantic, mechanical discipline,"[60] he repeatedly stages and even celebrates the mechanical discipline that marks a range of ancient forms, or these forms' residual survivals in modernity, of which the Latin class celebrated in "Emerald Uthwart" was the representative instance. Mechanical work was, after all, widely associated throughout the nineteenth century with teaching as well as trade, and with the teaching of ancient languages in particular—"dead Vocables," as Thomas Carlyle's protagonist calls them, remembering that all his subjects, but first and foremost "his Greek and Latin were 'mechanically' taught," to deanimating effect:

> "My Teachers," says he, "were hide-bound Pedants, without knowledge of man's nature, or of boy's; or of aught save their lexicons and quarterly account-books. Innumerable dead Vocables (no dead Language, for they themselves knew no Language) they crammed into us, and called it fostering the growth of mind. How can an inanimate, mechanical Gerund-grinder, the like of whom will, in a subsequent century, be manufactured at Nurnberg out

of wood and leather, foster the growth of anything; much more of Mind, which grows, not like a vegetable (by having its roots littered with etymological compost), but like a spirit, by mysterious contact of Spirit; Thought kindling itself at the fire of living Thought? How shall *he* give kindling, in whose own inward man there is no live coal, but all is burnt out to a dead grammatical cinder? The Hinterschlag Professors knew syntax enough; and of the human soul thus much: that it had a faculty called Memory, and could be acted on through the muscular integument by appliance of birch-rods."[61]

Though plainly satirical, this moment in *Sartor Resartus*, in a chapter called "Pedagogy," collates several commonplaces in the critique of "cram," a critique that intensified, as we have seen, during Pater's tenure at Oxford. Carlyle's passage also points to a contradiction latent in many versions of this critique. A mind, which is, according to Carlyle, a terrible thing to render inanimate, grows "not like a vegetable ... but like a spirit, by mysterious contact of Spirit." But that the mind is said to grow at all means that it remains in some sense organic; this mind is bodily even if not directly accessible, as the sadistic Hinterschlag Professors suppose, "through the muscular integument." Moreover, Carlyle effectively makes "dead grammatical cinders" indistinguishable from "etymological compost," pointing up the organicity that always animates the trope of language death. In order to be compostable, even the most inanimate and mechanical language must have been alive and vegetal once, and those who impart this language must likewise contain "live coal" somewhere within them. Carlyle invites readers to literalize this phrase almost to the point of incoherence, for though strictly speaking coal is organic, as "live" it is always on its way to burning out.[62] It follows that, as Pascoli will note,[63] any language that might be said to be living is already going the way of lexicons, just as the distinction, tenuous from the first, between "Language" and "Vocables" is already in the process of coming undone.

In Victorian England as in Carlyle's fictional Germany, the charge that too many teachers trained the "faculty called Memory" at the expense of "Mind" would echo in the discourse of educational reform.[64] We have already encountered a version of this charge in Mill's *Autobiography*, with its dismissal of "mere exercises of memory." In the teaching of English rather than Latin, and when it came to the education of public school students rather than home-schooled prodigies like Mill, reformers likewise opposed "instruction by rote" or "word-teaching only," which they thought, even without the appliance of birch-rods, would militate against the formation of upstanding citizens, of "earnest and truthful men."[65] Consider the account written by James Kay-Shuttleworth, who contrasts "the rote teacher" with the "master" who is instead "accustomed to regard himself as the interpreter of nature, as the engrafter of thoughts and not of words, and who is endeavoring to form the character of his pupils by inspiring them with an earnest love for truth."[66] From such a modern master, "pupils will gladly take much upon authority with a lively confidence," whereas "from the rote teacher they take nothing but words; he gains no confidence; it is difficult to love him, because it is not obvious what good he communicates."[67] What is "lively" in this teaching serves to shore up the teacher's "authority," and we can note in passing, returning to the terms I analyzed in the Introduction to this book, that the engrafting of thoughts is clearly more intrusive, not less, than the engrafting or enforced mechanical repetition of mere words, or what Kay-Shuttleworth here calls "word-teaching only." Though outwardly apparently deadening in its mechanicity, this teaching could in fact sustain possibilities for thought. This, at least, becomes Pater's view and is what he means when he refers, in "Emerald Uthwart," to the "complication of influence" that an "older method" of teaching affords (*MS* 205).

With his affinity for dead languages, dictionaries, and rituals of various kinds, the late Pater was by all accounts "difficult to love" like the "rote teacher" described by Kay-Shuttleworth. Hence Oscar Wilde's question, posed just after Pater's death: "Was he ever alive?"[68] Recall, too, that in his rendering of Pater, one early biographer found fault with the lexicon-loving author's reliance on words that were "anything but living and social."[69] But *Marius* everywhere attests to Pater's interest in the social function of words, phrases, and rites whose status as "living" matters less than their status as surviving. It is this latter status from which Marius will learn and to which Pater will repeatedly direct his reader's attention.

Beginning early in his career, Pater made "survivals" bear considerable conceptual weight.[70] Derived from the work of anthropologist Edward Burnett Tylor, who originated what became known as the "doctrine of survivals," this understanding of "survivals" sought to account for "the presence of the past in the present."[71] For Tylor and his followers, "survivals" named cultural practices and beliefs that remained operative long after they had lost their relevance, utility, or significance—indeed, often "in the very teeth of common sense"—as when "an idea, the meaning of which has perished for ages, may continue to exist simply because it has existed."[72] Tylor's *Primitive Culture* thus associates survivals with superstitions, both historically and etymologically: "The very word 'superstition,' in what is perhaps its original sense of a 'standing over' from old times, itself expresses the notion of survival. But the term 'superstition' now implies a reproach, and though this reproach may be often cast deservedly on fragments of a dead lower culture embedded in a living higher one, yet in many cases it would be harsh, and even untrue."[73] The Tylorian anthropologist should therefore be curious rather than dismissive and should treat such surviving fragments as "facts ... to be worked as mines of historic knowledge."[74]

The presence of "survivals" in *Marius* is marked and decisive from the first. In fact, the novel begins with a disquisition on the "survival" of a "religion of usages and sentiment rather than of facts and belief" (*M* 37):

> Glimpses of such a survival we may catch below the merely artificial attitudes of Latin pastoral poetry; in Tibullus especially, who has preserved for us many poetic details of old Roman religious usage.
>
> > At mihi contingat patrios celebrare Penates,
> > Reddereque antiquo menstrua thura Lari:
>
> —he prays, with unaffected seriousness. (*M* 37)

A prayer—"Something liturgical," as Pater's narrator goes on to call it—sets the tone for the novel as a whole (*M* 37). And it matters that this prayer in the form of a lyric, attesting to the "survival" in the country of what in the city is already obsolete, also addresses a practice precisely: not an inward state but rather what it befalls the speaker (*mihi contingat*) to do. The lines quoted here bear on a custom that, like one of Tylor's survivals, if not with quite the same longevity, continues to exist simply because it has existed. Pater's point is that the Roman poet gives no theological reason—and feels no need to give any such reason—for the burning of incense and the honoring of household gods in keeping with a ritual calendar that also figures in Tylor's chapter on "Survival in Culture." There the anthropologist adduces Ovid to account for the still-circulated "saying that marriages are unlucky in May": "Ovid mentions the vulgar Roman objection to marriages in May, which he not unreasonably explains by the occurrence in that month of the funeral rites of the Lemuralia."[75]

This is a striking point of comparison between Pater's *Marius* and Tylor's *Primitive Culture*. But, of course, there are important differences between the two works as well: in citing Tibullus, Pater's narrator takes care to distinguish surfaces from depths, and to remark on tone and "attitudes" as well as content, whereas Tylor offers the better-known Ovid's lines without commentary, solely and strictly as evidence of an ancient folk belief. These differences of course make disciplinary and generic sense: *Marius* is not an ethnography, after all, but rather a fictional study of *Sensations and Ideas*, and one that explicitly takes "sentiment[s] ... rather than ... facts" as its objects (*M* 37). But I would argue that the differences between Tylor's text and Pater's are both more complex and more consequential. In addition to stopping short of the mining of historical fragments for facts in which Tylor's method culminates, Pater's deeply pedagogical deployment of survivals in *Marius* also reverses the terms of the Tylorian hierarchy. Tylor's "fragments of a dead lower culture embedded in a living higher one" come to take precedence: the "dead" culture is repositioned above the "living" one, becoming the site of the lesson that the latter must learn. Touching on the present and befalling it (*contingans*), imposing "a year-long burden of forms" (*M* 38), giving direction and dictation (as both Flavian and Marcus Aurelius will in Pater's novel), the past that has "perished for ages" stands over the present in more ways than one.[76]

The etymological plot begun in *Primitive Culture* thickens in ways the Latinist Pater would have appreciated, because the "original sense" of superstition was not, *pace* Tylor, "a 'standing over' from old times." The English word is in fact derived from the Latin *superstes*, meaning most simply standing over, in a physical rather than temporal sense. *Superstes*'s "semantic motivation" is unknown, according to the *Oxford English Dictionary*, but "Cicero suggested . . . that superstitious people (*superstitiosi*) were so called because they practiced excessive religious devotion in order that their children might survive (*superstites essent*), but this is probably a folk etymology. . . . In classical Latin *superstes* was used," the *OED* continues, "with reference to a soldier standing over the prostrate body of a defeated enemy."[77] In the case of superstition, then, as in that of "survival" (from the Latin *supervivo*, where the prefix "super" likewise indicates primarily "physical position above or on top of something"),[78] uprightness belongs to the body that lives on, lording it over by simply *standing* over the body of the vanquished or of the children who take the latter's place on the horizontal plane.

For his part, Pater's protagonist never graduates from this lower position in order to accede to an upright or victorious one.[79] "To the last, Marius is seeking."[80] He survives, to be sure, in transitive and intransitive senses: he outlives both parents, an early, life-threatening illness, and a plague that ravages whole towns as well as much of Rome itself. The plague also kills Flavian, Marius's beloved teacher and friend, and the scene of Flavian's death indeed offers Pater's protagonist the opportunity to become *superstes*: to stand over the body that he also watches over. (During Flavian's last night, "Marius lay down beside him," but the next morning finds "Marius standing by the dead, watching," and he struggles for a whole day in this "effort to watch by" his friend's corpse [*M* 101].) His vigil, though, gives way not to greater literary independence but to another humbling textual apprenticeship: having taken dictation from the charismatic, then the "almost abject" Flavian (*M* 101),

Marius follows an imperial summons to Rome, where he becomes Marcus Aurelius's eager "*amanuensis*" (*M* 124). Here he also falls in with the Christian soldier Cornelius, ethically superior but still importantly comparable to Flavian in that he wields power over Marius with a "charm, rather physical than moral": "And wholly different as was this later friendship . . . from the feverish attachment to Flavian, which had made him at times like an uneasy slave, still, like that, it was a reconciliation to the world of sense, the visible world" (*M* 166). So Pater's narrator characterizes Cornelius—uneasily indeed, since one friendship cannot be both "like" and "wholly different" from another. This contradiction suggests that, at this point in Pater's "relentlessly circuitous" narrative, Marius *has* been made slavish again after all: the language of servitude, "dominion," "fascination," and "sway" first associated with Flavian is transferred onto Cornelius in an almost psychoanalytic sense (*M* 64).[81] This is also to say that, having matured, Marius regresses to dependence, in another instance of *Bildung* become *Bindung*: "Again, as in his early days with Flavian, a vivid personal presence broke through the dreamy idealism, which had almost come to doubt of other men's reality, reassuringly, indeed, yet not without some sense of a constraining tyranny from without" (*M* 130).[82]

Following a short-lived phase of verticality, Marius is thus effectively lowered again as he is set to work for two charismatic men: the emperor *cum* "lecturer" whose meditations he compiles (*M* 121) and the soldier with whom he "[i]dentif[ies] himself" (*M* 289). It is as though his upright phase—Marius's brief stint as a *superstes*—were meant to underscore with its very brevity the importance of these returns to the baseline. Here he will remain until his last mechanical exercises and his martyrdom, for even at their most spiritual, the lessons that Marius learns in Rome tend toward something other than uplift. It's not that these lessons keep him in his place; he is not so much stationary as stationed time and again in places where the past's survival is also its standing over the present, the persistence of perpendicularity.

By this I mean that Pater makes Marius repeatedly encounter and increasingly cede to "a weighty tradition," "a remnant of right conduct" aligned with convention, derived from ritual, and positioned "over and above" the protagonist himself (*M* 178). By virtue of this position, the past's remnants or survivals become capable of correcting Marius's "own elaborately thought-out intellectual scheme," the scheme painstakingly outlined in the first two parts of Pater's novel (*M* 176). Part the Third in *Marius* opens with two chapters that stage a veritable if still "pagan" conversion: "Stoicism at Court" and "Second Thoughts." These especially dense chapters constitute the pedagogical centerpiece as well as the philosophical turning point in Pater's text. (I have already quoted from them while gesturing toward the possibility of a quarrel between *Marius* and Mill.) With good reason, then, the first of these chapters presents a scene of instruction—one of many in the novel, but one that uniquely stays with Marius for the whole length of a lesson: a public lecture on stoicism given by Marcus Aurelius's beloved teacher, Cornelius Fronto. Whereas Flavian's teachings on style are delivered piecemeal across several chapters, and the novel elsewhere quotes an address by the emperor in its entirety and still elsewhere imitates Platonic dialogue, Fronto's lecture is reported indirectly, filtered all the while through Marius's thoughts. This filtering lets Pater's narrator register the effects of instruction in a sustained way and with particular vividness: Marius's mind wanders, but it does so along lines that the "Stoic professor" lays down (*M* 177), in a "style" that looks backward to "the authority of approved ancient models" with its "long, skillfully modulated sentences" and forward to Pater's own "Style" in that Fronto's is also "a management, by which subtle, unexpected meaning was brought out of familiar terms, like flies from morsels of amber" (*M* 176). The speaker's words themselves become repositories of past meanings, "brought out" again in the narrative present, just as the aged, surviving Fronto himself embodies another era.

"And it happened with Marius, as it will sometimes happen, that this general discourse to a general audience had the effect of an utterance adroitly designed for him" (*M* 176). But though seemingly "designed for him," Fronto's discourse in fact *displaces* Marius: it speaks to his current preoccupations but does so precisely by alienating him from "his own elaborately thought-out intellectual scheme." Marius has just been deeply disturbed by the spectacle of gladiatorial games ("the novel-reading of that age," Pater's narrator opines), which force him to confront the limits of Aurelius's ethical system and of "pagan" morals more generally. It is therefore an implicitly proto-Christian answer to this system that Marius, led by Fronto, discovers in "the old morality" (*M* 176). Put another way, *Marius* presents Christianity itself as the second coming of this morality. This means that Pater's protagonist's learning is still learning from the past even when he comes into contact with "the future" (*M* 170).

Fronto's lecture reminds Marius of resources that have long since been available to him (and that remain available because, as we read later, "the boy-priest" in him "survived" [*M* 234]), leading him out of the "revolt against accustomed modes" that his intellectual quest had previously entailed (*M* 177). By recalling these modes, which themselves recall the conventions from which the "Conclusion" wanted to be free, Pater's protagonist rediscovers "how much the manner, because the heart itself, counts" (*M* 177). "Over and above ... natural affection or self-love or fear," "there is a remnant of right conduct, what he does, still more what he abstains from doing, not so much through his own free election, as from a deference, an 'assent,' entire, habitual, unconscious, to custom—to the actual habit or fashion of others, from whom he could not endure to break away" (*M* 178). These others become, a page later, those "whose faces averted from him, would be more than he could endure" (*M* 179), and Pater's repeated emphasis on the unbearable nature of the separation that Marius avoids tightens the bond between these others and the "observances, customs, usages" that Fronto claims are indispensible (*M* 178). It is as if these usages *became* the others that they embody, the souls with whom they keep Marius in touch. Hence the feeling of utter loneliness that overtakes Marius as he contemplates what it would mean "to break away." The realization that the "revolt" implied by his "'antinomianism'" must entail such loneliness leads Marius to regroup—if not to retreat outright, then at least to rethink his youthful strategy (*M* 177). One person's "elaborately thought-out intellectual scheme" turns out to be insufficient, and Marius therefore, following Fronto, looks to the past, engaging in an "assent entire, habitual, unconscious, to custom."

"Entire, habitual, unconscious," and mechanical: Pater reintroduces this last word in his next chapter, "Second Thoughts," where he also importantly reintroduces the language of freedom and constraint. Here, again, under new Cyrenaic "masters" (*M* 186), Marius assents to "some curtailment of his liberty" (*M* 188). The teaching methods of "the old Cyreniacs" are mechanical (M 186). To repeat: "The authority they exercised was that of classic taste—an influence so subtle yet so real, as defining the loyalty of the scholar—or of some beautiful and venerable ritual, in which every observance is become ... almost mechanical" (*M* 188). "Second Thoughts" thus recalls the tone-setting moment on *Marius*'s first page, when Pater's reader first encounters a "religion of usages and sentiment rather than of facts and belief" (*M* 37). Such encounters recur throughout the text: "Roman religion, as Marius knew, had, indeed, been always something to be done, rather than something to be thought, or believed, or loved; something to be done in minutely detailed manner, at a particular time and place, correctness in which had been a long matter of laborious learning with a whole school of ritualists" (*M* 137). Likewise are the evolving and syncretic rituals of the early Christians lovingly described as so many "action[s]" (*M* 248): even when Pater's narrator emphasizes Christianity's new aspiration to the status of "fact" (*M* 248), Marius's attention remains reserved for the outward elements of this worship: gestures, "*vestimenti*" (*M* 249), "hymns, prayer, silence," Latin choruses lovingly quoted (*M* 248). Throughout the novel, Pater's narrator signals Marius's adherence to the "school of ritualists" (*M* 137). "Stoicism and Court" and "Second Thoughts" consider the implications of this adherence.

That one neither can nor should aspire to break with the past is the old news that *Marius*'s two key chapters bear as they distill Pater's effort to counter progress using the resources of ritual. Ellis Hanson clarifies the stakes of Pater's interest in these resources, highlighting the convergence of orthodoxy and radicalism in the author's return to Rome "at a time when ritualism was a major political battle." Hanson further notes the feminizing disdain with which "young men who, like Pater, sought out ritualistic churches" were treated by "disapproving Protestants."[83] Hanson's reference to Protestantism provides a key context for the novel, helping us to specify the religion of "facts and belief" against which Pater positions Roman *and* early Christian rituals.[84] Programmatically, then, with its would-be liturgy, *Marius* contests "the Protestant doctrine that correct belief must be more highly valued than correct practice."[85]

In recent decades, anthropologists have traced the legacies of this consequential doctrine, which they have described as instrumental to the construction of "the moral narrative of modernity" and thus indirectly to the consolidation of national and colonial rule.[86] For Webb Keane, this narrative insists that "progress is not only a matter of improvements in technology, economic well-being, or health but is also, and perhaps above all, about human emancipation and self-mastery." To "become modern" is therefore to "realize the true character of human agency." "What makes this a specifically Protestant strand" or doctrine, Keane concludes, "is that the narrative tends, often only by implication, to link moral progress to practices of detachment from and reevaluation of materiality," including the materiality of language, or what Keane elsewhere calls "the recalcitrance of semiotic form."[87] Keane argues that as inward faith becomes privileged over outward, ritual performance—and "facts and belief" over what Pater calls "usages"—the modern subject is increasingly "abstracted from material and social entanglements in the name of greater freedom."[88] This process of abstraction leads to the elevation of "Mind" over "the faculty called Memory" and mechanical exercise.[89] It thus also leads to educational philosophies like Mill's, to "intellectual scheme[s]" like the one that Marius rethinks (*M* 176), and to "antinomianism[s]" like the early Pater's (*M* 177).

As the "Conclusion" makes clear, the Paterian subject never was free from material entanglements; even in the early text, this subject is thoroughly enmeshed in the physical world to which he is susceptible and by which he is made.[90] But the "Conclusion" does imagine a subject who is abstracted from what Kean calls "social entanglements," freed from the encumbrances of "what is only conventional," in Pater's words (*R* 120). The decisive, counter-progressive shift in Pater's work thus becomes visible in his later attempt to affirm a subjectivity that is socially *and* materially entangled. With their radical recasting of "what is only conventional" as the past from which Marius cannot "endure to break away," "Stoicism at Court" and "Second Thoughts" rehearse this shift (*M* 178). It stands to reason that these chapters center on pedagogy, for the shift they effect—away from "antinomianism" and toward an acknowledgment of the claims of convention—implies a valorization of transmission. This shift accounts as well for Pater's effort to rehabilitate the "mere exercises of memory" that Mill emphatically went without. Such exercises encode the past not left behind; they enact the "assent" to custom that Fronto advocates (*M* 178) and enforce the "curtailment of . . . liberty" that Marius learns painstakingly to accept (*M* 188). Pater privileges "exercises of memory," then, because they register the social entanglements that he seeks to affirm, entanglements that key strands in progressive educational thought would deny. Marius's lesson is therefore the reader's as well; Pater's narrator provides readers with a version of the schooling that Marius receives.

But for all its "modernisms" (*M* 269), *Marius* is not Joyce's *A Portrait of the Artist as a Young Man*. Pater's narrator does not, as in Joyce's conceit, recognizably grow, change, learn, or recollect "together" with his protagonist.[91] In fact, the distance that divides the narrator from the character whose "mental pilgrimage" he recounts remains unbridgeable; the difference between the two undeniable (*M* 110). That there can be no final rapprochement between the narrator's London and Marius's Rome is part of Pater's point. Hence his narrator's frequent prolepses and anachronisms. These mark the narrator's separation from the narrated world of the past, his coming from a present in which rites need to be explained and dead vocables translated. Still, his coming from this present does not make him fully one with it; the narrator treats English, after all, "as a learned language,"[92] in keeping with Pater's recommendation in "Style." His erudition is evident at every turn, on show as scholarship become stylishness, as the means by which he is kept in touch with "ancient models" (*M* 176). The narrator's disquisitions are, therefore, to the reader what Fronto's discourse and the Cyrenaics' teachings are to Marius: they place "over and above" the past that one might otherwise pretend to *be* above, and to have left behind. In this sense, it is the reader who, though always kept at a distance from Marius, engages in exercises with him; Pater's narrator, for his part, administers these exercises "one after another" (*M* 396).

I have noted the novel's intimacy with the Marius who takes dictation. Crucially, though, this intimacy never leads to an effacement of the distinction between character and narrator. On the contrary, by maintaining a separation between them, Pater installs a survival at the heart of his narrative. If Marius and the narrator really were identified or interchangeable with one another, then historical difference would be denied. Likewise, if the novel's nineteenth century and its Rome really were typologically identical or equivalent, then there would be no way to account for the text's interest in survivals.[93] In fact, though, like Fronto, Carlyle's "mechanical Gerund-grinder," or Kay-Shuttleworth's "rote teacher," Pater's narrator *becomes* a survival.[94] And it is, Pater suggests, through the mediation of such survivals that the past should be studied: neither fully internalized nor "engrafted," but rather read, reread, recited, and valued for its difference from the present that returns to it, going back over it again, mechanically.

Through this valorization of anachronism—of the ritual, liturgical, and mechanical—Pater reorders the civilizational hierarchy that he might at first appear merely to reinforce. An "importance attached to forms or observances" was a hallmark of traditional education, including in the British colonies; it stood opposed to modern knowledge and reformed education.[95] Pater asks readers to attend to the resources that remain available as survivals in modern as well as ancient worlds. In *Marius*, even more than in Tylor,[96] these are "forms" (*M* 38), not contents; usages, not facts; customs, not beliefs—or beliefs that are only superstitions, not substantiated. They are the repositories of pasts. They remain, as Marius learns, things "to be done," and means by which we might yet become something.

Each Mind Keeping

"What is this song or picture, this engaging personality presented in life or in a book, to *me*? What effect does it really produce on me? Does it give me pleasure, and if so, what sort or degree of pleasure?" (*R* 3; emphasis in original). For the young Pater, these questions exemplified "the aim of the true student of aesthetics" (*R* 3). Such a student understood, as Pater wrote in the Preface to his *Studies in the History of the Renaissance*, that "Beauty ... is relative," not abstract or absolute (*R* 3). The critic could not but begin with his own experience of a "song or picture"; his task was therefore to produce an account of that experience, to analyze and explain objects on the basis of it. In this sense, it's hard to think of a better or more brilliant student of Pater's than Roland Barthes. The author of *The Pleasure of the Text* and the unapologetic *Roland Barthes by Roland Barthes* inherits and endlessly reinflects the questions posed in Pater's Preface. Especially later in his career, Barthes gives himself permission—and no doubt enjoys the institutional permission—explicitly to tarry with the question of what an object means to *him*. He makes himself "the measure of... 'knowledge'": "So I resolved," he writes, to take just one example, "to start my inquiry with no more than a few photographs, the ones I was sure existed *for me*."[97]

And yet it's hard to imagine any place farther from the utopia that ends Barthes's *How to Live Together* than Pater's utopian version of ancient Sparta in "Lacedaemon," a lecture to which I have already referred. The late Barthes thus continues to learn from the early Pater but would seem to share nothing with the later "aesthetic critic," with the Pater who valorizes mechanical exercise. Reading the two writers' late utopias together, however, makes it possible to bring out the late Pater's specificity. To this end, and in order to assess what Pater may still have to teach us, I offer a concluding, comparative account of two sets of late lectures.

In the last of his lectures on living together, Barthes says that he has come to understand that "a utopia of idiorrythmic Living-Together is not a social utopia. Now, from Plato to Fourier," Barthes continues, "all written utopias have been social: an attempt to fix upon the ideal organization of power."[98] Refusing the rigidity that this "attempt to fix upon" implies, Barthes claims instead simply to be "setting out some ... principles of the idiorrhythmic Good."[99] This is in keeping with the "protocol" of the lecture course as a whole: with programmatic provisionality, as Barthes has said from the first and repeats by way of conclusion, *How to Live Together* sets out principles, or rather strikes poses, adopting in place of decisiveness "the mobile posture of someone at work (not thinking of the end result)."[100] Far from "fetishiz[ing] the goal as a privileged place, to the detriment of other possible places," Barthes lets the latter proliferate as he pursues "*Paideia*," defined as the "eccentric path of possibilities, stumbling among blocks of knowledge."[101] The worker, then, is also a stumbling student, grouped with others including "athletes, orators, statues."[102]

Pater's lectures on *Plato and Platonism*, including "Lacedaemon," assemble figures like these as well, making a virtue of nearly Barthesian "mutability" as they, too, consider workers, students, athletes, orators, and statues.[103] Unlike Barthes's "protocol," though, Pater's approach seems nothing if not ends-driven, "an attempt to fix upon" a model, if not quite an ideal, in the ancient, ascetic past. This may account for the comparative ease with which we assimilate and apply Barthes's more easy-going and open-ended model of multiplicity. This social model—which isn't, in fact, according to Barthes, either social or a model—makes almost no demands apart from the demand for "distance and respect, a relation that's in no way oppressive but at the same time where there's a real warmth of feeling"; it has, Barthes says repeatedly, plenty of rules but no regulations.[104] And it is worth asking after this model's critical appeal at a time of ongoing economic deregulation and state withdrawal from social provision.

We know that one entailment of such deregulation has been coercive legislation and policing, and that the expansion of a certain kind of "freedom" has in fact been wholly compatible with, for example, mass incarceration. In light of this compatibility, it may be worth pointing to one last moment in Barthes's lectures on living together. In a glaringly odd passage, Barthes wonders whether his own "idiorrhythmic fantasy," his vision of "a distance permeated, irrigated by tender feeling," might be "perhaps, in its way, taking the differences in historical context and ideology into account, comparable to what Plato was getting at under the name of *Sophronistery*."[105] Here Barthes is referring to the *sophronisterion* in Plato's *Laws*: what his translators call a "house of correction" but is elsewhere rendered as a "reformatory" or "a place where people learn moderation." This was to be a prison *cum* boarding school where "curable wrongdoers would undergo a process of reeducation" by means of nightly assemblies during which officials would admonish them.[106]

Given Barthes's methodological disclaimers, it would obviously be unfair—because against the stated spirit of the lectures—to read this reference to the *sophronisterion* as at all definitive. Still, the reader is hard-pressed to think of any set of "differences in historical context and ideology" that would suffice to make Plato's vision comparable to Barthes's own. Barthes, again, says early on that "the exact opposite of idiorrhythmy" is the rhythm that defines places like "barracks, boarding schools."[107] And there can be no denying the oppressiveness of the relation in and by which, in the Platonic institution, sense is beaten into the inmate-students to be cured. This institutional oppressiveness recalls the memorably tyrannical mother who, in Barthes's introduction, "walks at her own pace, unaware of the fact that her son's rhythm is different," wielding power "through disrhythmy, heterorhythmy"—except that the *Sophronistery* makes this mother look tame.[108]

Returning to Pater, we can compare the residents of this *sophronisterion* to the prisoners to whom Pater refers in the "Conclusion," when he writes of utter and ineluctable solitude as constitutive of experience: "Experience . . . is ringed round for each one of us by that thick wall of personality through which no real voice has ever pierced on its way to us, or from us to that which we can only conjecture to be without. Every one of those impressions is the impression of the individual in his isolation, each mind keeping as a solitary prisoner its own dream of a world" (R 119). Pater here defines and universalizes the predicament of solipsism. We've neither heard nor made ourselves heard—neither seen nor been seen—through the prison wall that surrounds us. What matters most, for Pater, is that the confinement remains solitary, so that, perforce keeping its own private dream, the mind "can only conjecture," not perceive, what is or must be outside it. In such a context, there can be no nightly, Platonic admonitions; or rather, admonitions can only be provided by the mind turned against itself—unless it benefits from the cure that Pater prescribes, a cure whose end is, the "Conclusion" says, "Not the fruit of experience but experience itself." Thus the very "experience" that he has just confined to a "narrow chamber" Pater proceeds to render limitless in his turn from lament to exhortation: "Our one chance is in expanding [life's] interval, in getting as many pulsations as possible into the given time" (R 121). The youthful Pater's answer to radical isolation involves the expansion of the "individual mind." In this sense, as in its attempt to graduate from "what is only conventional" (R 120), the "Conclusion" bears the traces of philosophical liberalism.[109]

But it's possible to hear another echo in the figure of "each mind keeping as a solitary prisoner its own dream of a world," because to keep is to "guard, defend, protect, preserve, [and] save," as one does with a secret, but also to "preserve in being or operation; to maintain, retain, or continue to hold" as one does with time or a tune.[110] In other words, Pater's solitary dream may also be a *rhythm*, and its keeping may therefore be the upholding of an idiorrhythmic practice in Barthes's sense. I have suggested that, for all its undeniable promise, such a practice might be limited by its relation to living together. Barthes posits a kind of negative freedom—a freedom from imposition, impingement, or heterorhythmy—as a precondition for the realization of "the idiorrhythmic Good."[111] I'm less interested in asking whether we can do without a vision of this Good than in asking after Barthes's desire to do without its others: without, again, heterorrhythmy and all the rest, a desire belied by the *sophronisterion* secreted in How to Live Together.

What would it mean to take these as given, to begin not with the solitary prisoner, "individual mind," or Barthes's independent *idios*, but rather with the child dragged along, to Barthes's dismay, by his mother or another? What would it mean not to suspend the world outside Pater's prison or conjure it away, but rather to accept the social surround that both precedes and shapes "each mind"? I have argued that Pater's late work offers answers to these questions as it turns and returns to the school. Recall the child dragged along by the bad mother in Barthes's account. If, for Barthes, the imposition of rhythm begins at home, for Pater it really gets underway in school. According to Pater, the young child in Sparta

> left his home, his tender nurses in those quiet old suburban houses early, for a public school, a schooling all the stricter as the years went on, to be followed,

even so, by a peculiar kind of barrack-life, the temper of that, a sort of military monasticism (it must be repeated) would beset him to the end. Though in the gymnasia of Lacedaemon no idle by-standers, no—well! Platonic loungers after truth or what not—were permitted, yet we are told, *neither there nor in Sparta generally, neither there nor anywhere else, were the boys permitted to be alone*. If a certain love of reserve, of seclusion, characterized the Spartan citizen as such, it was perhaps the cicatrice of that wrench from a soft home into the imperative, inevitable gaze of his fellows, broad, searching, minute, his regret for, his desire to regain, moral and mental even more than physical ease. And his education continued late.... (*PP* 221; emphasis added)

Until age thirty at least, Pater will go on to specify. This passage appears near the beginning of Pater's lecture on Spartan society, which centers on Spartan public schools. That phrase itself, "public schools," is, of course, like "suburban houses," anachronistic, a superposition of the ancient educational system onto the abiding English one, which Pater, sounding old-school indeed, regards as continuing at the best of times the best traditions of its past, those that Plato so admired. I single out this moment in Pater's "Lacedaemon" because of the stipulations that it takes to be primary: if the duration of the "military monasticism" into which the young student is thrown "must be repeated," then the terms of this stipulation (which I have italicized) bear repeating as well: "*Neither there nor in Sparta generally, neither there nor anywhere else, were the boys permitted to be alone.*"

The reader may trip over the lack of logical contradiction between this part of the sentence and the clauses that precede it. Pater's presupposition here seems to be that, like whatever else would happen in gymnasia, exercise inherently, or at least ordinarily, entails taking turns and invites spectators. Pater appears to assume, in other words, that accompanied exercise would typically entail or invite one person's standing by and looking on and that simultaneous, synchronized workouts like those required by Spartan schoolmasters would have been difficult to coordinate. The automatic thing would be for one boy or bystander to linger and Platonically to lounge for the duration of the other's exercise. Instead, togetherness without turn-taking, sociality without cease or caesura, are the consequences of the Spartans' prohibition on solitude, which leaves no child behind. This is at once school without recess and punishment without reprieve; the admonition's not nightly but rather all day, and Pater's prisoners are now anything but solitary.

But no sooner do we learn about this ban than we read of a "love of reserve" that, Pater writes, must be its result or residue later in life. More precisely, we encounter the scar, the "cicatrice," left by the system of rules, both military and monastic, by which Spartan sociality is enforced. Here the protection from or barrier to relation becomes the very medium of relation. "Cicatrice" is a Latinate word that grates against the Germanic "wrench" in the immediate vicinity. "Cicatrice" is also, to state the obvious, a word that, in English, calls a lot of attention to itself; it's like those words about which the author's biographers complained: plucked from dictionaries and deposited directly into Pater's prose, these words threatened, or perhaps aspired, to upstage all surrounding ones. This is a good example of why Pater's detractors called his style "insubordinate": it wore down collective entities, both social and syntactic, for the sake of their individual members, who were therefore no longer members but rather so many mutineers. Again, "the unity of the book," one wrote representatively, "is decomposed to give place to the independence of the page, ... the page is decomposed to give place to the phrase, and the phrase to give place to the independence of the word."[112] It's thus as if the word "cicatrice" were encoding some of the reserve or distance from the immediate world that it's meant to name.[113]

But the context of Pater's lecture makes it clear that this distance is paradoxically the *product* of closeness: again, the scar that the latter leaves behind. For all its apparent lexical independence, the cicatrice is otherwise (grammatically and semantically) altogether dependent on the social world that not only surrounds it but also creates it in the first place, marking a skin that we are not invited to imagine could ever remain unscathed. This inscription instantiates Jean Laplanche's "priority of the other."[114] If Barthes, responding to this priority, wants to escape from the top-down imposition of a rhythm by power, then the late Pater, despite his association with "retreat," wants to think of ways to live together that might follow, rather than flee, from this imposition. For, again, the temper of the "barrack-life" into which the Spartan boy is thrown must "beset" him before it can give way to another arrangement,[115] one that no longer militates against but instead facilitates seclusion, or what remains of it: an old wound. That this besetting is rhythmic is shown by the pride of place given to music in Pater's Sparta, where dance is "the perfect flower of their correction" (*PP* 225), and music serves "everywhere, not to alleviate only but actually to promote and inform, to be the very substance of their so strenuous and taxing habit of life" (*PP* 200).

For this reason, Pater writes, "Those who in other places had lost their taste amid the facile splendours of a later day, might here go to school again" (*PP* 213), where "here" points both to Sparta and to the page itself, the text of the lecture that he is delivering. Pater's account itself thus becomes an instrument of education, and if his aesthetic state sounds unappealing as well as unbearably masculinist relative to Barthes's, then it may help to remember once more the "Conclusion" to which an earlier Pater was led in his book on the Renaissance. Instructively, that text's liberal individualism is replaced in *Plato and Platonism* by a regimentation that is formative, rather than ruinous, of "each mind." Reserve remains available in Spartan schools as the outcome, not the avoidance, of this regimentation. Like Marius in a later age and the boys reciting Horace in the English public school in "Emerald Uthwart" still later, the students in "Lacedaemon" are meant to show what ritual and repeated, material and mechanical exercise can enable, all it can entail that is not the repetition of the same. In this way, Pater makes the case for why we might yet go to school again, in a phrase.

2. Among *Fanciulli*
Poetry, Pedantry, and Pascoli's Paedagogium

"Tu sei antichissimo, o fanciullo!" [You are so very ancient, o little boy!]
—Giovanni Pascoli, *Il fanciullino*

Well-beloved and widely assigned by generations of Italian schoolteachers, Giovanni Pascoli has also been read for decades as having preached the gospel of the Child.[1] If Pater has been remembered mainly through phrases, Pascoli has been remembered as the author of little, onomatopoetic, and easy-to-remember lyrics and of the essay and *ars poetica Il fanciullino*, which seeks to provide these lyrics with an aesthetic, historical, and psychological justification. First published serially in 1897, then brought out in book form in 1903, *Il fanciullino* pays homage to the small child who lives in all of us—the little, little boy, as we might render the essay's doubly diminutive title term—and argues that poetry derives its peculiar power from its ability to speak to this *puer aeternus*, in his language.[2]

Il fanciullino's commitment to this language is so firm and programmatic that the text openly enacts the poetic phenomena it describes. Written in dialogue form, Pascoli's essay lets the little, little boy speak in verse, in his own voice. Thus allowed to have his say, the *fanciullino* periodically interrupts the exposition, like an improbably eloquent infant demanding attention:

Io poco voglio; pur, molto: accendere
io su le tombe mute la lampada
  che irraggi e conforti
    la veglia dei poveri morti.

Io tutto voglio; pur, nulla: aggiungere
un punto ai mondi della Via Lattea,
  nel cielo infinito;
    dar nuova dolcezza al vagito.[3]

[I want a little bit; or rather, a lot: to light
on the mute tombs the torch
   that might light up and comfort
      the vigil of the poor dead.

I want everything; or rather, nothing: to reach
A point on the worlds of the Milky Way,
   in the infinite sky;
      to give new sweetness to the cry.]

Here the *fanciullino*'s petulance, registered in the repetition of "Io ... voglio," is unmistakable, but offset by the way in which he cannily, chiastically reframes what he wants as really nothing much: merely "poco," to begin with; then even less, "pur, nulla." In their oscillation between a little and a lot, and all and nothing, these lines make a *fort/da* game of what the essay's longer prose passages claim is poetry's key tendency: the tendency to effect an adequation between need and desire, and world and mind, so that the reader comes to sense that the "little" that one can expect to receive is plenty, and conversely that the "nothing" that life seems to grant is, in fact, "infinite."

Such insights would seem to be anything but childish. On the contrary, they would seem to be attainable only as the fruit of mature philosophical reflection. Yet Pascoli's language makes these insights seem accessible even—perhaps especially—to the untutored. Rhyme here works to achieve neat resolution and therefore to discourage the kind of tarrying with complexity typically associated with negative capability. Pascoli's rhymes here instead align "conforti" with "morti," assuaging in advance the reader's fears for the latter, and they open the infantile "vagito" up to the expansive but somehow still cradling "infinito," a far cry here from the ego-annihilating expanse of Giacomo Leopardi's "L'infinito." Moreover, despite one instance of hyperbaton ("io su le tombe mute la lampada") and the lightly paradoxical back and forth or *fort/da* I have already referred to (whereby "poco" becomes "molto," and "tutto" "nulla"), the lines make few syntactic, lexical, or logical demands. Lines like these thus appear to address a minimally educated reader, whereas much of Pascoli's prose in *Il fanciullino* is obviously erudite. Such lines would seem to be so simple that even the simplest or youngest of readers would learn from them and very likely learn them by heart—and this, on account of their sweetness as well as their being served light.[4]

For like the *stilnovisti* who, inaugurating the Italian vernacular lyric tradition, made sweetness their shared poetic principle, Pascoli—here acting as ventriloquist or medium for the little, little boy—elevates *dolcezza* to the point where it does more than help the medicine go down. Sweetness becomes the means by which the infant's cry is made new—which is to say, made newly audible as something other than a primal scream. Indeed, whereas Lacanians and Leopardians alike might hear the infant's cry as announcing the human being's originary and irreparable misalignment with the world, or the demand always already in excess of any possible satisfaction, Pascoli picks up another signal altogether.[5] For him, the *vagito* is so susceptible of sweetening that it comes to bear the promise of satiation; in its poetic rendition, at least, the cry says that there will be enough. Rewritten by the *fanciullino* and transposed into his sweeter register, the *vagito* can be heard to repeat at a distance the injunction to grown men delivered in Pascoli's preface to the *Primi poemetti*: "Uomini, insomma contentatevi del poco" [Men, in a word, be content with the little bit].[6]

That such sweetened verse sometimes becomes cloying, just as this injunctions become cliché, matters less for my purposes here than that, with phrases like "*nuova dolcezza*," this verse signals its participation in the very canon that *Il fanciullino*'s (self-)infantilizing argument forswears.[7] I have emphasized the densely intertextual nature of the lines that I have quoted—their gesturing toward Leopardi as well as the *dolce stil novo*, to say nothing of the prayers to which they also indirectly point—less to recast their simplicity as deceptive than to give a sense of Pascoli's intimacy with the traditions on which he draws. Pascoli sustains this intimacy with tradition even at his most *fanciullesco*, his most childish.[8] The poetics of the *fanciullino* thus does not pretend to shed the layers of literary history in order to channel the *vagito* in its primal purity. Instead, Pascoli calls attention to his (late) place in the long history of lyric in which he participates, making a virtue of the poetic necessity of rendering the preverbal cry in writing.

So it turns out that the little, little boy is hyperliterate. This strange fact, related as it is to Pascoli's everywhere-apparent erudition, has of course not escaped critics' attention. Still, Pascoli's reception has tended to downplay the ways in which the poet's erudition becomes the *fanciullino*'s own. Similarly, critics have tended to ignore the products of what I am calling Pascoli's "pedantry" in favor of what they consider his more canon-worthy work. This has even, and improbably, meant aligning Pascoli's Latin poems (which are nothing if not learned) with his famously accessible vernacular verse, privileging the latter and distinguishing the former from mere academic "exercises."[9] Thus even critics who have read *Il fanciullino* against the grain, redefining its central figure as ambivalent, dead, or nonexistent—or giving the letter, rather than the voice, pride of place—have not addressed the contexts of the little, little boy's literacy.[10] They have treated the letter in Pascoli's essay and the fact of the boy's being lettered as matters of language as such rather than as embedded in any kind of institutionality. Sidelining the polemics, the teaching practices, and indeed the poetics that emerged from within the specific institution that was the school—and effectively consigning Pascoli's work on and among schoolchildren to a secondary, negligible place—these readings have insisted on the *fanciullino*'s blankness and purity.[11]

In this chapter, I claim that Pascoli looks to the child not because the latter is blank or pure or prior to all forms of institutionality, but rather *because he is educable in a particular sense*, awaiting less the development of his individual faculties than an actualization of the collective past that has the potential to enable release from what Pascoli sees as the present's impasse. This form of educability becomes vividly apparent if we take the relatively minor *Paedagogium*, rather than *Il fanciullino*, to be emblematic of Pascoli's project. Before turning directly to *Paedagogium*, a short narrative poem written in Latin the year *Il fanciullino* was first published in full (1903), I situate the text in several key contexts, past and present. First looking to an essay by Giorgio Agamben that takes Pascoli's "Pensieri scolastici" as its point of departure, I then ask what "scholastic," an adjective that Agamben elides, might have meant for the poet and his contemporaries, which also means asking why Pascoli's work has elicited an ongoing scholastic response.[12] I then show that *Paedagogium* offers implicit answers to these questions, answers that are surprising not least because of their distance from the *dolcezza* or straightforward sweetness that Pascoli's readers, following the *fanciullino*, have been led to expect.

Va, pensiero

> . . . the path in which he treads
> Is choked with grammars.
>
> —William Wordsworth, *The Prelude* (1805)

With good reason, then, in light of *Il fanciullino*'s lesson, as this lesson has been understood and passed on, Pascoli has been regarded as the high priest of the Italian strain of what William Empson, following Wyndham Lewis, calls "child-cult." Empson characterizes this cult as pastoral's last redoubt in modernity and traces its emergence to modern, scientific rationality's becoming so widespread as "to seem narrow and unescapable."[13] Child-cult, according to Empson, "depends on a feeling . . . that no way of building up character, no intellectual system, can bring out all that is inherent in the human spirit, and therefore that there is more in the child than any man has been able to keep."[14] In Pascoli's case, I have begun to show, this "more" is paradoxical in that it has to do with the capacity to make do with less, a capacity that atrophies, according to Pascoli, as the child matures and the inner *fanciullino* who survives him is forgotten, his voice drowned out by the adult world's demands. Empson's formulation nevertheless nicely captures what most readers have made of Pascoli's poetics of the *fanciullino*. By this account, the child is less the "father of the man" than the latter's loser son, whose lot is precisely *not* to get to "keep / [his] heritage."[15] For, as Empson notes, the realization of the child's potentials, his "building up" and *Bildung*, entail the relinquishment of at least some of "all that is inherent" in him. Education thus defined requires a squandering of inner riches and given possibilities that is also a veritable sacrifice: of "native poetry" if not of the child himself.[16] "I remember believing," Empson confides, "that I should have to die in order to grow up, and thinking the prospect very disagreeable."[17]

Critics have thus tended to read Pascoli as mourning—or as commemorating in the effort to hold onto or regain—the "more" whose renunciation Empson locates at the origin of "child-cult." The poet has been seen, in other words, consistently to record and variously to respond to "the progressive and inevitable loss of [childish] capability through time."[18] I have begun to argue, however, to the contrary, that Pascoli makes particular modes of building up and bringing out, to redeploy Empson's phrases, central to his poetics. This is not to say that he wholeheartedly embraces or imparts intact an already-extant "intellectual system." But he insists on his location within such a system in ways that the received critical narrative obscures even when it emphasizes Pascoli's investment in tradition.[19] There is a pedagogical specificity to the system that the poet's work indexes, one that the celebration of the *fanciullino* forgets even at its most sophisticated. The system in question is, I will show, a school system, and attention to the scholastic contexts within which he worked lets us see Pascoli's child anew. In fact, attention to this school system shows us that the figure that we took to be a version of the small, speechless "Seer blest" addressed in Wordsworth's "Intimations" ode turns out to be much more like that English poet's infant prodigy, whose path is "choked with grammars." Again, that is, Pascoli's painstaking child is hyperliterate. And Pascoli's readers are schooled as well.

Before considering the traces of the school system left in *Paedagogium* and elsewhere in Pascoli's work, however, I want to ask what happens when these traces are ignored. This will also mean establishing the persistence of the critical account according to which Pascoli assigns redemptive power—rather than, say, homework—to the child as such.[20] That even the most astute followers of the *fanciullino* continue to see Pascoli as a "child-cult" leader—more concerned with the "more" that is lost with time's passage than with the labor of "bringing out" what's left—is illustrated by Agamben's "Pascoli and the Thought of the Voice," to which I now turn.

Agamben frames his essay as a meditation on one of Pascoli's more startling claims: that "la lingua della poesia è sempre una lingua morta. Curioso a dirsi: una lingua morta che si usa a dare maggior vita al pensiero!" [the language of poetry is always a dead language. Strange to say: a dead language that is used to give greater life to thought!] (quoted in *EP* 62; *CI* 62).[21] This claim—made, again, in a polemical piece by Pascoli called "Pensieri scolastici"—prompts Agamben to situate "Pascoli's poetry in a dimension in which what is at issue is no longer simply his poetics but his dictation: the dictation of poetry, if we mean by this term (which we take from the vocabulary of medieval poetics, but which has never ceased to be familiar to the Italian poetic tradition) the experience of the originary event of speech itself" (*EP* 63; *CI* 62). Thus from the outset Agamben displaces Pascoli's poetics—or rather, "no longer simply his poetics," where the "simply" signals that poetics have been demoted, left behind. Perhaps taking his cue from Pascoli's dehistoricizing "always" ("the language of poetry is *always* a dead language," Pascoli writes), Agamben seeks to divest poetic language of all historical engagements and encumbrances, and instead to restore it—or show that Pascoli has already restored it—to a prior, indeed an "originary," location.[22]

Proceeding in typically paratactic fashion, Agamben draws on Paul and Augustine, connecting Pascoli's "dead language" to Paul's reflections on *glossolalia*, or speaking in tongues, and to Augustine's understanding of the *vocabulum emortuum*, or "dead word." Each of these terms designates a word that has shed its semantic weight but is not for all that nonsensical. According to Agamben, it is crucial in both Augustine and Paul that the reader or listener retain a sense that the foreign or outmoded word once signified, or still signifies somewhere, in some other context. This sense prevents the reader or listener from dismissing or tuning out the alien word, the instance of *glossolalia* or example of a *vocabulum emortuum*, as mere sound. Whereas Paul cautions Christians against the "barbarous" incomprehension that results from such a word's use—a speech situation in which words can be heard to signify without being understood—Augustine credits the dead word with the salutary potential to activate the soul's curiosity and even incite its love, a love Agamben predicates "as will to know": "The more the word is registered, without being fully so, the more the soul therefore desires to know that residue of knowledge" (quoted in *EP* 63; *CI* 62). The *vocabulum emortuum* has a claim on the latent "desire to know" greater than that of the already-known word, on the one hand (for, Augustine maintains, the soul "does not love" the "syllables he already knows"), or, on the other, the nonsense word or mere sound or "voice": for if the soul "knew only the existence of this voice and not *that it signified something*, the soul would have nothing to search for once it had perceived the sensible sound as best it could. But since the soul already knows that there is not only a voice but also a sign, it wants to have perfect knowledge of it" (quoted in *EP* 63–64; *CI* 62–63; emphasis added).

Passages like these do shed light on Pascoli's "lingua morta," even while they are clearly continuous with Agamben's abiding interest "in the very fact that human beings speak, that there is language and opening to sense beyond, before, or, rather *in* every determinate event of signification."[23] Augustine's *vocabulum emortuum* constitutes, after all, an "event of signification" that highlights this basic fact with singular clarity: in order for the search for the dead word's signification to begin, the fact "that it signified" must first be known or at least intuited. So this first step's status as a separate step in the process of coming to know the dead word's meaning—its being a precondition without which this process would never get underway—lets Agamben underscore "that there is." Indeed, "that there is language" is, in the passage from Augustine that Agamben discusses, not merely a precondition; it is even a fact privileged over signification, which becomes little more than an afterthought, the mere "residue of knowledge." For Augustine as well as for Agamben, then, the process of desiring to know matters more than its end result, knowing itself. Pascoli, recast as Augustine's legatee, comes to teach a "lesson," or a series of them, in this specific sense (*EP* 74): he seeks not to impart knowledge in a once-and-done way, but rather to awaken and keep alive the desire for lessons. Hence Pascoli's "greater life for thought," as Agamben understands it.

Critics since Gianfranco Contini, to whom Agamben dedicates his essay, have noted the paradoxical convergence of "pregrammatical" and "postgrammatical" elements in Pascoli's poetry.[24] This poetry privileges, on the one hand, words that are onomatopoetically imitative of nature—of birdsong, most famously—or outright "infantile," and, on the other, learned constructions of various kinds: obscure ornithological terms; dialectal and sometimes even apparently idiolectal usages requiring glossaries; foreign-language phrases; Latinisms and entire texts written in Latin. Agamben works to show that both of these types of utterances can be defined as "dead" in Augustine's desire-activating sense, since both "pre-" and "postgrammatical" structures stage "language's departure from its semantic dimension and its return to the original sphere of the pure intention to signify (not mere sound, but rather language and thought of the voice alone)" (*EP* 67). Thus Agamben argues, *contra* Contini, that onomatopoeia is not, in fact, truly "pregrammatical" but rather grammatical through and through, where the "*gramma*, the letter, which itself does not signify," becomes "the cipher of an intention to signify that will be accomplished" (*EP* 69)—but where this accomplishment, again, is secondary to the "desire to know" first stimulated by the cipher. "It is therefore not truly a matter of phono-symbolism," Agamben continues, countering another commonplace in Pascoli criticism, "but rather a matter of a sphere so to speak beyond or before sound, a sphere that does not *symbolize* anything as much as it *indicates* a pure intention to signify, that is, the voice in its originary purity. This is an indication that has its place neither in mere sound nor in signification but rather, we might say, in pure *grammata*, in pure letters" (*EP* 67; emphases in original).

But what are "pure letters"? And what is "a pure intention to signify"?[25] How could a signifying intention, however inspiring, ever attain purity, shedding all the baggage of the semantic and all ties to the pragmatic on the way to language's "original sphere"? Admittedly, all of this is, in Agamben's account, implicitly aspirational, rather than accomplished: using the language of departure and return, Agamben foregrounds Pascoli's movement toward prior "purity" rather than the poet's fixed abode there. But the fact remains: Agamben's is a "voice" in a vacuum, or at least one suspended in an "originary" state, uncontaminated by the signification to which it nevertheless points. For, as Agamben repeats, Pascoli's poems everywhere engage in an indexical operation: they indicate more than they symbolize. Importantly, though, "Pascoli and the Thought of the Voice" treats indexicality as a matter of pointing to *intention*—the "pure intention to signify"—rather than to *institutions*, sites within the social world. In his desire to highlight the "desire to know," Agamben denies the importance of such places, where there is no "pure letter," because the letter is always and irretrievably caught up in scenes of "intersubjective violence," in struggles for and negotiations with literacy.[26]

Of course, Agamben's interest is first and foremost in Pascoli's disclosure of structural, rather than historical, "experience" (*EP* 74; *CI* 72). It is therefore unsurprising that the philosopher, writing in a Heideggerian vein, sets aside questions relating to context and instead treats Pascoli's "thought of the voice" as though it were an instantiation or emanation of the "other breath" in "What are Poets For?": "The other breath is no longer solicitous for this or that objective thing; it is a breath for nothing."[27] Agamben amends this "for nothing" just slightly, to accommodate the purpose that, following Pascoli, he allows poetry to serve: that of giving "greater life to thought." My point, however, is that for Agamben this purpose does not and cannot constitute an "objective thing," since, in its capacity as "dictation" rather than mere "poetics," poetry has long since left all such things behind. I have referred to Jacques Derrida's notion of "the violence of the letter" in order to suggest that there are resources available within philosophy for nuancing Agamben's account, even for taking his decontextualizing reading, so to speak, back to school.[28]

To point out that Pascoli *was*, even in his verse, solicitous of objective things is thus not necessarily to refuse philosophy, any more than it is to suggest, with soulless literal-mindedness, that Pascoli's work was fully determined by the "present and practical, . . . real and useful" claims against which he protested.[29] It is instead to note that something critical (in both senses) falls away from Pascoli's poetics when such solicitations are ignored in the rush to "metaphysics" (*EP* 74). My next section elaborates this claim by rereading "Pensieri scolastici." Whereas Agamben seeks to preserve the *fanciullino*'s purity, returning to Pascoli's essay in another context makes it possible to see how this figure is set to work as poetry itself is "used to give greater life to thought."

Dust Called Erudite

> Dunque, lo Stato pedagogo? [So, the pedagogue State?]
>
> —Giovanni Gentile, "L'unità della scuola media e la libertà degli studi"

Suzanne Stewart-Steinberg has emphasized the centrality of the school in Italian political discourse following unification.[30] She shows that, given its belated formation and its trailing behind northern European nations when it came to modernization—whether defined as revolution, Reformation, or industrialization—Italy imagined itself, during the last decades of the nineteenth century, as "a state [still] in search of a nation" (*PE* 1). In this context, schools became the means by which a national character was to be built (*PE* 17) and the fact of historical belatedness made up for. At least, this was the idea: in the work of theorists and practitioners ranging from Francesco de Sanctis to Maria Montessori, pedagogical projects of various kinds came to represent the cures for what ailed Italians, for the "decadence" previously deemed, as in de Sanctis's worried diagnosis, all but "incurable" (quoted in *PE* 15). "For De Sanctis," Stewart-Steinberg writes, "the school must provide a training in nationhood, just as the nation itself must function as a great school" (*PE* 17). Meanwhile, for Montessori, "even when the focus was on the literal education of children, . . . the metonymic referent was in fact a nation composed only of children," but children who were to be educated *out* of "perpetual infancy" (*PE* 3). A double movement in these educational theories thus put new pressure on "the literal education of children" while also *generalizing* education—to the extent of rendering it figurative, or metonymic, in Stewart-Steinberg's gloss—so that it was seen to take place in all spheres of civic life, rather than simply in schools. Anticipating Gramsci's redrawing of the boundaries of the classroom to encompass all "relations of hegemony"—his contention that "the educational relationship should not be restricted to the field of . . . strictly 'scholastic' relationships" but rather "exists throughout society as a whole"—the progressive pedagogies that Stewart-Steinberg considers also had practical implications for generations of Italian (and not only Italian) youth.[31]

These were new schools, then, for Italy's new national dispensation. This is also to say that the reformers' projects positioned themselves against *old* schools, the institutions of classical education that came to be seen increasingly as outmoded relics of an obsolete past. This past, its critics contended, ought to have been left behind long ago. And it was a past that the newly modern nation would finally enable its citizens to outgrow, if only, paradoxically, in and through a process of national nursery building. The reformers proposed progressive solutions to problems that they blamed the old schools for having worsened, if not caused: the problems of historical belatedness, on the one hand, and, on the other, of the bankruptcy or even the nonexistence of national character. The old schools could not possibly have produced citizens equipped for participation in modern political life when these schools sought first and foremost to ensure the maintenance of an ossified tradition. Such maintenance was achieved by means that would come to be associated with "instruction" over and against the "education" that was, in some influential reformers' accounts, including Giovanni Gentile's, *Bildung*-inspired and thus northern European in its provenance, forward-looking and thus in touch with the times. True education in this vein promoted individual and collective progress, moving the young scholar, in Gentile's words, "ever forward, ever farther, . . . and making him in this way ever more a man." By contrast, the methods of instruction—"material, mechanical, spiritually worthless," intellectually contentless, developmentally arresting, dead, "fragmentary and inorganic"—tended to impede the nation's advancement as well as that of the child left behind.[32] Whatever their differences—and these were considerable, since they came from the right and the left alike—the reformers were united in defining classical education as a thing of the past and in making the old school, understood as a place good for nothing but "the learning by heart of Latin grammar," the target of their critiques.[33] All agreed that this institution should give way to one better suited to the needs of the modern nation.

These reformist critiques were made that much more urgent by the fact that classical schools had enjoyed hegemonic status after the Italian state's formation. Far from being always already marginal, these schools had been seen as central, as the best purveyors of culture to members of the administrative as well as learned professions. Classical schools, by this account, were crucial for those who would constitute the ruling classes. They would fashion leaders who could guarantee the functioning of the new nation, and they were not merely for those who, in their dustier way, would keep the memory of the classical tradition alive, or at least on life support, through study (*IC* 19–20). As education was democratized, then, so, too, was instruction in Greek and Latin made into the means by which *all* social classes were to be elevated—with the result, in the reformers' later view, that many were schooled in irrelevance, given unrealistic expectations, or otherwise rendered ill-equipped for modernity.

Still, this schooling first had to prevail in order to have a chance to fail. A phase of relative stability for the classical school had preceded the reformers' perception of its disappointing results. High hopes for the old school had initially been circulated and taken seriously.[34] As Gaetano Bonetta notes, during the early years of the post-unification liberal regime, classical studies in elementary and secondary schools were thought to fulfill a crucial nation-building function, such that to these studies alone some public figures attributed the "power to be able to bring to fruition the educational goals of a cultural and political nature that were necessary for the development of the nation" (*IC* 19). By means of study in Greek and Latin, a starry-eyed 1879 *disegno di legge* imagines, a national middle class could be consolidated; without this study, on the contrary, no "chain of union" capable of uniting this class could be forged, nor could leaders create "a common atmosphere... in which all the minds of the nation could breathe" (quoted in *IC* 20).

But if during the years immediately following the founding of the nation, the classical school was seen to promise fresh air—and even to be the medium without which the minds of the nation would never breathe free—by the turn of the century the situation had changed, and reformers with various intellectual priorities and political allegiances had come to see the school as asphyxiating for its students and impeding for the progress of the newly united nation. Hopes had been dashed. It now became clear that the classical curriculum was confining. There was, indeed, one V. E. Orlando opined, no other way to express what it was: "Now the systems currently in force have constrained (that's the word) a whole multitude within the classical school, a multitutde of people who even a half century ago felt no need to obtain a degree."[35] Thus, for some opponents of the old school, it was precisely this institution's becoming democratic that had led, by way of a "deplorable and pernicious crowding," to this school's decline.[36]

For others, including those whose initiatives Stewart-Steinberg privileges, the old school's decline stemmed from its remaining stuck in its ways, committed to a dated model of culture, and closed to the scientific and vocational alternatives that modernity both opened up and made requisite, rather than elective. Whatever their differences, though, again, critics of the old school were united in their sense of this school's failure to deliver on its promises. They were also agreed on the disastrous consequences of this failure, seeing in it the "collapse of an Italian cultural politics that had been mobilized for the 'construction of the nation.'" Bonetta concludes that "at the end of the nineteenth century," the limits of "traditional classicism" became abundantly clear: "Too much faith had been placed," after unification, "in the diffusion of a cultural patrimony erroneously held to be national, one that only with difficulty took root in the 'common sense' of the people. It was necessary, in short, to change course" (*IC* 50).

But if this sense that an impasse had been reached and that it was therefore time to change directions was widespread, it was by no means universally shared. The reformists were united not only in their recognition of a crisis in cultural politics, but also in their opposition to those for whom change to the old school's time-honored curriculum spelled disaster. A reformist consensus had emerged, then, but reformists still had a war to wage, a "struggle" to pursue,[37] given the antagonism that had by then hardened into an "ancient and inevitable antithesis between conservatives and reformists."[38] In this way, even moderns were forced to admit that their quarrel with the ancients had become ancient.

First published in 1896 in *La rassegna scolastica*—a journal for teachers, advertised as "dedicated to Primary and Secondary Schools"—Pascoli's "Pensieri scolastici" plainly emerges from within this embattled context.[39] From the first, the essay identifies itself as part of a counteroffensive or rearguard action meant to defend the much-maligned old school: "Because the war is against dead languages, against the liberal arts," and it is being waged "in the name of the present and practical, of the real and useful."[40] With hyperbole that verges on the hysterical, Pascoli all but declares that the sky is falling:[41] "The work of demolition has begun: with one stone removed, another will fall, and a third will collapse. Thus the house will be smashed amid a cloud of that dust that they call erudite [Così si sfascerà la casa tra un nuvolo di quella polvere che chiamano erudita]."[42] The joke here is on the reformers, because dust was, in their discourse, what attached to those in Pascoli's camp—the pedants who adhered to traditional methods—not to their own modern and progressive educational undertakings. That the reformers are here said to be the ones *producing* such dust—sending it up from the edifice that they're speedily destroying—means that their claim to be cleaning house is rendered suspect. At the very least, in Pascoli's image, the progressive educators are complicit in making the messes that they undertake to fix. If it weren't for the demolition, erudite dusts long since settled might still be there—Pascoli implicitly grants that libraries might still need airing out—but they would not constitute a cloud.

Such is the place, though—the impasse—from which the poet begins, as he surveys a scholastic scene characterized by widespread discouragement on the part of teachers, caused by distrust or faithlessness (*diffidenza*) on the part of students and parents. The latter, Pascoli complains, do not believe in "the utility, never mind the necessity," of classical studies anymore, now that dead languages have fallen into disfavor, or rather come under attack.[43] Worrying about the fate of poetry in this context—and here the poet makes the claim that Agamben analyzes, the claim that "the language of poetry is always a dead language . . . : a dead language that is used to give greater life to thought!" where the exclamation mark is already, implicitly enlivening—Pascoli suggests that the assault on classical education and on dead languages more broadly is underwritten by an ideology of modern exceptionalism, a historical arrogance that he proceeds to deride in no uncertain terms: "It seems to almost everyone that he is living . . . in a solemn moment in human history, one in which what was never before seen or thought of should be realized; and in which the facts of experience and of history do not count for anything anymore in the face of the exception of our age."[44] At such a juncture, to try to counter the ideology of progress by insisting on the past's importance is to lose the battle in advance. "Almost everyone," by this account, already assumes that such insistence is merely reactionary, and it is difficult, even for Pascoli, to imagine how, in a field thus set up, the "facts of history and of experience" could ever compete with the new and never-before-seen. To be for the new is to breathe free in a rush of collective fate-determination and intergenerational rupture. To side with tradition, with "experience and history," on the contrary, is to struggle to breathe in an atmosphere of dust, among pedant parents.

All of which makes it necessary to refuse the terms deployed by the enemies of the old school. At the same time, though, this situation also leads the counter-progressive Pascoli to dismiss the "usual reasons so easily repeated" to defend tradition.[45] In place of the standard defenses—the appeals to the moral authority of the classics or their character-building or citizen-forming function—"Pensieri scolastici" proposes a much bolder and broader set of arguments:

> One must be persuaded that our studies are rooted in such a primitive and tenacious human sentiment, and respond to such an intimate necessity of our

being, that despite the passing of time and the changing of its forms society will never be able to exclude dead languages and ancient literatures from the education of its "best" children.

Crucially, Pascoli's wording here leaves open the possibility that these arguments are meant to have more strategic value than essential validity. According to this logic, one "must be persuaded" of the old school's speaking to "primitive and tenacious" parts of ourselves not because it necessarily *does* speak in this way, but rather because one has to believe *something* if one is to keep teaching Greek—and to make the case for such teaching—"in the face of the exception of our age" and the widespread *diffidenza* to which faith in this exception leads. I note the potentially instrumental status of the reasons that Pascoli sets forth in order to correct Agamben's tendency to treat the poet's claims as though they always bore on the essential. Ultimately, though, I am less interested in distinguishing tactics from truth claims than in understanding the *generalizing* movement that the passage initiates.

This movement continues as Pascoli returns to while also revising his earlier claim that "the language of poetry is always a dead language":

> Dead languages! ancient literatures! Where is the language that cannot be called dead or dying? Not only each writer, but also each speaker, tends to use the words from the common fund in his own way: a metaphor is, for its part, already the transformation of a language. It begins with one and with a few, then with many, and finally [ends] with everyone: the ideological transition [or trespass] by which a word dies to one sense and is born to another.... Where is the present of a language? πάντα ῥεῖ. How could the expression of a thought, especially in intellectual needs, be fixed even for the duration of a generation, if in going forward we didn't face backward from to time?[46]

Here it is not merely "the language of poetry," but rather language as such that is said—exasperatingly—to be "dead or dying." Pascoli figures linguistic change as so constant and unstoppable as to preclude any fixed linguistic "present," and he implies that, since such a present is constitutively lacking, language must be always already past, and literature effectively "ancient," even at the moment when a word is first "born to" a new sense. This conclusion is striking not least because of the way in which it undoes the very opposition that "Pensieri scolastici" would appear to require in order to defend instruction in dead languages. That is, Pascoli seems to argue himself into a corner, for if all languages, ancient and modern, were really already dead, and all literatures really already ancient, then there would be no pressing need to preserve the *particular* dead languages and ancient literatures at the center of the classical school's curriculum. It's not clear, then, why Greek and Latin should continue to be privileged once they are defined as mere illustrations of a universal linguistic phenomenon. Wouldn't this make *all* instruction, conducted in whatever language, instruction in dead language, and thus render Pascoli's whole argument irrelevant, his breath wasted?

At the end of the passage that I have just quoted, Pascoli provides an implicit answer to these objections. That "ideological" change is unstoppable means that all languages are "dead or dying" if you stop to think about it. And dead languages—that is, languages like Greek and Latin—turn out crucially to enable you to stop to think about it. Reverting to the would-be Heraclitean notion—also, interestingly, a cliché—that everything is in flux ("πάντα ῥεῖ," "panta rhei"),[47] Pascoli in fact *arrests* the flow of his prose, performing in advance the "fixing of expression" that his next sentence will go on to address. Even while the text seems to take for granted a reader with good-enough Greek, the code and alphabetic switch here require that this reader engage in a mental adjustment and therefore a slowing-down, however slight. This readerly gear shift, then, both precedes and makes possible the passage from flow to fixity by which Pascoli reinstates the specificity of the classical school's dead languages. No sooner has he summoned one of these ancient languages onto the scene than he has set it to work, in and as a backward turn that prepares the reader for the explicit defense of backward turns to follow. The Greek phrase lets the reader practice, if only briefly, one such turn herself.

Pascoli's "panta rhei" thus functions as a password thanks to which the requirements of logic are finessed and the strictures of argument are opened. There is no apparent logical reason the last of the questions that I have quoted ("How could the expression of a thought ... be fixed even for the duration of a generation, if in going forward we didn't face backward from to time?") should follow the one before it ("Where is the present of a language?"). If language has no present, then it can *never* be fixed, for by definition it eludes all attempts at arrest. But on the other side of "panta rhei," again, such fixing suddenly seems both necessary and achievable. The backward turn (named in a conditional contrary to fact, a construction that seems to underscore the turn's precarious status in Pascoli's present) becomes the instrument that makes fixing possible. Without it, Pascoli implies, there would only be Babel—only, that is, the very condition of presentless fluidity and unfixed expression that his argument has just seemed to declare universal.

So the Greek phrase descends like a *deus ex machina* to come to "our" rescue, to ensure that "intellectual needs" will still be met, if only provisionally, provided that the backward turns be allowed to continue. Perhaps Pascoli means here, by placing the two questions together and bridging them with Greek, that a "literally" dead language, one of the ancient languages, becomes an aid to thought because it is more dead than dying, and thus provides a relatively stable point of reference for speakers who must perforce deploy "dying," rather than dead, language in everyday speech. But if this is the idea, then Pascoli's *use* of dead language—his writing, in texts like *Paedagogium*, not only in "the language of poetry," but also in a well-wrought and hard-won neo-Latin of his own—works against such stabilization. The poet's Latin corpus puts the dead language back into circulation, or rather keeps it in circulation among the hyperliterate. Even while singing the praises of dead languages, Pascoli prevents at least one of these languages from becoming veritably dead, destabilizing it, if only unwittingly, by adding, "in his own way," new usages to the old, by making new transformations by means of new metaphors. Here again, then, the argument of "Pensieri scolastici" is undone. But perhaps this, too, was Pascoli's point: if there can be no present in any language, then neither can there be a past that's truly dead and past. That is, of course, unless the reformers have their way, and backward turns, and thoughts enlivened by dead languages, become extinct definitively in the ongoing, oddly dusty forward march.

Doing Tenses

> ... et dixit ad me vade [Then he said unto me, Depart]
>
> —Acts 22:21, Pascoli's motto for *Paedagogium*

I have suggested that "Pensieri scolastici," which everywhere *refers* to the problem of the school, also *registers* Pascoli's engagement with this problem.[48] I have argued, in other words, that the school makes its presence felt in Pascoli's essay not only at the level of *propositions*, by being repeatedly named and discussed, but also, more interestingly at the level of *pragmatics*, in the *use* the text makes of dead language.[49] I have highlighted this use's contradictory nature, which is in keeping with the contradictions in the field that Pascoli's essay considers. These resulted in part, unsurprisingly, from the contested nature of this field, in which reformers were for generations pitted against classicists. But other contradictions were traceable to the competing demands placed on the school *within* each of the opposing camps. On each side of the new school / old school—or the living / dead—divide, the school was asked to do an awful lot of work. It was recruited to save not only its students, but also the nation as a whole, whether from the decay and centuries-old irrelevance against which the reformers fought or from the "demolition" of the past that the classicists feared would result from reform. The school, whether reformed or classical, was to be both itself and a model or miniaturization of the nation—and this even when the latter aim came into conflict with or forestalled the realization of the former. There can be no complete citizen-formation, let alone any but a nominal graduation, when "the school of the nation" is always in session, and the teacher's work never done (*PE* 14). Or, as Pascoli would lament in another context but still apropos of making Italians, when it seems that "men who are already formed [gli uomini fatti] do not listen and do not look anymore," and it therefore becomes imperative for men to be boys.[50]

There is nothing new or unique about schools' being made to shelter broad collective aspirations, of course. As the crucibles in which citizens and subjects were to be forged, schools had long since borne the weight of such hopes. But Stewart-Steinberg's account makes it clear that in the newly formed nation, under the pressure of a belated modernity, these aspirations became especially burdensome and pervasive. They thus inevitably informed discourses like Pascoli's. Whereas Agamben thinks that Pascoli's work indicates "a pure intention to signify, that is, the voice in its originary purity" (*EP* 67), I am working to show that the poet in fact points to another sphere, one much less pure and much more conflictual: the school, which had become a battlefield. In "Pensieri scolastici," this means that the "dead language" cannot suffice unto itself but must be shown to operate everywhere even while it retains crucial importance on its own, "literal" terms. In this way, Pascoli's essay registers its participation in the post-unification debates on education, debates in which the school had to be omnipresent while remaining a concrete and delimited space. Pascoli's text does this in a mode of transposition that I have characterized as indexical, because it points to without naming key features of the context in which it emerges and to which it responds.

A different kind of indexicality becomes central to the Latin poem *Paedagogium*, which points not only to the present of its production, but also to the remote past, a past that both remains and returns in the form of a trace. "Both remains and returns" because crucially the past here returns without fully having gone away, reappears without really having disappeared first; it reemerges after having been written off or sidelined rather than forcefully repressed. Here, then, are the facts of the trace, the index in question: Pascoli's poem takes as its inspiration an ancient graffito discovered during the course of excavations on the Palatine in 1856. *Paedagogium* thus centers on an indexical record, or at least a document that combines indexical qualities with iconic and narrative ones.[51] The graffito that inspired *Paedagogium*,

76 Among *Fanciulli*

unlike the majority of those uncovered by archaeologists along with it, does not simply use a proper name indexically to attest to the past presence of someone: Apollonius (116), Demetrius (98, 111), Marianus (150), Silvanus (137), or whomever. Nor is the graffito that interested Pascoli simply a phallus (131) or single figure (133). Instead, combining image and text, the graffito tells a story, while still fulfilling an indexical function. It shows two figures, one a little, little boy standing beneath the other, who is seen from behind: a crucified animal-human hybrid with the head of a donkey and the body of a man. With his right arm raised (in the posture known as *iactare basia*, or throwing kisses), the boy prays, as the inscription beside and below him explains in "badly executed letters": Αλεξαμενὸς σέβετε θεόν [*Alexamenos sebete theon*; Alexamenos worships God] (P 210–11) (Figure 3).

Writing *Paedagogium*, Pascoli undertook to narrate how this graffito came to be. Collected in the *Poemata christiana*—which Pascoli had planned more neutrally to entitle *Carmina*, *Res Romanae*, or simply *Roma*—*Paedagogium* is

Figure 3. A Rendering of the Alexamenos Graffito. Giulia Sacco, "Il graffito blasfemo del *paedagogium* nella *Domus Augustana* del Palatino," in *Le iscrizioni dei cristiani in Vaticano*, ed. Ivan Di Stefano Manzella (Vatican City, 1997), 192.

one in a series of historical portraits meant to render, in Latin, the experience of early Christians living (and especially dying) under the Roman Empire. Beginning with the earliest conversions, the *Poemata* proceed to recount the founding of the first Christian communities, the persecutions of early Christians, the decline of "pagan" religion, and the continuation of Christianity into the Middle Ages.[52] (These poems were projected as part of an even more sweeping cycle of short narrative poems or *poemetti* written in Latin, which would trace all of Roman history from the city's mythical origins to what Pascoli called its "fine non definitiva" [nondefinitive end], with a slight but telling gesture toward the possibility of the eternal city's living-on in later Latin.)[53] Together with one other poem (*Pomponia*), *Paedagogium* represents the phase of persecutions in early Christian history.[54] Strikingly, though, persecution here takes the unspectacular form of bullying: one small boy scrawls the figures in the graffito and writes out the accompanying caption in an effort to humiliate—indeed, to out—Alexamenos.

Pascoli's *poemetto* treats a victim and an aggressor: Alexamenos and the graffitist, named Kareius. Both boys are young captives housed in the imperial *paedagogium* named in the poem's title, which refers not to an abstraction—not, that is, to pedagogy in the current sense—but rather to "the place where boys of servile birth intended for pages were educated" (as well as to "the boys in" such a place and more generally "boys reared for vice" or "*delicati pueri*").[55] Pascoli's protagonist is introduced as choosing homework over play, in keeping with his key characterization in the poet's preparatory notes—"Alexamenos è così studioso!" [Alexamenos is so studious!],[56] an exclamation to which I will return. Alexamenos prefers, he says, not to join in his schoolmates' game but instead "versus ediscere" (*P v.* 32), to learn verses by heart, in order to be ready to recite them to a punishing "praeceptor" (*P v.* 55). The lines that he commits to memory are these, from the *Aeneid*, lines that themselves enjoin memory:

Tu regere imperio populos, Romane, memento
(hae tibi erunt artes) pacique imponere morem,
parcere subiectis et debellare superbos.

[Roman, remember by your strength to rule
Earth's peoples—for your arts are to be these:
To pacify, to impose the rule of law,
To spare the conquered, battle down the proud.][57]

Only the three words italicized in the verses I have quoted are included in the text of *Paedagogium*. Yet these words alone suffice to trigger, or to test, the reader's memory. The irony in Pascoli's citation, like much else in his poem, is unsubtle: Alexamenos, who is to learn the lines by heart, is emphatically not the Roman addressed by Virgil. He is one of the subjected whom this magnanimous Roman spares as he rules over the peoples of the empire, building order and disarming the proud.

But the boys in his school do not spare the Chaldean-born, Greek-speaking Alexamenos.[58] Instead they ridicule him for reciting prayers to the Christian God and then give him a thrashing. Or rather, they begin to give him a thrashing, but they are interrupted by a caring "custos," who confines the bully in the lead, a "Gallum rebellem" [rebellious Gall] named Kareius (*P v.* 74), to a narrow room, where he almost literally does time. He does tenses. Put in solitary, Kareius pitches a fit that culminates—since a stylus is conveniently ready to hand—in his carving the blasphemous image and scrawling the caption that accompanies it: "Alexamenos worships God" (*P v.* 99).

In this way, Pascoli stages the scene of writing that results in the Palatine graffito. And here, in another moment of unsubtle if endearing irony, *Paedagogium* gives the lie to the idea that the events the poem records, once past, are "nec iam reditura," "now not to return again" (*P v.* 105). Anger's giving way to the acceptance of punishment, and the fit's to graffiti, make it possible for a remoter past to return, propelling the rest of the poem's narrative, as Pascoli's speaker announces:

> Quidquid erat nuper, nihil est: effluxit: at adsunt
> quae procul atque olim, nec iam reditura, fuerunt. (*P vv.* 104–5)
>
> [Whatever just now was, is nothing: it has vanished: but present are things that were long ago and far away, that now will not return.]

Strangely beautiful though they are, these densely adverbial, strictly untranslatable lines read a bit like grammar exercises—and not merely because they're written in the language of the classical grammar school. The convergence of *erat, est,* and *fuerunt*—the imperfect, present, and preterit tenses of *sum*, in both singular and plural forms, with the prefix-modified, present-tense *adsunt* added in for good measure—in just two lines cannot but recall drill sentences aimed at consolidating students' command of Latin tenses, and their grasp of the conjugation of *sum* in particular. A far cry from Virgil's, Pascoli's Latin thus interpellates the reader not as a Roman but rather as a pupil. However much it may seek "to give greater life to thought," the dead language here perforce participates in this reader's instruction—where, as in the Italian educational reformers' critiques of it, instruction names something other than teaching *tout court*. Only with great difficulty, after all, can one build on lines in which human agents have gone underground, lines that merely make whatever happen, as *quidquid* and *quae*.

To say this is not, however, to discount the lines' importance for the poem as a whole—or the poem's importance, for that matter. What *Paedagogium* activates not despite but because of Pascoli's pedantry, and what these lines illustrate with particular vividness, is instruction's capacity to render a reordering of tenses that is also a counter-progressive rearrangement of historical times. If in the lines I have just quoted the historical present—a tense typically thought to enliven the distant past, to mark narrative moments of special importance—gives way to the preterit, just as in *Paedagogium* as a whole the vernacular long since forged gives way to Latin, this is because, for Pascoli, as "Pensieri scolastici" already insists, that which is *olim* or remote is no less crucial than the much more recent *nuper*. In *Paedagogium* the former persistently displaces the latter, leading to a repudiation of progressive time and its entailments, among them the idea of a self, or nation, that only faces the future, having finally shed the dead weight of the past.

The poem's staging of this displacement is, I have claimed, neither mourning for nor melancholic attachment to the "more" that "there is in the child" according to Empson: that which, in "child-cult," tragically exceeds what "any man has been able to keep."[59] Instead, *Paedagogium* models the relationship to history that it also suggests can only be sustained within the institutional frame of the old school—that is, in Empson's words, in the place of a particular kind of "building up" and "bringing out."[60] Out indeed: it is as if, according to the logic of the *poemetto*, the return of the past—also the making of the mark that will return as past in the future—is only possible within the narrower frame within the institutional frame that is the cell in which Kareius is confined. The boy's punishment is what brings about his conversion, which in turn leads to his joining Alexamenos in the martyrdom that will happen offstage, only hinted at in Pascoli's poem itself. Confinement is, then, paradoxically what makes it possible for strictures to give way—for the impasse of the present to become something other than a dead end. "La scuola deve abolire la prigione" [The school must abolish the prison], Pascoli proclaims elsewhere,[61] however improbably a prison abolitionist *ante litteram*, using the discourse of "abolition" against itself. (In Pascoli's time and place, "abolition" named measures to eliminate compulsory Greek instruction.) And the school *does* abolish or at least overwrite the prison in *Paedagogium*—but not for long. For although Kareius's inscription, coinciding with the return of the past, causes his anger to abate and thus enables both a conversation with Alexamenos and a provisional release from punishment, the reader knows that worldly punishment is soon to follow, the boys being early Christians, and this being Rome.

In *Paedagogium*'s last lines, Kareius moves forward to accompany poor Alexamenos, the student formerly known as a "puer ambitios[us]" (*P v.* 51), now singled out as "pestifer unus," the only pestilential, as in Christian, student in the school (*P* 187). This charge then prompts the converted young Gaul's correction, his "ecce alium":

> "Falleris: ecce alium" exclamat Kareius, et offert
> se fratri, iunctaque manu *comitatur euntem*. (*P vv.* 188–89; emphasis added)
>
> ["You are wrong: here is another," Kareius exclaims, and he goes to meet his brother, and with joined hands accompanies the one going away.]

So *Paedagogium* concludes, with a citation of the *Aeneid* (VI.863) that is also a vindication of learning by heart. This citation aligns Pascoli's speaker less with Aeneas, to whom the words belong in Virgil's poem, than with Alexamenos, whose assigned *versus* ("tu regere imperio" and all the rest) are from just ten lines earlier in the *Aeneid*.[62] At the end of the relay that Pascoli has staged—a relay in which verses are passed first from the *praeceptor* to Alexamenos, then to Pascoli's speaker as he approaches Kareius, converted following his punishment—the poem itself becomes "studious," following the lead, but also taking the hand, of the little, little boy whose lines it has learned by heart. The pupil's homework has become the poet's heritage, handed down again for the reader to learn or to leave behind.

Studious Youth

> ... perché ciò che fu e quelli che furono pare sempre bello e paiono sempre buoni a quelli che sono. [... because that which was and those who were—it always seems beautiful, and they always seem good to those who are.]
>
> —Pascoli, *Il fanciullino*

When homework becomes a poetic heritage in this way, the scholastic chore leaves its trace in the text that might seem to work to transcend it.[63] The mere, mechanical, scholastic exercise thus also marks a limit to the transcendence for which Pascoli's patently redemptive poem would appear to strive, and toward which it would appear to lead. This, I would argue, is ultimately what distinguishes *Paedagogium* from the products of the Fascist *puericultura* that it might seem to anticipate. Whereas, according to Barbara Spackman, styles of "Fascist Puerility" tend to spiritualize both the child and the nation,⁶⁴ *Paedagogium*'s spiritualization—its commemoration of the martyrdom of two early Christian captive boys—is inseparable from the poem's materialization as a text to be studied, one that also thematizes study. (Recall Gentile's characterization of instruction as "material, mechanical, [and] spiritually worthless," among other things.)⁶⁵ Latin verb forms that the reader has long since memorized are repeatedly recalled, and all but drilled, in a poem that both stages and itself engages in memorization: stages in Alexamenos's "versus ediscere," and engages in the poem's concluding words: "comitatur euntem."

If this conclusion ensures that *Paedagogium* remains stubbornly material even in its reach for the transcendent, then Pascoli's adherence to the prenational language of Rome amounts to a resistance to the still-young nation's effort to appropriate and thus domesticate, to back-date and thus effectively eternalize, its past. Far from being eternalized through spiritualization, as in the discourses of the Fascist regime, Italy is in *Paedagogium* implicitly *historicized*. The nation is, in other words, shown to be a historical rather than timeless, a material rather than essentially spiritual, entity. That the vernacular is *not* retrofitted to render *Roma* means that Pascoli's Italian reader is denied the satisfaction, or frustrated in the expectation, of finding himself mirrored in the remote Roman past. *Paedagogium* linguistically preserves this past's difference from the national present, reminding Italians of what came before and remains distinct from the nation.

Pascoli's poem preserves the distinction between the tense of the past and that of the nation in another way as well, by centering on a "studious" protagonist. Remember the *incipit* in Pascoli's preparatory notes: "Alexamenos is so studious!" And recall Alexamenos's opting out of child's play because of his commitment to *versus*. "Unfortunately, in Italy no one studies except for the professors (so they call us)," Pascoli writes in his 1896 essay "La scuola classica."⁶⁶ Studiousness thus acquires, before *Paedagogium*, a specific—and a not strictly national—valence in Pascoli's work as it addresses itself to the poet's present. In this present, the "studious youth" form in every sense a minor collectivity.⁶⁷ In his essays on education, Pascoli repeatedly imagines this collectivity's becoming major, converting its current losses into gains in a utopian future. But this is a future in which public schools will offer Sanskrit as well as Greek and Latin:⁶⁸ a future that refers to the remote past—crucially, the prenational past that the national present can neither fully subsume nor finally bring back to life. As "Pensieri scolastici" insists, there is no word that doesn't die even as it passes over into a new sense, and in this passage or "trapasso" give greater life to thought.⁶⁹

Pascoli's approach in *Paedagogium* and in essays like "La scuola classica" and

"Pensieri scolastici"—his programmatic preservation of the past's difference from the present and of the dead language's difference from the living—contrasts starkly with Gentile's effort to enlist Latinity in his nation-building project. This project was—symptomatically, given the national context that I sketched out earlier—first and foremost a pedagogical initiative, realized legislatively in the Riforma Gentile of 1923 but already conceptually delineated in the essay "L'unità della scuola media e la libertà degli studi."[70] Published in 1902, Gentile's essay represents a third way between progressive reform and classicist reaction, positions that I have so far characterized, following Orlando's account of "ancient antithesis," in dichotomous terms.[71] Gentile's "L'unità della scuola media," that is, both decries the libertarian tendencies of progressive reform and implies a critique of classicism, even while it appears to pledge allegiance to the classical school. Gentile's attack on the "material, mechanical," and dead methods of instruction—the attack in *La riforma* from which I have already repeatedly quoted—is latent in the philosopher's early text.[72]

"L'unità della scuola" takes pains first to equate language as such with the national language, then to render dead languages living and subservient to the national language.[73] Greek and Latin must absolutely be taught, according to Gentile, who here opposes the "utilitarian" reformers, whose democratizing and modernizing calls for increased vocational and scientific instruction he derides.[74] Gentile thus remains in this limited sense a classicist, but his differences from Pascoli are more instructive. For the reasons that Gentile gives for retaining Latin and Greek are reasons of state—also by definition reasons of spirit, since it is the former that, in Gentile's account, guarantees the autonomy and actualization of the latter. The philosopher, unlike the poet, has no patience for the discourses that declare ancient languages dead; still less is he interested in versions of Pascoli's claim that such languages are instructive precisely in their deadness. If these languages are worth teaching—and they are, Gentile thinks—then they must remain alive and well:

> Is Latin dead or alive? If Italian is a transformation of Latin, then the latter is as living as Italian, because, if Latin were dead, then Italian would lack all of the substance of its being, and this would therefore be a dead abstraction: a transformation not inhering in any subject! And whoever remembers classical Latin's contacts with Greek, and the enormous influence of the syntax (not to say the lexicon and morphology) of the latter on the former, and the originary relations between the two languages, and the enormous influence of Greek literature on Latin literature—can any such person distinguish Latin from Greek? The two languages deserving of our veneration, far from being dead, live and will live forever in the immortal Greco-Italic spirit, with the national language

and for the national language, since the being that becomes is not annulled in the being that it has become.[75]

Pascoli, too, in "La scuola classica," makes the case for Latin's inseparability from Greek,[76] but he does so without ever suggesting that the ancient languages should be learned—let alone that they "live and will live forever"—for the sake of the vernacular. Pascoli does not claim, in other words, that these languages should be studied alongside but also, in Gentile's second, more forceful formulation, "*for* the national language." This formulation in fact belies the Hegelian-sounding explanation that follows it. Even if the ancient languages are not altogether annulled in the process of their becoming vernacular, Greek and Latin are definitively rendered subservient to "the national language," of which Gentile speaks proleptically, not to say wishfully—that is, as though there were one.[77] Gentile's nationalist pedagogy *cum* progress narrative leaves no room for the possibility that these ancient bondsmen may yet overthrow their modern lords.[78] The future of Greek and Latin is, instead, in "L'unità della scuola," resolutely national. Rushing toward this future, Gentile bypasses and effectively rules out the real life-and-death struggle staged in Hegel's dialectic, since the triumph of life—the victory, that is, of the living, national language—is guaranteed from the start.

That Pascoli, by contrast, tarries with the negative, at least in his educational and Latin writings, should by now be clear.[79] I have shown that these writings dramatize the return of the remote past in various guises: as the Sanskrit to be taught in future utopian classrooms in "La scuola classica";[80] as the more banal-seeming backward turn that lets the present stop to think in "Pensieri scolastici";[81] and, most strikingly, as the graffito that is already "procul atque olim," long ago and far away, at the moment of its first inscription in *Paedagogium* (*P v.* 105). In each of these cases, the past interrupts and unsettles the present. What separates Pascoli's vision of Latinity from Gentile's is thus, to begin with, the power that the poet attributes to the past: not only, as in Gentile, "not annulled," Pascoli's remote past acts on the present in ways that the latter cannot fully command, either at the level of (national) language or at that of (progressive) history. On its own terms and in its own dead language, the past makes a claim on us. This claim, for Pascoli, derives not from the past's having paved the way for and thus come to belong to the nation that is the birthright of the students of the present, as in Gentile's account, but rather from its *being different from the present and usable as such*.

Here again, then, as in Pascoli's "Pensieri scolastici" (where the dead language is, again, "*used* to give greater life to thought"), the use of dead language to serve pedagogical ends is crucial. But this use should be rigorously distinguished from the kind of appropriation or projection, underwritten by progress, in which Gentile's account engages and for which it calls.[82] In and through this process, the "now" subsumes the "then" in which it recognizes itself. Gentilean pedagogy is thus presentist as well as progressive. Pascoli's poetics, on the other hand, emblematized by *Paedagogium*, places faith in the force of the past, channeled but not finally controlled by the preceptors and pedantic pupils of the present. Against Gentile's philosophy of actualism, the poet thus envisions a form of actualization in which the remote past, *reditura* or to return again, after all, preserves the possibility of the present's—and the nation's—differing from itself (*P* v. 105).

I adapt this non-actualist—that is, non-Gentilean—notion of "actualization" from Walter Benjamin, for whom *Vergegenwärtigung*, actualization or "making-things-present," represents a corrective to positivist historicism and the relationship to the past that it establishes. In the "Paralipomena to 'On the Concept of History'"—but also throughout his late work—Benjamin protests against the "false aliveness of the past-made-present" that positivist history tends, in his view, to produce.[83] This false aliveness is, he writes, "secured at the cost of completely eradicating every vestige of history's original role as remembrance [*Eingedenken*]."[84] Rebecca Comay glosses this last term as follows:

> Memory, *Eingedenken*—the "*Ein-*" prefix signifying here in fact precisely the opposite of the unifying inwardness of a thought affirming its self-actualization as a culture returning to itself in the recollection of its own formation or *Bildung* (the opposite, in a word, of the Hegelian *Erinnerung* which it lexically recalls)—Benjamin's *Eingedenken* is no longer strictly inward (*Ein-*) and no longer strictly thought (*-Denken*). It announces, rather, a mindfulness or vigilance which refuses to take in (or be taken in by) a tradition authorizing itself as the continuity of an essential legacy, task or mission to be transmitted, developed or enacted.... *Eingedenken* marks the impasse or "standstill" of thought as such: the "flow" of inference is interrupted.... In "blasting open" the continuum, *Eingedenken* inaugurates repetition as the return of that which strictly speaking never happened: it announces the redemption of a failed revolutionary opportunity at the moment of most pressing danger. "Hope in the past." ... Such repetition arrests the apparent continuity of inherited power relations by remembering precisely what official historiography had to repress.[85]

Comay's gloss indirectly brings the contrast between Gentile's reform and Pascoli's classicism into further relief. The former inherits "Hegelian *Erinnerung*" as Comay defines it, even while it elides crucial episodes in the *Phenomenology*—ignoring, again, the life-and-death struggle and the reversibility of lordship and bondage in which this struggle results. Gentile's reform indeed centers on "the unifying inwardness of a thought affirming its self-actualization as a culture returning to itself in the recollection of its own formation." By contrast, Pascoli's pedagogy—and his *Paedagogium*—can be aligned with Benjamin's *Eingedenken*.

This alignment might at first seem counterintuitive, given Benjamin's well-rehearsed engagements with "the tradition of the oppressed" as well as his efforts to counter what Comay calls "the continuity of an essential legacy, task or mission to be transmitted, developed or enacted."[86] How, one might wonder, could a poem written in the language of Rome and resurrecting the iconography of early Christianity—in the interest of continuing both—ever be heard to resonate with Benjamin's understanding of remembrance and its rupturing effects? How could *Paedagogium*—or any text, for that matter, written in prize-winning, latter-day Latin—be seen to instantiate anything but the "continuity of inherited power relations"?[87] I have suggested that these questions are difficult to answer unless Pascoli's educational writings are taken into account, together with the broader polemical context that these writings register. Essays like "Pensieri scolastici" make Pascoli's Latin writings legible as something more than a series of reactionary gestures. Rearguard actions though they undoubtedly were, these essays worked to interrupt "the 'flow' of inference" dictated by discourses of progress, including Gentile's. They also sought to produce in the midst and in the place of this flux an "impasse or 'standstill'" akin to Benjamin's—again, in order simultaneously to produce the possibility of this standstill's giving way to something else: an out.

But whereas Benjamin privileges blasting open and bursting apart over most kinds of continuity, Pascoli argues for a pause in the name of persistence. Likewise, whereas Benjamin foregrounds the violence of historical repression, Pascoli seeks to counter the more banal processes that I have called sidelining and writing off: he wants to rescue from destruction not, in Comay's words, what "official historiography had to repress," but rather what this historiography has, in its accelerated forward movement, simply deemed useless, declared obsolete, left for dead. Still, this declaration is hyperbolically rendered in Pascoli's prose; the sidelining of the classical school thus becomes violent, is effectively recast as an impending catastrophe in texts like "Pensieri scolastici."

Pascoli's poem can be further illuminated by Benjamin's writing in another mode—as when, in a sketch for the *Arcades Project*, he refers to, or indeed remembers, "Leopardi 13." In this context, Benjamin offers "Leopardi 13"—the thirteenth of the poet's essayistic *Pensieri*—as another alternative to progressive history. Without elaborating any specific claims about the Leopardian text, Benjamin implies that it has the potential to model a nonprogressive history—that it has the potential to impart alternative "techniques of nearness" leading to alternative forms of actualization or *Vergegenwärtigung*.[88]

Strikingly, although Benjamin associates the text with anecdotes precisely, Leopardi's thirteenth *pensiero* is altogether lacking in anecdotal specificity. Rather than recording a concrete set of circumstances, the *pensiero* meditates on the observance of anniversaries, and it comes to center on certain unnamed "sensitive men" for whom this observance is especially important, even sustaining.[89] Here Leopardi sums up, having made a study of his subject: "And I have noted, questioning many men about this subject, that sensitive men, and men used to solitude, or to conversing internally, tend to be very respectful of anniversaries and to live, so to say, on remembrances of this kind, and always returning and saying to themselves: on a day of the year like the present one, this or that thing happened to me."[90] The vagueness of this concluding sentence—in which the events commemorated by Leopardi's "sensitive men" are not even indirectly named, but merely gestured toward as "questa o questa cosa"—makes a collectivity out of otherwise solitary walkers, here significantly labeled *studiosissimi*: very respectful, devout, observant, "obsessed," but also, like Pascoli's Alexamenos, "so studious."[91]

These "sensitive men" merely repeat themselves in order to sustain themselves. And if there is something redemptive about the end result of their observance of anniversaries, whereby "the sad thought of the annulment of what was is medicated in part [è medicato in parte il tristo pensiero dell'annullamento di ciò che fu]," this redemptiveness would appear, in its very partiality, to stop short of Benjaminian total reckoning. Still, Comay's definition of Benjamin's *Eingedenken* lets us see its surprising intimacy with Leopardi's poetics, and with Pascoli's poetics as well. *Eingedenken* is, again, according to Comay, "no longer strictly inward (*Ein-*) and no longer strictly thought (*-Denken*). It announces, rather, a mindfulness or vigilance that refuses to take in (or be taken in by) a tradition authorizing itself as the continuity of an essential legacy." Neither strictly inward nor strictly thought, the all but automatic "riandando e dicendo" practiced by Leopardi's studious men remind Benjamin of the surprising potentials of repetition.

Under certain circumstances, "Leopardi 13" suggests, repeated action and rote saying can realize the return of the past, or at least bring about the recognition that the past's disappearance has not been an annulment. Here, on another scale and in another register altogether, Leopardi anticipates the lesson of *Paedagogium*. Both texts make the case for studiousness, for memorization as a mode of "mindfulness or vigilance," which alone can preserve the possibility of the past's return and the present's remaining medicable. Crucially, this possibility is not guaranteed in either Leopardi or Pascoli by a "tradition authorizing itself as the continuity of an essential legacy." Gentile's Latinity represents one such tradition. Pascoli provides a corrective to this tradition's inwardness and appropriativeness, in that *Paedagogium*, in Comay's terms, "refuses to take in (or be taken in by)" a tradition thus essentialized. The poem instead imagines a mode of actualization that does not subsume the past in the language of the present and the nation, but that both addresses and forges a collectivity all the same. *Paedagogium* addresses pupils, and it makes a match and a minor community of the boys become brothers, brought together by "whatever,"[92] just as Leopardi's "uomini sensibili," these studious boys' secular and vernacular forebears, ultimately share nothing more substantial than "this."

I began this chapter by distinguishing between the sense of satiation in Pascoli's *Il fanciullino* and the dissatisfaction expressed by Leopardi, among others. I conclude, by contrast, with a gesture toward the partial compatibility of the two poets' projects. In at least one of his moods or modes, in the thirteenth of his *Pensieri*, Leopardi imagines the maintenance, rather than the obliteration, of the memory of the past—and this by those he calls "very studious [*studiosissimi*]." He imagines, that is, a provisional alternative to the ruin projected most spectacularly in "La ginestra": an alternative that, I have shown, takes the form of rote, ritual *riandando*, returning or going back over again, rather than spontaneous recollection. Pascoli, for his part, imagines—and, in his poem's last line, joins by imitating—a studious child, one with a penchant for memorization, in order to counter the "work of demolition" that he thought modernity had initiated: a work that took down the past together with the old school that was this past's repository.[93]

The differences, though, between Leopardi's "uomini sensibili" and Pascoli's pedantic boys are as important as the studiousness that these sets of figures have in common. Whereas Leopardi's men are grown, Pascoli's *pueri* are emphatically still growing (and not nearly as satisfied as *Il fanciullino* would suggest they should be). Likewise, whereas the former study in solitude, the latter live together. The reader's only access to Pascoli's boys is thus both collective and institutional; she encounters them only in the *collegio* in which they reside as captives.[94] During the time that separated the *Pensieri* (first published posthumously in 1845, but compiled between 1831 and 1835) from *Paedagogium* (brought out, again, in 1903), the Italian state was founded, even if the Italian nation had not yet become full-fledged. And during this same time span, classical schools underwent a phase of growth followed by one of perceived decline, a period of democratization followed by one of divestment. It was in this latter context—a context of decline and *diffidenza*, in which the very survival of classical studies was felt to be under threat, and the old school was barely able to parry the blows dealt by modernity[95]—that Pascoli returned to the Roman imperial school, recast as a last redoubt of what Benjamin would call "hope in the past."[96]

Franco Moretti writes in another context but of roughly the same historical phase: "Youth relapses into 'apprenticeship' in the narrowest sense: *school*, replete with teachers and homework."[97] According to Moretti, the eclipse of the European *Bildungsroman*, which had long worked through the personalization of social relations, coincided with the school's becoming prevalent as one of several "social institutions [beginning] to appear as such"—beginning to appear, that is, without being embodied or "personalized" in characters.[98] "In the ... often uselessly painful tests enforced by the school," Moretti continues, "the individualized socialization of Western modernity seems to collapse back into archaic initiation rituals," as in Joyce's *Portrait* or Robert Musil's *Confusions of Young Törless*.[99] Moretti's account lets us see that Leopardi's men "used to solitude" still participate in the process of "individual socialization," despite their obvious distance from the heroes of nineteenth-century *Bildungsromane*. Pascoli's *pueri*, by contrast, attest to the "collapse" and "relapse" that Moretti locates at the turn of the twentieth century. The task of *Paedagogium* was to turn this collapse to scholastic profit: to imagine a school whose painful tests and archaic rituals, far from being useless, would again be put to use.

3. "Copied Out Big"
Instruction in Joyce's Ulysses

"Steeled in the school of old Aquinas," in the words of his own youthful boast,[1] James Joyce also returned to this old school time and again in his fiction. One of his Jesuit instructors is said to have taught the Greek word *epiphany* "as an aside in his Latin class," and this lesson or digression would give rise to some of Joyce's first formal experiments, the brief sketches called "Epiphanies."[2] These showings-forth are set in truant moments, for the most part, as are the "stories of childhood" that open *Dubliners*.[3] But the schoolroom proper becomes the scene of some of the most memorable passages in Joyce's subsequent works, works that also feature various other spaces made over in the schoolroom's image. From the painful schooldays of Stephen Dedalus in *A Portrait of the Artist as a Young Man* to the two catechisms of *Ulysses* and the "Nightlessons" offered in *Finnegans Wake*, scenes of instruction recur in Joyce's texts.[4] They do so, admittedly, with spectacular variations as Joyce experiments with a wide range of changeful narrators and protean narrative forms. But for all their changefulness, Joycean scenes of instruction retain a kind of coherence. Consistently, these scenes signal the author's commitment to reimagining the educational institutions whose monumentalizing treatment of texts like *Ulysses* Joyce also famously anticipates.

"I've put in so many enigmas and puzzles that it will keep the professors busy for centuries arguing over what I mean, and that's the only way of insuring one's immortality."[5] To readers from Virginia Woolf to Leo Bersani and beyond, this boast confirms both Joyce's bad faith and his bad form. By this account, Joyce's aspiration to greatness, his bid for academically secured immorality, prevents *Ulysses* from being, in Woolf's often-quoted verdict, "first rate," making the novel instead "underbred, not only in the obvious sense, but in the literary sense."[6] Countless readers since have complained that this bid also "spoils" the experience of reading *Ulysses*. Consider, for instance, this recent, representative confession from Daniel Mendelsohn: "What spoils *Ulysses* for me, each time, is the oppressive allusiveness, the wearyingly overdetermined referentiality, the heavy constructedness of it all. Reading the book is never pleasurable" because it is "like being on one of those Easter egg hunts you went on as a child—you constantly feel yourself being *managed*, being carefully steered in the direction of effortfully planted treats."[7] *Ulysses* is thus infantilizing as well as off-puttingly bookish; with its excessive, even "oppressive," organization, Joyce's novel *manages* when it ought to delight and move.

The reviewer's main complaint is ultimately that *Ulysses* leaves "ordinary readers" in the lurch, abandoning these readers in favor of the "literary theorists" whom it fully—indeed, "effortfully"—intends to keep busy.[8] The criticism that *Ulysses* itself calls "the speculation of schoolboys for schoolboys" continues apace, spurred by Joyce's text (*U* 9.53).[9] But this critical enterprise fails to speak to the scholastically uninitiated or to those whose initiation came to an end with their graduation from formal schooling those who no longer see themselves as schoolchildren.

Here, however, it's worth recalling Stephen Dedalus's pointed response to the charge of mere scholasticism leveled at him by a fellow reader in "Scylla and Charybdis": "The schoolmen were schoolboys first" (*U* 9.56). Perhaps, in light of this response, it's not really the case that Joyce only addresses certain hyperliterate readers while neglecting others. Perhaps instead he works to render *every* reader hyperliterate, to turn all of his readers (back) into students. Perhaps, that is, Joyce asks *every* reader to consult the schemas that ruin the reviewer's pleasure because he wagers that something happens in and through this process of consultation, that the frustrations this process entails are somehow formative. At least some of these frustrations derive from the *limitations* that the schemas put in place: calculating, inviting, or predetermining interpretations in advance, if only by prompting resistance to interpretations that they offer, *Ulysses'* schemas deprive readers of a long-cherished liberty, undermining our freedom to be self-taught.[10] The schemas fence us in; they contribute to "our sense of being in a bright and yet somehow strictly confined apartment rather than at large beneath the sky."[11]

But there is another sense in which the schemas constitute what one early review calls a "limitation imposed" by Joyce.[12] Referring to the schemas means remaining within or at least returning repeatedly to the institutions that seek to guarantee the author's immortality, as predicted. Whether they employ editors, commentators, or professors, these institutions now pass on the outlines of Homeric analogies and other Joycean conceits together with the text of *Ulysses* itself. In this way, another cherished freedom is curtailed, for the reader can no longer sustain her belief in being alone—and "at large"—with the literary work. On the contrary, she must keep company with countless others crowded into a small apartment that becomes "strictly confined," claustrophobic indeed.

In keeping with the possibility that these sources of confinement might not "spoil" Joyce's project but instead constitute its pedagogical crux, this chapter takes on the "overdetermined referentiality" of *Ulysses* by looking at the most overdetermined and referential, the most maligned, the most often skipped, and arguably the most "wearying," of the novel's eighteen episodes: "Oxen of the Sun." Here, more than anywhere else in the novel, "enigmas and puzzles" proliferate. "They are numerous, complex, and perhaps too elaborately contrived," and Joyce is at his showiest, making a spectacle of his overbearing erudition.[13] There is thus no more direct route, no comparable royal road, to the "heavy constructedness" of *Ulysses* to which Mendelsohn objects. But if my approach to this constructedness is in this sense head-on, I will be approaching a text whose pedagogy is backward even while it represents a feat of modernist experimentation.

Indeed, "Oxen" both continues and radicalizes the "retrogressive progression" of *Ulysses'* previous episode, "Nausicaa." "Oxen" is from the first so programmatically retrograde that it begins by returning to the ancient language and the repetitive form of the "incantation."[14] At the same time, Joyce adulterates this form by combining incantatory repetition with a modern place name: "Deshil Holles Eamus. Deshil Holles Eamus. Deshil Holles Eamus" (U 14.1). So the episode begins, reverting, in a sort of Latin "Let us go then" (as in T. S. Eliot's "Prufrock"), to a language that long predates any modern's mother tongue. And not for nothing, for although "Oxen" is set in the National Maternity Hospital in Holles Street—a place of protection for "proliferent mothers"—the episode is organized by a split between mothering and mouthing off, which is what its male characters do—criminally, if Joyce's own framing of the episode is to be believed. "Am working hard at *Oxen of the Sun*, the idea being the crime committed against fecundity by sterilizing the act of coition," Joyce wrote to Frank Budgen.[15]

Early on, Joyce's narrator announces a regression to the womb: "Before born babe bliss had. Within womb won he worship" (U 14.60). But importantly this Anglo-Saxon alliteration begins only after the narrator has taken pains to put the *natio*, or birth, back into the nation, in a recapitulation of received ideas, an account of what "the most in doctrine erudite ... constantly maintain": namely, that "by no exterior splendour is the prosperity of a nation more efficaciously asserted than by the measure of how far forward may have progressed the tribute of its solicitude for that proliferent continuance which of evils the original if it be absent when fortunately present constitutes the certain sign of omnipollent nature's incorrupted benefaction" (U 14.10–17). To ask, as one must, what is going on in a sentence like this one is also, infantilized, to cry for help.

Ostentatiously overwritten, absurdly Latinate, and grotesquely involuted in its syntax, as any ordinary reader would be quick to notice, the sentence that I have just quoted also slyly takes back what it purports "efficaciously" to assert. The most telling of several inversions makes the subject of a subordinate clause follow, rather than precede, the very verb that would announce sequence: far from registering "how far forward [the tribute] may have *progressed*," the sentence in fact regresses. The tribute paid by the nation to its own "continuance" appears, then, from the first as not having progressed very far at all. Instead, this tribute—which in advance would render to the nation that which is the nation's—interrupts the account that it would initiate, forcing the reader to circle back and begin again, in order mentally to translate this English prose from Latin, or into Latin and then back into English. Unless, that is, the reader simply forges ahead:

> It behooves every most just citizen to become the exhorator and admonisher of his semblables and to tremble lest what had in the past been by the nation excellently commenced might be in the future not with similar excellence accomplished if an inverecund habit shall have gradually traduced the honorable by ancestors transmitted customs.... (U 14.21–26)

Here Joyce relies on variation as well as inversion to complicate the passage from the past into the future, or rather to show how this passage already will have been complicated without anyone's willing it—in fact, despite injunctions to will the contrary. The syntactic parallel between "what had *in the past* been" and "what might be *in the future*" is only slightly off—but off enough to suggest that the latter traduces the former, and the former, the latter. Derived from the Latin *traducere*, "to lead across, transfer, degrade," Joyce's "traduced" hints at the betrayal latent in every tradition, every transmission.[16] But the verb also gives the lie to—and indeed queers—the fictions of production and reproduction that "every most just citizen" is here enjoined to exhort.

In what is, then, both a critique of "chrononormativity" and a send-up of "reproductive futurism" *ante litteram*,[17] Joyce suggests that, "universally," ancestors will have been betrayed (U 14.7), and similarity will have given way to difference.[18] Likewise will "semblables" "tremble." That those last two words share a central set of letters makes their differences from one another that much more striking in a passage ostensibly about the urgent need to forestall change as such, to guarantee the "continuance" thanks to which the nation might remain identical to itself—to enforce the "law of heredity" according to which national "semblables" must retain their resemblance.[19]

But if my reading so far sounds like it will set up a familiar celebration of "proliferent" difference as prevailing by wearing away at singular institutions, here I need to begin again, because "Oxen" is not simply a study in the sort of inevitable "self-changingness that gives the slip to the rigidifying structures of the social order."[20] For although the episode enacts change at every turn, it does so by inhabiting—and calling on readers to inhabit—the very rigid structures and social orders that it satirizes, the same orders and structures whose endless alteration it stages. Joyce suggests that such alteration is enabled by the institution that might seem only to dictate self-identity: the old school, whose techniques "Oxen" everywhere redeploys. Against progressive educators' insistence that we leave this school behind in the name of ease and independence, "Oxen" looks to outmoded scholastic forms and in this way strictly limits itself and its readers. Making constant demands, the episode sets readers to work and cultivates dependencies in two senses: highlighting its own reliance on a range of textual sources, "Oxen" also forces us to consult schemas and commentaries, to become so many "schoolboys."

The strand in Joyce's reception that I have sketched, from Woolf to Mendelsohn, deeply resents these supplementary texts and would cast them off as so many constraints, of a piece with the "puzzles and enigmas" that Joyce couldn't keep himself from putting in. Hence, for instance, Woolf's aversion to Joyce's tricks and Mendelsohn's to "being *managed*." This tradition of reception repeats progressive education's demand that learning be made easy—a demand that Joyce both flagrantly violates and pointedly acknowledges. For although "Oxen" reverts to the old school's methods and preserves its constraints, the episode also gestures toward the ostensibly free and easy education that it refuses. Buck Mulligan becomes this education's advocate. The narrator in "Oxen," by contrast, becomes its counter-progressive opponent. Finding in Walter Pater a model of weight-bearing transmission—effortful, rather than easy—Joyce contrasts Mulligan's understanding of aestheticism and development with his own arduous pedagogical project. "Oxen" thus affirms what Mulligan and many right-thinking readers of *Ulysses* would negate: the past that weighs heavily and that must be repeated, imitated, altered, laboriously copied out again.

His Swaddling Bands

Scenes of instruction early in *Ulysses* set the stage for the later episode's handling of "the studious" and its effort to enforce studiousness (*U* 14.1380). These scenes begin with "Nestor," *Ulysses*'s second episode, set in the school where Stephen works as a teacher. Here, during class, Stephen lets his thoughts wander as his students badly mangle Roman history and barely manage to recite lines from Milton's *Lycidas*. After the lesson ends, a slow learner named Cyril Sargent stays behind, "showing an open copybook" to Stephen (U 2.123–24). "Ugly and futile," Cyril needs help. He has been told to copy out math problems whose solutions he does not understand. For his part, Stephen thinks of the boy's dead mother, his own, and mother love more generally: "*Amor matris*: subjective and objective genitive. With her weak blood and whey-sour milk she had fed him and hid from sight of others his swaddlingbands" (U 2.164–66). It's typical of the overeducated Stephen to translate lived and carnal relations into grammatical terms. What matters most here, however, is that his doing so marks the scene of teaching as *missing* the mother who nevertheless remains in attendance if only as a memory or a thought.

Like the "legend" or inscription "*Fœtus*" that the younger Stephen encounters in an empty anatomy theater in *A Portrait of the Artist as a Young Man*,[21] "*Amor matris*" emphasizes the absence of the very figure that it conjures. The phrase names the dead mother in a dead language, but it also highlights this language's particular amenability to formal analysis. The phrase immediately triggers Stephen's grammatical gloss, and this gloss just as immediately registers the formal study that Stephen has undergone. Even more than the Latin phrase itself, "subjective and objective genitive" sounds like it comes from another teacher or from a textbook. It thus encodes the past in a different way from the phrase that it accompanies; "subjective and objective genitive" points not only to two different kinds or valences of mother love, but also to the scholastic contexts in which this love, abstracted from any particular mother or child, becomes an object of study.

All the while, Cyril continues to copy out his sums. Beautifully drawing attention to the *sum*, the Latin "I am," secreted in these sums, Barry McCrea has read "Nestor" as a tale of two modes of transmission, one genealogical, the other queer. McCrea stresses Stephen's determination to graduate from the scene "of perfect reproduction, of copying, of writing out again," and he aligns such rote reproduction with Stephen's employer, the headmaster Deasy.[22] Deasy, who has given Cyril the assignment that he completes under Stephen's distracted watch, engages in both copying and collecting, and McCrea argues that both processes stand for "pointless accumulation," "offering no possibility of . . . transformation," only an endless repetition of the same. For McCrea, both Stephen and *Ulysses* move away from these processes until they arrive at "Ithaca," which represents the culmination of the progressive growth that the novel charts. By this account, *Ulysses* counterintuitively comes home by running away: "nongenetic genealogies," or queer intergenerational relations, "usurp paternity and marriage by offering a grid on which to plot the protagonists' positions and changing but consistent identities across time (the sum of their *sum*s, but not from a copybook)."[23] Bloom and Stephen are, for McCrea, "not from a copybook," or no longer from one, because by the time they reach "Ithaca," they have forged a bond outside kinship and conjugality and a pair of identities that adds up to more than an assigned *sum*.

But in an important sense, the catechism of "Ithaca" represents a continuation, rather than an overcoming, of the copying out first imagined in "Nestor." For all its undeniable humor and its endless scope and creativity, as a protracted if patently impossible text for memorization, the catechism remains a copybook. It retains even while it radically reworks the form of the "treatise for instruction" whose answers are to be reproduced in a rote fashion:[24] a catechism's answers are emphatically not adapted to suit the styles of individual worshippers, but repeated verbatim under the sign of the impersonal *sum* of someone else. Thus, even while *Ulysses* seems increasingly to privilege spontaneous over learned and "deficient" over compliant forms[25]—to lead inexorably toward Molly's "more than once cover[ing] a sheet of paper with signs and hieroglyphics which she stated were Greek and Irish and Hebrew characters" (*U* 17.676–78)—the distinction between copying and transformation never becomes definitive.

Neither, for that matter, does the difference between reproductive and queer relations that McCrea identifies, finding in the latter alternatives to the "perfect reproduction" of the same.[26] As I have noted, "Oxen of the Sun" begins by enacting the impossibility of this sameness, exposing the difference that inevitably overtakes the effort to sustain "semblables" (*U* 14.23). And yet "Oxen" relies programmatically on repetition. Joyce devises queer forms of repetition that are not strictly reproductive but that refer both to reproductive functions and to the techniques that McCrea associates with "perfect reproduction." These are also the techniques of instruction. Joyce's engagement with the old school as the site of displaced "*Amor matris*" thus also opens onto a reading of the strange persistence of the reproductive in *Ulysses,* and of the repetitive and copied-out in the queer. This is the reading that I undertake here, returning to "Oxen."

Labors of Pedagogy

Joyce meant for the phases of gestation and birth to organize the form of "Oxen." His aim in writing the episode was, as he wrote to Frank Budgen and as almost all commentaries begin by repeating, to map the "progression" of English prose styles onto "the natural stages of development in the embryo and the periods of faunal evolution in general" in a series of strained parallels that only further strained credulity the further they extended, becoming so many Joycean stretch marks: "Bloom is the spermatozoon, the hospital the womb, the nurse the ovum, Stephen the embryo."[27] If, as his detractors complain, the author often makes heavy weather of the Homeric analogies in *Ulysses* as a whole, in "Oxen" he belabors his analogical procedure to the breaking point.

Leo Bersani raises this objection, among others, in his essay "Against *Ulysses*." Here Bersani argues that, far from being subversive, Joyce's novel stages a reactionary reconsolidation of "cultural authority," and that "Oxen" advances this agenda with particular shamelessness:[28]

> Consider "Oxen of the Sun," which may be the most difficult and the most accessible episode of the novel. Once we have identified all the referents in this virtuoso pastiche of prose styles from Sallust to modern slang, what else does the episode give us? How does its language enact its sense? While the narrator is engaging in this stylistic tour de force, several of the characters—including Bloom and Stephen—are sitting around drinking and talking in a maternity hospital, where Mrs. Purefoy is going through the final moments of a long, hard labor. With some help from a letter Joyce wrote to Frank Budgen as he was working on "Oxen of the Sun," critics have proposed a series of parallels between the evolution of English prose and (1) biological gestation and birth, (2) the development of the embryonic artist's prose style, (3) faunal evolution, and (4) Stephen's rebirth as an artist. The episode may be the most extraordinary example in the history of literature of meaning unrelated to the experience of reading and to the work of writing.[29]

It's strange that Bersani, elsewhere a champion of willed readerly as well as writerly poverty,[30] here equates "the experience of reading" with the production, or the consumption, of "sense," as if there could be nothing instructive about language that does not deliver meaning.[31] For Bersani, the bookish *Ulysses*, whose politics are distilled in "Oxen," instead burdens its readers with all the heaviest baggage of the oppressive "cultural inheritance" that it not only leaves intact, but also actively preserves. But this is still to remain wedded to the programmatic statements that Joyce made to Budgen and thus to consolidate, if only unwittingly, the authorial "control" whose exercise Bersani wants to contest.[32] In fact, the parallels listed in Joyce's letter to Budgen are eclipsed in "the experience of reading" through which "Oxen" interpellates its reader as pupil.

This interpellation begins with the episode's first, Latinate paragraphs, which require readers to engage in a sort of reverse translation—minimally, to grasp that Joyce's English sentences are being modeled after Sallust's Latin periods.[33] Even this minimal, provisional grasp presupposes some sense of what the original periods sound like. Only armed with this sense—or with a commentary—is it possible to begin to parse Joyce's English. The practice of reverse translation, recommended for the "making of *Latines*" in the English-speaking world since Roger Ascham's sixteenth-century teachers' manual *The Scholemaster*, is already scholastic in its provenance—that is, already instructional in Giovanni Gentile's disparaging sense.[34] But "Oxen" becomes increasingly scholastic as it proceeds, even while it continues Joyce's engagement with maternity in earlier episodes, including "Nestor." The form that this engagement takes in "Oxen" scandalizes Bersani, because it looks to him like a repudiation of the feminine as such. Joyce, however, complicates this contrast between male *otium* and female reproductive labor. For while Stephen may find "a refuge from his labours of pedagogy" in the Holles Street hospital (*U* 14.1214–15), here *Joyce's* pedagogical labor is intensified.

Critics have noted that, together with the many primary source texts whose styles it imitates, "Oxen" parodies the literary anthologies of Joyce's day. "[I]ntended mainly for the use of young students" rather than adult readers, these texts tended to make history into a matter of linear progression and organic development, with prose "specimens" leading from the fourteenth century to "the present day" or to the recent past in which the present was readily recognizable.[35] Even when the compilers of these anthologies prescribed "attentive toil" in reading,[36] their chronologically arranged selections unfolded more or less seamlessly, with only authors' names and birth and death dates and the titles of their works coming between selections. Although Joyce also consulted more explanatory and editorializing literary histories, he took the humbler extract-collections as models for "Oxen."[37] These provided the episode with its scaffolding, and what results is a sort of abbreviated anthology of prose styles, one from which the informational signposts have been removed and above which a narrative and allegorical overlay has been added. Again: "Bloom is the spermatozoon, the hospital the womb, the nurse the ovum, Stephen the embryo."[38]

This, Joyce said, was his conceit. Recent readings have emphasized, however, that Joyce complicated this approach by using the tropes of progress and development against themselves, as in the episode's introductory paragraphs, which undercut the continuity that they pretend to exhort and "traduc[e]" the productivity that they might at first seem to celebrate (*U* 14.24). Joyce substitutes a "profoundly anachronistic method" for the anthologists' confidently forward-looking procedure and in this way ruins the succession of styles that he claimed to have recreated.[39] The episode's prose keeps getting ahead of itself, and, conversely, having advanced in literary history, "Oxen" stylistically and even linguistically regresses—most spectacularly when Latin punctuates the episode's concluding "afterbirth," made up mainly of slang and ersatz ad copy: "*Silentium!* Get a spurt on" (*U* 14.1457). Joyce accounted for another kind of relapse in the text by pointing to a source in the animal world: "The double-thudding Anglo-Saxon motive recurs from time to time . . . to give the sense of the hoofs of oxen."[40]

This kind of repetition or backward-looking motif is in keeping with Stephen's stated interest in recasting developmental advance as "retrogressive metamorphosis" (*U* 14.390), an interest that Stephen shares with both Bloom and Joyce himself. But the intimate relation of this interest to the backward forms of instruction has not yet been critically recognized. This is perhaps because "Oxen" does not appear to thematize the school—at least not as explicitly as it thematizes sexuality, on the one hand, and history, on the other. "Oxen" has fittingly become a focal point for scholars interested in Joyce's handling of each of these themes.[41] Yet, as Hugh Kenner notes, "student-talk" makes up the episode's "chief material."[42] More importantly still, the transposition and transcription of this talk into a series of painstakingly learned styles constitutes its demanding method.

Demanding, I mean, both for Joyce—who claimed to be engaged in his own "long, hard labor" while writing the episode, which gave him more trouble and caused him more pain than any he had previously composed—and for the reader.[43] Harriet Shaw Weaver, one of the first to respond to "Oxen," wrote to Joyce that "the reading of it is like being taken the rounds of hell."[44] Subsequent generations of readers, including Bersani, have concurred—that is, when they have not given in to the understandable temptation to bypass the episode altogether. There is indeed something hellish, or punishing at the very least, about the experience of reading "Oxen," which, for all its humor, impedes our movement at every turn.

Sending us back to school very late in the day on which *Ulysses* takes place—it is already 10:00 p.m.—"Oxen" also blocks our path to "Circe" and its more pleasurable punishments, not with unbroken monotony, but rather by taking us through circuitous, repetitious "rounds."[45] The episode thus makes the past perceptible as dead weight. It makes the past, more precisely, into a pensum not finally assimilable to meaning.[46] A pensum—whose name derives, like the Latin verb *pensare*, to think, from *pendere*, to weigh—is a scholastic punishment that often takes the form of text copied out, paradigmatically, lines of poetry.[47] Chris Ackerley gives a more capacious definition: "*Pensums*: in the parlance of the Public School, the fagging, detentions, lines, and small senseless demands that so intrude upon time. It was Flaubert's name," Ackerley adds, "for the chore of writing *Madame Bovary*."⁴⁸ It seems fitting, then, that in the opening scene of Flaubert's novel, a Headmaster assigns two pensums: "Five hundred lines for the entire class," and, for the "*new boy*" Charles Bovary, "the verb *ridiculus sum*" to be copied out twenty times.⁴⁹ Joyce reprises this scene of punishment explicitly in *A Portrait*, when the flustered Father Arnall singles out a student who wrongly claims that "the noun *mare*" "has no plural," then fumes, "Copy out your themes again the rest of you."⁵⁰ So, too, does "Oxen" revisit Bovary's "*ridiculus sum*."

And a ridiculous sum of styles is indeed the result, for the pastiches in "Oxen" keep exposing the absurdity of their models. This might seem to suggest that Joyce is engaged less in copying out than in sending up, or even, in Andrew Gibson's more activist formulation, in "writing back"—less in reproducing, that is, than, again, in *traducing* the authors whose prose he imitates.⁵¹ If Joyce or his narrator in "Oxen" undertakes to complete a pensum, then he doesn't complete it well; instead, like a student doing impressions of his teachers throughout detention, he remains defiant. Browne, he says, in so many words, is a bore, and Burke a mere windbag. But I would argue that critical attention to Joyce's subversions of textual authority has tended to obscure the procedures modeled on the pensum that are central to the episode's construction.

Attending to these makes it possible to recognize that "Oxen" does seek to administer "direct instruction" (*U* 17.698). Joyce locates unspent, unsuspected potentials in the very instructional methods that Giovanni Gentile, like Rousseau and John Dewey, sought to clear away. The reformers' efforts to dispense with such residual forms, to sanitize and streamline education, is closely if surprisingly related to the setting of "Oxen": the maternity hospital or "Manse of Mothers" (*U* 14.455). In this narrative context, the episode's "technic"—the stylistic tour-de-force that stages "Embryonic Development," according to the Linati Schema—serves ironically to underscore the sterility of the narrator's discourse. Again, this discourse's tendency to traduce there where reproduction is loudly called for (*U* 14.24) is also its manifest failure to reproduce itself, as each style keeps spilling over into other styles that are not its "semblables" (*U* 14.23).

Yet inasmuch as they are modeled on the styles of others, "Oxen"'s styles *do* reproduce. Or at the very least they gesture—for all their obvious and parodic imperfection—toward what McCrea calls "perfect reproduction."⁵² Each paragraph in "Oxen" is the product of a process distinct from but crucially related to the reproduction that happens in Holles Street, "in the high sunbright wellbuilt fair home of mothers when, ostensibly far gone and reproductitive, it is come by her thereto to lie in, her term up" (*U* 14.68–70). Here the Joycean neologism "reproductitive" condenses the relation-in-distinction that I am trying to describe. Not quite reproductive, but not quite not, "reproductitive" stops short of the episode's would-be Anglo Saxon "double thudding" but engages in the same phonemic stuttering that will lead, in this same sentence, to "thereto to." At the same time, though, "reproductitive" also does more than stutter, since it mimics the form of the *frequentative*, a verbal inflection that signals "the frequent repetition of an action."[53] In Latin, frequentatives rely on the addition of a "-t" or "-it" to a verb's simple form, as when *canare* (to sing) becomes *cantare* (to keep singing); *dicere* (to say) becomes *dictare* (to dictate); or *agere* (to do or drive) becomes *agitare* (to put into motion, and here the frequentative is retained in the English "agitate"). The insertion of these same letters into "Oxen"'s Latinate English not only draws attention to the dead language latent in the living; Joyce's archaizing neologism also describes the work of Joycean instruction itself.

The iterative frequentative "reproductitive" shows how Joyce at once inscribes his text within and marks its distance from reproduction. Supplementing the reproductive—in the Derridean sense, both adding to and supplanting, both requiring and replacing it—the "reproductitive" organizes "Oxen"; it becomes the sign under which the episode unfolds.[54] Ostensibly gathering to worship at the altar of biological reproduction, Joyce's "studious" characters (U 14.1380)—and even more so his readers—end up engaging in another set of rituals. These belong to the school rather than the maternity ward, and this makes their recurrence in "Oxen" that much more striking. Joyce has the forward-looking medical institution—guarantor of the "reiteratedly procreating function ever irrevocably enjoined" by Genesis and the nation alike (U 14.31–32)—shelter the more frequent and backward form of reiteration that inheres in the techniques of the old school. These techniques enjoin not increase and multiplication, but going back over what has gone before.

Midway through the episode, Bloom reflects on this distinction as he considers the schoolboy humor of the medical students in the maternity ward: "Singular, communed the guest with himself, ... that the puerperal dormitory and the dissecting theatre should be the seminaries of such frivolity" (U 14.896–99). "Such frivolity" may be another name for the "crime committed against fecundity" that Joyce said "Oxen" was to illustrate: "Am working hard at *Oxen of the Sun*, the idea being the crime committed against fecundity by sterilizing the act of coition."[55] But rather than simply sterilizing, "Oxen" makes writing "reproductitive."

Embryo Philosophers

Given Joyce's hard work and sustained if impious adherence to his stylistic sources, I have been arguing that "Oxen"'s "most conspicuous practice" is, in fact, copying out, not "writing back."[56] If the gestalt of the text's styles is defiant, as Gibson and others contend, their individual instances—the stylistic episodes within the narrative episode—remain derivative. To say this is not to deny the inventiveness of the episode as a whole; it is instead to specify that this inventiveness remains inseparable from imitation, just as the narrative of "Oxen" is impossible to disentangle from its obtrusive stylistic presentation—even while the two, style and narrative substance, never quite sync up. Far from being a mere decorative overlay or distraction, the stylistic pastiches in "Oxen" constitute its defining feature and insinuate its argument. Countering the progressive stipulation that we should—together with the idea that we ever could—get out from under the past, Joyce insists in this way that repeated and formative, frequent and "reproductitive" returns to it remain indispensable.

Long since sustained by the old school and reenacted in "Oxen," such returns are what progressive education recasts as obsolete in order to leave them behind. Yet at the same time, the discourse of educational reform, beginning with Rousseau and continuing well past Joyce's day, also recasts *itself* as reproductive; time and again, reformers pretend to forswear the repetition of the past for the sake of fertility. For progressive educators, later called "developmentalists,"[57] traditional education and the Latin class that is its emblem thus become sterilizing. Cultural contraceptives, these old institutions are held responsible for broad collective stagnation, for national failures to innovate. But they also stand accused more pointedly of what Joyce, framing "Oxen," calls "crime[s] committed against fecundity."[58] Rousseau's *Émile*, for instance, links bad education to declining birth rates, and Dewey sees such education as evolutionarily redundant. For both thinkers and their reform-minded followers, the old school thwarts the procreation it should serve; it separates itself, and its students, from the reproduction with which it should coincide.

In these progressive educational theories, reproduction importantly refers not to the maintenance of the same. Rather, it names a process of continual improvement, whether social or evolutionary or both, as in Dewey. Reproduction becomes the optimization rather than the mere preservation of life, as in the ideology that Lee Edelman will call "reproductive futurism."[59] Consider the logic of the impassioned defense of breastfeeding that opens *Émile*, where Rousseau argues that nursing lays the foundation for an education properly realigned with nature. Indeed, Rousseau at times even gives readers to understand that breastfeeding suffices to *constitute* this education, capable on its own of bringing about thoroughgoing reform: "Let mothers design to nurse their children, morals will reform themselves, nature's sentiments will be awakened in every heart, the state will be repeopled."[60] Repopulated, that is, by newly moral, newly natural, "lively and animated" men, women, and children. For Rousseau, reform, which begins at home, thus means innovation first and foremost. It also rules out repetition by definition, as *Émile* will proceed to explain. *Émile*'s first pages at first seem to advocate a return to a past state of affairs, to a time when women were mothers. Plainly, however, these pages instantiate Rousseau's "archeoteleological concept of nature," according to which the return to origins and the achievement of destiny coincide.[61] And here *telos* trumps *arche*, just as reform trumps recurrence: "Thus from the correction of this single abuse," Rousseau writes, referring to mothers' reliance on wet nurses, "would soon result a general reform; nature would soon have reclaimed all her rights" (*E* 46; trans. modified). The "all" tips the reformer's hand: Rousseau has in mind the wholesale restoration of a nature not only prior to culture, but also after it. Fully reproductive, the nature that has "reclaimed all her rights" will have left culture and its props behind.

At the same time, though, Rousseau makes his *Émile* the purveyor of a system of acculturation continuous with nature as origin and end. Addressed to mothers (*E* 37), the treatise proposes an educational method based on mother love—and this even though, remarkably, "Émile is an orphan" (*E* 52). Therefore, no dead language, no scholastic abstraction—nothing like Joyce's "*Amor matris*: subjective and objective genitive" (*U* 2.163)—can come between the pupil and his teacher, who "inherit[s] all [parental] rights" (*E* 52). This twist—that an orphan models the ideal reception of teaching as naturalized mother love—already complicates the philosopher's claims about breastfeeding.[62] But these complications do not trouble Rousseau, determined as he is to reimagine education as liberation.[63] "All our practices are only subjection, impediment, and constraint" (*E* 42), he complains. These cannot but lead to "sad and sterile childhood[s]" (*E* 112). For this reason, *Émile* does away with the cultural baggage in which "Oxen" revels: reverse translations, anthologies, pensums. Instead, the treatise thoroughly integrates the nursery, the schoolroom, and the natural world in the interest of fertilizing there where the old school sterilizes.

Joyce need not have had Rousseau's exhortations on breastfeeding in mind when he wrote "Oxen"—rather than, say, the exhortations of his contemporaries, ranging from advocates of racial purity to nationalists urging that Ireland be "repeopled" after the ravages of famine, emigration, and anticolonial struggle.[64] The Rousseauist legacy persisted in Joyce's day, with biology supplanting nature as a gauge of the good in right-thinking educational theories as well as in theories of purity and population.[65] Dewey's *Democracy and Education* vividly attests to the ongoing subsumption of cultural transmission by reproduction—and nature's replacement by biology—in the discourse of educational reform. First published in 1916, the year of *Portrait*'s release, Dewey's text responds critically to Rousseau but seeks, like *Émile*, to refute theories that define "education as recapitulation and retrospection," as repetition and recall, as imitation.[66] Dewey argues that these theories rely on a faulty understanding of evolution: far from necessitating the "retraversal" of stages previously surpassed in phylogeny, individual development according to Dewey in fact benefits from increasingly "short-circuited growth," which streamlines ontogeny. For Dewey, progressive education takes its cue from such streamlining precisely; this makes it possible to eliminate unnecessary "retraversing," whereas conservative educational models deliberately retain such retraversing tendencies. Dewey thinks that these lead to wasteful expenditures of energy—recall the "fagging, detentions, lines, and small senseless demands that so intrude upon time"—for students whose growth is thereby stunted.[67]

Dewey's appeal to embryonic development in this context is especially instructive when it is read alongside "Oxen"'s rendition of the same process. Here is Dewey:

> Embryonic growth of the human infant preserves, without doubt, some of the traits of lower forms of life. But in no respect is it a strict traversing of past stages. If there were any strict "law" of repetition, evolutionary development would clearly not have taken place. Each new generation would simply have repeated its predecessors' existence. Development, in short, has taken place by the entrance of short-cuts and alterations in the prior scheme of growth. And this suggests that the aim of education is to facilitate such short-circuited growth. The great advantage of immaturity, educationally speaking, is that it enables us to emancipate the young from the need of dwelling in an outgrown past. The business of education is rather to liberate the young from reviving and retraversing the past than to lead them to a recapitulation of it. . . . A biologist has said: "The history of development in different animals . . . offers to us . . . a serious of ingenious, determined, varied but more or less unsuccessful efforts to escape from the necessity of recapitulating and to substitute for the ancestral method a more direct method." Surely it would be foolish if education did not deliberately attempt to facilitate similar efforts in conscious experience so that they become increasingly successful. (*DE* 85–86)

By a barely detectable sleight of hand, the philosopher concludes this passage by outbidding the evolutionary biology to which he appeals. "A biologist has said," Dewey admits, that animal development bears witness to many "'more or less unsuccessful efforts to escape,'" to go without recapitulation after having outgrown it. But the stress here, in the sentence Dewey quotes, falls on failure, not success. This is where progressive education, defined as emancipation, comes in: sponsoring "short-circuited growth," such education looks to biology for inspiration, but it parts ways with natural science at a crucial juncture, for it spares students the labor of recapitulation, of repetition.[68] In this way, it succeeds where evolution falls short. The growing student's efforts are "similar" to those of the developing animal, but "increasingly successful" and so less beholden to the repetitive rhythms of animal life. Progressive education thus improves even on embryonic growth.

Ease, moreover, marks the passage from the old school to the new. Dewey does not go so far as to suggest that progressive education will liberate students from work as such as well as from "reviving and retraversing the past." But he clearly implies that a heavy burden is lifted when the latter processes go the way of ancestral methods. Meaning now accrues to the education thus streamlined, which becomes power-enhancing rather than pensum-like, intrinsically rewarding rather than a long series of imposed chores: "We thus reach a technical definition of education: It is that reconstruction or reorganization of experience which adds to the meaning of experience, and which increases the ability to direct the course of subsequent experience" (*DE* 89–90).

If "Oxen" indeed seems to create "short-cuts and alterations in the prior scheme of growth" of English prose as it condenses whole epochs into mere paragraphs, these paragraphs are anything but facile. Laborious and long, they are instead modeled on a set of scholastic chores, on the copying out of past styles liable to be felt as impositions, hindering rather than helping the reader to advance. In order to advance at all, this reader must be willing to go without—to lose, rather than gain in, meaning—as Bersani complains. But if we recognize that what Bersani calls "the work of writing" and "experience of reading" alike in "Oxen" return to the old school's rituals—which, as rituals, privilege practice over signification—then it becomes possible to reassess the Joycean text, which programmatically puts us through motions without positing, as does Dewey, that a surplus of meaning will result.[69]

Indeed, "Oxen" creates—and satirically exaggerates—tension between the terms that progressive education works to reconcile. Joyce belabors the seam that Rousseau, Dewey, and Gentile will away in their effort seamlessly to integrate language and sense, transmission and reproduction, culture and biology. "Oxen" instead insists on the divide between these terms. This divide, Joyce suggests, is insuperable but not, for all that, static or sterile. After all, it generates the text of "Oxen" itself, born from the relation-in-distinction, the contact and collision between the labor-intensive maternity ward and what Bloom calls the "seminary of frivolity" (*U* 14.899).

Briefly, this frivolity—the assembled students' carousing, "the general vacant hilarity" (*U* 14.799)—touches on "a discourse" reminiscent of Rousseau's (*U* 14.797). And we are, in fact, in the loose chronology of the episode's styles, in the age of *Émile*, though the medical students' debate now centers not on wet nursing but on the use of contraceptives. Against this use, one student advocates nakedness, just as *Émile* had advocated that babies be freed from constraining swaddling clothes (*E* 43):

> Dame Nature, by the divine blessing, has implanted it in our heart and it has become a household word that *il y a deux choses* for which the innocence of our original garb, in other circumstances a breach of the properties, is the fittest nay, the only, garment. The first ... is a bath—But at this point a bell tinkling in the hall cut short a discourse which promised so bravely for the enrichment of our store of knowledge. (*U* 14.790–98)

The bell in the maternity ward announces a labor in progress. The event of childbirth truncates the praise of "dame Nature," as if to suggest that the student's Rousseauist discourse can bring itself to name a bath, but can accommodate neither the unseemly act of sex nor the agonizing scene of "hard birth" (*U* 14.114). The brave new dream of an "enrichment of our store of knowledge" inseparably yoked to reproduction is therefore, for Joyce, predicated on the denial of the facts of sexuality and labor.

Of course, the students' "ribaldry" in "Oxen" (*U* 14.806) everywhere breaches "the properties" that govern sex. But Joyce refutes Rousseau and Dewey even more forcefully through his handling of labor. Although "Oxen," too, avoids the agonizing scene of birth—although, again, we only hear about Mina Purefoy's labor secondhand—this labor is transposed as Joyce sets himself and his reader to work, often agonizingly. By "transposed" I mean both altered and preserved: against the tendency shared by Rousseau and Dewey to foreclose labor, to make education a matter of (fake) freedom and facilitation, "Oxen" makes labor central to "the experience of reading." Joyce thus implies that if reproduction and education, maternity and imposed style, share anything, it is their status as an "ordeal of ... duress" (14.878).

This is not to suggest that for Joyce the two kinds of labor, maternal and textual, are the same. On the contrary, in "Oxen," the "reproductitive" is precisely *not* coextensive with the reproductive. The former is more frequently repeated, more repetitive. But both are laborious. Rendering the instruction that is an ordeal, Joyce denies the Deweyan and Rousseauist claim that hard labor in education is both obsolete and avoidable. To do this, though, he needs a language not made up of household words.

Manner of Oxenford

At a key moment in "Oxen," Joyce invites readers to see the absurdity that marks attempts to deny the divide between education and reproduction. During a discussion of infant mortality's causes and possible cures, the ever-campy Buck Mulligan proposes to redecorate the "puerperal dormitory" so thoroughly as to make it into a school centered on "Kalipedia," or the study of beauty:[70]

> Kalipedia, he prophesied, would soon be generally adopted and all the graces of life, genuinely good music, agreeable literature, light philosophy, instructive pictures, plastercast reproductions of the classical statues such as Venus and Apollo, artistic coloured photographs of prize babies, all these little attentions would enable ladies who were in a particular condition to pass the intervening months in a most enjoyable manner. (U 14.1251–56)

The model for this new school would seem to be classical, or at least in keeping with a received understanding of Paterian classicism. But the style being imitated here is that of the Darwinian Thomas Henry Huxley, and Mulligan presents his vision of a future academy as the antidote to an unhealthy and underreproductive modernity. Forward thinking, not really backward looking, "Kalipedia" serves to remedy an age in need of airing out. Before his prophecy, Mulligan blames infant death and the deterioration of Irish stock on "the sanitary conditions" that result from the inhalation of "the bacteria which lurk in dust" (U 14.1243–45):

> These factors, he alleged, and the revolting spectacles offered by our streets, hideous publicity posters, religious ministers of all denominations, mutilated soldiers and sailors, exposed scorbutic cardrivers, the suspended carcases of dead animals, paranoic bachelors and unfructified duennas—these, he said, were accountable for any and every fallingoff in the calibre of the race. (U 14.1245–50)

Mulligan (like Gentile) renders classicism and progress compatible, calling for revival without recapitulation, optimization of "the race" rather than repetitive traffic with the dead and "suspended." He is a queer character, to be sure, but one evidently co-opted at this point into reproductive futurism. Queerness comes to reside elsewhere—in the old school—as the detritus of progressive discourses like Dewey's reappears in Mulligan's sanitizing speech, instructively. For to clear away this detritus in order to create the conditions under which "prize babies" may become models—to do this, as Mulligan proposes, is to call for "increasingly successful" fructification, freed from the ways of "the lower forms of life" (DE 85).

Since these are the ways that *Ulysses* itself has followed at least since Bloom's first appearance together with his cat and beloved "beasts and fowls" (*U* 4.1), this moment in "Oxen" constitutes a joke at Mulligan's expense. "A onelegged sailor" appears in "Wandering Rocks" (*U* 10.7), prompting Father Conmee to think, "but not for long, of soldiers and sailors whose legs had been shot off by cannonballs" (*U* 10.12). The butcher shop in the earlier "Lestrygonians" is, of course, full of "the suspended carcases of dead animals," which themselves recall "the bloated carcass of a dog" that appears briefly in "Proteus" (*U* 3.286). Stephen, as that early episode attests, is himself a "paranoic bachelor," and we gather in "Nausicaa" that the limping Gerty MacDowell may go on to become an "unfructified duenna" by choice. All of the "factors" that Mulligan blames for "fallingsoff" and that "Kalipedia" pretends to leave behind have therefore figured elsewhere in the novel, whose earlier episodes Mulligan recapitulates—ironically, given his call for an education-during-reproduction that would do away with redundancy. This is also a call for the streamlining of education along Deweyan lines: its integration with reproduction and subsumption by evolution defined as advance, a progressive process that outbids even the evolution "desiderated by the late ingenious Mr Darwin" (*U* 14.858–59). In this sense, Mulligan's prophecy for "Kalipedia" remains consistent with his own earlier "project" (*U* 14.701): "to set up a national fertilising farm" (*U* 14.685). The farm and the school alike maximize fertility. Both places make procreation into progress, into the adaptive and efficient "short-circuited growth" that Dewey celebrates (*DE* 85).

Technologies of cultural, rather than biological, reproduction also appear in Mulligan's fantasy hospital *cum* school, where "prize babies" are shown in "artistic coloured photographs" and Venus and Apollo appear as "plastercast reproductions." As in the "light philosophy" to be assigned, the past is rendered weightless in Mulligan's ideal maternal world, where everything has been translated into commercialese, becoming graceful, "genuinely good," "agreeable," "light," "most enjoyable." This is education as facilitation indeed: even while mothers-to-be become students in Mulligan's vision, they are spared the scholarly labors that Joyce's readers undergo, to say nothing of Joyce's own "labours of pedagogy" (*U* 14.1214–15). Labor has given way to ease for this lying-in under "Kalipedia," during which history repeats itself only as Muzak.

Mulligan, then, has awoken from Stephen's nightmare, and the future he beholds in "Oxen" is all sweetness and light. We have seen, by contrast, that, despite its humor, "Oxen" puts up punishing resistance palpable as weight. Figures of weight recur in critical responses to the episode. Christopher

Ames, for instance, recasts Edmund Wilson's charge of "dead weight" as praise[71] and writes that in "Oxen" Joyce develops "strategies for transforming the oppressive weight of literary tradition into a creative source."[72] John Gordon writes of "Oxen" as "onerous,"[73] and Robert Spoo, for his part, thinks of each of the episode's styles as exerting "pressure."[74] Spoo also notes that etymologically "nightmare" has "'the sense of . . . crushing weight on the breast.'"[75] and this observation lets us realign Stephen's well-worn definition of history with Marx's claim that "the tradition of all dead generations weighs like a nightmare on the brain of the living."[76] Joyce's critics have tended to suggest that *Ulysses* ultimately sheds this weight and have tended to see "Oxen" as the place in the novel where the burden of the past is both acknowledged and, progressively, cast off, with Joyce "registering the laughter of minds freeing themselves from historical bondage."[77] But this optimistic account forgets the abiding nightmarishness of the Joycean text:[78] a nightmarishness that, in "Oxen," takes the form of stylistic and scholastic encumbrance.

Pointedly, Joyce uses such dead weight to narrate a scene of birth, thus underscoring the contrast between Mulligan's ideal, classicizing academy for "Kalipedia" and the old-school "seminar[y]" that is "Oxen" (*U* 14.899). Whereas the former does away with dust, "dead animals," and all that it opposes to optimal fertility, "Oxen," like "Hades," lets such miscellaneous dead, ugly, and futile matter in, circulating cultural and material waste while also activating less-than-optimal affects like boredom and frustration. And the contrast between "Oxen"'s old and Mulligan's new school is further clarified when Joyce reaches the era of aestheticism in the chronology of his episode's prose styles. Precisely where we might expect a further send-up of Mulligan's preciosity—in Joyce's pastiche of Pater—we get another scene altogether instead: a "'Nativity' scene" less reproductive than "reproductitive."[79]

Here Bloom, "chewing the cud of reminiscence" (*U* 14.1041–42), recognizes Stephen, whom he has seen years before, when Stephen was still a boy, accompanied by his mother. Recognition then gives way to a recollection rendered in vintage Paterisms:

> The stranger still regarded on the face before him a slow recession of that false calm there, imposed, as it seemed, by habit or some studied trick upon words so embittered as to accuse in their speaker an unhealthiness, a *flair*, for the cruder things of life. A scene disengages itself in the observer's memory, evoked, it would seem, by a word of so natural a homeliness as if those days were really present there (as some thought) with their immediate pleasures. A shaven space of lawn one soft May evening, the wellremembered grove of lilacs at Roundtown, purple and white, fragrant slender spectators of the game

but with much real interest in the pellets as they run slowly forward over the sward or collide and stop, one by its fellow, with a brief alert shock. And yonder about that grey urn where the water moves at times in thoughtful irrigation you saw another fragrant sisterhood, Floey, Atty, Tiny and their darker friend with I know not what of arresting in her pose then, Our Lady of the Cherries, a comely brace of them pendent from an ear, bringing out the foreign warmth of the skin so daintily against the cool ardent fruit. A lad of four or five in linseywoolsey (blossomtime but there will be cheer in the kindly hearth when ere long the bowls are gathered and hutched) is standing on the urn secured by that circle of girlish fond hands. He frowns a little just as this young man does now with a perhaps too conscious enjoyment of danger but must needs glance at whiles towards where his mother watches from the *piazzetta* giving upon the flower-close with a faint shadow of remoteness or of reproach (*alles Vergängliche*) in her glad look. (*U* 14.1356–78)

"They were all together once in Eden," Kenner paraphrases, "Bloom and a not yet unfaithful Molly, Stephen and a not yet spectral mother," figured here in the pointedly pretentious German parenthetical "not as the wraith who haunts [Stephen's] thoughts today, but as the Mater Gloriosa who summons Goethe's errant Faust aloft."[80] But the Eternal Feminine to which Kenner refers is present here only as a negative image or faint echo, for "*alles Vergängliche*" means "all that is transitory." And Joyce, honoring the young Pater, attends to such fleeting impressions, "moments as they pass."[81] The "May evening" that Bloom recalls is thus passing even while "wellremembered": the involuntary memory prompted by Stephen's expression never stays still but keeps shifting with the passage's pronouns and tenses: "you saw . . . with I know not what of arresting in her pose."

The pastiche is as appreciative as it is irreverent, as docile as it is defiant. On the one hand, it brings out the laughable affectation always latent in Pater's mannerisms, heightening the pathos in his pathetic fallacies, as when Joyce's narrator points "yonder about that grey urn where the water moves at times in thoughtful irrigation" (*U* 14.1366–67). But on the other hand, Joyce evinces a tolerance of and even a tenderness for Pater's stylistic tics: his arch hesitations and hedges; his archaisms, over the top though these may be; the grating of words derived from Anglo Saxon against longer, Latinate ones, as recommended in Pater's own "Style."[82] That Joyce's appreciation results from painstaking study is shown by the passages that he copied out from Pater in one of his Trieste notebooks.[83] Here Joyce occasionally transcribed single, striking phrases ("a marvelous tact of omission"), but more often extended descriptions of places and ceremonies, both Roman and early Christian

(5r; *IP* 6). All of the transcriptions are taken not from *The Renaissance*, but rather from later works: *Marius the Epicurean* and the stories collected in *Imaginary Portraits*. The transcriptions date from 1919 and 1920, years that included the composition of "Oxen," and they are surprisingly scrupulous. Cross-outs and self-corrections are rare, and, though his ink sometimes runs low, Joyce's handwriting remains consistent.

Some elements from these transcriptions make their way untransformed into the "Oxen" pastiche, as when "wellremembered roses" (4v; *M* 95, where Joyce has omitted the hyphen, rewriting Pater's compound in his own fashion) become "the wellremembered grove of lilacs at Roundtown." At other times, the influence of the copied-out passages remains evident even after Joyce's transformation of the source texts, as when Joyce seems to get the idea for the Goethean shorthand or shibboleth "*alles Vergängliche*" from Pater's looser adaptation of phrases from the same poet: "She was like clear sunny weather, with bluebells and the green leaves, between rainy days, and seemed to embody *Die Ruh auf dem Gipfel*, all the restful hours he had spent of late in the woodlands and on the hilltops" (6r; *IP* 148). Joyce transcribed several such passages about the weather, and almost all of them take pleasure in the formation of hybrids between the natural and human worlds, or between landscapes and built environments, which everywhere frame "the unbuilt country" (6r; *IP* 10). Unlike Rousseau, then, Pater nowhere envisions a nature cleansed of culture. Various kinds of cultural and especially ritual props instead recur in Pater's prose, inspiring Joyce's "grey urn."

Consistently, Joyce's selections assemble sacred and profane, Roman and Catholic, "remains" (6r; *IP* 69), which proliferate in the passages from Pater that Joyce copied out. Consider the "battlefield of mouldering human remains" whose "odour rose plainly above the plentiful clouds of incense" in one of the Oxford don's *Imaginary Portraits* (6r; *IP* 69); or the "dead bodies ... hastily buried during the plague" in *Marius*. Even natural objects become relics of a kind, products of decay as much as of growth. Hence the "secular trees themselves" that, Joyce copies, "will hardly last another generation" (6r; *IP* 32); and the olive trees that appear in an extended *descriptio loci* from *Marius*, "fretted and twisted by the ["the" added by Joyce] combining forces of life and death, into every conceivable caprice of form" (6r; *M* 209).

These transcriptions show that although Joyce pokes fun at Pater, he has taken time and pains to learn his style intimately so as to imitate it. And the resulting pastiche underscores the contrast between Mulligan's aestheticist paradise, his school-sanitarium, and the very different version of aestheticism that Joyce's narrator reprises as he picks up on Pater's commitment to the "combining forces of life and death" (6r; *M* 209). Far from being all sweetness and light, like Mulligan's Kalipedia, Pater's prose makes room, even at its most precious, for "weak people" (6r; *IP* 67); for "misshapen features" (7r; *M* 282); for "the dwindled body" of a king's corpse (6r; *IP* 69). Indeed, in Joyce's Pater, sovereigns and subjects alike keep being brought down, or falling off. In *Marius*, for instance, a plague descends on Rome, and wolves, "led by the carrion scent," devour the bodies claimed by disease (5r; *M* 153). These are precisely the kinds of sights, scents, and descents banished from the republic of "Kalipedia."[84] Mulligan's "most enjoyable manner" of educating mothers thus contrasts markedly with Pater's mannerism, and the latter, surprisingly, turns out to be truer to the life that includes death, the life that interests both Bloom and Stephen.

This makes their encounter under the sign of Pater—or rather, their coming together again, accompanied by the realization that they had already seen one another before—overdetermined rather than arbitrary. The Paterian context of their reunion not only highlights the preoccupation with death and decay that Stephen and Bloom share; it also inscribes recapitulation into the novel's central relationship. Just as Stephen's frown in the narrative present repeats his expression from his childish past, so Joyce's rendering of the past's return is the product of his going back over Pater. *Pace* Dewey, then, neither Joyce's characters nor his readers have been freed from "retraversing" "the outgrown past."

To be sure, all of the episode's styles embody obsolesced pasts not left behind. But the past that Pater embodies is, elsewhere in *Ulysses*, expressly associated with pedagogy, and with a particular old school. Bloom's encounter with Stephen in the Holles Street Maternity Hospital follows two previous missed connections: one in the newspaper office in "Aeolus" and another at the National Library in "Scylla and Charybdis." In the latter episode, Mulligan sees Bloom and thinks that he is heavily cruising Stephen: "He looked upon you to lust after you.... O, Kinch, thou art in peril. Get thee a breechpad. // Manner of Oxenford" (*U* 9.1210–12). That last phrase looks forward to "Oxen," but it also refers to a whole late Victorian proto-gay subculture, one in which Pater figured prominently.[85] The appearance of Pater's manner in "Oxen" constitutes a reappearance in this sense as well: Pater turns "Oxen" into "Oxenford."

Before "Oxen," Stephen has been told to cover his ass when Bloom's around, but it is in fact his face that attracts Bloom's attention and awakens his memory. Still, the pederastic or Oxonian possibility first proposed by Mulligan never fully goes away. Neither do the props and "remains" that Pater multiplies in the encumbered descriptions that Joyce copies out, then recapitulates (6r; *IP* 69). These Paterian passages "copied out big" register the history whose weight cannot simply be shed (*U* 14.635): the past at once evolutionary and imperial, linguistic and political, that progressive education would have us bypass and thus deny, free us from "retraversing," exempt us from copying out.[86] Far from liberating us from all that the discourse of progressive education would have us leave behind, Joycean instruction keeps us in surprisingly close touch with what Dewey calls "the lower forms of life." In "Oxen," at Oxenford, these forms include not only Homeric oxen and "Kerry cows" (*U* 14.546), but also Paterian "queerities" (*U* 14.528). Joyce looks to these "queerities," in fact, to counter "Kalipedia," with its sublimations and fructifying stipulations. And it is this affirmation of queerness—or of the queerness of instruction's very negativity—that distinguishes "Oxen" and *Ulysses* from, say, T. S. Eliot's rightist modernist classicism. It is not, then, to be clear, the old school as such that Joyce seeks to affirm. It is instead a particular, queer version of this school, one associated with though not at all exclusive to Pater, whose potential he recognizes and whose queerness "Oxen" lets us see instructively.

Gathering those who are not strictly reproductive, "Oxen" is also queer if by "queer" we mean, with Edelman, at odds with identity. And yet, in "Oxen," copying out becomes a way of changing, not remaining the same. Joyce thus lets us complicate Edelman's recent definition of education as "compulsory reproduction."[87] Although "Oxen" toys with compulsion and traffics in both reproductive themes and repetitive forms, what results is not the kind of "good education" that Edelman has in mind.[88] What results is not, that is, the kind of education that progressive reformers from Rousseau to Dewey advocate and align consistently with reproduction. Counter-progressive and "reproductitive," "Oxen" instead delivers something closer to instruction in Gentile's sense, radically recast. Such instruction is already "bad education," not least because it makes identification (without identity) into a matter of endless *alteration* through imitation—an imitation that, for Joyce, is unavoidably laborious.[89]

In this sense, "Oxen" stages a sort of dress rehearsal for the dream that is "Circe": there, as David Kurnick shows, identities become altogether detached from the acts that would define them in waking life, and this results in "a hollowing out of character at the site of its supposed fastening."[90] For Kurnick, the utopianism of "Circe" inheres in this very "hollowing out," even while the episode's pathos derives from the reader's painful awareness of its social impossibility. "Oxen," I have argued, makes a different site of identity's supposed fastening—the school—into the place of its perpetual (if still socially impossible) alteration, the institution that might sponsor, rather than rule out, what "Circe" calls "self-pretence" (*U* 15.4412).

Whereas the progressive school enjoins us to be ourselves and only ourselves—just as Émile is "entirely for himself" (*E* 39)—the old school reimagined in "Oxen" makes alternatives available, perhaps against all odds. Requiring the "retraversing" of the past that progressive education forswears but that "Oxen" enforces (*DE* 85), Joycean instruction also requires the self "to traverse not itself" (*U* 15.2117). This much Rousseau already knew: "The foundation of imitation among us comes from the desire always to be transported out of ourselves. If I succeed in my enterprise, Émile surely will not have this desire. We must, therefore, give up the apparent good which imitation can produce" (*E* 104). But what if this desire were intractable? What if imitation were prior to, even constitutive of, desire? Then the student could no longer be "entirely for himself." He could no longer stand alone. Instead, like the "underbred" Joyce requiring his exegetes,[91] or *Ulysses* leaning on its schemas, or the reader of "Oxen," an anti-Émile, endlessly consulting source-texts and commentaries without ever understanding clearly, he would remain dependent.[92] To the last, when it came to progress, he would remain behind.

4. *Salò* and the School of Abuse

Salò Our Contemporary

If, as my last chapter argued, Joyce strikingly suggests that it is the old school, not the new, that comes to shelter queer forms of life, in Pier Paolo Pasolini's last film, *Salò o le 120 giornate di Sodoma* (1975), forms that we might take to be queer have been institutionalized, made into the rules and not the exceptions, the norms and not their transgressions. Yet I show in this chapter that, far from abandoning the old school, the film compels viewers to inhabit it and in this way remains continuous with the confining "Oxen of the Sun." While there was an idiosyncratic utopianism or a wishfulness in Joyce's approach to instruction, however, Pasolini's approach becomes veritably dystopian. Still, despite this tonal or temperamental difference—and despite the decades that separate *Ulysses* from *Salò* and the significant and far from straightforward shift from page to screen, from novel to film—both works share an impulse and an aim in their recourse to the old school. Like Joyce, that is, Pasolini returns to and redeploys the forms of instruction in order to counter a prevailing discourse of progress. And in Pasolini's case, as in Joyce's, this effort has proven difficult to see for critics accustomed to valorizing not the counter-progressive but the progressive.

To be sure, readings of *Salò* typically unfold under the sign not of progress but of "prophecy" defined as prediction. According to these readings, *Salò* predicts the future that is our present. In this chapter, I will be telling a different story, one about Pasolini's pedagogy and its relation to the past. This will also be an effort to make sense of the filmmaker's claim that *Salò* was "conceived as a rite."[1] For, as I will show, the kinds of teaching that organize *Salò* are associated with ritual and repetition rather than advancement and innovation. Pointedly backward, they are characterized by coercion, constraint, and corporal punishment rather than their progressive alternatives. By such outmoded educational means—by administering a version of the instruction that it thematizes—*Salò* invites resistance, or sets resistance to work, as it seeks to redress a present marked by disavowal. But before beginning this account of the film, I will offer a fuller sense of the critical conversation to which my reading of the film responds and in which it participates.

There are, to schematize, two stories that are often told about the very end of Pasolini's career. The first story is pathologizing, and although it doesn't prevail the way it used to, versions of it still persist. Those who tell this critical story, whom I'll call the late Pasolini's detractors, argue that he went too far not only because he got himself killed the same year *Salò* was released, but also because he showed what shouldn't be shown.[2] He made us see—or tried to make us see—what we didn't want to see. He lingered with what we would and should leave behind. *Salò* stages an adaptation of the Marquis de Sade's 1785 text *The 120 Days of Sodom*, transposed into the short-lived Fascist Republic of Salò, in northern Italy (1943–45). The film is famously graphic, including long sequences of torture, killing, and various kinds of sexual violence—sequences whose construction is exquisitely precise, consistently painstaking.

According to the late Pasolini's detractors, it's this precision precisely that's perverse, or worse, because it's as if the camera had been recruited to participate in the process that the director claimed *Salò* had set out to decry: a process that is as aestheticizing as it is exploitative and destructive. Consider the early sequences in which the film's four Fascist libertines—representing the nobility, the church, the state, and finance—audition young victims of both sexes with scrupulous care, casting only the camera-ready for their orgies, orgies that are also lessons, this being a "School for Libertinage."[3] Or consider the awful series of tortures that unfolds in the film's penultimate sequence. These tortures, too, are stage-managed with the utmost care, and this proves that even when they're administering fatal punishments, Pasolini's libertines do not give their desire free rein but instead remain bound by the *regolamenti*, the regulations, that bind them together. So, too, does *Salò*'s camera remain, atypically for Pasolini, controlled, quiet, and methodical in its movements.[4] Registering the rules' continued force with its formal precision and fixity, the camera is also committed to *heightening* the libertines' choreography, to framing their already painterly compositions to good effect, as when, in a famous frame, we look with one of the libertines, through his binoculars, at the courtyard in which the tortures are taking place, where victims' bodies have already been carefully and symmetrically arranged (Figure 4). Since the binoculars are held backward, this is a strangely distancing subjective shot, but a key example all the same of the camera's aestheticizing work.[5] Through

Figure 4. The Courtyard in *Salò* (1975). Shown through backward binoculars.

this work, Pasolini's film mimics—it takes cues from and assists—the men who oversee the tortures. And, the story goes, for this irresponsible aestheticization, for *Salò*'s sustained, tasteless, and politically dangerous intimacy with power, the late Pasolini should never be forgiven.[6]

But there is, as I have indicated, another account according to which he has not only been forgiven many times over, but also recast as a prophet of current political or biopolitical realities. This second story is hagiographic, and it has been especially widely disseminated during the last two decades. Those who tell this story counter the late Pasolini's detractors by noting that, if *Salò* is hard to see, so, too, is our world of bare life and resurgent sovereignty, marked by unabashed exploitation and the end of the citizen-subject's autonomy.[7] Indeed, *Salò*'s defenders have argued cogently and often compellingly for the film's lasting relevance. They have also shown that Pasolini's late work speaks to a range of urgent contemporary debates. Seldom, though, have these critics stayed with *Salò*'s images or tarried with the uncomfortable question of complicity. There is instead a rush to bypass, an effort to look *through* rather than *at* the film in these accounts, which frequently refer not to the film's images but to what they signify.[8] And they have been seen to signify everything from "the eclipse of desire" in the present to "current methods of biopower," where the operative word in that last phrase is "current."[9] *Salò*, by this account, looks forward-looking, like our contemporary; made just over forty years ago, the film uncannily anticipates our politics and our predicaments today.

To be sure, critics who make arguments like these follow the lead of the allegorizing cover story that the director himself provided, as when he said that sex in the film was merely a "metaphor for power."[10] Indeed, Pasolini claimed repeatedly that he had sought, with *Salò*, to expose contemporary capitalist power at its purest, at its most "anarchic."[11] But if we take Pasolini at his word here—or rather if, forgetting that a metaphor asks to be *read*, we take him to mean that the film's images are so many veils to strip away or to see through—then it becomes difficult to account for the film's painstaking construction and even more for its insistent backwardness: its fascination with Fascism and its fixation on Sade; its staging of ritual tableaux and its retrograde interest in "sodomy." This interest contrasts starkly with the liberated—and still celebrated—sexual exuberance of the director's previous three films, the films in his *Trilogy of Life*. Some of the films that he made before the *Trilogy*, ranging from *La rabbia* (1963) to *Teorema* (1968), had in fact shown postwar capitalist power recognizably—that is, in images in which spectators might have recognized themselves. *Salò* is instead set in a past that, by most accounts, was never to be repeated, that was supposed to have been left behind. Surely it was therefore easy, from the first, for *Salò*'s spectators to regard the film as if it were not about them at all. *Salò* is, after all, most obviously about Fascist and Sadean power—that is, about forms of power whose apparent remoteness from the present might have proven reassuring to viewers who tended to relegate Fascism and Sade to pasts long since superseded. These same spectators might have tended to imagine sadistic sexual practices as confined to present worlds that they chose not to enter. Thus, if the film was meant to force spectators to recognize their present, then it is not clear why the film itself placed so many obstacles in the way of recognition, why it provided, in effect, so many alibis, rendering power in such spectacular and patently past forms when its goal was to decry a type of power that was all too present and banal.

Again, recent readings have more often praised *Salò* for its "proleptic insight" than they have attended to such obstacles and alibis.[12] That is, critics have tended to insist on *Salò*'s prescience and to defend the film on precisely these grounds—so much so, I would argue, that the film's pastness has been all but forgotten, and as has its pedagogy.[13] The film's backwardness, that is, has become difficult to learn from or even to see. But it is only by staying with what I am calling *Salò*'s backwardness that we can begin to learn its lesson. This means looking at—as well as reading—the film. Rather than labeling the late Pasolini either prophetic or apocalyptic, either "saving" or simply pathological, it means responding to *Salò*'s specificity and refusing the ostensibly politicizing but effectively pacifying claim that sex in *Salò* is a mere "metaphor for power."

This claim sanitizes, desexualizes, and deaestheticizes. It reassures us by giving us permission to feel that we are not implicated in, or at all ambivalent about, the film's brutality. But that we *are* thus implicated is clear if we look long enough. In this sense, Pasolini's detractors are onto something.[14] I say this although I will not be joining them in dismissing *Salò*. Nor, to be clear, will I be joining other critics who, adhering to neither of the two sets of views I have so far sketched, defend the film but declare Pasolini's "political analyses" altogether "failed."[15] Although I build on Armando Maggi's claim that "Pasolini's work teaches us a method of reading reality, not a set of historical beliefs,"[16] I do not think that this "method of reading" can dispense with Pasolini's critique of progress.[17] On the contrary, this critique motivates my reading of *Salò*, a film that is nothing if not backward: "behindhand in progress" sexually, politically, and, as I will show, pedagogically.[18] Following the film's own (backward) movement, then, from text to image,[19] I will contend that *Salò*'s force derives from its ways of implicating us by a range of formal means. These are also ways of *instructing* us, where "instruction" does not refer to content delivery.

Pasolini in Detention

Readers will recall that in the Italian context in particular, "instruction" was often, in the discourse of reformers up to and including the philosopher Giovanni Gentile, a disparaging name for what the old school was good for: nothing. A waste of time and talent, "instruction" stood opposed to the real education that, reformers argued, only the new school could provide. "Material, mechanical," repetitive and ritual, rote and redundant, coercive, contentless, useless, merely outward, and, most emphatically, "dead"—instruction was what progressive educators wanted to replace.[20] They called for an education about inwardness and individuality, one that would be capable of equipping Italian students for modernity, finally.

Two sets of facts are worth underscoring in this connection. First, while he was at work on *Salò*, Pasolini was also composing a text that he called a "trattatello pedagogico," or "little pedagogical treatise."[21] In this text, without addressing "instruction" directly, Pasolini calls Rousseau, whose *Émile* inaugurates the modern critique of the old school, "monstrous," and says that he prefers to dedicate his treatise instead to the "disdainful shade of de Sade"—as if the latter figure could counter the former.[22] Second, to review, in Italy the ranks of self-styled Rousseauists, of progressive educational reformers, included Fascists, chief among them Gentile. Gentile's own pedagogical treatises speak scathingly about "instruction" but soar rhetorically when calling for the modernization—and indeed the "liberation"—of Italian public education.[23] Again, Gentile in fact became minister of education under Mussolini and oversaw the implementation of a broad set of educational reforms to Italian public schools. (As I noted in the Introduction to this book, these reforms included the abolition of compulsory Latin for all students, and the surprising, instruction-advocating response from Antonio Gramsci that this measure prompted paves the way for Pasolini's radical repurposing of the old school, if only indirectly.) The framework that the Riforma Gentile put in place was among the structural features of the state that persisted after the end of the war and the fall of the Fascist regime.[24]

These reforms were continuous with a whole strand in Italian educational discourse in both the nineteenth and twentieth centuries, a long series of pedagogical theories that tried to yoke education to modernization and that made schooling a matter of catching up, of overcoming the national predicament known as *arretratezza*, or belatedness.[25] Such catching up was still compulsory in the postwar period and even in the 1970s. In fact, as Paola Bonifazio shows in *Schooling in Modernity*, her book about the state- and corporate-sponsored deployment of documentary film in postwar Italy, in this context the demand to catch up intensified.[26] This demand accompanied another that has been a central concern in recent scholarship in both Italian historiography and film studies: a postwar imperative to paper over the Fascist past, to render it a closed "parenthesis" in Benedetto Croce's infamous formulation, and to do this in order to reconstitute the nation as good object.[27] Even among communists, the need to lay claim to and enshrine the anti-Fascist Resistance trumped any real reckoning with the recent past or attempt to work through it.[28] Forward-thinking–sponsored filmmakers like those whose work Bonifazio studies and politicians on the parliamentary left alike thus shared in a consensus that pretended to leave the regime behind, that preserved "distinctions between the Fascist past and the democratic present,"[29] and that trained the national gaze on the present and future of progress defined as economic growth.[30]

Against this consensus, Pasolini loudly protested. He came to associate modernization with monoculture, with the mind-numbing inducements of television, with widespread "homogenization," "cultural genocide," and what he called, in a beautiful, lyrical, proto-eco-critical essay, "the disappearance of the fireflies."[31] For Pasolini, far from delivering the freedom that it promised, capitalist modernity entailed a destruction of older forms of life and led to a foreclosure of possibilities for thought and action, imagination and memory. Indeed, the essays that Pasolini wrote during the last years of his life go so far as to claim that what he alternately names neo-capitalism and neo-Fascism—that is, capitalism in its postwar, consumer-driven, global guise—is more totalizing, more pernicious, and in fact more Fascist than Fascism itself. Whereas the regime had ruled through "a superficial, scenic form of regimentation," Pasolini claims that under the new dispensation, which both is and isn't new, regimentation has become "real," an accomplished fact and no longer an aspiration.[32] Power now lays claim to hearts and minds as well as bodies, and the power thus internalized can level whole forms of life, including the forms of life of fireflies.

These are the forms of life that Pasolini's other films are famous for rendering. And the Pasolini we know how to love goes all over—first all over Italy, then all over the world—in search of cultures not yet conquered by modernity. This effort took him from the subproletarian *borgate* or suburbs surrounding Rome, where he began his film career in the early 1960s, to Yemen in the early and mid-1970s, where he filmed both a documentary on the modernization of the city of Sana'a, *Le mure di Sana'a* [*The Walls of Sana'a*] (1971), and *Il fiore delle Mille e una notte* [*The Thousand and One Nights*] (1974), the last film he made before *Salò*, other parts of which were filmed in Ethiopia, Iran, and elsewhere. Such were the lengths to which the filmmaker had to go, he noted, to find even momentary escapes from a capitalism and a conformism that now covered and stultified all of Italy and most of the rest of the world. So it was bound to feel like a betrayal when Pasolini announced that he would stop this travel because "integrating power" had become altogether inescapable.[33] This power left him with no alternative but to retreat, return, stay in.

Staying in, at least, is what he claimed to be doing in a text called "Abiura dalla *Trilogia della vita*," the "Abjuration" or "Repudiation of the *Trilogy of Life*." In this short essay, Pasolini takes distance from—indeed, renounces—the three features that he made before *Salò*, all of which had staged exuberant if not uncomplicated celebrations of youthful bodies and pleasures. No longer able to believe in the "progressive struggle" for sexual liberation, Pasolini finds that the films in the trilogy have been co-opted by capitalism operating through a "tolerance as vast as it is false."[34] In the "Abiura," Pasolini writes that he has come to realize that *any* affirmative handling of bodies and pleasures would be similarly co-opted, which is why he is herewith—in and through the "Abiura"—giving up the search for alternatives to what he finds in his immediate world. I quote the "Abiura" here in both the original Italian and the English translation, because it is truly a text over which to weep:

Dunque io mi sto adattando alla degradazione e sto accettando l'inaccettabile. Manovro per risistemare la mia vita. Sto dimenticando com'erano *prima* le cose. Le amate facce di ieri cominciano a ingiallire. Mi è davanti—pian piano senza più alternative—il presente. Riadatto il mio impegno ad una maggiore leggibilità (*Salò?*).[35]

[Therefore I am adapting to degradation and am accepting the unacceptable. I am maneuvering to rearrange my life. I am forgetting the way things were *before*. The beloved faces of yesterday begin to yellow. In front of me is—little by little without any more alternatives—the present. I re-adapt my commitment to a greater legibility (*Salò?*).]

Those are the essay's last sentences: six declaratives whose finality is finally if only subtly undermined by the question mark that hovers in the concluding parenthesis.

These sentences and the whole essay are by now well rehearsed. Roberto Esposito, Suzanne Stewart-Steinberg, and Rei Terada are just some of the many critics who have recently considered the text's relevance to contemporary conditions of impasse.[36] To my knowledge, though, no one has yet undertaken to read that weird parenthesis as a corrective to Croce's. Recall that, for the philosopher, a parenthesis names what's over and done with, a case that's closed. Here instead Pasolini's question about his own film hangs in the air and makes us hesitate before turning the page; it forces us to go back over to the last sentence to be sure we've understood. Which we haven't, quite, since neither, by his own indirect, interrogative admission, has the "I" who signs the declaration. The parenthetical question in the "Abiura" lingers, remains unresolved; far from effecting, it enigmatically *prevents* the achievement of closure and the abandonment of what's come before.

This is striking not least because Pasolini's avowed goal in the "Abiura" is to announce that he's abandoning the past, in two senses: he is both repudiating his own past projects and, since these were themselves projects of filmic recovery, renouncing the whole impulse to look for ways out of and life-giving alternatives to the postwar capitalist present. But let's return to the sentences that I have been reading. These are at once deliberative and affect-laden: the verb *manovrare*, calling as it does the Gramscian *guerra manovrata* or "war of maneuver" to memory, and the calculating notion of rearranging or more literally resystematizing, one's life—these grate against the "beloved faces of yesterday" that are now beginning to fade. It becomes impossible to tell whether accepting the unacceptable is a matter of pathos or one of resignation. Which suggests, of course, that it is both: the "Abiura" depicts a world in which all passion is spent, but it does so passionately rather than dispassionately, as when, in his penultimate sentence, the author considers the present that he sees before him "little by little without any more alternatives," where these phrases—suspended between dashes that sustain the hopes soon to be dashed—postpone the inevitable.

To postpone the inevitable is to do something other than simply accept it. This is Pasolini in detention, where "detention" also names "a keeping from going or proceeding; hindrance to progress; compulsory delay."[37] In this sense, the phrases "pian piano senza più alternative," phrases that are dilatory, detaining, even while they usher in the end, emblematize the "Abiura" as a whole. For the text protests too much, encircling the faces that it pretends to leave behind and remembering the forms of life that it claims to be forgetting. Although the "Abiura" would seem to give up on the belief in the past's persistence, the text everywhere betrays an ongoing attachment to all that it says that it forswears, and sustains the past that it would leave behind. In this way, Pasolini's essay, like his late poetry, looks to "schemi letterari collaudati" [proven or time-tested literary schemas],[38] drawing on what Anne-Lise François calls poetry's peculiar "power to conjure and linger with what it claims not to mean and not to have."[39] The text thus does something more than what it both purports and seems to do: repudiate, resign, renounce, relinquish. The "Abiura" is a poetic text for this reason and in this specific sense: the essay participates in the lyric mode that involves continuing the very thing that one claims to be discontinuing—as when Petrarch, of all people, announces at a particularly low point in his love life, "Mai non vo' più cantar com'io soleva" [I never want to sing the way I used to anymore].[40] But here the point is that the poet makes this announcement in a *canzone*—that is, precisely by singing the way he used to and the way he'll go on to for many, many poems to come. Recanting remains a form of *cantar*, of singing. The palinode—the kind of poem whose speaker says, "I take it back"—remains an ode.[41] And so does Pasolini's "Abiura," I am claiming.

Reading *Salò*

This way of reading—a *lectio difficilior* or reading in detention—has important implications for understanding *Salò*, and in what's left of this chapter I will indicate the difference it makes. That it is indeed *reading* that's at issue for any viewer of *Salò* the "Abiura" already suggests, in its last sentence: "I re-adapt my commitment to a greater legibility (*Salò?*)." But what is "legibility"? And how does it inform or organize *Salò*? The film offers a first answer in the form of an "Essential Bibliography" (Figure 5). If the "Abiura" is one

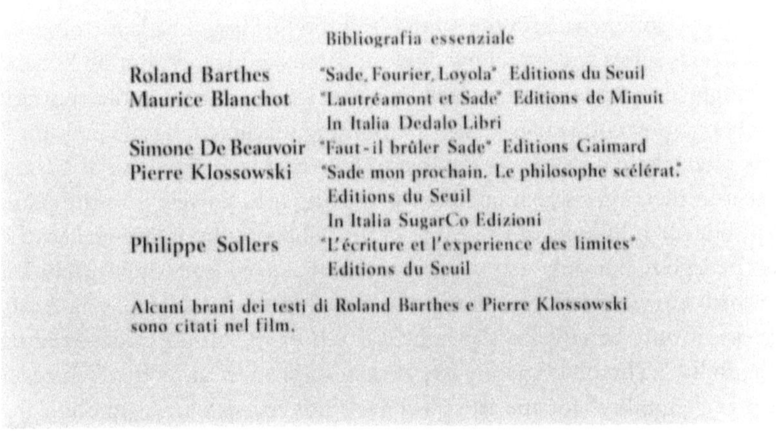

> Bibliografia essenziale
>
> Roland Barthes — "Sade, Fourier, Loyola" Editions du Seuil
> Maurice Blanchot — "Lautréamont et Sade" Editions de Minuit
>   In Italia Dedalo Libri
> Simone De Beauvoir — "Faut-il brûler Sade" Editions Gaimard
> Pierre Klossowski — "Sade mon prochain. Le philosophe scélérat."
>   Editions du Seuil
>   In Italia SugarCo Edizioni
> Philippe Sollers — "L'écriture et l'experience des limites"
>   Editions du Seuil
>
> Alcuni brani dei testi di Roland Barthes e Pierre Klossowski sono citati nel film.

Figure 5. "Bibliografia essenziale." *Salò* (1975).

text that mediates our access to *Salò*'s images, this list of sources, which appears near the end of the film's opening credit sequence, is another. The frame signals the film's desire to participate in, and to complicate, a French philosophical conversation.[42] James Steintrager has incisively compared the "Bibliografia" to the legitimating forewords that appeared before translations of Sade's works, forewords that were sometimes, in fact, the very texts named here by Pasolini.[43] (Simone de Beauvoir's essay "Must We Burn Sade?" and part of Pierre Klossowski's *Sade My Neighbor*, for instance, both still appear before the Grove Press English translation of *The 120 Days of Sodom*.) These prefatory gestures were meant to preempt censorship by establishing the high seriousness of the novels they introduced. If these novels were worthy of the attention of French philosophers, the thinking went (this at a time when French philosophers had not lost prestige), then obscenity charges would be defused in advance; "redeeming social value" would be guaranteed.[44]

There are several other ways to interpret Pasolini's invocation of these figures in Sade's reception and postwar "rehabilitation." And it is also interesting to note the figures left off the list, whose readings of Sade are implicitly deemed inessential: Horkheimer and Adorno, Bataille, Lacan.[45] What matters most, though, is simply the fact that the film begins by assigning required reading. At the outset, that is, *Salò* interpellates the viewer as pupil. But the question then becomes: what kind of a student is the viewer here enjoined to be or become? I cannot claim to be the only viewer at once ardent and compliant enough to have read, in order, all of the texts enumerated here, but I can attest, after having learned the hard way, that the exercise is a slog and ultimately unrewarding. So much so, in fact, that I would even call the bibliography somewhat sadistic: it holds out the thrilling if pedantic promise that the texts it lists will somehow disclose *Salò*'s significance. But no "essential" insight, no solution to the riddle, is in fact forthcoming. On the contrary, the bibliography constitutes a time-consuming misdirection, or a pensum.[46]

Like the schemas that Joyce devised to help readers make sense of *Ulysses*, but that in their very streamlined sense-making instructively miss the point of episodes like "Oxen of the Sun," *Salò*'s bibliography is integral to the film's pedagogy, but only gets viewers so far or indeed leads them astray. Yet it is worth tarrying with one of the texts listed in the bibliography, *Sade My Neighbor*, if only briefly, for the light it sheds on Pasolini's understanding of "legibility." The bibliography has already sufficed to show that, whatever else it is, "legibility" for the late Pasolini is not transparency: although the list of source-texts that begins *Salò* asks to be read, to read this list or the texts it includes is not to arrive at a clear or "essential" understanding of the film. It is to be left with questions that linger like the parenthetical with which Pasolini's "Abiura" ends. That text's concluding sentence bears rereading: "I re-adapt my commitment to a greater legibility (*Salò*?)." If, as I have argued, the "Abiura" preserves what it pretends to give up and keeps all that it pronounces dead, in fact, on afterlife support, then the essay's concluding claim can likewise be seen to hold onto the illegibility that it would seem to forswear for the sake of adaptation. This statement can be taken to mean, in other words, not that Pasolini pledges to *make his texts and films more legible*, but rather that he aims to *adapt to the regime of the legible*. This might mean precisely not producing texts that are easily read by a public demanding legibility; it might lead instead to texts that present themselves as *differently illegible* in a context now wholly governed by the order of the legible, in something like Roland Barthes's sense: "This circle, in which 'everything holds together,' is that of the readerly [*lisible*]."[47] Barthes deploys military language throughout his discussion of the "readerly," whose "meaning is a force."[48] Like the "integrating power" that Pasolini decried,[49] the readerly or legible, for Barthes, is both totalizing by definition and a regime of consumption; it seeks both to defend against and to destroy what opposes it.

Petrolio, Pasolini's last, unfinished fictional project, offers one model of illegibility, one that precedes and contrasts markedly with the "adaptation" announced in the "Abiura" and enacted in *Salò*. Sprawling and radically experimental, Pasolini's novel explicitly presents itself as a direct threat to the readerly order.[50] *Petrolio*'s narrator claims that his account "belongs by its nature to the order of the 'illegible,'" signaling the book's programmatic—

and frontal—assault on readerly norms and expectations.[51] *Salò* proceeds from a different and more complicated understanding of legibility. Here Pasolini shares less with the Barthesian critic, who counters the readerly order with the value of the writerly, than with the author imagined by Klossowski in a section of *Sade My Neighbor* on "How the Sadist Experience Renders Unreadable the Conventional Form of Communication." *Salò*'s approach is in keeping with Sade's procedure as theorized by Klossowski, who claims that the Sadean text stages "the irruption of nonlanguage in language" or, to rephrase, the irruption of the illegible in and only in the medium of the legible.[52] *Sade My Neighbor* also calls this process "the foreclosure of language by itself,"[53] and the figure of foreclosure (a word Klossowski does not use in its psychoanalytic sense) indicates that Sade's language is not finally or fully broken apart, as the earlier "irruption" might at first suggest, but rather continually repaired. For Klossowski, that is, Sade's language is no sooner opened than it is closed up again, recontained, reintegrated; this language is reinstated paradoxically in and through its breakage: "The logically structured language with which Sade expresses himself becomes for him the terrain of outrage, as it is the terrain of norms."[54] And it is crucial that for Klossowski Sade's terrain remains that of norms as well as outrage, even while his texts record crime after crime. By this account, Sade "never transgresses [the] laws [of language] except in the gesture whereby he reproduces them *in* their transgression."[55]

We can thus recognize in Klossowski's "conventional form of communication" the kind of legibility that Pasolini thought had become "greater" with time. The neo-capitalist or neo-Fascist context in which *Salò* sought to intervene was, in fact, for Pasolini, one in which all transgressions served in the end to reproduce the laws that they would have violated. Such is the effect of what Pasolini repeatedly names, with Herbert Marcuse, "repressive tolerance" or "false tolerance," which he characterizes as the recontainment of every effort to break with norms and the automatic conversion of disobedience into its opposite, as in the poet's remorseful address to the younger generation: "obbedisti disobbedendo!" [you obeyed disobeying!].[56]

This false tolerance was, then, a form of foreclosure. But according to Klossowski, "'Foreclosure' means that something remains outside."[57] Dialectically, the apparent negation of the outside becomes an affirmation of its continued existence. Indeed, there would be no need to foreclose that which did not threaten from without—in Sade's case, "the act to be done," Klossowski writes; in Pasolini's, past and lost forms of life.[58] "Something remains outside" in *Salò* as well, then, but this something cannot be accessed directly, as it still could in the *Trilogy*, as the "Abiura" insists. Any belief in the possibility of such direct access would imply a denial of foreclosure's extent. Instead, by the time of *Salò*, the outside could only be "produced within thought."[59] Another name for this outside might be "illegibility." And conversely, for the late Pasolini, "legibility" might be another name for foreclosure.

To adapt to *this* would mean finding ways to film the conversion of disobedience into obedience or transgression into law, while at the same time indicating that "something remains outside" nevertheless. *Sade My Neighbor* can therefore help us to account for Pasolini's return to school as well as his recourse to Sade.[60] Klossowski offers a vocabulary for understanding *Salò*'s not strictly Sadean engagement with—its effort to administer—instruction, which we can now redefine as a pedagogy of foreclosure, of hindrance or prohibition rather than (false) permission. Yet we have seen throughout the preceding chapters that "something remains outside" when this pedagogy is redeployed in counter-progressive projects, which preserve possibilities for "reserve" (in Pater), departure (in Pascoli), or desire and "self-pretence" (in Joyce). I have shown repeatedly that these possibilities remain not despite but because of an insistence on foreclosure or constraint as well as on the persistence of the past, its status as a weight to be borne.

So, too, does *Salò* respond to a foreclosing present, with a foreclosure that knows itself and that is undeniable, "scenographic."[61] And so, too, does the film recast the past as pensum. Finding progressive discourses and struggles complicit with the "real" foreclosure effected by the regime of the legible or readerly—a regime that he would have called, again, both neo-capitalist and neo-Fascist—Pasolini returns to and repurposes instruction, defined, as in the discourse of progressive educational theory, as a set of painfully inflicted tasks that impose on students', or viewers', time. To do this is also to counter the forgetting of the Fascist past and its structural persistence, to reintroduce temporal contradiction into a context of presentist consensus and "historic compromise."[62] Against the progressive claim that the past is past and closed, parenthesis-wise, *Salò* brings the bad old news of all that is *not* abandoned when old eras are declared ended and old fixations outgrown. In such a context, infliction and imposition become necessary because kinder and gentler teacherly means, a teaching style respectful of our space and our spontaneity and rooted in a belief in our freedom (recall that the Fascist Gentile claimed to be a great believer in our freedom), would not forcefully register the survival of the past from which we are not free.[63]

Now, there is also an account of our unfreedom in what I have called the allegorical reading of *Salò*, a reading authorized by Pasolini's own claim that sex in his film is only a "metaphor for power." But, if only unwittingly, proponents of this reading imply that we should look *through* *Salò*'s images to what they signify, symbolize, or metaphorize. Imagine reading, though, in a poem, *right past* the vehicle to access the tenor that it "hides," as if the latter weren't at all affected by the former.[64] By this account, again, *Salò* is not about this casting call or beauty pageant but about bare life; not about that whipping but about contemporary sovereignty. This argument, which effectively lets viewers off the hook, runs directly counter to mine. It is not a progressive argument, obviously, since it is about how much we have regressed in recent years, but like progressive educational theory from Rousseau to Gentile, it would spare us the work and the formative ordeal of returning to the past that *Salò* repeats. We can better understand the terms of this repetition and the value of the ordeal to which it leads by turning to another category, one related to instruction in ways that previous chapters have emphasized: ritual.[65]

Lands of Regret

Again, Pasolini claimed that *Salò* was "conceived as a rite."[66] Unlike many recent readers of the film, I take this claim seriously, as a prompt to think through the film's complex and programmatic engagement with ritual. I also take this claim to be more instructive, because more demanding, than the allegorizing or metaphorizing claim that I have already considered. If a metaphor can all too easily be treated as a means of content delivery—as, again, a vehicle or veil to be seen through in a search for tenors or referents—a rite, by contrast, is undergone as a process.[67] Or it is resisted. Or resistance becomes inseparable from the experience of undergoing it.

Rites recur in a book that *can* shed light on *Salò*—more, I would argue, than the books listed in the film's bibliography: anthropologist Ernesto De Martino's *La terra del rimorso*, or *The Land of Regret*. First published in 1961, De Martino's book gathers a range of ethnographic and historical reflections on *tarantismo*, the set of ritual practices associated with the treatment of poisonous spider bites in Puglia, in southern Italy. The text centers on the returns of malignant symptoms among the predominantly female *tarantate*, those supposedly bitten and rebitten by spiders, "bitten again" being another meaning of the *rimorso* in De Martino's title. De Martino is especially interested in these symptoms' ritual cures, cures that turn out to imitate symptoms so closely as to be indistinguishable from them.[68] These cures were, interestingly in the context of *Salò*, orgiastic in antiquity. Considering their social role in the present, De Martino reads these rites neither as matters of superstition nor instances of mental illness, but as ways of responding to what he calls "il cattivo passato che torna," "the bad past that returns."[69]

A passage from the anthropologist's conclusion underscores this return's relevance to De Martino's present:

> Today we know that the "prick" of remorse is not the attack of a demon or of a god, but the bad past that returns.... But precisely because we know these things—and the contemporary world has offered us too much of this bitter knowledge—*tarantismo* activates our interest once again and becomes a live question that concerns us intimately. On the other hand, precisely because our consciousnesses have never been so buffeted by the individual and collective past as they are today, and precisely because our souls are beset by the search for operative symbols that might be adequate to our humanism and to our sense of history ... *tarantismo* is not indifferent to us, but rather almost constrains us to measure with it the ensnared powers of our modernity. In this sense, if the Land of Regret is Puglia in that it is the elective fatherland of *tarantismo*, the pilgrims who visited it in the summer of '59 [De Martino himself and his team] come from a vaster land that in the end deserves to be known by the same name, a land that extends even to the limits of the world inhabited by men [*sic*].[70]

Note that what begins as a confident statement about the difference between "us" and those who still believe in gods, monsters, malevolent spiders, and miracle cures ends with a virtual erasure of this very difference. Locating the modern researchers, tellingly renamed "pilgrims" here, in a land that is also one of regret (though one that doesn't know itself), and then further widening the boundaries of this land so that it encompasses the whole inhabited world, De Martino all but undoes the distinction that he initially establishes between the backward and benighted *tarantate* and the modern, metropolitan pilgrims who have undertaken to observe them.

Yet on another level this distinction is preserved, or sublated, because it is the latter who stand to learn from the former, and it is difference that makes this learning possible.[71] Since souls in "our modernity" are tasked with searching for the kinds of "operative symbols" that remain operative in the realm of *tarantismo*, the remorseful Southerners effectively teach their northern visitors. Measured against—or rather *with*, as De Martino more forcefully writes—*tarantismo*, "our humanism and our history" cannot remain the same; they cannot, that is, after the lessons of the Land of Regret, remain the possessions of moderns who either claim to have superseded the past or rush to catch up with those who have. In this way, De Martino's text both thematizes and models a way of relating to the past that resists its subsumption by the present.[72]

Pasolini and De Martino clearly share an interest in the ritual resources available in nonmodern worlds.[73] Both suggest, moreover, that such resources might still be accessed and set to work to redress an ailing modernity.[74]

But Pasolini is typically said to have abandoned this hope by the time he made *Salò*.⁷⁵ I have shown, however, that the "Abiura," which purports to announce this abandonment, does something else as well. We can now say that that text dwells in the Land of Regret: it *enacts* the return of the bad past that De Martino traces through the Puglia of the *tarantate*, only then to argue that it happens everywhere, that the return is not regional.⁷⁶

This return structures *Salò*, including at the level of the image. A pair of sequences can illustrate this organizing principle. In the villa's main hall, where the libertines, their female storytelling assistants, and the guards and victims all gather for assemblies when what Sade calls "school" is in session, Signora Vaccari (who was, incidentally, born in a school) presides over two storytelling scenes. To begin with, the *narratrice* regales the congregation with an account of her early life. A victim has already disappointed one libertine, and now another victim masturbates the financier ineptly. Seeing this, Signora Vaccari breaks off her story, declaring that something must be done. Prompted by this declaration or by something else, a young curly-haired girl, looking dazed, suddenly runs to the nearest window and tries to jump out. Guards stop her, and we see her struggling as they carry her away—but only for several seconds, since it is mealtime, and after a dissolve the struggle is succeeded by the first of several banquet scenes.

Lunch is eventful. Victims working as waitresses are (in the film's language) "sodomized," as is the eager and ever idiotic financier. Two other libertines philosophize, and a *narratrice* reminisces. Out of nowhere, everyone sings a war song, in a beautiful hymnal rendition that briefly and arrestingly brings victims and libertines, servants and served, together.⁷⁷ After this, a mannequin is brought in, and the masturbation lesson promised by Signora Vaccari is finally given, to the delight of libertines, storytellers, and soldiers alike. At this point the viewer has all but forgotten about the escape, or suicide, attempt that has immediately preceded the meal. But the film provides an aggressive reminder, enacting the return of the diegetic "bad past." Back in the main hall, the whole group is shown: *signori* and storytellers, victims and soldiers, all gathered again silently around the altar, which now has its wings closed. After a sign is given, these wings, painted to look like curtains, open to reveal the would-be escapee, now dead. Two later shots show that the girl's throat has been cut, but Signora Vaccari quickly resumes her storytelling. A crude painting that sits atop the altar, anomalous in a villa famously full of modernist artworks, shows a haloed Madonna and her Child.⁷⁸ This painting was shown frontally in the background only once, very briefly during the scene before lunch, its appearance coinciding with the girl's attempt to escape. Now, the Madonna is more prominently visible, since the storyteller positions herself immediately before the painting. She then steps aside, then paces back and forth repeatedly, to reveal, then conceal, then reveal again the girl flat on her back who has become the painting's extension or its refutation. The dead body disappears from view, then reappears, is alternately covered and uncovered by Signora Vaccari's dress. Now you see her; now you don't (Figure 6); then again you do (Figure 7). The victim's intermittent visibility instantiates the return of the bad past that *Salò* stages. For the viewer, each reappearance becomes a brief experience of what De Martino calls *ri-morso*: a re-bite.

But the static image of the Madonna presides over these reappearances. The painting's sustained on-screen presence contrasts with the dead girl's disappearances and returns. The Madonna thus marks one place where *Salò* reflects on its own status as image, drawing on what Georges Didi-Huberman calls the tradition of "critical images." These he understands as primarily ritual, rather than representational, in their function.[79] More specifically, Didi-Huberman argues that critical images engage in "a perpetual 'putting to death'" in order to counter "the common desire" or collective determination to forget it.[80] The critical image constitutes an answer to, and an effort to undo, collective disavowal. Likewise, as both a rite and what Pasolini more specifically calls a "sacra rappresentazione"[81]—referring, backward, to a tradition traceable to early modern Tuscany, that birthplace of perspectival vision where, dialectically, Didi-Huberman locates resources for thinking the image otherwise—*Salò* seeks to counter the progressive wish to abandon the Fascist past.[82]

All That Behind

This wish is distilled in Michel Foucault's response to what he saw as the "sacralization" of Sade in the film: "It's time to leave all that behind." Foucault objects in particular to what he sees as the "sacralization" of Sade in *Salò*, the film's investment in "an erotics of the disciplinary type":

> After all, I would be willing to admit that Sade formulated an eroticism proper to the disciplinary society: a regulated, anatomical, hierarchical society whose time is carefully distributed, its spaces partitioned, characterized by obedience and surveillance.
>
> *It's time to leave all that behind*, and Sade's eroticism with it. We must invent with the body, with its elements, surfaces, volumes, and thicknesses, a nondisciplinary eroticism—that of a body in a volatile and diffused state, with its chance encounters and unplanned pleasures.[83]

Figure 6. Fort. *Salò* (1975).

Figure 7. Da. *Salò* (1975).

Foucault will later complicate this understanding of historical sequence, attending to sovereignty's survival after its ostensible eclipse, to its living on in the era of discipline, and to discipline's living on into the age of governmentality.[84] Still, there is something almost irresistible about the progressive invitation and interpellation, offered here with the poignant assurance of being on the present's side: "It's time to leave all that behind." By now we can recognize in this response to *Salò* a version of the impulse to abandon the past that I am arguing the film itself works to counter. In fact, *Salò* points up in advance the wishfulness of Foucault's thinking here, the utopianism of his search for "a nondisciplinary eroticism." The film also lets us see the progressivism that implicitly underwrites even queer theories inspired by Foucault's call for reinvented bodies and pleasures.

Leo Bersani, for instance, famously places complicity at the center of his account of gay male sexuality in essays like "Is the Rectum a Grave?"[85] This text takes pains to position its understanding of sex *against* the "pastoralizing impulse" that Bersani detects in his contemporaries' accounts—accounts of sex's radical potential to establish communal solidarities.[86] Seeking to correct what he takes to be the idealization operative in such accounts, Bersani offers instead a theory of gay male sex that sees it as working through the ruthlessness in which it traffics in order to become a paradoxically "hygienic practice of nonviolence."[87] In this practice, rigorously pursued, being penetrated by the other becomes a form of "self-debasement"[88] or "self-dismissal,"[89] in and through which gay men give up their entitlements as bearers of "proud subjectivity,"[90] practicing instead a willingness to relinquish the self capable of cleansing this self of other-directed violent drives. Hence "hygienic." Masochism of a particular kind becomes an answer to sadistic urges; the care of the self through the arrangement for its "shattering" can, in time, stem this self's impingements on the world.

Salò offers no perspective whatsoever from which sex could be seen to lead to such "shattering" or salutary weakening. The film thus makes it possible to see that "pastoralization," or something like it, lingers in Bersani's quest for a paradoxical kind of cleanliness. Bersani hopes that intimacy with and even careful contamination by male power can be made to yield a nonviolent result. *Salò*'s intimacy with its libertines is, by contrast, not finally purgative, but rather repetitive. The film compels us to take insistent if intermittent and uncomfortable pleasure in the old erotics from which Foucault wanted us to graduate.

Here again, a pair of sequences is illustrative, not least because it flagrantly violates the rule—or indeed the restraining order—that others see as operative in the film, whereby sex in *Salò*, since it's a mere "metaphor for power," can only take the form of "brutal assaults involving no foreplay, aimed at the humiliation of naked, defenseless, and otherwise inert bodies."[91] In the second of the film's two wedding scenes, an executive assistant named Guido helps the Bishop to officiate. The Bishop chants, while the other libertines march in, each beaming, arm in arm with a miserable-looking male victim. (*Salò* is thus evidently a province in which gay marriage has been legalized.) For his part, Guido remains obliging. While the ceremony is in session, the camera frames the Bishop's briefs covered by his gauzy red gown in a sustained close-up that contradicts the common wisdom according to which

Salò privileges long and medium shots. Having approached the Bishop from behind, Guido fondles him. Then there is a quick cut.

The film has so far trained viewers to expect nothing to follow from fondling in general, for it has never allowed anything resembling a "sex scene" to unfold. Hand job, instead, has been heaped upon hand job—but always interruptedly. The cut that concludes *Salò*'s second wedding startles, then, by opening onto coupling that is conventional if *contra natura*.[92] In this scene, the Bishop and his assistant are shown going at it by a camera that engages in an elaborate dance, a back-and-forth between nearness and medium distance that prompts us to admire, not only to recoil from, this instance of intergenerational intimacy (Figure 8). Sex is followed by kissing and tender talk, talk that both bespeaks consent and projects that consent into the future (Figure 9). And this from a director who claimed, in the "Abiura," to be giving up on and to "hate" bodies and their sex organs.[93] Here the camera gives the lie to the "Abiura"'s claim: those bodies and those organs are shot, and lit, lovingly.

To be clear, this moment of mutual satisfaction in the midst of "brutal assaults"[94]—and of consent in the midst of constant coercions—matters not because it renders the other sex acts shown in *Salò* any less diegetically demeaning or casts any doubt on their cruelty. Instead, the scene that I have been discussing matters because, if we look at and linger on the moments that Guido shares with the Bishop—rather than assuming that sex in the film holds no visual interest but simply allegorizes and anticipates—we begin to learn the lesson embedded in a scene that might at first look like a mere anomaly. Imagining a republic whose ruling elite do anything but *"abdicate power"*

Figure 8. Wedding Night. *Salò* (1975).

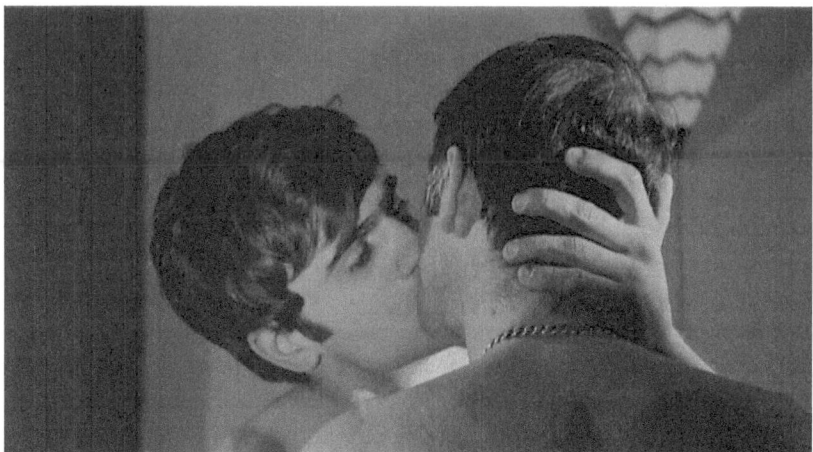

Figure 9. "Normal Love." *Salò* (1975).

when they engage in same-sex sex,[95] *Salò* also speaks to a reality in which disciplinarians are still at large and Fascism is still "real"—arguably more real than before.[96] One does not depose such figures or disempower this Fascism by saying, with Foucault, that it's high time to leave them behind.

This interpretive path through Foucault and Bersani thus leads, however improbably, back to school. *Salò*'s lesson was not that its viewers simply lived in the "bad past" represented by the film's Republic of Salò, but rather that they did not get to leave that past and place behind by deciding that, in keeping with progress, it was time to do so. For Pasolini, the old school, like *tarantismo* for De Martino, taught this lesson.[97] This is why Pasolini's return to Fascist "regimentation,"[98] a return "conceived as a rite," is also a return to instruction,[99] why *Salò* makes Sade's "School for Libertinage" into an old school that gives ritual form to the "bad past" denied by official discourses of progress. These discourses would have us bypass the experience of *rimorso* by which alone, according to De Martino, we might redress "our modernity."[100] *Salò*, by contrast, sets this remorse to work, renders it pedagogical. I have argued that it is as a remorseful and pedagogical ritual that *Salò* still operates most powerfully. "Ci riguarda da vicino" indeed, in De Martino's words—it looks at us up close and concerns us intimately—because, as the film's reception shows, the land of regret remains a place that we would abandon, that we pretend to have left behind. This place's claim on us is what *Salò* would have us learn the hard way.

Which brings us to the film's (famous) last word. At the end of the culminating courtyard sequence, Pasolini's screenplay delivers this death sentence:

"*Tutti i ragazzi vengono seviziati e massacrati*" [*All the children are tortured and massacred*].[101] But the short exchange that follows between two *ragazzi* gives the lie to the totalizing *tutti*, indicating that at least some of the young people gathered in the villa will survive. We are back indoors, where one of two guards changes the radio station. Cutting short the choral music, with words in Latin, that has accompanied the torture and is here shown to have been diegetic, the guard, named Claudio, looks pleased to find a much lighter, mid-tempo, instrumental piece. Now *this* is music to dance to, and it is familiar to the viewer, too, reprised from the film's opening credits. Smiling, Claudio asks his *compagno* if he knows how to dance. The latter says no, at which point the boys agree to give it a try, guns down. Still at first, the camera begins to follow their back-and-forth, which is awkward but not nearly as arrhythmic as the libertines' courtyard can-can, shown briefly during the previous scene. The boys' wordlessness gives way to small talk as the heartfelt music continues: one boy asks another, as if to deny or downplay the fact of their dancing or to dampen any remaining sense we may have of their queerness, "What's your girlfriend's name?" "Margherita," the other responds, and there is a fade to white: the end. Everything in *Salò* has built toward the climax of the courtyard massacre. But then the film concludes with this non sequitur, this triviality after torture, neither a bang nor a whimper.[102]

This moment is difficult to read, if not illegible. If the "Essential Bibliography" presents the viewer with one sort of challenge, if it assigns one sort of chore or pensum, then the film's concluding scene, accompanied by the same music, presents another. If the film begins by assigning required reading, then *Salò*'s enigmatic ending seems to compel repeated viewing. It is as if the film insists that it must be seen again in order for its ending to be understood, though this ending, like the bibliography, may also taunt and punish by withholding the meaning, the correct answer, that it seems to promise. The ending has of course occasioned various interpretations. Since the proper name "Margherita" is also a common noun—the name of a flower, a daisy—critics have heard it as another name for commonnes precisely.[103] For some, this has made *Salò*'s ending strangely hopeful, even "radically frivolous."[104] For others, the dancing lesson—I would add, the film's final ritual—has made *Salò* seem that much bleaker because it attests to the resumption of ordinary business—or indeed "'the birth of a nation'"—in the postwar period.[105] This reading honors the urgency of the film while also sharing in the logic of Pasolini's late polemics, which, to repeat, refused the distinction between the pre- and the postwar nation, insisting that the latter was born from, and therefore still guilty of, the ravages of the Fascist past, which wasn't even past but rather had become ever more real.

But "Margherita" may also point in another backward direction and may index another bad past's return. The name may extend rather than discontinue the instruction that *Salò* has all along administered. Especially because Latin words have just been sounding, before the final, instrumental music that accompanies the boys' dance, "Margherita" calls to memory the Latin word from which it derives: *margarita*, Latin for pearl, as in the "pearl salads" that late in the empire "the ancient Romans were given to eating ... during their orgies."[106] Or as in the injunction delivered in the gospel that Pasolini had adapted for an earlier film: "Neque mittatis margaritas vestras ante porcos ne forte conculcent eas pedibus suis et conversi dirumpant vos" [Neither cast ye your pearls before swine, lest they trample them under their feet, and turn again and rend you] (Matthew 7:6). Gentile, for his part, puts the inverse injunction into the mouths of his critics: "Studies, others say—study must be democratic! As if to say: *mittite margaritas*."[107] So—democratically, after all, then—Pasolini casts his pearl before us. To turn again and rend, not "to leave all that behind," becomes our task. And in this sense, those who read *Salò* as addressed to the present are right. The task remains. Again, it's time.

5. Schooling in Ruins
Glauber Rocha's Rome

The Problem to Change

The preceding pages have traced a series of attempts to counter progress from within the European frame. Pater's "survivals," Pascoli's dead languages, Joyce's dead weights, and the late Pasolini's ritual regrets all become, I have claimed, means of attempting to correct European modernity's rush to be rid of what impeded its own forward movement. But moving outside the European context lets us see what limits these projects: all originate in Europe or are imagined to originate there by those who would counter-progressively set them to work. For all his celebration of Sanskrit, for instance, Pascoli looks to the archives and artifacts of ancient Rome, both in his essays on education and in *Paedagogium*. Joyce gives up on "Guru English" for the duration of "Oxen of the Sun,"[1] and, following his filmic forays into other continents, Pasolini returns to the Italy that he had left behind in order to direct *Salò* (1975). Thus, even if most of the authors whose works I have analyzed depart imaginatively from Europe at other key moments in their careers, in their capacity as counter-progressive pedagogues, they remain provincial—provincial, that is, precisely in their Europeanness.[2] In their counter-progressive phases or late styles they avoid a reckoning with the non-European.

Throughout this book, I have stressed these authors' efforts to undermine discourses of purity, from Pater's "complication of influence" to Pasolini's erotics of complicity. By way of conclusion, I will acknowledge that these efforts only extend so far. Despite their interest in radical temporal alterity—in the remote or recent past that survives or returns in various forms—the spatial scope of the works that I have considered is, again, strictly and deliberately limited. Pascoli's captive Alexamenos is Chaldean, and a "black servant" appears briefly in *Salò*, standing as a reminder of Italian colonial power and the fantasies of miscegenation that it sustained.[3] But such narrative details barely register, given the programmatic narrowness of the texts in my counter-progressive canon—given what I have called, adapting Wordsworth, the "prisons into which they doom themselves."

These prisons entrap characters and readers or spectators alike, so that the latter, too, come to occupy the "cramping, narrowing" place that is Marius's mind;[4] the little cell where Kaireus does time and punishing tenses in *Paedagogium*; the sealed-off hospital ward in "Oxen"; and the enclosed Sadean villa in *Salò*. I have stressed that such narrowing fulfills a crucial pedagogical function across these spaces, furthering the counter-progressive effort to dwell in and on the obstructions that key strands in progressive pedagogy willfully deny. According to the logic of this effort, to sustain the student's sense of breathing free would be to participate in the progressive denial of the past, to shore up the founding pernicious fiction of liberal humanist pedagogy. I have argued instead that the obstructions throughout the texts I have treated—the sources of constraint and unfreedom that readers and spectators experience, variously identified with conventions upheld, verses recited, old prose styles copied out, and ostensibly deposed regimes—serve as powerful correctives to the ideology of progress. But I have not yet explicitly marked the limits of the counter-progressive strategies that I have located or asked whether a political narrowness—again, a provincialism, a forgetting of the non-European—might follow from a commitment to remaining behind in a close, confined, and European "angoletto morto" or dead little corner.[5] To this end, and with the aim of breaking the frame within which I have stayed so far, I turn finally to the work of Brazilian-born director Glauber Rocha, whose *Claro* (1975) imagines both captivity and collective, anticolonial jailbreak.

Like Pasolini, who claimed that *Salò* was "conceived as a rite,"[6] Rocha made a film conceived as a "ritual fact."[7] *Claro* and *Salò* thus have an aim and an abiding interest in common: ritual organizes both films, and Rocha acknowledged his debts to the Italian director. But Rocha also criticized Pasolini's approach to filmmaking, characterizing it as "still fundamentally paternalist," "colonial and patriarchal."[8] In *Claro*, a film combining narrative and documentary elements and shot in and around Rome during his unofficial exile, Rocha imagined an alternative approach.[9] He sought not merely, like Pasolini, to use the painful, ritual reenactment of the past to counter its forgetting or to reproduce present conditions of brutality so that these might be reckoned with rather than denied. He also worked to imagine a collective release from these brutal conditions: precisely the kind of release that *Salò* renders all but unimaginable.[10] To ask after the implications of *Claro*'s double movement, its dialectic of imprisonment and release, is thus also to disclose the limits of the counter-progressive poetics that culminates in Pasolini's last film.

I take *Claro* to represent at once the continuation and the end of this countertradition, but I do so provisionally, not least because *Old Schools* has concerned itself with deaths that are by no means definitive, with ends that are not once and done. I cannot therefore discount the possibility that the impulse to go back to the old school might emerge in other places and at other times, in other aesthetic works and to other political ends than those I have specified.[11] Still, significantly, *Claro* marks the point at which the repeated, pedagogical "retraversing" of the past comes to require a supplement.[12] Rocha's film shares the late Pasolini's commitment to retraversing—a commitment that I have argued was also Pater's, Pascoli's, and Joyce's—and in this way remains counter-progressive in its pedagogy. But at the same time, *Claro* exceeds the literary and cinematic projects that I have so far examined. Aspiring—like *Marius*, *Paedagogium*, "Oxen," and *Salò*—to the condition of instruction, Rocha's film also teaches that "in order for the problem to change," instruction must become barbarous as well as backward, must become cacophonous and collective as well as classical.[13]

This lesson does not simply follow from Rocha's status as an exile or from his film's thematization of that condition.[14] Nor is it only a product of *Claro*'s mixing of languages, its use of Italian, Portuguese, French, and English.[15] After all, *Ulysses*, too, engages in language mixing—"barbarism" in its oldest sense, according to the *Oxford English Dictionary*.[16] And Joyce, too, famously, considered himself an exile. Pascoli's pages in training all come from the provinces, as do Pasolini's captive youths and even, for that matter, Pater's Marius. A concern with displacement thus marks all of the works that I have studied so far, all of which also feature foreign languages. In these ways and in many others, counter-progressive pedagogy remains rich and strange, retains unspent potential. I would be lacking in the courage of my convictions, then, were I to end this book by lapsing into a progress narrative, one according to which a saving final figure, Rocha, would supersede those who came before him with his political maturity and aesthetic sophistication—as though we could leave the other figures behind. This is not, to repeat, the story that this chapter tells. Rocha works *with* and not merely against counter-progressive pedagogy, *with* and not merely against the techniques of the residual, repetitious Latin class. This class still, however improbably, makes *Claro* possible, organizing rather than simply appearing in Rocha's film. Still, *Claro*'s counter-progressive pedagogy is exceptional. What sets the film's engagement with instruction apart, though, is neither its multilingualism nor its meditation on exile, but instead its cacophonous and collective staging of what I have called the old school's dialectical potential. Rocha' produces and sustains a countermovement within the retraversing of the Roman past in which his film nevertheless engages, an intermittent but insistent interruption of the pilgrimage that *Claro* nevertheless makes. This Roman pilgrimage becomes at the same time the passage to another place, and in this way Rocha *counters counter-progress*, though not quite with progress.

New Dependencies

Rome, as we know, wasn't built in a day, but *Claro* very nearly was, if we are to believe the biographical accounts. These accounts tell us that, late in his exile, the filmmaker had almost no budget; that he recruited nonactors whom he then instructed to improvise; that he made a virtue of necessity by filming, *vérité*-style, what was already happening on the Roman streets: religious processions, labor demonstrations, groups of tourists, and so forth. Rocha's viewers often disparage the film that resulted: relegated to the film festival at Taormina, after having shown many films at Cannes, the director is said to have been in a period of creative "stagnation" marked by *Claro*, a minor work.[17] I am not suggesting that these accounts of how *Claro* was produced are untrue, only that they are incomplete. Moreover, their emphasis on the spontaneous, the spur of the moment, and the observational risks obscuring what's most fascinating and most provocative about the film, in my view. This is the way it sets rehearsal, repetition, and resistance to work as it both stages and delivers instruction.

Variations on the word "unbearable" recur in *Claro*'s first reviews.[18] And with good reason, for in some ways the film is arguably more trying to watch even than *Salò*.[19] *Claro* offers none of that film's awful spectacles of torture and coerced sex but also none of its "lateral divertissements."[20] Instead Rocha stages scene after long scene of screaming, with characters' voices raised in competition. He presents, and sometimes himself delivers, speech after drawn-out speech. The title *Claro* promises lucidity and literal light. It leads us to expect, if not enlightenment (this being a film by Rocha, after all), then at least explication, affirmation, and certainty, as in Stephen Dedalus's *claritas*.[21] In Portuguese as in Spanish, *claro* often signals emphatic agreement, introducing or abbreviating an "of course": *claro que sim*. As a noun, *claro* refers to a clearing, an open space. Beautifully yoked to the unknown and unknowable in *Claro enigma*, the oxymoronic title of a volume by the Brazilian modernist poet Carlos Drummond de Andrade,[22] the word *claro* as redeployed by Rocha floats free of any object that it might predicate or place it might name, as if to offer the light or illumination without the enigma this time.

In fact, though, the film is nothing if not obscure. It is thus as if someone were to say, "to be clear," only then to speak confusingly—and, again, in several languages. The promise of the title turns out to be false, casting doubt on the director's claim "to have made a film without ambiguities," prompted by a desire "to see clearly [*claro*] into the contradictions of the capitalist society of our time."[23] A poncho-wearing, French-speaking woman (Juliet Berto, who had starred in Jean-Luc Godard's didactic films *La chinoise* [1967] and *Le gai savoir* [1969], in which she had played "the daughter of Lumumba and the Cultural Revolution") appears in most of the film's scenes, but we never learn who she is or what she's after.[24] She offers us no guidance. Rocha's camerawork contributes further to *Claro*'s obscurity, abetting its programmatic plotlessness. More often than not, the film's frames are crowded, whether with cropped faces and limbs shot in close-up or with worshippers or tourists shown farther away, congregated in Vatican Square or gathered near the Forum. The ruins in the many location shots of the ancient city alternate with the kitschy objects that recur in the film's interiors. And *Claro* even features a single *vanitas*-like still life, in which meat sits atop a Roman capital. All of these assorted persons and things obstruct our view, so that we do not, in fact, see clearly.

Nor, *pace* Rocha, do we see only the contradictions of "our time." On the contrary, *Claro* draws attention to the layering of times and histories for which Rome's architecture is famous as an emblem of both civilization and its discontents.[25] The remnants of dead pasts everywhere pile up in *Claro*. And these combine with the other miscellaneous dead things that find their way into the frame and with the repeated phrases and rote gestures that recur in the diegesis to make the film into a veritable document of deadness, a far cry from the products of the "living spirit of Cinema Novo" repeatedly summoned in what is still Rocha's most widely read and frequently cited work: the manifesto for that movement, first presented in Genoa in 1965, "Uma estética da fome" [An Aesthetics of Hunger].[26]

Here the filmmaker calls for a Latin American cinema capable of opposing a Euro-U.S. film industry fully committed to "untruth and exploitation."[27] Accepting rather than denying its colonial situation in order to become fully anticolonial, the engaged cinema that Rocha envisions, born from the "politics of hunger," would undertake both to demystify and to arm: both to "*make the public aware of its misery [dar ao público a consciência de sua própria miséria]*" and to seek "freedom for Latin America."[28] At this early moment in his career, Rocha places faith in a version of what Gilles Deleuze, in *Cinema 2*, calls "becoming conscious." This Deleuze sees as a hallmark of classical political cinema, which seeks to initiate a process "of evolution from the Old to the New, or of revolution that produces a leap from one to the other."[29] We might also think in terms of the progressive process that Paulo Freire describes in *Pedagogy of the Oppressed*, where *conscientização* names the precondition for the entry of the oppressed into history, their "emergence" from a condition of imposed silence, or what Freire also calls their "humanizaton."[30] For Rocha, too, in "An Aesthetics of Hunger," becoming conscious, making "the public aware," is what Cinema Novo seeks to achieve. Awareness is a matter of recognition, of understanding, of the removal of obstacles to perception put in place by industrial cinema and a whole imperial apparatus of "economic and cultural conditioning." Though *Pedagogy of the Oppressed* postdates Rocha's manifesto, I would argue that there is something Freirean about the project that the manifesto articulates.

Still, there is also something counter-progressive about "An Aesthetics of Hunger":

> Undeniably, Latin America remains a colony, and what distinguishes yesterday's colonialism from today's is merely the more refined forms employed by the contemporary colonizer. Meanwhile, those who are preparing future domination try to replace these with even more subtle forms. The international problem facing Latin America is still that of merely exchanging colonizers [um pouco de mudança de colonizadores], so that any possible liberation will always be a function of a new dependency [sendo que uma libertação possível estará sempre em função de uma nova dependência].[31]

Reminiscent of Pasolini's insistence, in *Salò* and other texts that my last chapter addressed, that Fascism survived the war and even became more "real" than it had been before,[32] these claims are also comparable to the more recent demonstration of the persistence of antiblackness in the face of discourses of "post-raciality."[33] This makes sense, given that Rocha and these recent critics share a set of psychoanalytic sources. Channeling Fanon at several later moments in his manifesto and appealing to the language of the "*symptom*"[34] and the "*unconscious*" early on,[35] Rocha's argument here recalls the psychoanalytic attribution of lasting power to "mnemic residues." If, in Freud, these continue, through symptoms, to operate long after the end of the "experiences" that first laid them down, Fanon shows that such experiences cannot even be said truthfully to end in the colonial context, where "traumatisms" remain diffuse and complexes "*conscious*" rather than unconscious.[36] In "An Aesthetics of Hunger," Rocha makes a comparable suggestion even while gesturing toward the cinematic means by which neocolonial traumatisms might be worked through. Having noted these resonances, however, here I simply want to underscore the refusal of progress narratives implied by the assertion that throughout Latin America colonialism perdures, *permanece*.

Rocha delivers this verdict in a present tense that powerfully denies the relegation of the colonial situation to the past of the postcolony. But the moment in his manifesto that I have just quoted builds toward an equally powerful future tense, one whose placement in a grammatically subordinate clause does little, in fact, to attenuate its threat of permanent subordination. As long as change for Latin America takes the form of a mere exchange of masters (where the Portuguese, "um pouco de mudança," makes the change even more of a nonevent than mere exchange would be), liberation *will entail* another dependency. So Rocha claims, though in terms that make the advent of real liberation even less assured—terms that render the threat of ongoing dependency that much more threatening because not strictly conditional. The director says not quite, "*If* we don't stop thinking of change as exchange, *then* we'll always be dependent," but rather something more like, "The problem *is* that change still means exchange, *it being the case* that we'll always be dependent." Though apparently slight, the distinction, both linguistic and logical, is in fact highly significant—because Cinema Novo's project, as articulated in Rocha's manifesto, becomes an attempt to alter that future tense, to imagine a way out of the impasse that "the international problem" here designates: a liberation that would do away with dependency.

By the time Rocha made *Claro*, things had changed in ways that made such a liberating exit from dependency seem unachievable, a dependent future tense irrevocable, and an impasse permanent. One monologue in the film, in fact, bears witness to this very disillusionment: it begins with a former communist's memories of the heady time when he thought he could change the world and ends with his attempt to name "a vague feeling that remains, a sensation that doesn't end." The next speaker's monologue also bespeaks burnout: "The revolution continued, and I wasn't part of it anymore." And a third speaker complains in the next monologue in similar terms: "I lack a spontaneity that I *did* have before [Io manco (sic) una spontaneità che io ho *avuto* prima]." Here again, youthful energy gives way to exhaustion. This speaker will go on to insist that his lost spontaneity "is something that I *can* regain in myself, something that still exists in me, something that I think, returning here, I think, that really can be in me [è una cosa che io *può* (sic) ritovare in me, una cosa che esiste ancora in me, una cosa che credo, tornando qua, credo che, che può avere (sic) veramente ancora in me]."[37] He learned this, he says, from a child. And there is indeed something vaguely childish about his awkward and not strictly grammatical Italian. Like many others in *Claro*'s cast and like Rocha himself, this speaker is evidently still learning the language. But though this man's speech may be childish, it is anything but spontaneous. On the contrary, it is nothing if not rehearsed—forced, even. Moreover, the repetitiousness of his lines belies the spontaneity that they extoll, and their halting delivery suggests that the loss of what Rocha's early manifesto had called "living spirit" is more final than this speaker would allow.

What has become, then, of Rocha's revolution, of Cinema Novo's spontaneity? During the years that intervened between "An Aesthetics of Hunger" and *Claro*, Brazil's military dictatorship, which had already begun with the 1964 U.S.-backed coup that overthrew President João Goulart, became increasingly repressive. A decree issued in 1968, the Ato Instituional Número Cinco, consolidated executive powers and eroded all kinds of constitutional protections. The act intensified government censorship of the arts and journalism, outlawed demonstrations not preapproved by police, and suspended habeas corpus. These and the act's other provisions heightened the tensions that led to Rocha's departure from Brazil. Meanwhile, military governments continued to emerge—or to reemerge, to return like the name Porfirio Díaz in Rocha's *Terra em transe* [*Land in Anguish*] (1967)—in other Latin American countries, including Uruguay and Chile, which both witnessed coups in 1973. More generally, both in the Americas and in Europe, where Rocha spent his part of his exile,[38] the early 1970s were marked by both economic crisis and signs of the political retrenchment that would characterize the first phase of neoliberalization.[39]

These multiple social, economic, and political shifts are registered in Rocha's cinematic trajectory, which proceeds, or counter-progresses, from relative clarity to opacity.[40] Rocha transitions, that is, from a style in keeping with Cinema Novo's liberationist aims, as these are articulated in "An Aesthetics of Hunger," to a style foregrounding difficulty and blockage, one better suited, he thought, to an era of entrenched dictatorships and ascendant markets. (Compare Pasolini's "Abiura dalla *Trilogia della vita*.") In such an era, dependencies come to seem ineluctable, and old solidarities, desires, and aspirations are driven underground. Indeed, following the international success of his first films, Rocha abandoned "critical realism," as James Phillips explains, "in favor of an [increasingly] underground cinema": "The agony of hunger passes over" from the diegesis "into the cinematic image itself, convulsing it in *Land in Anguish* (*Terra em transe*) (1967) before overseeing its disintegration in the final provocations ... of *The Age of Earth* (*A idade da terra*) (1980)."[41] *Claro* comes between these two films, and its images take part in both of the processes that Phillips identifies: both convulsion and disintegration.

But *Claro* engages in another set of processes as well, and in my view more interestingly: processes that make the film's return to Rome and to school counter-progressive. Here the counterexample of Freire's pedagogy can bring the film's specificity—its status as a counter-progressive rejoinder—into relief. I suggested earlier that, with its commitment to "making the public aware" or, in Deleuze's words, to the spectator's "becoming conscious," Rocha's cinematic project as it is defined in "An Aesthetics of Hunger" could be considered Freirean. To be sure, I pointed to counter-progressive moments in that text as well, moments that indicated Rocha's awareness of the limits of awareness and of liberation. Still, these limits remained implicit in "An Aesthetics of Hunger," which is animated by a "living spirit" that Freire, too, might affirm.

In *Claro,* by contrast, far from modeling the pedagogy of the oppressed, Rocha seems to be systematically breaking with Freire's recommendations, flagrantly ignoring his progressive prescriptions. Far from removing obstacles to understanding and insight, he multiplies them: again, in the crowded and often tightly cropped frames that recur throughout the film, in the confusion of its languages, in the incoherence of its narrative. *Claro* offers nothing like the "unveiling of reality" (*Pedagogy* 81; *Pedagogia* 97), the aid to "clearer perception" or means of turning "com mais claridade" to totality (*Pedagogy* 104; *Pedagogia* 133), for which Freire calls. In both his own heavy-handed voiceovers recounting Roman history and the monologues of his characters, Rocha traffics in precisely the rhetoric that Freire warns against, often eloquently: the teacher "expounds on a topic completely alien to the existential experience of the students.... Words are emptied of their concreteness" or indeed their significance "and become a hollow, alienated, and alienating verbosity" (*Pedagogy* 71; *Pedagogia* 80–81). In this context, "The student records, memorizes, and repeats phrases without perceiving" what they really mean (*Pedagogy* 71; *Pedagogia* 81). Here Freire is describing anti-dialogic education, that is, the kind of education that he opposes—call it instruction—but he might also be describing *Claro.* By this I mean both that he could be giving an account of how the film functions diegetically—how its scenes of teaching work—and that we could take his words as characterizing our relation to the film: how it interpellates us as spectators-become-students. At both of these levels—both on-screen and in its address to us, its viewers—*Claro* is counter-progressive. Far from bringing about the "solution [or overcoming, *superação,* elsewhere translated as 'supersedence'] of the teacher-student contradiction" for which Freire keeps calling (*Pedagogy* 72; *Pedagogia* 82; cf. *Pedagogy* 80, 93), the film intensifies this contradiction from the first.

Now, since Freire is, even more than Dewey, someone whose recommendations many of us have internalized if not learned by heart—and for good reason—key questions are bound to arise, or to recur, at this juncture. Unlike the other progressive theories that I have considered in previous chapters, Freire's pedagogy does not center on the individual student; it is radical rather than liberal and is undeniably attentive to the structural problems of capitalist exploitation, immiseration, and inequality. Moreover, Freire, a reader of Marx as well as Fanon, does not for a moment let himself lose sight of the fact that the achievement of collective liberation is bound to be a long and laborious process, a painful undertaking fraught with real danger. To be sure, then, *Pedagogy of the Oppressed* is not simply a sequel of Rousseau's *Émile* or of Dewey's *Democracy and Education*. In many key ways, it is another kind of book altogether, one that prompts us to interrogate the coherence of the progressive educational tradition as a whole. We thus have that much more reason to ask: Why would Rocha, champion of the vernacular Cinema Novo, a radical leftist whose outspoken dissidence led him, like Freire, to flee Brazil's military dictatorship, not only break with Freire's pedagogy of the oppressed but also return to the old school, and to Rome? Is this simply a symptom of creative "stagnation," as one biographical account concludes "definitively"?[42] Or the sign of political regression? To be sure, Rocha shared with Pasolini the vocation of gadfly or career contrarian, and this contrarian impulse led him to cinematic extremes. What I am calling his return to school in *Claro* could be seen as one of these. But to say this is less to interpret than to discount by pathologizing *Claro*'s engagement with the old school. I am arguing that this engagement is instead programmatic, and in what's left of this chapter, I will specify *how Claro* seeks, *contra* Freire, to school us, and to what end.

Rulers' Ends

I have called the process guiding *Claro*'s diegesis "pilgrimage," and I have hinted at some other, formal ways in which the film does not, in Phillips's words, fall apart, convulse itself, or disintegrate, but rather repeats itself, stages returns. There is, first and most obviously, the repetitiveness of *Claro*'s monologues. But then there is the serial organization of these monologues that makes one come after and echo another. Consider, too, the film's overall structure: *Claro* begins in Rome, then swerves away from the city for a seaside interlude. But Rocha's camera returns to the place it has thus left behind; his film enacts the return to Rome that it thematizes. A moment late in the film miniaturizes—and recapitulates—this return at another scale, at the level of the single take: as the camera pans, white washes out the rooftops of Rome (Figure 10), but only briefly. These rooftops no sooner fade than they return, as Rocha restores the shot to its initial contrast (Figure 11). Now you see Rome; now you don't; then again, you do. The joke is on the spectator, but

Figure 10. Fort. *Claro* (1975).

Figure 11. Da. *Claro* (1975).

Rocha's fake-out fade-out is also deeply serious. The shot attests to Rome's permanence in the face of our desire for the end of the *imperium*—a desire that *Claro* also, paradoxically, works to produce. Here, though, the film suggests that the city may indeed be eternal if its erasure—in Phillips's terms, its disintegration—is so short-lived.[43] At the very least, Rome must be reckoned with and not denied. This is the lesson of the shot, which compels us to return to the place that returns.

Readers familiar with Rocha's trajectory will already sense that we are here apparently at some distance from the explosive "*guerrilla cinema*" that he theorized in texts like "The Tricontinental Filmmaker" and sought to realize in films like *Der Leone Have Sept Cabeças* [*The Seven-Headed Lion*] (1970), even more than in his best-known films, in which he took "the first steps toward . . . guerrilla cinema": *Barravento* (1962), *Deus e o diablo na terra do sol* [*Black God, White Devil*] (1964), and *Terra em transe*.[44] This cinema was both rooted in and responsive to the Third World. To make a film in the Third World at all—just to register the light there—was or ought to be, Rocha claimed, political, anticolonial, committed.[45] Being there would thus seem to be a precondition for making "tricontinental" or Third Worldist films. Rome's fading and return in *Claro* therefore raises several questions: What is Rocha doing here, not only *not* in the Third World, but in what he calls "the center of imperialism"? Why does he ask us not only to linger in Rome but also to bear witness to the city's returns? And why call Rome the heart of empire in any case, anachronistically in 1975, when, as Rocha himself had noted, empire's contemporary capital was in Hollywood or Washington, D.C.?[46]

Or, to ask the question in another way, what kind of a lesson is taught by the shot that shows Rome fade only to return? Strikingly, one answer Phillips offers is "classical." To be sure, though, Phillips uses this as a term of art. Considering the director's career as a whole, Phillips argues that "Rocha's work is classical not because it recalls the 'perfection' of classical art"—on the contrary, turning underdevelopment to aesthetic profit, it does no such thing—"but because it recreates the anarchic conditions in which," according to Hannah Arendt, "the Greek cities differentiated themselves from the despotism of their Persian and Egyptian neighbors. In this anarchy, the Greek is a citizen and not a subject, a means to the ruler's ends."[47] But attending to *Claro* has already made it possible to see that, though changeful, cacophonous, and crowded, the film is not, in fact, "anarchic." Repetition governs Rocha's film, both in its diegesis and at the level of the image. Note, too, that Phillips concludes by reinstating a version of the very distinction that he seeks to overturn. Although he affirms "indeterminacy" and "undecideability,"[48] he in fact decides in advance on the difference between Greeks, on the one hand, and Persians and Egyptians, on the other.[49] The latter are, Phillips asserts, only "means to the ruler's ends," whereas "anarchic conditions" allow for the elaboration of Greek freedom, the realization of Greek self-definition and neighborly differentiation.

But this is effectively to deny the barbarous even while defending the "anarchic." The "barbarous," of course, originally names that which is "not Greek," and later what is "not Greek nor Latin; *hence* not classical or pure."[50] Notwithstanding the distance Phillips takes from the standards of formal perfection, his account of Rocha's films comes to privilege purity after all, in its privileging of politics in the "Greek" sense: Rocha's "is a pure cinema to the extent that it is a political cinema," Phillips claims.[51] The political, for Phillips, participates in the movement typically but, he writes, only "improperly understood as the affair of aestheticism," in an inversion whose implication is clear but, by virtue of that very clarity, not borne out in *Claro*:[52] it is politics, "properly" understood, that models the open-endedness and the freedom from instrumentality that the aesthetic, in aestheticism, wrongly claims for itself alone. Rocha's "pure cinema" would thus constitute a corrective to the aestheticist "refusal to engage in political struggles."[53] At once becoming political and revealing cinema's "essential politicality,"[54] Rocha's films would undermine the attempt, associated (and often reductively made synonymous) with figures like Pater, to delimit a separate aesthetic space; these films would offer a sustained critique of aesthetic autonomy.[55]

This is a powerful and persuasive account of Rocha's cinema. But according to its logic, the director never really amends his early position, never recognizes the ineluctability of dependency, broadly defined. Dependency instead attaches to the Persians and Egyptians of the world, the barbarians. Rocha, for his part, according to Phillips, turns the wretched of the earth into so many Greeks. To repeat: "Rocha's work . . . recreates the anarchic conditions in which the Greek cities differentiated themselves from the despotism of their Persian and Egyptian neighbors. In this anarchy, the Greek is a citizen and not a subject, a means to the ruler's ends."[56] But matters in *Claro* are, as I have said, considerably more complicated, much less clearly "differentiated." For one thing, such distinctions would have had a different resonance—and a plainly colonial provenance—in Latin America, where attempts to define "Latinity" and to defend civilization against barbarism had likewise relied on appeals to Greek freedom.[57] Additionally, though—and in an apparent tension or even outright contradiction with its anticolonial aims—*Claro* evinces a fascination with the figure of the despot. As in *Salò*, this figure becomes closely associated with the figure of the director: "his majesty Eisenstein!," as Berto ironically proclaims.[58] But whereas the director-as-despot only lurked *behind* Pasolini's images—in the casting call evoked by the libertines' painstaking selection of the beautiful *fanciulli* or in the figure of the Bishop who officiates at the gay wedding and recalls the priest played by Pasolini himself in *Edipo re* [*Oedipus Rex*] (1967)—Rocha makes his own voice audible and his own body visible. Moreover, he makes his own directorial "despotism" manifest, rather than latent like Pasolini's.

Claro begins, in fact, with a long outdoor sequence, at the end of which Rocha kicks Berto, repeatedly, while she's down (Figure 12). The kicks are playful, but troubling still: Rocha's gestures signal the force and even the coerciveness of the directions he gives, even as they insist on his embodiment, exposing him to the gaze of both the diegetic and the viewing publics.[59] The sequence also literalizes what in Chapter 1 I called the "persistence of perpendicularity," a feature that recurs in all of the counter-progressive pedagogical projects I have considered, beginning with Pater's, which aligned the teacher with the *superstes* and the pupil with his prostrate counterpart. Upright, Rocha stands over the horizontal Berto. And the latter keeps returning to this position after rolling over and being dragged along, at times pulled up so that parts of her body form diagonals within the frame. The sequence thus insists visually on the perpendicular formed by the two bodies, Berto's and Rocha's. Framed by an unsteady camera against the backdrop of the Colosseum, the director's repeated kicks draw the assembled tourists' attention, as if to underscore the fact that the spectacle now unfolds outside the ancient amphitheater, not within it. And Rocha seems to warn *Claro*'s spectators at the outset that his film will entail a certain violence, someone's submission, however provisional and playful that submission may be.

At other moments, though, Rocha seems to critique violence and submission precisely as he looks to empires both present and past. An anomalous,

Figure 12. Rocha and Berto, Kicked While She's Down. *Claro* (1975).

English-language exchange between two Americans refers to the Vietnam War. A black woman and a white soldier, her lover, appear in bed. Beset by waking nightmares, the soldier complains that "the sensation of this killing" is killing him. Yet this brief acknowledgment is the only one he can manage; mostly he denies knowing anything at all about killing or those he killed. "You've killed people that I loved," the woman laments; "you've killed *me*!" And again later, in the face of her lover's repeated denials, she repeats herself: "You have killed my people! You have killed my people!" To which the soldier can only respond, reverting at once to denial and the imperial drill, that he has "fought with the greatest, the greatest in the world." "The war can't be lost," he screams; "I've got to go on! I've got to go on!" The empire will regroup, and its forward march will continue apace, Rocha suggests, despite defeats and psychic disturbances.

Indeed, *Claro* takes pains to underscore the millennial continuity of imperial power. An earlier shot of the Piazza del Campidoglio centered on the misidentified equestrian statue of Marcus Aurelius,[60] locates—or more accurately fixes: *fixa*—the heart of imperialism past and present in Rome. In this static shot about stasis, this fixed image of imperial fixity, Rocha repeats emperors' names even while he mangles chronology. And the misidentification and mangling are themselves interesting, as further examples of instruction's privileging of form or process over content. For his part, Freire would surely find this so much "hollow, alienated, and alienating verbosity": "The center, the center of imperialism, Augustus Octavian, result of Rome's imperialist conquest of the Third World, Augustus Octavian, Caesar Augustus, democratic imperialism, the seat of imperialism, located [*fixado*] here." And before a cut, Rocha captions the image on which his own camera has remained fixed after having been mobile throughout the film's first, long sequence: "this image, the last image of the West, the last image of the West [esta imagem, a última imagem do occidente, la ultima immagine dell'occcidente]" (Figure 13). The claim or would-be demonstration that the Roman Empire never ended thus comes up against the sudden proclamation that this empire's fall is imminent.[61] But here again the repetitiousness of the words spoken in the film, this time by Rocha, gives the lie to his concluding, conclusive label. The image will, in fact, not be the West's "last" in any sense. On the contrary, *Claro* will go on to attest to the persistence of old structures architectural and authoritarian.[62]

In a much longer sequence more obviously reminiscent of *Salò*, for instance, a Fascist-sympathizing man in drag played by director and dramaturge Carmelo Bene, reprising his own role in *S.A.D.E.*, another adaptation of Sade's *120 Days of Sodom*, eats gelato, drinks, and smokes while deliver-

Figure 13. "The Last Image of the West." *Claro* (1975).

ing a lecture about later emperors. Bene's character addresses the unnamed young woman played by Berto, whose poncho looks even more incongruous indoors than it does on the streets of Rome. Recounting the formation of militias during the reign of Septimus Severus, Bene refers in passing to the "libertinage, the Sadean evolution, let's say, of the police." His speech continues:

> Septimus Severus opened the door, he made the Ministry of the Interior.... He made the Ministry of the Interior into a legion.... Many legions, my dear, many. There were many.... Now, Pertinax the emperor who follows Septimus Severus, right, does the same. Then a wicked emperor, Caracalla, morbid, and so on. Basically, the important fact until you arrive at the Stoics, that is the Antonines—the Antonines who with Christianity, basically destroy power, that is they break power apart, but voluntarily. Decadence is beautiful.

This last sentiment is one that Bene has already expressed. In fact, the sentence—"La decadenza è bella," which easily could have appeared in *Salò*'s screenplay, as a line to be spoken by one of that film's libertines—is one that he repeats verbatim. After a cut here, Bene is shown standing, bottle in hand. The cut suggests that we may have been spared more of his monologue, but the speech still shows no signs of abating: "Then you have to ... you'll have to wait centuries for a *duce* to come, a *dux*. Aetius, Aetius, Atilla's rival, Atilla. Aetius was the first *duce*." Bene's translation of *duce* into *dux* and back again indicates his character's nostalgia for the Fascist past as well as the remoter

Roman world. In his speech as in the discourse of the regime, ancient Rome presages and provides the sanction for Fascism; Mussolini represents the second coming of Aetius.[63]

To be sure, this is hardly a history lesson.[64] For one thing, Bene gets his facts wrong: Pertinax was not Septimus Severus's successor, for instance, but his predecessor. We are clearly at a far remove from an avowedly pedagogical project like the late Roberto Rossellini's.[65] Still, the scene retains a pedagogical form inasmuch as Berto, seen and not heard throughout the long monologue, models the receptiveness of the pupil, if not the attentiveness of the good one. In this sense, she stands in for the film's spectator as well. Like her, *Claro*'s viewer can hardly be expected simply and uninterruptedly to pay attention to Bene's tirade. The *mise en scène* is as distracting, though not nearly as elegant, as anything in *Salò*. There are mirrors prominently featured in the drag queen's decked-out apartment reminiscent of those in the Salonian libertines' villa, and statues and paintings that are no less visually obtrusive for being obviously cheap. Then there are the sources of distraction within the monologue itself: frequent self-interruptions, drinking from the bottle, ice cream, opera. The distractions multiply as the scene proceeds: Bene's voice, now repeatedly intoning "Italy for me! [Italia a me!]," competes with "Casta diva," which starts playing loudly midway through the monologue. Bene's performance, meanwhile, becomes ever more grotesque.

Throughout his speech, Berto stands beside him, moving a small statuette of a *putto* in circles: first this way, then that; then this way again, then that (Figure 14). She keeps at this for several minutes before speaking. Still seen and not heard, she continues to move the statue mechanically, even after Bene has collapsed from drunkenness. Then when her monologue finally begins, she keeps up the circular motions, moving her own body instead of the statuette. Her speech is elusive, apocalyptic rather than nostalgic. She speaks of annihilation, of ends without beginnings, and of irretrievable pasts (Figure 15). She speaks of not knowing anymore, of not having words adequate to account for anything, of language that is no longer language. She is not, therefore, simply *imitating* the triumphalist speech that she and we have just been made to sit through. Nor is it ever clear what she is doing in the same apartment with Bene to begin with. Needless to say, the kind of instruction that Berto receives here could never lead to anyone's becoming conscious in Freire's sense. I am therefore not claiming that the apartment sequence stages such a coming-to-consciousness or a simple transfer of knowledge or of language. But, reminding us of the relation between rote and rotation, her circling during and after Bene's speech suggests that perhaps she has learned something, if not what Bene's diva intended, after all. And perhaps we have learned something as well.

Figure 14. Seen, Not Heard. *Claro* (1975).

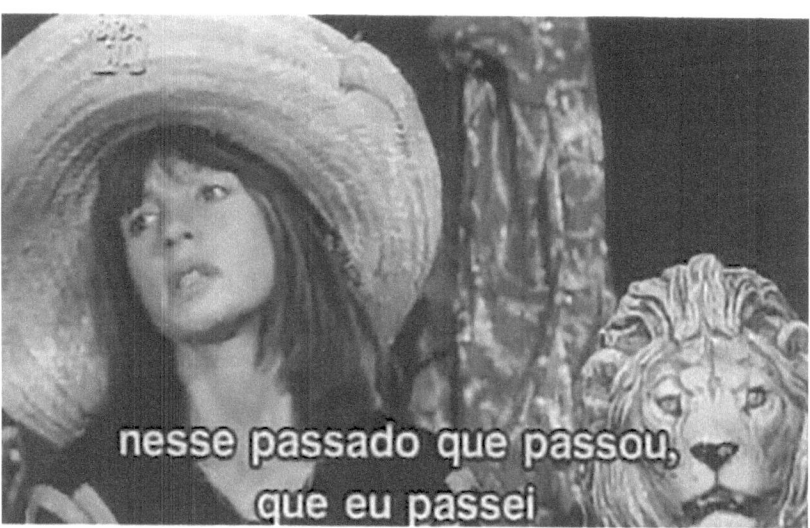

Figure 15. Non Sequitur. *Claro* (1975).

But what? Simply that repeated gestures can help us to survive educational ordeals? By this account, Berto's movements would be the gestural equivalent of doodling: means of keeping her body occupied or ways of trying to protect her mind from the numbness that Bene's lecture would otherwise induce. Yet this does not seem quite right—if only because Berto's gestures during the lecture are enthusiastically performed, not perfunctory. She is either complying with someone's orders, whether Rocha's or Bene's or both, or acting voluntarily, like the Antonines to whom Bene refers: "scardinano il potere, però volontariamente." But that we have seen Berto kicked repeatedly by Rocha makes the latter, voluntary alternative less plausible. In that early scene, too, her movements had been circular: she had rolled, or been made to roll, on the ground. From this we can infer that the motions weren't voluntary to begin with, even if they may be now. Her circular movements bear—or maybe they just *are*—the trace of the kicks that she has received.

The setup is highly, even exaggeratedly gendered, both in the apartment, drag notwithstanding, and outside the Colosseum. Rocha would thus seem to participate in the same paternalism of which he accuses Pasolini—as if his kicks were for Berto's own good in the end.[66] At the same time, though, Berto's is the view—and the monologue—that the film would affirm. Her speech on world-ending, the failures of language, and the fate of the past—a speech that distills so many of *Claro*'s concerns—responds to and continues in another, more lyrical register Rocha's earlier, voiceover call for the fall of Rome. This fact does not exempt Rocha from the kind of critique that he aimed at Pasolini, of course, but it does coexist enigmatically with the "mechanical coercion" that *Claro*'s first scene registers and to which Berto's later gestures indirectly refer.[67] It is as though the scene outside the Colosseum showed not degradation, but a kind of *delegation*—as though Berto had become in that inaugural scene Rocha's representative as well as ours. It is as though he, too, had been kicked while down—or hungry—and this had kept him circling, repeating himself and the past. But as Jean Laplanche and Jean-Bertrand Pontalis note, delegation implies more than the faithful imitation of such gestures, more than the execution of someone else's orders: "Though in principle [she] is nothing more than the proxy of [her] mandator, the delegate ... enters in practice into a new system of relationships which is liable to change [her] perspective and cause [her] to depart from the directives [she] has been given."[68]

Last Images

Like the progressive theorists whose texts I have considered throughout this study—like Rousseau, Mill, Gentile, Dewey, and Freire—several of Rocha's critics give voice to a desire for "the exteriority of liberty and nonliberty."[69] These critics write, in other words, as though there could and should be a definitive separation between freedom and constraint, liberation and dependency, spontaneity and repetition. Representatively, Phillips claims, again: "Rocha's work ... recreates the anarchic conditions in which the Greek cities differentiated themselves from the despotism of their Persian and Egyptian neighbors. In this anarchy, the Greek is a citizen and not a subject, a means to the ruler's ends."[70] The wish expressed here as in much progressive educational theory is for a hard and fast distinction, for a permanently sustainable difference between citizens and subjects, such that the former would no longer have to be the latter. Rocha's cinema, for Phillips, trains us to be citizens by producing the anarchy that lets us know that we are not mere "means to [any] ruler's ends." But to say this is to refuse to undertake the motions that *Claro* assigns. These motions entail not *sorting out* amid anarchy, but rather two types of *circling*: one that leads back to Rome and another that leads Berto to move the *putto* statuette, then her own body, repeatedly this way, then that, after she has been moved by Rocha.[71]

Far from privileging spontaneity, this first moment in the film marks "the priority of the other."[72] Borrowing this phrase from Laplanche, I have used it to characterize the counter-progressive pedagogical project. I have argued that this project takes "the priority of the other" as given and, against persistent, "ipsocentric" progressive educational efforts to disavow this other, makes this into the prioirty of the preceptor—as if the other whom the infant encountered in its first contacts with the adult world provided the model for the later others who are teachers.[73] Recall Flavian in Pater's *Marius*; the punishing *praeceptor* in Pascoli's *Paedagogium*; the hardworking, heavily demanding narrator of "Oxen"; or *Salò*'s libertines. Rocha inherits these figures' pedagogical function. Lording it over by simply standing over Berto, initiating her repetitive, rote movements, Rocha likewise lords it over *us* by lecturing to us, even while presenting "the last image of the West." Yet *Claro* also illustrates the transformation—and negation—that such instruction can sponsor. For Berto's monologue repeats Rocha's with a difference: again, she sets his kicks to work even while, moving in circles, she seems still to reel from them.

In this sense, she resembles Pascoli's *pueri*, who find an exit in the very impasse of their scholastic punishment, or Pater's Spartan schoolboys, whose social scars become the sites of their "reserve."[74] She exemplifies, in other words, the counter-progressive determination to locate ways out even in what look like the most imprisoning of situations—and to imagine those ways out as immanent to scenes of imprisonment and freedom as arising within constraints. More immediately, though, she resembles the piazza "born during the Fascist period" shown late in *Claro*. This public square becomes a site of solidarity for "all the population, entirely [tutta la popolazione, per intero]," but only after it has been marked by the regime, which had razed the buildings in the neighborhood to create room for tourists. A resident explains to Berto that, "on the basis of the situation of marginalization, a social structure was created, a very special structure [tutta particolare], but one that was also very strong, very combative."

The paradox here is easy to miss but worth underscoring: the collective whose experience the Roman woman recalls is at once particular and general. Pointedly, this group encompasses "tutta la popolazione, per intero" but remains at the same time "tutta particolare," where *particolare* means "special," as it often does in spoken Italian, but also "partial." These terms, "population" and "particularity," and their pointed coming-together here recall Deleuze's brief discussion of Rocha in *Cinema 2*. Although he does not engage with *Claro* specifically, Deleuze offers a still-resonant account of Rocha's turn away from the position staked out in texts like "An Aesthetics of Hunger." Early on, Deleuze writes, Rocha could sustain his belief in "a united or unified people."[75] But this belief gave way to a sense of the irreducible plurality—and particularity—of peoples. According to Deleuze, "modern political cinema," as forged by Rocha and others, proceeds from the recognition that "*the people are missing.*"[76] Missing, that is, constitutively: not only in the making, awaiting "invention,"[77] the people are *always* multiple and heterogeneous. It follows that no amount of "awareness" will bring about the collective oneness that classical cinema both presupposes and enacts.[78] It is not enough, then, to become conscious, where, as in classical cinema, this marks the first step toward belonging to a people moving forward; for those in the Third World made into "perpetual minorities," such narratives of advance become untenable:[79] "There is no longer a 'general line,' that is, of evolution from the Old to the New, or of revolution which produces a leap from one to the other."[80]

It is, Deleuze writes, in the context of this discrediting of progress narratives that Rocha rethinks his youthful stance: "The death-knell for becoming conscious"—for the progressive if not fully Freirian project of Rocha's early cinema—"was precisely the consciousness that there were no people, but always several peoples, an infinity of peoples, who remained to be united, or should not be united, in order for the problem to change."[81] The hesitation here—"remained to be . . . , or should not be"—is crucial,[82] not least because it registers the difficulty that inheres in the effort to renounce the classical dream of unity. This dream informs Deleuze's first phrase, only to be given up in his second, more forceful formulation. That the people "should not be united" means that no single voice or language, no one "speech act" or "collective utterance," should ever be thought to suffice to effect unity, whether it is addressed to Greeks, Persians, or Egyptians; Romans or Brazilians; ancients or moderns.[83]

To be sure, unity was never what the counter-progressive pedagogue sought to achieve. The old school as reimagined by this modern teacher was always a repository of difference, and the use of this school's techniques in the scenes of instruction that I have studied was always meant to enable the present to alter itself. The old school redeployed in modernity was always, in this sense, meant to shelter dissidence, to enable resistance. Still, in their commitment to constraint, in their returning to and remaining within Latinity, in their insistence on the inseparability of memory and imagination—in all of these ways, the works that I studied in previous chapters all foreclosed the possibility that, as Deleuze writes, the problem would change. *Claro*, by contrast, reopens this possibility as it makes its way through Rome, moving circuitously from the Colosseum to the neighborhood whose reoccupation the Roman woman addressing Berto recounts near the end of the film.

But if, as I have claimed, in its opening scene, *Claro* acknowledges a Freudian or Lacanian insight that Deleuze himself might deride (for, Deleuze opines elsewhere, "Freud has always been a Roman"),[84] then the late, problem-changing lesson remains just that: a lesson and not a free-for-all. To the last, that is, Berto is listening,[85] even while "she sees; she has learnt to see."[86] To repeat: "On the basis of the situation of marginalization, a social structure was created, a very special structure but one that was also very strong, very combative." Though particular, again, the combat is collective and communist, and *Claro* builds toward a resounding affirmation of it. In the climactic and cacophonous scenes that follow the account of the formation of local solidarities that I have just quoted, Rocha shows rallies, red flags everywhere, protestors assembled in struggle and in celebration after the United States' defeat in Vietnam, marked by the fall or liberation of Saigon. These, however, do not constitute scenes of unity, given the superimpositions that follow and conclude *Claro*, superimpositions that bring together faces, bodies, murals, headlines, Ho Chi Minh. These figures, *Claro* makes clear, will not be united, although they may share the frame, vie for attention, coexist incommensurably. But neither do the rallies or the superimpositions that follow constitute scenes of anarchy, if only because *Claro* prepares for them by pointing to the *emarginazione*—the attempt at forceful relocation and minoritization—from which the collective struggle results. The condition of being (almost) made a means to rulers' ends thus precedes and even constitutes the precondition for struggle, and anticolonial victory, and the latter retains the memory of the former. Without apologizing for the regimes that necessitate such rebellions,[87] Rocha indicates the possibilities for thought and action that they can unwittingly bring into being. Staging their returns repeatedly, he shows throughout *Claro* that such regimes must be reckoned with, like Rome itself.

The capacity for this reckoning is what the old school as redeployed by Rocha seeks to impart. It is also what progressive education precludes when it disavows conflict or posits, as Freire does repeatedly, "the solution of the teacher-student contradiction" as both its precondition and its promise. Rocha takes this contradiction to be irreducible, though not irreversible,[88] and he suggests that its disavowal leads to a situation that is paradoxically *more* colonial, not less, given his contention, already in "An Aesthetics of Hunger," that colonialism in its contemporary "refined" forms is a matter of internalization, of psychic more than territorial conquest,[89] or of what we long ago, with Joyce, learned to call "indirect suggestion implicating selfinterest."[90] In *Claro*, a return to Rome turns out to sustain, rather than rule out, anticolonial possibility precisely because it requires acknowledgment of the difficulties involved in bringing about the fall of Rome on any scale.

The film counters—and radically complicates—Freirean pedagogy in another way as well. If Freire's educational theory is undeniably compelling and has been broadly enabling, there's a sense in which it deprives students of a prior capacity that Rocha in fact grants—and this although he appears to be the less generous, the less student-affirming, of the two figures.[91] I mean the capacity to space out, to distract oneself, *to dream*, as in Rocha's 1971 manifesto "An Aesthetics of the Dream."[92] In this sense, Berto's silence, which gives way to her stunning non sequitur of a speech,[93] feels qualitatively different from what Freire calls the "structure of mutism in the face of the overwhelming force of ... limit-situations [estrutura costituinte do mutismo ante a força esmagadora de 'situações-limite,' em face das quais o óbvio é a adaptação]" (*Pedagogy* 106; *Pedagogia* 136).[94] Previous critiques of Freire have in fact noted that his emphasis on the "silence" of the oppressed verges at times on a denial of their subjectivity. "The irony," according to one of these critiques, is "Freire's suggestion that the silent oppressed [have] to be 'taught' to surrender their passivity and their fear." By this account, "Freire's radical pedagogy [is] marred by a false notion of dialogue, insofar as it depends on the ... 'teacher-vanguard' to enter the imprisoned community from without to initiate reflexive speech, to rupture the silence of the oppressed, and to release the long-trapped flow and exchange of ideas [and] language."[95] As if the silence had until then been total, the trap airtight, and the prison impenetrable. In this way, Freire arguably reinstates a version of the contradiction, the hierarchical verticality (*Pedagogia* 117), that he had sought to overcome through dialogue and horizontality.[96]

For his part, Rocha insists that "dreaming is the only right that cannot be denied [o único direito que não se pode proibir]."[97] This means that even, perhaps especially, in Rome, when we are compelled to return, the dream recurs. And dreaming, of course, cannot be taught.[98] Here again, then, we see the dialectical twist that marks all of the efforts to reimagine the old school that I have considered—because in the end the instruction that *Claro* administers turns out to be anything but merely "top down" (*Pedagogy* 94).[99] Giving its student-spectators something to come up against, the film prompts resistance rather than preempting it. Far from ruling out such resistance, *Claro* sustains it programmatically, drawing on cinema's capacity to deliver an experience of duration that is at once collectively undergone and conducive to individual spacing out, drift, or dreaming. In this way, again, the "imposition" (*Pedagogy* 93; *Pedagogia* 116) that knows itself to be imposed, the educational chore—or the didactic film—that understands itself to be laborious and mechanical, turns out to be paradoxically, if only potentially, more freeing than the progressive alternative.

This dialectic or dream, this conversion of imposition and intrusion into possibility, constitutes the counter-progressive legacy. And this is what the pedagogical projects that I have studied all leave behind: a process rather than a property. Pater might call this process "something to be done," underscoring its status as a task to be accomplished and begun again.[100] Pascoli might teach us to recognize it as homework, repeatedly assigned. Joyce would no doubt urge us, in the end, to "try it on," or copy it out big.[101] And Pasolini would seek, in his paradoxical way, to preserve this process in and through its repudiation, its abjuration. Each of these authors *would* thus have prepared us, after all, to revisit Rome again with Rocha, to see *Claro* without understanding clearly. What they could not have prepared us for, though, because they could only barely glimpse, is the decline and fall that Rocha's film projects, the ruin for which it stands as a last image that is not the West's.

Acknowledgments

There was something self-fulfilling about this book's argument, it turned out. I wrote about the value of a certain kind of slog, and sure enough the work of revision became a slog: a long, drawn-out, and difficult process. Throughout this process, though, I had the good fortune to be accompanied by teachers, mentors, colleagues, students, friends, and family members who made the completion of this pensum into a pleasure.

I am grateful to Barbara Spackman, who taught me what it could mean to read closely and critically. D. A. Miller made it possible for me to hear myself think. I could not have written this book without the example and provocation of his singular intelligence. To Judith Butler, whose encouragement has been as sustaining as it was at first surprising, I owe more than I can say. I thank C. D. Blanton for reading my work early, often, and with tenacity. Conversations with Anne-Lise François don't just have a way of happening; they are a way of happening.

I might never have tried to write a book like this one if it weren't for Jenny Davidson's early encouragement. Brent Hayes Edwards offered later inspiration at Columbia, and his work and teaching continue to inspire. So, too, do the work and teaching of Robert Kaufman and Stefania Pandolfo. I thank them both for formative seminars and mind-changing conversations. Heartfelt thanks as well to Kathryn Bond Stockton for the difference her teaching has made. I first read Gramsci with care in a seminar taught by Gayatri Chakravorty Spivak, to whom I offer belated thanks.

Research for this book began at the University of California, Berkeley, where it was supported by the Program in Critical Theory and the Doreen B. Townsend Center for the Humanities. Later support came from the Pembroke Center for Teaching and Research on Women at Brown University and the International Consortium of Critical Theory Programs.

At Brown, it was a pleasure and a privilege to be in conversation with the one and only Joan Copjec and with Denise Davis, Jacques Khalip, Azeen Khan, Ellen Rooney, Suzanne Stewart-Steinberg, Drew Walker, Elizabeth Weed, and Soyoung Yoon. Thanks to Massimo Riva for the invitation to present work on Pasolini, and to Ronald Martinez for inviting me to share my chapter on Pascoli with Brown's Italian Studies Colloquium. I thank all of the participants in that colloquium for their earnest and open-minded engagement, especially Carolina Castiglione and, again, Suzanne. My time at Brown also brought me into contact with the brilliant Lorenzo Fabbri, with whom it has been a pleasure to collaborate. Heartfelt thanks as well to Humphrey Morris and all of the members of the Psychoanalytic Practices working group at Harvard.

Back in Berkeley, it has been an honor and an adventure to work with the incomparable Breana George. Thanks to Katharine Wallerstein for her keen eye and constant solidarity, and to my other officemates: Rebecca Dizon, Patty Dunlap, Khai Nguyen, and Brandon Schneider.

This book bears the marks or scars of several years of soul-corroding scarcity in the fields in which I work. For offering advice, encouragement, invitations to collaborate, and, in some cases, paid work during these often difficult years, I thank Albert Ascoli, Athena Athanasiou, Natalia Brizuela, Gisela Catanzaro, Rodrigo De La Fabián, Bill Dixon, Samera Esmeir, Banu Karaca, Erica Kaufman, Carla Marcantonio, Leticia Sabsay, Poulomi Saha, Elena Tzelepis, and Sophie Volpp.

I am thrilled to be joining the departments of Comparative Literature and Italian at the University of St. Andrews and am especially grateful to Seán Allan, Bettina Bildhauer, Emma Bond, Derek Duncan, Ian Smith, Saeed Talajooy, and Derek Woollins for their willingness to take my work seriously.

Thanks to my students at Brown, Bard, and UC Berkeley, especially all the students in my seminar on "Seeing Red: 1975 in Italian and World Cinema" in 2017.

I will always be grateful to Andrew Parker for introducing me to Tom Lay at Fordham University Press, and to Tom for taking such consistently good care of my manuscript. For their more recent care work, I thank Eric Newman and Aldene Fredenburg. I am grateful to Sarah Guyer and Brian McGrath for including my book in the Lit Z series. My at first anonymous peer reviewers, Jean-Michel Rabaté and John David Rhodes, truly a dream team, made the manuscript stronger with their sharply perceptive responses and suggestions for revision.

Thanks to Colin Brant and Joshua Park for coming through to help with film stills at the eleventh hour. I am grateful to Andrea Poulsen, speaking of film stills, for the gift of this book's cover image and even more so for the gift of her friendship.

Parts of the Introduction and Chapter 3 first appeared as "'Copied Out Big': Instruction in Joyce's *Ulysses*," on *Modernism/modernity*'s Print Plus platform, in vol. 3, Cycle 3 (2018) (copyright © 2018 Johns Hopkins University Press). An earlier version of Chapter 4 was published as "*Salò* and the School of Abuse," in *Postmodern Culture* 26, no. 3 (2016) (copyright © 2016 Johns Hopkins University Press). I thank the Johns Hopkins University Press for permission to reprint both texts, and Debra Rae Cohen and Eyal Amiran for the improvements they made to these chapters.

★ ★ ★

Friends convinced me that this book was worth writing and shared their insights, observations, and sensibilities. Time spent with Joshua Branciforte was and is always energizing. Paco Brito understood what I was trying to say long before I did. Or rather, he generously saw in this book the best version of what it could be. Ashley Brock offered beautifully perceptive readings both early and late, and help with Glauber in particular. Kathryn Crim was right there with me. Jordan Greenwald reminded me of the imaginative resources that remained available when I felt resourceless. Katie Kadue, who taught me everything I know about the importance of exercise, read more iterations of this book's chapters than anyone else. I cannot imagine a better, sharper, or more sensitive reader, or any possible world in which this book could exist without her emails. Marianne Kaletzky more than once enlivened this book's composition and was a true comrade in her willingness to think through its implications repeatedly. Jocelyn Saidenberg offered perspectives on poetry, psychoanalysis, and teaching as well as depths of understanding in dark times. Shaul Setter inspired my thinking from a distance. Luckily, Laura Wagner was close by, always able to reframe arguments and situations. Althea Wasow believed in this book even when I was a mere wannabe. Thanks to Sima Belmar, Emily Drumsta, Ross Lerner, Suzanne Li Puma, Emily O'Rourke, Yosefa Raz, Joel Street, Kris Trujillo, Michelle Ty, for a late-breaking conversation, Saskia Ziolkowski..

I am grateful to everyone at Hot 8 Pasadena, my other school.

For homes away from home and various other forms of soul sustenance, thanks to Claire McDonnell, purveyor of many deep and meaningfuls, James Lee, Julia and Miguel Wu, Daniel Esquivel, Ricardo Tejeda, Ifeolu Babatunde, Stefano and Francesca Beltrame, Sara Beltrame and Marco Gobbi Kraft, Karen Cresci, Fabián Alfonso, Ben Joseph, Judy Berkman, Jenny Weissbourd, Alan Glazer, and Noel, Maire, and Aoibheann McLoughlin.

Con profundo agradecimiento, I thank la familia Diaz, both in California and in San Rafael, Huejúcar, Jalisco, México. For their hospitality, their sense of humor, and their willingness to welcome me into the family, thanks especially to Arcelia Diaz Flores, Juan Carlos Dias, Araceli Rojas, Donna Dias, Mia and Sigi, Reyna Diaz and Ashley, Josemar Diaz, Rebecca Ramos and Guillermito, Suzie Diaz, Angie and Ezra Mateo, Diana Diaz, Ivan Rivera,

Bertha Diaz Flores, Nancy Trujillo, Juan Luis Diaz, Rosa Trujillo, Chon Flores, Yolanda Diaz, Heriberto Diaz, Luz María Trujillo, Vanessa Diaz, and Marilu Diaz.

It is a dream come true to call Katie O'Donnell, Jessie Hawk, and August Hawk O'Donnell family. To Katie and Jessie: thank you for sharing the years that made it possible for me to first imagine this book, years that began in a very small apartment in San Francisco, circa 2008.

Nietzsche writes that it is only in love, "that is to say in the unconditional faith in right and perfection that love produces," that we can create. So if there is anything creative about these pages, it is thanks to Freddie Diaz, who sustains my faith in right.

This book is dedicated with love to my parents and first teachers, Bob Glazer and Martricia McLaughlin, and to Ryan and Mariele McGlazer.

Notes

Unless otherwise noted, all translations are my own throughout.

Introduction: On Counter-Progressive Pedagogy

1. James Joyce, *Ulysses: The Corrected Text*, ed. Hans Walter Gabler, with Wolfhard Steppe and Claus Melchior (New York: Vintage, 1986), 17.698. My epigraph is taken from 17.699–702. Further citations are given parenthetically in the text, with episode numbers followed by line numbers.

2. In his early essay "Drama and Life" (1900), Joyce rejects the claim "that the drama should have special ethical aims, . . . that it should instruct, elevate, and amuse. Here," Joyce continues, "is another gyve that the jailers have bestowed"; Joyce, "Drama and Life," in *Occasional, Critical, and Political Writing*, ed. Kevin Barry (New York: Oxford University Press, 2000), 26–27.

3. Giovanni Gentile, *La riforma dell'educazione: Discorsi ai maestri di Trieste* (Bari: Laterza, 1920), 186.

4. Penelope Deutscher, *Foucault's Futures: A Critique of Reproductive Reason* (New York: Columbia University Press, 2017), 44; Lee Edelman, *No Future: Queer Theory and the Death Drive* (Durham, N.C.: Duke University Press, 2004), 30.

5. Lee Edelman, "Learning Nothing: *Bad Education*," *differences* 28, no. 1 (2017): 129.

6. Gentile, *La riforma*, 186, emphasis added.

7. Ibid.

8. This assertion may at first seem jarring and implausible, but the "irony" of the Fascist philosopher's promotion of progressive educational ideals has not gone unnoticed by educational historians. Madan Sarup, for instance, writes, "It is an interesting irony that the reforms, though carried out by a Fascist government, tended towards the 'liberalization' of education. Accounts of the principles underlying [Gentile's] reforms read like summaries of progressive educational theory, what we would now call 'child-centered' ideas"; Sarap, "Education and Social Change: The Work of Gramsci," in *Marxism/Structuralism/Education: Theoretical Developments in the Sociology of Education* (New York: Routledge, 1983), 133. See also Eden K. McLean, *Mussolini's Children: Race and Elementary Education in Fascist Italy* (Lincoln: University of Nebraska Press, 2018), 27.

9. Gentile, *La riforma*, 188.

10. For Marinetti's affirmation of the futurist "love of progress, of freedom," see F. T. Marinetti, *Democrazia futurista: Dinamismo politico* (Milan: Facchi, 1919), 211. For another characterization of the "dominant critical model in modernist studies" as in keeping with "Futurism's dictates," and for a critique of this tendency in the field, see

Louise Hornby, *Still Modernism: Photography, Literature, Film* (Oxford: Oxford University Press, 2016), 8–9.

11. The definitions of "progressive pedagogy" and "progressive education" are contested. In this book, I define these terms broadly and consider diverse educational theories and practices "progressive." I do this not to elide the differences between, say, Rousseau and Gentile or Dewey and Paulo Freire, whose liberatory or critical pedagogy, discussed in Chapter 5, is often distinguished from Deweyan and other liberal progressive models. My aim is instead to draw attention to the premises, priorities, and polemical targets that these various approaches share. All present themselves, for instance, as modernizing and humanizing alternatives to an old school whose methods are characterized as mechanical, rote, repetitive, uncreative, constraining, oppressive, and even deadening. Frances Ferguson's account of early progressive educational theory identifies several other key continuities. This education, Ferguson writes, "presented itself as a staged progress for the individual but also for knowledge in general. It continually limned education as an initiation into the process of extending knowledge past what it had been; and, in the process, it created generations as forceful entities that would not so much carry the knowledge of their predecessors but would render it obsolete"; Ferguson, "Educational Rationalization/Sublime Reason," *Romantic Circles, Praxis Series* (August 2010), https://www.rc.umd.edu/praxis/sublime_education/ferguson/ferguson.html.

12. For a sense of the reach of Gentile's text, see Donald T. Torchiana, "'Among School Children' and the Education of the Irish Spirit," in *In Excited Reverie: A Centenary Tribute to William Butler Yeats*, ed. A. Norman Jeffares and K. G. W. Cross (London: Macmillan, 1965), 123–50. Torchiana discusses Yeats's admiration for Gentile and his support for Irish attempts to imitate Gentilean reforms. Yeats relied on an English translation of *La riforma* whose publication postdates *Ulysses* (132), but in Trieste Joyce would have enjoyed earlier and less mediated access to Gentile's published lectures and the debates in which they participated. On Joyce's language teaching, see Elizabeth Switaj, *James Joyce's Teaching Life and Methods: Language and Pedagogy in "A Portrait of the Artist as a Young Man," "Ulysses," and "Finnegans Wake"* (New York: Palgrave, 2016).

13. Antonio Gramsci, *Quaderni del carcere,* ed. Valentino Gerratana (Turin: Einaudi, 2007), 3:1544; *Selections from Prison Notebooks*, ed. and trans. Quinton Hoare and Geoffrey Nowell Smith (New York: International, 1971), 37. Further citations are given parenthetically in the text, using the abbreviation *QC* for the original Italian and *PN* for the English.

14. "For [in instruction] the learner is not a passive and mechanical recipient, a gramophone record [poiché il discente non è un disco di grammofono]—even if the liturgical conventionality of examinations sometimes makes him appear so. The relation between these educational forms and the child's psychology is always active and creative, just as the relation of the worker to his tools is active and creative" (*QC* 1549; *PN* 42; trans. modified).

15. Gentile, *La riforma*, 167.

16. Ibid., 188.

17. Gramsci, *PN* 24; the phrase is taken from Hoare and Nowell Smith's introductory notes to their selection of Gramsci's educational writings.

18. Ibid., 24.

19. See Simonetta Falasca-Zamponi, "The Myth of Rome," in *Fascist Spectacle: The Aesthetics of Power in Mussolini's Italy* (Berkeley: University of California Press, 1997), 90–99; especially 91.

20. Thanks to Robert Kaufman for helping me to see this.

21. T. S. Eliot, *What Is a Classic?* (London: Faber and Faber, 1945), 29.

22. Ibid., 28.

23. Ibid., 31.

24. Jean-Jacques Rousseau, *Émile, or On Education*, trans. Allan Bloom (New York: Basic, 1979), 112.

25. Ibid., 42.

26. Ibid., 112.

27. Ibid., 37.

28. "There is no subjection so perfect as that which keeps the appearance of freedom. Thus the will itself is made captive. The poor child who knows nothing, who can do nothing, who has no learning, is he not at your mercy? Do you not dispose, with respect to him, of everything which surrounds him? Are you not the master of affecting him as you please? Are not his labors, his games, his pleasures, his pains, all in your hands without his knowing it? Doubtless he ought to do only what he wants; but he ought to want only what you want him to do. He ought not to make a step without your having foreseen it; he ought not to open his mouth without your knowing what he is going to say"; Rousseau, *Émile*, 120. If Rousseau makes room for this acknowledgment, his followers are seldom as self-aware. See also Diane Berrett Brown, "The Constraints of Liberty at the Scene of Instruction," in *Rousseau and Freedom*, ed. Christie McDonald and Stanley Hoffmann (Cambridge: Cambridge University Press, 2010), 159–73. On Gentile as "liberal" and Rousseauist, see Gramsci, QC 2349. For some of Gentile's reflections on freedom in education, see *La riforma*, e.g., 58–59. And for an earlier account attesting to the centrality of freedom in Gentile's educational theory, see "L'unità della scuola media e la libertà degli studi," in *La nuova scuola media*, ed. Hervé A. Cavallera, vol. 40, *Opere complete di Giovanni Gentile* (Florence: Casa Editrice Le Lettere, 1988), 1–39.

29. The process of radicalization that this book traces is thus also an increasing valorization of the old school's dialectical potential. By 1975, I show, in both Pasolini's *Salò* and Rocha's *Claro*, we return or counter-progress to the old school not because it's simply *good* for us to do so, but because, according to Pasolini and Rocha, there's something potentially good or salutary about how *bad* it is to spend time there, how much formative boredom, blockage, frustration, and limitation a return to the old school entails. I return to these questions in Chapter 3 through an engagement with Edelman, "Learning Nothing," 124–73.

30. Baidik Bhattacharya, "Interview with Gayatri Chakravorty Spivak," in *The Postcolonial Gramsci*, ed. Neelam Srivastava and Baidik Bhattacharya (New York: Routledge, 2012), 223–32. "The entire business of taking Latin away from the *Latinitas* of Mussolini . . . has a pretty old-fashioned argument behind it, but the important thing is to sabotage it to a different end, the old-fashioned tools have lasted" (230–31).

31. Gayatri Chakravroty Spivak, "Introduction," in *An Aesthetic Education in the Era of Globalization* (Cambridge, Mass.: Harvard University Press, 2012), 20, 29.

32. Spivak, "Scattered Speculations on the Subaltern and the Popular," in *An Aesthetic Education*, 436. Spivak quotes from *PN* 8, 10; in the Italian, these sentences appear in QC 1515, 1517.

33. Theodor Adorno and Hellmut Becker, "Education for Autonomy," trans. David J. Parent, *Telos* 55 (1983): 109.

34. For a notable exception, see Molly Nesbit, *Their Common Sense* (London: Black Dog, 2000).

35. See, for example, Annamaria Palmieri, *Maestri di scuola, maestri di pensiero: La scuola tra letteratura e vita nella seconda metà del Novecento; Pasolini, Sciascia, Mastronardi* (Rome: Aracne, 2015), and Angelo Restivo, *The Cinema of Economic Miracles: Visuality and Modernization in the Postwar European Art Film* (Durham, N.C.: Duke University Press, 2002), 150–59; on Pascoli, see Lylia Loce-Mandes, *Pascoli educatore* (Rome: Ciranna, 1959). I consider further examples in Chapters 2 and 4.

36. Michael Warner, "Uncritical Reading," in *Polemic: Critical or Uncritical*, ed. Jane Gallop (New York: Routledge, 2004), 19. One classic account of modernity as an exit from constraints can be found in Immanuel Kant, "An Answer to the Question 'What Is Enlightenment?,'" in *Groundwork for the Metaphysics of Morals*, ed. Lara Denis, trans. Thomas K. Abbott (New York: Broadview, 2005), 119–26. But for a reading of Kant that emphasizes "the enabling function of constraints" in the third critique in particular, see Tracy McNulty, *Wrestling with the Angel: Experiments in Symbolic Life* (New York: Columbia University Press, 2014), 249–55.

37. Edward Said, *On Late Style: Music and Literature against the Grain* (New York: Vintage, 2006), 24.

38. Ibid., 22.

39. Ibid., 23.

40. Ibid., 17.

41. Ibid., 17, 12, 14; emphasis in original.

42. Ibid., 17.

43. Pier Paolo Pasolini, "Abiura dalla Trilogia della vita," in Lettere luterane (Turin: Einaudi, 1976), 71.

44. Ibid., 76.

45. I take these terms from Raymond Williams, "Dominant, Residual, and Emergent," in *Marxism and Literature* (Oxford: Oxford University Press, 1977), 121–27. It will become clear why I refer to the old school as "residual" rather than use another of Williams's terms, "archaic"—and this despite my emphasis elsewhere on the institution's status as the purveyor of a dead language whose power inheres precisely in its deadness. Williams writes, "The residual, by definition, has been effectively formed in the past but is still active in the cultural process, not only and often not at all as an element of the past, but as an effective element of the present" (122). I hope the reader hard-pressed to see how Latin could in any sense still be "active" in turn-of-the-century Dublin or in postwar Italy will refer to this book's individual chapters. Here the "residual" takes various forms, appearing, in Pater, for instance, as "superstitions" and "survivals," and in Pascoli as the specific, scholastic traditions threatened by the regime of utility. I account for the recurrence of Latin—as opposed to Greek, say, or Sanskrit or any other ancient language—across these varied texts in part by pointing to its preservation by a range of

institutions both religious and secular. In Italy, in Ireland, and in Pater's England, differently, as well as in Rocha's Latin America, Latin remained available if sidelined; it was actively used in ecclesiastical and boarding-school contexts, though long since defunct as a lingua franca. The dead language was, in this importance sense, still alive, still circulating, although, again, following Pascoli, I will also go on to stress its deadness, defined as its difference from the living. For another take on the residual in modern European culture, one that emphasizes the recalcitrance rather than the radical setting to work of the old and the academic, see Arno Mayer, *The Persistence of the Old Regime: Europe to the Great War* (New York: Pantheon, 1981), especially Chapter 4, "Official High Cultures and the Avant-Gardes," 189–274.

46. Massimiliano Biscuso and Franco Gallo, "Potenza emancipativa e disattivazione della riflessione leopardiana," in *Leopardi antitaliano*, ed. Massimiliano Biscuso and Franco Gallo (Rome: Manifesto, 1999), 39.

47. Anne-Lise François, *Open Secrets: The Literature of Uncounted Experience* (Stanford, Calif.: Stanford University Press, 2007), 254.

48. Ibid., 22. On the openness that is really closure, see, for instance, Fredric Jameson, *Representing "Capital:" A Commentary on Volume One* (New York: Verso, 2011), 146.

49. Barry McCrea, *Languages of the Night: Minor Languages and the Literary Imagination in Twentieth-Century Ireland and Europe* (New Haven: Yale University Press, 2015), xii.

50. Benjamin Conisbee Baer, "—*Your Ghost-Work*": Figures of the Peasant and the Autochthon in Literature and Politics, 1880s–1940s (Ph.D. diss., Columbia University, 2006), 5.

51. Jean Franco, *César Vallejo: The Dialectics of Poetry and Silence* (Cambridge: Cambridge University Press, 1976), 168.

52. See also Jennifer Scappettone, *Killing the Moonlight: Modernism in Venice* (New York: Columbia University Press, 2014), which shows that "the residual Venetian forms that appear to constitute hindrances to both modernization and high-modernist invention become the materials of experimental salvage" in a range of Anglo-American and Italian modernist works (41).

53. Robert Kaufman, "Aura, Still," *October* 99 (2002): 45–80. Kaufman explains "the critical negation formally enacted by aesthetic aura" in terms that resonate with, because they have influenced, this book's account of modernist engagements with outmoded educational forms. The old school, like the aura according to Kaufman, affords a "protocritical" and "provisional, enabling distance from . . . reigning concepts" (66) after its eclipse by progressive education—whether this eclipse is merely threatened or already accomplished.

54. See, however, McCrea's brief but suggestive remarks on "the peasantry and the aristocracy as a double alternative to middle-class progress"; *Languages of the Night*, 142. On the appropriation of the Latin class by elites during the eighteenth and especially the nineteenth centuries, see Françoise Waquet, "Class," in *Latin or the Empire of a Sign: From the Sixteenth to the Twentieth Centuries*, trans. John Howe (New York: Verso, 2001), 207–29. And for a fascinating account that locates the anti-democratic shift in Latin instruction earlier, in the displacement of scholastic educational traditions (older old schools) by humanist classicism, see Anthony Grafton and Lisa Jardine, *From Humanism to the Humanities: Education and the Liberal Arts in Fifteenth- and Sixteenth-Century Europe* (Cambridge, Mass.: Harvard University Press, 1986).

55. On the "elitism" of late style, see Said, *On Late Style*, 20–21.

56. Waquet, *Latin or the Empire of a Sign*, 233.

57. See Louis Althusser, "Ideology and Ideological State Apparatuses (Notes towards an Investigation)," in *Lenin and Philosophy and Other Essays*, trans. Ben Brewster (New York: Monthly Review Press, 1971), 152–57, on "the *educational ideological apparatus*" as "the ideological State apparatus which has been installed in the *dominant* position in mature capitalist social formations" (152, emphases in original).

58. Pierre Bourdieu and Jean-Claude Passeron, *Reproduction in Education, Society, and Culture*, trans. Richard Nice (London: SAGE, 1977), 210.

59. Ibid.; emphasis in original.

60. Judith Butler, "Theatrical Machines," *differences: A Journal of Feminist Cultural Studies* 26, no. 3 (2015): 37.

61. Stefania Pandolfo, "Testimony in Counterpoint: Psychiatric Fragments in the Aftermath of Culture," *Qui Parle* 17, no. 1 (2008): 110. See also Gayle Salamon, *The Life and Death of Latisha King: A Critical Phenomenology of Transphobia* (New York: New York University Press, 2018), 96: "Arguably the greatest value of a school is its ability to become an elsewhere." Another argument for the school as elsewhere can be found in Jan Masschelein and Maarten Simons, *In Defense of the School: A Public Issue*, translated by Jack McMartin (Leuven: E-ducation, Culture & Society Publishers, 2013).

62. "But what would it mean if teaching ... is precisely what one is asked to get beyond?" Harney and Moten ask. Here they mean teaching defined as pedagogical labor, but also, more broadly, the condition of being taught. Their question is thus not only whether scholars today are urged to get beyond the often implicitly feminized work of teaching to focus on value-adding, entrepreneurial research. For the answer to this question is obvious. They wonder more generally what would follow from the recognition that we have all long since been enjoined to "get beyond" the scene of teaching, to leave it behind in the name of an impoverished autonomy. Stefano Harney and Fred Moten, "The University and the Undercommons," in *The Undercommons: Fugitive Planning & Black Study* (Wivenhoe, UK: Minor Compositions, 2013), 27.

63. Maurizio Bettini makes a case for the denaturalizing potentials of teaching Greek and Latin in the Italian context today in *A che servono i greci e i romani?* (Turin: Einaudi, 2017), which emphasizes the "otherness" of the ancients, refusing accounts that treat classical studies as a matter of enshrining "identity" or returning to "roots"; see, e.g., 81–94, 145–47. This is a Gramscian but also, incidentally, a Hegelian position. See Hegel's comments on "the centrifugal force of the soul" and "why the soul must always be provided with the means of estranging itself from its natural condition and essence, and why in particular the young mind must be led into a remote and foreign world": "For it is the mechanical that is foreign to the mind, and it is this which awakens the mind's desire to digest the indigestible food forced upon it, to make intelligible what is at first without life and meaning"; G. W. F. Hegel, "On Classical Studies," trans. Richard Kroner, in *Early Theological Writings* (Philadelphia: University of Pennsylvania Press, 1971), 328. See also Rebecca Comay, "Hegel's Last Words," in *The Dash—The Other Side of Absolute Knowing*, by Rebecca Comay and Frank Ruda (Cambridge, Mass.: MIT Press, 2018), 75.

64. Chris Ackerley, *Demented Particulars: The Annotated "Murphy"* (Edinburgh: Edinburgh University Press, 2004), 114.

65. Paulo Freire, *Pedagogy of the Oppressed*, trans. Myra Bergman Ramos (New York: Continuum, 2005), 75; *Pedagogia do oprimido* (Rio de Janeiro: Paz e Terra, 2014), 86. The Portuguese original refers to the teacher's learning or "knowing with the students, as they know with him": "Saber com os educandos, enquanto estes soubessem com ele, seria sua tarifa."

66. Compare Gramsci, QC 1537; PN 33. Stefano Harney considers "decollectivisation" in labor and learning, in "Al-Khwariddimia, or A Partial Education," paper presented at "The Critical Tasks of the University," a conference held at the Università di Bologna, June 2017. See also Harney's discussion of individuation and the distinction between "total" and "partial education" in "Stefano Harney (part 2)," an interview by Michael Schapira and Jesse Montgomery, *Full Stop* (August 2017), http://www.full-stop.net/2017/08/10/interviews/michael-schapira-and-jesse-montgomery/stefano-harney-part-2/.

67. *Design Thinking for Educators*, http://www.designthinkingforeducators.com/design-examples/; quoted in Megan Erickson, "Edutopia," *Jacobin* 17 (Spring 2015), https://www.jacobinmag.com/2015/03/education-technology-gates-erickson/. For more on neoliberalism and education, see Wendy Brown, "Educating Human Capital," in *Undoing the Demos: Neoliberalism's Stealth Revolution* (New York: Zone, 2015), 175–200; and on the neoliberal ethos of self-appreciation more generally, see Michel Feher, "Self-Appreciation; or, The Aspirations of Human Capital," *Public Culture* 21, no. 1 (2009): 21–41; especially 29–31. For another account of how, after the uprisings of the late 1960s and 1970s, "capital was able to renew its psychic, ideological, and economic energy" through "the absorption of creativity, desire, and individualistic, libertarian drives for self-realization," see Franco "Bifo" Berardi, *The Soul at Work: From Alienation to Autonomy*, trans. Francesca Cadel and Giuseppina Mecchia (Los Angeles: Semiotext[e], 2009); the sentence I have quoted appears on page 96. See also 74–75, 77. This account makes it possible to observe—anachronistically, of course—that in a sense the old school may be to the new what the Fordist factory, with its "mechanical and repetition-based model" of productivity (90), is to the diffuse, digitized post-Fordist workplace. Or rather, Berardi's claim makes it possible to see that, from the perspective of the present, we can and should reread earlier discourses of "self-realization," including progressive educational theories, asking whether they, too, might thwart collective resistance while claiming to promote individual creativity.

68. Recent indications of this at the level of policy range, for instance, from current U.S. Education Secretary Betsy DeVos's "student-centered funding pilot program," implemented under the Obama-era Every Student Succeeds Act, to the European Union's Bologna Process, which regulates the ongoing reform of higher education, and in which the discourse of student-centered learning figures prominently. See U.S. Department of Education, "Secretary DeVos Announces New Student-Centered Funding Pilot Program," February 2, 2018, https://www.ed.gov/news/press-releases/secretary-devos-announces-new-student-centered-funding-pilot-program; and European Commission, *The European Higher Education Area in 2015: Bologna Process Implementation Report* (Luxembourg: Publications Office of the European Union, 2015). In *Race and the Origins of Progressive Education, 1880–1929* (New York: Teachers College Press, 2015), Thomas Fallace confirms that "child-centeredness" remains central in the education of educators today: "The progressive educational idea that teachers should nourish

a child's natural and instinctual curiosity (i.e., child-centeredness) . . . is still the leading approach espoused by most colleges of education."

69. Although I have been inspired as well as instructed by McNulty's *Wrestling with the Angel*, I do not share her sense that "we generally have no difficulty affirming the importance of constraints" in education (1). On the contrary, I observe a tendency, extending from *Émile* into the present, to see constraints in education not as conducive to freedom, but as leading to or constituting practice for a lifetime of lamentable unfreedom. This is also, I think, a tendency to equate nonprogressive forms of education with the "internalizing [of] rules and norms" precisely (2). The tendency against which McNulty argues—the tendency to define freedom "solely in negative terms, as a freedom *from* limits or constraints"—thus shapes our discussions of education as well, in my view (1; emphasis in original).

70. On "complication of influence," see Walter Pater, "Emerald Uthwart," in *Miscellaneous Studies: A Series of Essays* (London: Macmillan, 1895), 205.

71. On modernist cinema, see, for example, András Bálint Kovács, *Screening Modernism: European Art Cinema, 1950–1980* (Chicago: University of Chicago Press, 2007). Although neither *Salò* nor *Claro* figure in Kovács's study, both engage meaningfully with the late modernist, post-neorealist film tradition that he outlines. Both films also evince key features of cinematic modernism as it is generally defined, including notably self-reflexivity and a privileging of the director's perspective, or what Kovács calls "the auteurial text" (395). With its insistence on the diegetic presence of modernist artworks, moreover, *Salò* constitutes a reflection on the broader modernist legacy. I discuss this legacy as first and foremost a history of responses to modernization, rather than limiting my treatment of modernism to the high modernist decades represented in *Old Schools* only by *Ulysses*. In this sense, I follow the expansive handling of modernism in works like McCrea, *Languages of the Night*, and Scappettone, *Killing the Moonlight*. See also T. J. Clark's defense of "limit cases" in *Farewell to An Idea: Episodes from a History of Modernism* (New Haven: Yale University Press, 1999), 7. On the peculiar fate of "modernism" in the Italian context, see Paolo Valesio, "Foreword: After *The Conquest of the Stars*," in *Italian Modernism: Italian Culture between Decadentism and Avant-Garde*, ed. Luca Somigli and Mario Moroni (Toronto: University of Toronto Press, 2004), ix–xxxiii.

72. Muriel Spark, *The Prime of Miss Jean Brodie* (New York: HarperPerennial, 2009), 36; emphasis added.

73. Gentile, *La riforma*, 186.

74. David Lodge, "The Uses and Abuses of Omniscience: Method and Meaning in Muriel Spark's *The Prime of Miss Jean Brodie*," in *The Novelist at the Crossroads and Other Essays* (Ithaca, N.Y.: Cornell University Press, 1971), 131.

75. Ivan Illich calls this etymology "pedagogical folklore" in "Vernacular Values," *Philosophica* 26, no. 2 (1980): 79. It is both strange and telling that Illich discounts any "folklore" in a defense of the vernacular. This discounting is in keeping with his insistence on the (for him gendered) distinctions between home and school, the mother tongue and acquired speech, "the living speech of the unschooled" (95) and the "inevitably dead and useless" language of learning (81). My thanks to Anne-Lise François for drawing my attention to Illich's fascinating if deeply problematic text.

76. I note, however, the recurrence of repetitive, citational forms, forms that are often though not always also pedagogical, in Spark's fiction both early and late. From the "morning and evening exercise prescribed by the Chief Instructress of the Poise Course" in *The Girls of Slender Means* (New York: Alfred A. Knopf, 1963), 57, to the composition of schoolboyish verse in *The Mandelbaum Gate* (1965), from the practice of commonplacing in *Loitering with Intent* (1981) to the prayer recited every day at noon by the heroine of *A Far Cry from Kensington* (1988), Spark keeps returning to forms of repetition and imitation "prescribed" by instructors and institutions of various kinds. These returns index Spark's interest in what Sianne Ngai calls the common "linkage of femininity with imitation and iterability"; *Ugly Feelings* (Cambridge, Mass.: Harvard University Press, 2005), 149. According to the logic of this "correlation," Ngai explains, "to be feminine is to be ... an entity inducing imitation in others while at the same time appearing 'after the fashion' of a previously established model" (ibid.). In addition, and relatedly, the repetitive forms that recur in Spark's fiction attest to her career-long engagement with the social life of the phrase, the derivative status of language, the fact that our language is always someone else's first. They call attention, in other words, to the ineluctability of imposition or what Jean Brodie calls "intrusion." (Such intrusion can, of course, take more or less violent forms: more in *The Comforters* [1957] or differently *The Driver's Seat* [1970]; less, for instance, in *The Prime of Miss Jean Brodie* or *The Abbess of Crewe* [1974].) See Spark, *The Abbess of Crewe* (New York: New Directions, 1995), 71. On language as imposition, see also, for example, Jacques Lacan, *The Sinthome: The Seminar of Jacques Lacan, Book XXIII*, ed. Jacques-Alain Miller, trans. A. R. Price (Cambridge: Polity Press, 2016), 78; and on education as imposition, Adam Phillips, "Learning to Live: Psychoanalysis as Education," in *Side Effects* (New York: Harper Perennial, 2006), 147. That repetitive, instructional forms recur in Spark's fiction does not mean that they structure these novels, which feature without enacting, or thematize without practicing, counter-progressive pedagogy.

77. Spark, *Prime of Miss Jean Brodie*, 1.

78. Ibid., 21; Pater, *Plato and Platonism* (London: Macmillan, 1901), 198.

79. For an overview of this tradition, see Waquet, *Latin, or the Empire of a Sign*. Far from entailing uncritical adherence to norms, "tradition" can be seen not only to allow for but also to entail internal contradiction as well as the kind of boundary crossing that I allude to here. Giorgio Agamben has argued that a tradition betrays itself by definition; Agamben, "Tradition of the Immemorial," in *Potentialities: Collected Essays in Philosophy*, ed. and trans. Daniel Heller-Roazen (Stanford, Calif.: Stanford University Press, 1999), 104–15, especially 105. Talal Asad, in another context, refuses the claim "that traditions are essentially homogeneous" and maintains on the contrary that "widespread homogeneity is a function, not of tradition, but of the development and control of communication techniques that are part of modern industrial societies"; Asad, "The Idea of an Anthropology of Islam," *Qui Parle* 17, no. 2 (2009): 22. Sameness is thus wrongly attached to the past by a present that claims difference for itself alone, just as closure is ascribed to tradition by a modernity that pretends to monopolize openness.

80. See Spivak, "Rethinking Comparativism," in *An Aesthetic Education*, 474, which proposes that "we acknowledge as comparativist any attempt the text makes to go outside its space-time enclosure, the history and geography by which the text is determined."

81. Walter Benjamin, "On the Concept of History," trans. Harry Zohn in *Selected Writings*, vol. 4, *1938-1940*. ed. Howard Eiland and Michael W. Jennings (Cambridge, Mass.: Belknap, 2006), 395. For a more recent set of reflections on this sort of present, see Harry Harootunian, "Remembering the Historical Present," *Critical Inquiry* 33, no. 3 (2007): 490.

82. Pasolini, "Abiura dalla *Trilogia della vita*," 75. Here Pasolini worries "that Italy is on the whole a depoliticized country, a dead body whose reflexes are nothing but mechanical."

83. Edwin R. Wallace, *Freud and Anthropology: A History and Reappraisal* (New York: International Universities Press, 1983), 24–25.

84. This phrase recurs in Jean Laplanche, *Essays on Otherness*, ed. John Fletcher (New York: Routledge, 1999), e.g., on 74.

85. Pandolfo, *Knot of the Soul: Madness, Psychoanalysis, Islam* (Chicago: University of Chicago Press, 2018), 136.

86. Sigmund Freud, "Analytic Therapy," Lecture XXVIII, in *The Standard Edition of the Complete Works of Sigmund Freud: Introductory Lectures on Psycho-Analysis*, vol. 16, *1916–1917*, trans. and ed. James Strachey, with Anna Freud, Alix Strachey, and Alan Tyson (London: Hogarth, 1963), 451. Here importantly Freud associates both education and psychoanalysis with work: "The work of overcoming resistances is the essential function of analytic treatment; the patient has to accomplish it and the doctor makes this possible for him with the help of suggestion operating in an *educative* sense. For that reason, psychoanalytic treatment has justly been described as a kind of *after-education*." To be sure, Freud also famously defined teaching as impossible and took distance from actually existing pedagogies of various kinds. But on why the psychoanalytic "critique of pedagogy" does not follow from "a desire to do away with pedagogy altogether," see Shoshana Felman, "Psychoanalysis and Education: Teaching Terminable and Interminable," in *Jacques Lacan and the Adventure of Insight: Psychoanalysis in Contemporary Culture* (Cambridge, Mass.: Harvard University Press, 1987), 69–97.

87. On the provisionality of the transference, see, for instance, Sigmund Freud, "Remembering, Repeating, and Working Through (Further Recommendations on the Technique of Psycho-Analysis, II)," in *Standard Edition of the Complete Psychological Works of Sigmund Freud*, vol. 12, *1911–1913*, trans. and ed. James Strachey, with Anna Freud, Alix Strachey, and Alan Tyson (London: Hogarth, 1958), 154.

88. On the "adult" as opposed to the parent, see Laplanche, *New Foundations for Psychoanalysis*, trans. David Macey (Oxford: Basil Blackwell, 1989), 124. On the absconding of the adult, see Bernard Stiegler, *Taking Care of Youth and the Generations*, trans. Stephen Barker (Stanford, Calif.: Stanford University Press, 2010), and Massimo Recalcati, *L'ora di lezione: Per un'erotica dell'insegnamento* (Turin: Einaudi, 2014).

89. For recent and moving reflections on the role of resistance in psychoanalysis, see Comay, "Resistance and Repetition: Freud and Hegel," *Research in Phenomenology* 45, no. 2 (2015): 237–66. See also Jacques Derrida, "Resistances," in *Resistances of Psychoanalysis*, trans. Peggy Kamuf, Pascale-Anne Brault, and Michael Naas (Stanford, Calif.: Stanford University Press, 1998), and Jacqueline Rose, *The Last Resistance* (New York: Verso, 2007).

90. I borrow the phrase "scenes of teaching" from Spivak, "Ethics and Politics in Tagore, Coetzee, and Certain Scenes of Teaching," in *An Aesthetic Education*, 316–34. For

different reflections on the scene of teaching, see Jane Gallop, ed., *Pedagogy: The Question of Impersonation* (Bloomington: Indiana University Press, 1995). See also Recalcati's discussion of Pasolini's distinction between "scenographic" and "real" forms of regimentation in *L'ora di lezione*, 12; for the distinction in its original context, see Pasolini, "Fascista," ed. Massimo Fini, in *Scritti corsari* (Milan: Garzanti, 1977), 286.

91. Jacques Rancière, *The Ignorant Schoolmaster: Five Lessons in Intellectual Emancipation*, trans. Kristin Ross (Stanford, Calif.: Stanford University Press, 1991), 8, 9.

92. For key texts in queer theory that question linear progress, generationality, and other kinds of normative development, see Edelman, *No Future*; Heather Love, *Feeling Backward: Loss and the Politics of Queer History* (Cambridge, Mass.: Harvard University Press, 2007); and Elizabeth Freeman, *Time Binds: Queer Temporalities, Queer Histories* (Durham, N.C.: Duke University Press, 2010). For related but differently inflected refusals of developmental narrative within gay studies, see D. A. Miller, *Place for Us: Essay on the Broadway Musical* (Cambridge, Mass.: Harvard University Press, 1998), and Christopher Nealon, "Queer Tradition," *GLQ* 14, no. 4 (2008): 617–22.

93. Sigmund Freud, "Thoughts for the Times on War and Death," in *The Standard Edition of the Complete Psychological Works of Sigmund Freud*, vol. 14, *1914–1916*, trans. and ed. James Strachey, with Anna Freud, Alix Strachey, and Alan Tyson (London: Hogarth, 1957), 285.

94. Ibid., 286.

95. On the simultaneity of backward and forward movement in analysis, see Derrida, "Resistances," 19–20.

96. W. H. Auden, "In Memory of Sigmund Freud," in *Collected Poems*, ed. Edward Mendelson (New York: Vintage, 1991), 274.

97. Rancière, *Ignorant Schoolmaster*, 119. For a critique of Racière's text as both totalizing and "curiously innocent about the drive of assimilative power," see Nivedita Menon, "The University as Utopia: Critical Thinking and the Work of Social Transformation," *Critical Times* 2, no. 1 (2019): 85–105. See also Samir Haddad, "Shared Learning and The Ignorant Schoolmaster," *Philosophy of Education Yearbook 2015*: 175–82.

98. Ibid.; trans. modified.

99. Giacomo Leopardi, "La ginestra," in *Canti*, ed. Fernando Bandini (Milan: Garzanti, 2010), 309; emphasis in original.

100. Pasolini, *Gennariello*, in *Lettere luterane* (Turin: Einaudi, 1976), 27.

101. Gramsci, *QC* 2:1317.

102. William Wordsworth, "Nuns Fret Not at Their Convent's Narrow Room," in *The Major Works*, ed. Stephen Gill (Oxford: Oxford University Press, 2000), 286.

103. On capitalist presentism, see, for instance, Moishe Postone, *Time, Labor, and Social Domination: A Reinterpretation of Marx's Critical Theory* (Cambridge: Cambridge University Press, 1996), 299–300; Jonathan Crary, *24/7: Late Capitalism and the Ends of Sleep* (London: Verso, 2013), e.g., 19; Fredric Jameson, "The Aesthetics of Singularity," *New Left Review* 92 (2015): 101–32; Sianne Ngai, "Theory of the Gimmick," *Critical Inquiry* 43 (2017): 466–505. According to Enzo Traverso, "'Presentism' has a double dimension. On the one hand, it is the past reified by a culture industry that destroys all transmitted experience; on the other hand, it is the future abolished by the time of neoliberalism: . . . the dictatorship of the stock exchange, a time of permanent acceleration—borrowing the words of Koselleck—without a 'prognostic structure'"; Traverso, *Left-*

Wing Melancholia: Marxism, History, and Memory (New York: Columbia University Press, 2016), 8. (But on acceleration's impermanence and for a different reading of the present as impasse, see Benjamin Noys, "Stasis Today," in *Malign Velocities: Accelerationism and Capitalism* [London: Zero, 2014], 59–62.) Harry Harootunian relies on a less chronologically specific definition of presentism, associating it, for instance, with modernism's "progressive devaluation of the past and all that came before it," its desire, underwritten by capitalism, "to guarantee a definitive separation from the present's antecedents"; Harootunian, "Remembering the Historical Present," 488. The works that I discuss in *Old Schools* all reconsider this devaluation and this desire.

1. Surviving *Marius:* Pater's Mechanical Exercise

This chapter's epigraphs are taken from: Hugh of St. Victor, *Hugh of St. Victor on the Sacraments of the Christian Faith (De Sacramentis)*, trans. Roy J. Deferrari (Eugene, Ore.: Wipf and Stock, 2007), 157, 159; and Simone Weil, "Reflections on the Right Use of School Studies with a View to the Love of God," trans. Emma Craufurd, in *The Simone Weil Reader*, ed. George A. Panichas (New York: David McKay, 1977), 50.

1. All phrases in this sentence are taken from Walter Pater, *Studies in the History of the Renaissance*, ed. Matthew Beaumont (London: Oxford University Press, 2010), as follows: "To burn always ...," from the "Conclusion," 120; "She is older ...," from "Leonardo da Vinci" 70; "*All art* ...," from "The School of Giorgione," 124 (emphasis in original); "Failure is to form habits," from the "Conclusion," 120: "art for art's sake," from the "Conclusion," 121. Further citations from *The Renaissance* are given parenthetically in the text, using the abbreviation *R*.

2. First published in 1877, "The School of Giorgione" was included in the third edition of Pater's *The Renaissance* (1888). On the phrase "art for art's sake" as it first appears in Swinburne's *William Blake: A Critical Essay* (1868), see Beaumont's notes in *R* 179.

3. W. B. Yeats, Introduction to *The Oxford Book of Modern Verse, 1892–1935* (New York: Oxford University Press, 1936), v–xlii.

4. Pater, *Plato and Platonism* (London: Macmillan, 1901), 198. Further citations are given parenthetically in the text, using the abbreviation *PP*. Pater forswears "phraseworship" in "Style"; Pater, "Style," in *Appreciations, with an Essay on Style* (London: Macmillan, 1895), 26. Further citations are given parenthetically in the text, using the abbreviation *A*.

5. Pater, *Miscellaneous Studies: A Series of Essays* (London: Macmillan, 1895), 214–15. Further citations are given parenthetically in the text, using the abbreviation *MS*.

6. Quoted in Linda Dowling, "The Fatal Book," in *Language and Decadence in the Victorian Fin de Siècle* (Princeton: Princeton University Press, 1986), 133.

7. Pater, *Marius the Epicurean*, ed. Michael Levey (New York: Penguin, 1985), 137. Further citations are given parenthetically in the text, using the abbreviation *M*.

8. Webb Keane, *Christian Moderns: Freedom and Fetish in the Mission Encounter* (Berkeley: University of California Press, 2006), 6.

9. On the centrality of education in English liberalism, see, for instance, Uday Singh Mehta, *Liberalism and Empire: A Study in Nineteenth-Century British Liberal Thought* (Chicago: University of Chicago Press, 1999), e.g., 199.

10. John Stuart Mill, *Autobiography*, ed. John M. Robson (New York: Penguin, 1989), 44. Mill's *Autobiography* was first published in 1873.

11. Ibid., 44–45. For more on Pater and Mill, see Dowling, *The Vulgarization of Art: The Victorians and Aesthetic Democracy* (Charlottesville: University Press of Virginia, 1996), 79–80. Dowling shows that "Mill's electrifying sanction of both a rich and various individuality and a bold personal liberty against the crushing despotism of habit and the mass [sic] came to be incorporated in works barely mentioning his name," including Pater's *Renaissance* (79). This chapter focuses on the texts written after *The Renaissance*, in which habit becomes associated with something other than crushing despotism and bold personal liberty is no longer Pater's priority. In "'To Surrender Himself, in Perfect Liberal Inquiry': Walter Pater, Many-Sidedness, and the Conversion Novel," *Victorian Studies* 53, no. 2 (2011): 231–53, Sebastian Lecourt considers this same later phase in Pater's work but argues against reading his "turn to collectivity and tradition as a straightforward rejection of the liberal individualism with which Dowling associates him" (243). Although I agree that nothing in Pater's work is straightforward, my reading differs from Lecourt's in that I see Pater as countering, rather than merely amending, "liberal individualism." For his part, Benjamin Morgan argues that even in his early work Pater does not affirm individualism but rather "vigorously interrogates the foundations of individuality"; Morgan, "Aesthetic Freedom: Walter Pater and the Politics of Autonomy," *ELH* 77 (2010): 751.

12. Jean-Jacques Rousseau, *Émile, or On Education* trans. Allan Bloom (New York: Basic, 1979), 112.

13. Ibid., 117.

14. Giovanni Gentile, *La riforma dell'educazione: Discorsi ai maestri di Trieste* (Bari: Laterza, 1920), 167.

15. William F. Shuter writes, "Appearances to the contrary, 'Emerald Uthwart' was less a defense of a traditional mode of education against the threat of change than an effort to impose the patina of antiquity on a relatively recent educational innovation"; Shuter, *Rereading Walter Pater* (Cambridge: Cambridge University Press, 1997), 87. The innovation Shuter has in mind is Hellenization, and his reading of the story emphasizes its engagement with Greek sources. Shuter shows that such sources had not, in fact, long formed part of the curriculum in English public schools. My emphasis has been on the role of Latin, rather than Greek, in "Emerald Uthwart": a role whose importance Shuter understates, even while he notes that actually existing public schools centered on Latin instruction.

16. Giovanni Pascoli, *Prose*, ed. Augusto Vicinelli, vol. 1, *Pensieri di varia umanità* (Milan: Mondadori, 1946), 636; Joyce, *Ulysses*, 14.1245; Antonio Gramsci, *Quaderni del carcere*, ed. Valentino Gerratana (Turin: Einaudi, 2007), 3:1546.

17. Roland Barthes, *Roland Barthes by Roland Barthes*, trans. Richard Howard (New York: Hill and Wang, 2010), 67.

18. Ellis Hanson, "Pater Dolorosa," in *Decadence and Catholicism* (Cambridge, Mass.: Harvard University Press, 1997), 180. For biographical context on the other "crisis of 1874," a scandal involving the disclosure of a "homosexual romance" at Oxford, see Billie Andrew Inman, "Estrangement and Connection: Walter Pater, Benjamin Jowett, and

William M. Hardinge," in *Pater in the 1990s*, ed. Laurel Brake and Ian Small (Greensboro, N.C.: ELT, 1991), 1–20.

19. Jacques Khalip, "Pater's Sadness," *Raritan* 20, no. 2 (2000): 137.

20. See, for instance, Giles Whiteley's Conclusion, in *Aestheticism and the Philosophy of Death: Walter Pater and Post-Hegelianism* (London: LEGENDA, 2010), 148.

21. The *locus classicus* is T. S. Eliot's "Arnold and Pater," *Bookman* 72, no. 1 (1930): 1–7. But see also, for instance, Katie Hext, *Walter Pater: Individualism and Aesthetic Philosophy* (Edinburgh: Edinburgh University Press, 2013), 175, which attests to the continuing vitality of the "retreat hypothesis" (e.g., 185). On the liberal provenance of the claims made in Pater's "Conclusion" and throughout *Renaissance*, see Dowling, *Vulgarization of Art*, 75–89.

22. See Regenia Gagnier, "The Law of Progress and the Ironies of Individualism in the Nineteenth Century," *New Literary History* 31, no. 2 (2000): 326–30; Heather Love, "Walter Pater's Backward Modernism," in *Feeling Backward: Loss and the Politics of Queer History* (Cambridge, Mass.: Harvard University Press, 2007), 53–71; and Morgan, "Aesthetic Freedom."

23. Shuter, *Rereading Walter Pater*, 79.

24. For a recent reiteration of these charges, see Ruth Livesey, *Socialism, Sex, and the Culture of Aestheticism in Britain, 1880–1914* (Oxford: Oxford University Press, 2007), e.g., 28–29.

25. Shuter, *Rereading Walter Pater*, 79.

26. Matthew Kaiser, "Marius at Oxford: Paterian Pedagogy and the Ethics of Seduction," in *Walter Pater: Transparencies of Desire*, ed. Laurel Brake, Lesley Higgins, and Carolyn Williams (Greensboro, N.C.: ELT, 2002), 196.

27. For other readings of Pater as proto-gay, see Khalip, "Pater's Sadness," and Love, "Walter Pater's Backward Modernism."

28. For a more recent and explicit return to and revision of the "retreat hypothesis," see Rachel O'Connell, "Reparative Pater: Retreat, Ecstasy, and Reparation in the Writings of Walter Pater," *ELH* 82, no. 3 (2015): 969–86. This reading turns away from retreat defined as "capitulation, withdrawal, and defeat" in order to privilege "retreat as refuge and shelter, as a site of peace and calm, and as a space of one's own" (971). Yet O'Connell's compelling claim that Pater "interprets overwhelming disciplinary regimes as spaces of ecstasy" (971) already complicates the notion of "a space of one's own": if the regimes precede, and constitute the preconditions for, the spaces in which one takes distance from them, then the latter are not strictly separable from the former. This is what I undertake to show later in this chapter, in my reading of Pater's "reserve."

29. Yeats's reading remains continuous with those of Pater's contemporaries. After its first appearance Pater's book was seen either to pose a threat, in the opinion of detractors, or, for apologists, to merit praise precisely on account of its author's status as "master" or teacher. Favorably reviewing *The Renaissance* shortly after its publication in 1873, John Morley claimed, "It is assuredly good for us to possess such a school"—and this even if Pater's "doctrine" could matter only to an initiated few; Morley, "John Morley on Pater," in *Walter Pater: The Critical Heritage*, ed. R. M. Seiler (New York: Routledge, 1980), 70. Another reviewer countered that, like other apologists, Morley merely repeated "the gospel according to Mr Pater," and in this way made "an admi-

rable" but untrustworthy because altogether uncritical "Ali to Mr Pater's Mohammed"; See "Z: Modern Cyrenaicism, 'Examiner,'" in *Walter Pater: The Critical Heritage*, 75. Here, as the charge of Morley-Ali's adherence is meant to show, the heretic is also, just as importantly, the founder of an institutional religion. So, too, for Morley, the philosophical rebel was also the purveyor of a doctrine and the founder of a school.

30. Yeats, Introduction, viii.

31. Ibid.

32. This phrase tropes the famous claim made in Pater's "The School of Giorgione": "*All art constantly aspires towards the condition of music*" (R 124; emphasis in original).

33. Thomas Wright, *The Life of Walter Pater* (New York: G. P. Putnam's Sons, 1907), 2:112.

34. Edward Thomas, *Walter Pater: A Critical Study* (New York: Mitchell Kennerley, 1913), 213.

35. Raymond Williams, "Mechanical," in *Keywords: A Vocabulary of Culture and Society*, rev. ed. (New York: Oxford University Press, 1983), 202. Williams notes that the word "mechanical" "was earlier in English than *machine*," although after the mid-eighteenth century it becomes inseparable from the latter (201).

36. Quoted in Stefano Evangelista, "Rome and the Romantic Heritage in Walter Pater's *Marius the Epicurean*," in *Romans and Romantics*, ed. Timothy Saunders, Charles Martindale, Ralph Pite, and Mathilde Skoie (Oxford: Oxford University Press, 2012), 320. Evangelista reads *Marius* as continuous with, not critical of, Rousseau's foundational text.

37. Rousseau, *Émile*, trans. Allan Bloom, 112.

38. Mill, *Autobiography*, 45.

39. Alfred Tennyson, In Memoriam A. H. H., in *Selected Poems*, ed. Christopher Ricks (New York: Penguin, 2007), sect. V, vv. 1–8, p. 100.

40. *OED*, s. v. "exercise." In *Marius*, Pater again activates this sense of "exercise" indirectly: "He felt there ... the genius, the unique power of Christianity: in exercise then, as it has been exercised ever since" (M 235).

41. Here I am remembering the moment in Jacques Derrida, "Signature Event Context," trans. Alan Bass, in *Limited, Inc.*, ed. Gerald Graff (Evanston, Ill.: Northwestern University Press, 1977), 1–23, when Derrida refers to "a certain conventionality intrinsic to what constitutes the speech act itself." "'Ritual,'" Derrida goes on to claim, "is not a possible occurrence ... but rather, *as* iterability, a structural characteristic of every mark" (15). This claim resonates with the concerns of this chapter, which, however, follows Pater in finding some rituals more ritual than others.

42. And to the extent we have not, this is because the other side or doubled valence of the "mechanical" is, like the educative potential of ritual, already latent in "Winckelmann"—in other words, because that essay is more complicated than it has been taken to be, and not because *Marius* simply confirms our received sense of religion's opiate-administering simplicity; see, again, Dowling, *Vulgarization of Art*, 79.

43. I note that the "dark chambers" that here make up Marius's mind recall the prisons into which Pater dooms the individual subjects of his "Conclusion." I discuss these "solitary prisoners" and Pater's move away from this model of subjectivity in the last section of this chapter. Pater famously framed *Marius* as a sort of retraction of

his "Conclusion"—or rather as a substitute for his initial retraction, a second-order retraction that enabled him to restore his afterword after having suppressed it: "This brief 'Conclusion' was omitted in the second edition of this book, as I conceived it might possibly mislead some of those young men into whose hands it might fall. On the whole, I have thought it best to reprint it here [in the third edition].... I have dealt more fully in *Marius the Epicurean* with the thoughts suggested by it" (*R* 177). Importantly, *Marius* thus represents a processual working-through rather than a once-and-done recantation. Rather than beginning where the Pater of the "Conclusion" leaves off, Marius must retraverse various phases, including a phase called "hedonist" (*M* 119–20), before arriving at the broader understanding meant to signal his graduation from the solipsistic conclusions reached in *The Renaissance*.

44. See, for instance, Mill, *Autobiography*, 45.

45. Quoted in Shuter, *Rereading Walter Pater*, 80. For a study of the fate of the examination in Victorian literature and its broader role in British culture during the 1860s and 1870s, see Cathy Shuman, *Pedagogical Economies: The Examination and the Victorian Literary Man* (Stanford, Calif.: Stanford University Press, 2000). Shuman attends to the ambivalence of the exam as well as to its prevalence; drawing on the work of educational historians, she notes that the exam's effects were anything but straightforwardly democratizing: "The mid-nineteenth-century craze for exams ... owed much, of course, to the huge network of bourgeois campaigns to reform and rationalize British institutions, from Parliament to the Church of England. Support for examinations, however, by no means equaled support for democracy.... Historians of Victorian education agree that, for the most part, examinations legitimated older class and gender hierarchies, rather than transforming them" (10). Although undoubtedly "there is some link between the growing power of the middle class in mid-nineteenth-century British culture and the examination revolution," of which the reforms at Oxford were a part, "the extent and nature of this link" remains debatable: "Victorian educational reform was, after all, a thoroughly top-down phenomenon, which 'came from traditionally dominant classes—the landed gentry and aristocracy, assisted by the specific expertise of representatives of the professional groupings linked traditionally with these classes'" (220).

46. Shuter, *Rereading Walter Pater*, 82.

47. "Progress is such improvement as can be verified by statistics, just as education is such knowledge as can be tested by examinations": these definitions, offered by a zealous reformist in W. H. Mallock's satirical novel *The New Republic* (New York: Scribner, Welford, & Armstrong, 1878), 23, neatly attest to the exam's close association with progressive reform.

48. Compare the "magnificent retrieval of freedom just where one might least have thought to find it" in Douglas Mao's account of Pater's understanding of the aesthetic; Mao, *Fateful Beauty: Aesthetic Environments, Juvenile Development, and Literature, 1860–1960* (Princeton: Princeton University Press, 2008), 80.

49. Pater, Introduction, in *The Purgatory of Dante Alighieri (Purgatorio I-XXVII): An Experiment in Literal Verse Translation*, by Charles Lancelot Shadwell (London: Macmillan, 1892), xx.

50. Already in 1873, Morley wrote of Pater's "doctrine," favorably comparing it to

those of Newman and Ruskin on grounds that "it escapes their cramping narrowness"; see "John Morley on Pater," 70.

51. An emphasis on inwardness and affect characterizes many recent takes on Pater, including Khalip, "Pater's Sadness," 137, and Love, "Walter Pater's Backward Modernism." Even while they stress feeling's susceptibility to various kinds of externalization, these readings ultimately privilege interiority in Paterian aesthetics. Without discounting Pater's everywhere apparent interest in forms of inwardness, I want to highlight another interest: an interest in the "machinelike exteriority, the outward turn, which is retained in the German word for learning by heart, *aus-wendig lernen*"; Paul de Man, "Sign and Symbol in Hegel's *Aesthetics*," *Critical Inquiry* 8, no. 4 (1982): 773.

52. Yeats, Introduction, ix.

53. On Shakespeare and his adapters, see Richard Halpern, "Hamletmachines," in *Shakespeare among the Moderns* (Ithaca, N.Y.: Cornell University Press, 1997), 227–88; on Blake and Wordsworth, see Steven Goldsmith, "Strange Pulse" and "Wordsworth's Pulsation Machine, or the Half-Life of Mary Hutchinson: Interlude on 'She was a Phantom of delight,'" in *Blake's Agitation: Criticism and the Emotions* (Baltimore: Johns Hopkins University Press, 2013), 226–67. Pater himself writes that Wordsworth "often works up mechanically through a poem" to "the few perfect lines, the phrase, the single word perhaps" that makes the poem worthwhile (*A* 41). Apropos of Tennyson's "sad mechanic exercise," Peter McDonald writes, "If 'mechanic' brings with it ideas of eighteenth-century regularity, these include the notion of poetry in the shadow of Pope, where couplets and diction alike were often held to work automatically"; McDonald, "Alfred Tennyson: Memory and Hope," in *Sound Intentions: The Workings of Rhyme in Nineteenth-Century Poetry* (Oxford: Oxford University Press, 2012), 170. Hugh Kenner's *The Counterfeiters: An Historical Comedy* (Garden City, N.Y.: Anchor, 1973) reads Pope and Swift as belonging to the same historical moment as Joyce, a moment defined by the rise of rationalism and the proliferation of all manner of simulating machines. On Yeats's mechanical bird, see Daniel Tiffany, *Toy Medium: Materialism and Modern Lyric* (Berkeley: University of California Press, 2000), 17–21.

54. Williams, "Mechanical," 202.

55. William Wordsworth, Preface, in *Lyrical Ballads, with Pastoral and Other Poems*, in *The Major Works*, ed. Stephen Gill (New York: Oxford University Press, 2008), 600, 604.

56. Susan Sontag, "On Style," in *Essays of the 1960s & 70s*, ed. David Rieff (New York: Library of America, 2013), 32.

57. According to Paul de Man, "There can be no use of language which is not, within a certain perspective[,] . . . radically formal, i.e., mechanical, no matter how deeply this aspect may be concealed by aesthetic, formalistic delusions"; de Man, "Excuses (*Confessions*)," in *Allegories of Reading: Figural Language in Rousseau, Nietzsche, Rilke, and Proust* (New Haven: Yale University Press, 1979), 294. For a recent instance, indebted to Derrida, see Forrest Pyle, "What the Zeros Taught: Emily Dickinson, Event-Machine," in *Art's Undoing: In the Wake of a Radical Aestheticism* (New York: Fordham University Press, 2014), 105–42.

58. Dowling, "The Fatal Book," 111.

59. Ibid., 125.

60. Quoted in Shuter, *Rereading Walter Pater*, 80.

61. Thomas Carlyle, *Sartor Resartus* (London: Ward Lock, 1910), 115–16.

62. Williams notes that "mechanical" comes to be opposed to "organic" only after having been nearly synonymous with it; Williams, "Mechanical," 202.

63. Pascoli, *Prose,* 641.

64. It would also echo in the colonies. On the colonial career of this distinction and the role of the critique of "cram" in the Indian context in particular, see Sanjay Seth, "Changing the Subject," in *Subject Lessons: The Western Education of Colonial India* (Durham, N.C.: Duke University Press, 2007), 17–45.

65. Sir James Kay-Shuttleworth, *Four Periods of Public Education: As Reviewed in 1832–1839–1846–1862* (London: Longman, Green, Longman, and Roberts, 1862), 320, 321.

66. Ibid., 321.

67. Ibid.

68. Richard Ellmann, *Oscar Wilde* (New York: Vintage, 1988), 52.

69. Thomas, *Walter Pater,* 213.

70. Robert Crawford, "Pater's *Renaissance,* Andrew Lang, and Anthropological Romanticism," *ELH* 53, no. 4 (1986): 873–74; Shuter, *Rereading Walter Pater,* 101–2; Lecourt, "'To Surrender Himself,'" 232, 236.

71. Dowling, "Walter Pater and Archaeology: The Reconciliation with Earth," *Victorian Studies* 31, no. 2 (1988): 215. For another discussion of the temporality of survivals, see Georges Didi-Huberman, "The Surviving Image: Aby Warburg and Tylorian Anthropology," *Oxford Art Journal* 25, no. 1 (2002): 59–70.

72. Edward B. Tylor, "Survival in Culture," in *Primitive Culture: Researches into the Development of Mythology, Philosophy, Art, and Custom* (London: John Murray, 1871), 1:63–64.

73. Ibid., 64-65.

74. Ibid., 64.

75. Ibid.

76. Ibid.

77. *OED,* s.v. "superstition."

78. *OED,* s.v. "super-."

79. On the place of uprightness, or "ascent," in the discourses of both liberalism and imperialism and for an account of an alternative ethos of unheroic sacrifice and abjection, see Leela Gandhi, *The Common Cause: Postcolonial Ethics and the Practice of Democracy, 1900–1955* (Chicago: University of Chicago Press, 2014).

80. See Levey, Introduction to Pater, *Marius the Epicurean,* 23. See also Michael Tondre, "The Impassive Novel: 'Brain-Building' in Walter Pater's *Marius the Epicurean,*" *PMLA* 133, no. 2 (2018): 329–46.

81. Matthew Potolsky emphasizes the role of "sway" in *Marius,* especially in the episodes involving Flavian, Marius's teacher, whose "charismatic pedagogy" Potolsky takes to counter that of the novel itself; see Potolsky, "Fear of Falling: Walter Pater's *Marius the Epicurean* as a Dangerous Influence," *ELH* 65, no. 3 (1998): 707. I borrow the apt phrase "relentlessly circuitous" from Tondre, "The Impassive Novel," 337.

82. Potolsky notes another way in which Pater seems to negate his protagonist's advancement: "Despite [Marius's] renunciation of Flavian's aestheticism, and despite his movement at the end of the novel toward an acceptance of Christianity, he dies of the very plague—'broken out afresh' at his return home . . . —that killed his former teacher.

Marius's intellectual development seems, in this respect, but an extended incubation period for the germ planted by Flavian's teaching"; Potolsky, "Fear of Falling," 716.

83. Hanson, "Pater Dolorosa," 179. For an account of the complex relationship to Victorian discourses of masculinity that also addresses "aestheticism as ritual" in a different sense, see James Eli Adams, "Gentleman, Dandy, Priest: Masks and Masculinity in Pater's Aestheticism," in *Dandies and Desert Saints: Styles of Victorian Masculinity* (Ithaca, N.Y.: Cornell University Press, 1995), 183–232.

84. Lecourt calls this Pater's "anthropological turn" in Pater's work, in "'To Surrender Himself,'" 147.

85. Talal Asad, "Toward a Genealogy of the Concept of Ritual," in *Genealogies of Religion: Discipline and Reasons of Power in Christianity and Islam* (Baltimore: Johns Hopkins University Press, 1993), 58; see also Saba Mahmood, *Politics of Piety: The Islamic Revival and the Feminist Subject* (Princeton: Princeton University Press, 2005), xiii–xv.

86. Keane, *Christian Moderns*, 6 *et passim*. See also Seth, "Changing the Subject," 28.

87. Keane, *Christian Moderns*, 6, 176. In *Feminist Aesthetics and the Politics of Modernism* (New York: Columbia University Press, 2012), Ewa Płonowska Ziarek offers a differently inflected account of the fate of materiality under the pressure of what she calls "political formalism," or "the violent abstraction of commodity form and citizenship" (184). Ziarek also considers efforts to reclaim "damaged materialities" in modernism. Eyal Amiran reads the modernist desire for a "pure materiality of language" in *Modernism and the Materiality of Texts* (Cambridge: Cambridge University Press, 2016). For Amiran, such materiality, prior to both signification and motivation, importantly "never materializes" (1). But the search for it forms part of modernism's broader "project to register the transition from universalism to contingency," where the acknowledgment of contingency undermines the claims of "the abstract subject" (x). Pater's work can be considered modernist not least because it participates in this acknowledgment and this undermining.

88. Keane, *Christian Moderns*, 76.

89. Carlyle, *Sartor Resartus*, 115–16. Kay-Shuttleworth makes the connection between the valorization of inward faith and the work of educational reform more explicit. To rely on "rote teaching," he writes, is "to undermine the basis of an unwavering faith in revelation, by provoking the rebellion of the human spirit against authority in matters in which reason is free"; Kay-Shuttleworth, *Four Periods in Public Education*, 320.

90. See also Morgan, "Aesthetic Freedom," e.g., 739, 748.

91. This is Carolyn Williams's claim in "Historical Novelty and *Marius the Epicurean*," in *Transfigured World: Walter Pater's Aesthetic Historicism* (Ithaca, N.Y.: Cornell University Press, 1989), 204.

92. Pater, "English Literature: Four Books for Students of English Literature," in *Essays from "The Guardian"* (London: Macmillan, 1901), 115.

93. On equivalence in Pater, see Sigi Jöttkandt, "Effectively Equivalent: Walter Pater, 'Sebastian von Storck,' and the Ethics of Metaphor," *Nineteenth Century Literature* 60, no. 2 (2005): 193–97.

94. Carlyle, Sartor Resartus, 115; Kay-Shuttleworth, *Four Periods of Public Education, 321*.

95. Seth, "Changing the Subject," 36.

96. For Asad, the doctrine of survivals serves as an example of Protestant-inspired "decoding," or recasting ritual as a matter of symbol rather than social practice; Asad,

"Toward a Genealogy of the Concept of Ritual," 59. My reading exempts Pater from this charge, since it attends precisely to his investment in religion as practice.

97. Roland Barthes, *Camera Lucida: Reflections on Photography*, trans. Richard Howard (New York: Hill and Wang, 1981), 8–9.

98. Barthes, *How to Live Together: Novelistic Simulations of Some Everyday Spaces; Notes for a Lecture Course and Seminar at the Collège de France (1976–1977)*, ed. Claude Coste, trans. Kate Briggs (New York: Columbia University Press, 2013), 130.

99. Ibid., 131.

100. Ibid., 133.

101. Ibid.

102. Ibid.

103. Ibid.

104. Ibid., 119.

105. Ibid., 132.

106. Danielle Allen, "Plato's Paradigm Shifts," in *The World of Prometheus: The Politics of Punishing in Democratic Athens* (Princeton: Princeton University Press, 2002), 280.

107. Barthes, *How to Live Together*, 9.

108. Ibid.

109. See, again, Dowling, *Vulgarization of Art*, 75–89.

110. *OED*, s. v. "keep."

111. Barthes, *How to Live Together*, 131.

112. Quoted in Dowling, "The Fatal Book," 133.

113. This reserve is, incidentally, like the reprieve from determination that I located earlier, elsewhere in "Lacedaemon," in that it, too, affords relief from a repetitive system of education but also turns out to be made possible by this same system. For another reading of reserve in Pater, see Adams, "Gentleman, Dandy, Priest," e.g., 189, 196.

114. Laplanche, *Essays on Otherness*, ed. John Fletcher (New York: Routledge, 1999), e.g., 74.

115. Compare Pater's citation, in "Style," of this moment in Flaubert's correspondence: "I am reading over again the Æneid, certain verses of which I repeat to myself to satiety. There are phrases there which stay in one's head, by which I find myself beset, as with those musical airs which are for ever returning, and cause you pain, you love them so much" (*A* 28–29).

2. Among *Fanciulli*: Poetry, Pedantry, and Pascoli's *Paedagogium*

This chapter's epigraph is taken from *Il fanciullino*, in *Prose*, ed. Augusto Vicinelli, vol. 1, *Pensieri di varia umanità* (Milan: Mondadori, 1946), 17.

1. Already in 1920, Benedetto Croce worried about the damage that would be done by the introduction of Pascoli's work (the carrier, Croce thought, of the worst of "our sicknesses and our vices") into Italian school curricula; see Croce, *Giovanni Pascoli: Studio critico* (Bari: Laterza, 1920), 107. By 1959, however, the proud schoolteacher and Pascoli partisan Lylia Loce-Mandes could declare the battle won: "Now Pascoli's poems have happily entered our schools and everyone can see that the end of the world that the philosopher feared did not come about, and would that nothing less elevated

and less poetic would appear in our scholastic texts than Pascoli's poems!"; Lylia Loce-Mandes, *Pascoli educatore* (Rome: Ciranna, 1959), 118.

2. The word *fanciullino* is a diminutive form of *fanciullo*, which derives from *fancello*, itself (*fan[ti]cello*) a diminutive form of *fante*. For a translation of the *fanciullino* as the (genderless) "little child," see Rosa Maria La Valva, *The Eternal Child: The Poetry and Poetics of Giovanni Pascoli* (Chapel Hill, N.C.: Annali d'italianistica, 1999). On the figure of the *puer aeternus* in Pascoli's work, see, for instance, Elio Gioanola, "Puer aeternus," in *Giovanni Pascoli: Sentimenti filiali di un parricida* (Milan: Jaca, 2000), 167–90. See also Croce's dismissal of Pascoli's art as encapsulated in the image of an "amplesso del *poeta ut puer* e del *puer ut poeta*"; Croce, *Giovanni Pascoli*, 69.

3. Pascoli, *Il fanciullino*, in *Prose*, 54; italics in original.

4. Gianfranco Contini begins his essay "Il linguaggio di Pascoli" this way: "All of my listeners know the work of Giovanni Pascoli by heart [*a memoria*]"; see Contini, "Il linguaggio di Pascoli," in *Poesie*, by Giovanni Pascoli (Milan: Mondadori, 1969), 1:lxii.

5. For Lacan, the cry "already constitutes" a demand, and the demand by definition "bears on something other than the satisfactions it calls for," which is to say that it is both in excess of need and strictly unsatisfiable; see Jacques Lacan, "The Signification of the Phallus," in *Écrits: The First Complete Edition in English,* trans. Bruce Fink, with Héloïse Fink and Russell Grigg (New York: Norton: 2006), 580. Although the (Latinate) word *vagito* appears nowhere in Leopardi's *Zibaldone*, in passages like the following the poet attends to the comparable *pianto*, which signals that infancy is anything but adequate to the world in *Il fanciullino*'s sense: "Thus as soon as the baby is born, it happens that the mother at the moment of placing him in the world, consoles him, quiets his crying, and lightens the weight of the existence that she has given him. And one of the chief duties of good parents during the infancy and early youth of their children is that of consoling them, of encouraging them to live, since the pains and ills and passions they suffer are, during those years, much more serious than those which long experience, or just a long time alive, assuages. And in truth it happens that the good father and the good mother, seeking to console their children, must make amends as best they can and lighten the damage that they have done by procreating"; Giacomo Leopardi, *Zibaldone di pensieri*, ed. Anna Maria Moroni (Milan: Mondadori, 1972), 2:805.

6. Pascoli, *Poesie*, 1:170.

7. *Il fanciullino* disparages the Italian poetic tradition, beginning with Dante, for lovesickness, among other faults.

8. Here I am implicitly countering the surprisingly still-influential account according to which Pascoli was, after his father's assassination, unable to sustain intimacy of any kind except with his sisters, to whom he therefore clung with incestuous persistence; see Adolfo Agostini, *La psicosessualità di Giovanni Pascoli* (Saluzzo: Minerva Medica, 1962). For more recent (and only slightly less pathologizing) versions of this account, see Gioanola, *Giovanni Pascoli*, and Carlo Di Lieto, *Il romanzo familiare del Pascoli: Delitto, 'passione,' e delirio (il vero volto di un grande, sventurato poeta)* (Naples: Guida, 2008). And for a critique of the tendency to emphasize Pascoli's "family romance," see Maria Truglio, *Beyond the Family Romance: The Legend of Pascoli* (Toronto: University of Toronto Press, 2007).

9. According to Truglio, Pascoli's "turn to Latin . . . reveals an agenda quite opposite to that of an alienating elitism. Linked to the retrieval of infancy, it is, paradoxically,

another version of pre-grammaticality. . . . Pascoli's linguistic use of Latin and thematic turn to the classics become, then, not an exercise [*sic*] in erudition but ways in which he effects a turn backwards"; Truglio, *Beyond the Family Romance*, 63 (emphasis added). I follow Truglio in emphasizing backward turns but am less sure than she is that the poet's Latin texts are not so many exercises.

10. On the *fanciullino*'s ambivalent status, see ibid., 116; and for a reading of Pascoli's figure as dead—also a reading that emphasizes writing rather than speech—see Giorgio Agamben, "Pascoli e il pensiero della voce," in *Categorie italiane: Studi di poetica e di letteratura* (Bari: Laterza, 2011); "Pascoli and the Thought of the Voice," in *The End of the Poem*, trans. Daniel Heller-Roazen (Stanford, Calif.: Stanford University Press, 1999), 62–75. Further citations from Agamben's essay are given parenthetically in the text, with the abbreviation *CI* pointing to *Categorie italiane* and *EP* to *The End of the Poem*.

11. Although Loce-Mandes's *Pascoli educatore* helpfully gathers quotations from the poet's editorials on education and anthologies for schoolteachers, the book does not offer a sustained reading of the place of the school in the poet's work. Loce-Mandes's chapter on the *fanciullino*, moreover, both rehearses critical commonplaces and unaccountably—but, in my view, tellingly—sets the school aside.

12. My model here is John Guillory's reading of Gray's "Elegy Written in a Country Churchyard," in "Mute Inglorious Miltons: Gray, Wordsworth, and the Vernacular Canon," in *Cultural Capital: The Problem of Literary Canon Formation* (Chicago: University of Chicago Press, 1994), 85–133, which locates traces of the school in Gray's poem, while also asking what about the poem enabled it to "[establish] itself in the [modern] school system" (86). For another account of the process by which modern poetry has been "remade for consumption in the classroom," see Virginia Jackson, *Dickinson's Misery: A Theory of Lyric Reading* (Princeton: Princeton University Press, 2005); the phrase I have just quoted is from 262n32. And for another perspective on what this classroom "consumption" can mean, see Yopie Prins, "Swinburne's Sapphic Sublime," in *Victorian Sappho* (Princeton: Princeton University Press, 1999), 112–73; especially 121–40.

13. William Empson, *Some Versions of Pastoral* (New York: New Directions, 1974), 260. For a distillation of Wyndham Lewis's denunciation of the modernist "Child-cult" (to which Empson refers only in passing), see Lewis, "A Brief Account of the Child-Cult," in *Time and Western Man*, ed. Paul Edwards (Santa Rosa, Calif.: Black Sparrow, 1993), 51–52. This section's epigraph is taken from William Wordsworth, *The Prelude* (1805), in *The Major Works*, ed. Stephen Gill (New York: Oxford University Press, 2000), vv. 324–25, p. 442.

14. Empson, *Some Versions*, 260–61.

15. I refer here to the famous and even clichéd claim in Wordsworth's "My Heart Leaps Up When I Behold" that "The Child is the father of the man," and to one of many addresses to the infant "Seer blest" in the "Ode: Intimations of Immortality from Recollections of Early Childhood": "Thou best philosopher, who yet dost keep / Thy heritage"; Wordsworth, *Major Works*, 246, 300. On "loser sons," see Avital Ronell, *Loser Sons: Politics and Authority* (Champaign, Ill.: University of Illinois Press, 2012); and on Pascoli's relationship to Wordsworth, see Truglio, *Beyond the Family Romance*, 58–61.

16. Empson, *Some Versions*, 260.

17. Ibid., 268.

18. Truglio, *Beyond the Family Romance*, 65.

19. For one account that stresses Pascoli's relationship to tradition, see Pier Paulo Pasolini, "Pascoli," in *Passione e ideologia* (Milan: Garzanti, 1973), 267–75, which concludes that an "obsession" with the maintenance of the same wins out over various innovative "tendencies" in Pascoli's work.

20. This feature of Pascoli's reception is in keeping with a broader tendency in criticism and theory to value childhood—youth broadly defined, from infancy to adolescence—for its supposed capacity to disrupt or even destroy the claims of knowledge. See, for instance, Giorgio Agamben, *Infancy and History: The Destruction of Experience*, trans. Liz Heron (New York: Verso, 1993), 13–72; Geoff Gilbert, "Boys: Manufacturing Inefficiency," in *Before Modernism Was: Modern History and the Constituency of Writing* (New York: Palgrave Macmillan, 2004), 51–73; Ronell, *Loser Sons*, especially chapter 6, "On the Unrelenting Creepiness of Childhood: Lyotard, Kid-Tested"; and section II of Christopher Fynsk, *Infant Figures: The Death of the 'Infans' and Other Scenes of Origin* (Stanford, Calif.: Stanford University Press, 2000), 49–130, which centers on Maurice Blanchot's definition of the *infans* as "that in us which has not yet begun to speak and never will speak"; see Blanchot's *The Writing of the Disaster*, trans. Ann Smock (Lincoln: University of Nebraska Press, 1986), 67. To suggest that these texts participate in a latter-day version of child-cult is perhaps to go too far—but perhaps not. For these critical accounts all endow the child (again, variously defined, as *infans*, adolescent, or in between) with the power to save us from our adult selves or at least to curb those selves' cognitive pretensions. Unlike these accounts, I emphasize the fact that Pascoli's child *will* speak—and read. In this sense, my chapter's understanding of the child is closer to Kathryn Bond Stockton's in "The Smart Child Is the Masochistic Child: Pedagogy, Pedophilia, and the Pleasures of Harm," in *The Queer Child, or Growing Sideways in the Twentieth Century* (Durham, N.C.: Duke University Press, 2009), 61–88, although I address the sexuality of Pascoli's poetic children only indirectly. It matters, in my view, that Stockton's child is from the first a pupil, rather than a pure blank slate or an experience of originary infancy or ontological priority, or whatever else. I bracket the *locus classicus* in queer theory—Lee Edelman's *No Future: Queer Theory and the Death Drive* (Durham, N.C.: Duke University Press, 2004)—because I do not think that Pascoli's child functions as a figure for futurity in Edelman's sense. Instead, the *fanciullino* brings old news; as I have emphasized, he arrives from the past, always already *antichissimo*.

21. Pascoli, *Prose*, 636. Agamben slightly misquotes Pascoli here, and his translator follows him. I have restored Pascoli's wording by quoting from the text in the collected *Prose* and provided my own, more literal translation, while indicating where the quotation appears in Agamben's essay in both Italian and English.

22. "Origin" is a term of art for Agamben, who writes elsewhere of Proto-Indo-European: "It is an origin, but an origin that is not diachronically pushed back into the past; rather, it guarantees the synchronic coherence of the system"; Agamben, "Project for a Review," in *Infancy and History: The Destruction of Experience*, trans. Liz Heron (New York: Verso, 1993), 166.

23. Agamben, "Tradition of the Immemorial," in *Potentialities: Collected Essays in Philosophy*, ed. and trans. Daniel Heller-Roazen (Stanford, Calif.: Stanford University Press, 1999), 104.

24. Contini, "Il linguaggio di Pascoli," in Pascoli, *Poesie*, 1:lxix.

25. For a critique of "pure intention," see Jacques Derrida, *Voice and Phenomenon: Introduction to the Problem of the Sign in Husserl's Phenomenology*, trans. Leonard Lawler (Evanston, Ill.: Northwestern University Press, 2011), 29.

26. Derrida, "The Violence of the Letter," in *Of Grammatology*, trans. Gayatri Chakravorty Spivak (Baltimore: Johns Hopkins University Press, 1997), 127.

27. Martin Heidegger, "What Are Poets For?" in *Poetry, Language, Thought*, trans. Albert Hofstadter (New York: Harper & Row, 2001), 137.

28. Although *Of Grammatology* is not typically read as concerned with concrete educational initiatives, it is worth noting that Derrida's critique of Claude Lévi-Strauss's "Writing Lesson" raises questions about the latter's implications for the ongoing "struggle against illiteracy" (132). Compare the way in which Derrida's discussion of dictation in "Che cos'è la poesia?" is in surprisingly close touch with the pedagogical practice of dictation, unlike Agamben's "Pascoli and the Thought of the Voice" and "The Dictation of Poetry," in *End of the Poem*, 76–86, both of which treat dictation as a matter for poet-philosophers; see Derrida, "Che cos'è la poesia?," trans. Peggy Kamuf, in *A Derrida Reader: Between the Blinds*, ed. Peggy Kamuf (New York: Columbia University Press, 1991), 221–37.

29. Pascoli, *Prose*, 636.

30. Suzanne Stewart-Steinberg, *The Pinocchio Effect: On Making Italians, 1860–1920* (Chicago: University of Chicago Press, 2007). Citations are given parenthetically in the text, using the abbreviation PE. I rely heavily on Stewart-Steinberg's study, although she focuses on the progressives' initiatives in all their variety rather than on the classical school as such. For broader context and an account that centers on the latter, see Gaetano Bonetta and Gigliola Fioravanti, eds., *L'istruzione classica (1860–1910)* (Rome: Ministero per i beni culturali e ambientali, Ufficio centrale per i beni archivistici, 1995), especially Bonetta's introductory essay, "L'istruzione classica nell'Italia liberale," 17–94, which I cite hereafter parenthetically, using the abbreviation IC. This section's epigraph is taken from "L'unità della scuola media e la libertà degli studi," in *Opere complete di Giovanni Gentile*, ed. Hervé A. Cavallera, vol. 40, *La nuova scuola media* (Florence: Casa Editrice Le Lettere, 1988), 1–39.

31. Antonio Gramsci, *Selections from Prison Notebooks*, ed. and trans. Quinton Hoare and Geoffrey Nowell Smith (New York: International, 1971), 350.

32. Giovanni Gentile, *La riforma dell'educazione: Discorsi ai maestri di Trieste* (Bari: Laterza, 1920), 186.

33. I quote from Hoare and Nowell Smith's introduction to the educational writings collected in Gramsci, *Prison Notebooks*, 24.

34. V. E. Orlando's slightly later "La riforma della scuola classica," *Nuova Antologia* 119 (September–October 1905): 635.

35. Ibid., 634.

36. Ibid., 635.

37. Ibid., 633.

38. Ibid., 631.

39. I quote from an advertisement for the journal published in the *Giornale della libreria, della tipografia, e delle arti ed industrie affini* 9 (1896): 424. Here Pascoli is listed among notable frequent contributors to the *Rassegna*.

40. Rather than refer to Pascoli's essay "Pensieri scolastici" in its original context of publication, *La rassegna scolastica* 2, no. 6 (December 16, 1896): 122–24, I cite from the more widely available volume: Pascoli, *Prose*, 636–44. It's worth noting, however, that the issue of *La rassegna* in which Pascoli's "Pensieri" first appeared distills the debates on education whose contours I have sketched: together with Pascoli's essay and another impassioned, backward-looking polemic by Gino Toscano, "Scuole normali e riforme . . . impossibili!," a much more sober text appears: "Appunti sulla Scuola primaria," by G. Giansiracusa (130–32). This latter essay expresses the kind of utilitarian views that Pascoli's "Pensieri scolastici" decries, indicating that the *Rassegna* made space for modernizing reformers as well as for their classicist opponents—in keeping with the journal's stated aim of becoming a "an open arena for every discussion" and a representative microcosm. See the mission statement in the journal's inaugural issue, "Il nostro programma," *La rassegna scolastica* 1, no. 1 (October 1, 1895): 1.

41. Pascoli's fears were to prove exaggerated, as is shown by the fact that instruction in Latin and Greek is still relatively widespread in Italian secondary schools today. See Maurizio Bettini, "I classici come enciclopedia culturale e come antenati: L'insegnamento del latino nella scuola superiore," *California Italian Studies* 2, no. 1 (2011), http://escholarship.org/uc/item/3ps870vk#page-1. See also Table 1 in Bonetta's Introduction to *L'istruzione classica*, 95, which shows that weekly hours devoted to Latin, having peaked in 1891, did not significantly decrease between 1894 and 1923, during which time even weekly hours dedicated to instruction in Greek remained steady.

42. Pascoli, *Prose*, 636.

43. Ibid.

44. Ibid., 637.

45. Ibid., 638.

46. Ibid., 641.

47. On the cliché as defense against catastrophe, see Anne Carson, "Variations on the Right to Remain Silent," *A Public Space* 7 (2008): 179–87.

48. The epigraph beginning this section is quoted in Orazio Aiello's Introduction to Giovanni Pascoli, *Paedagogium*, ed. Aiello (Palermo: Epos, 2001), 46.

49. Here I am relying on a distinction of Michael Silverstein's; see Silverstein, "How Knowledge Begets Communication Begets Knowledge: Textuality and Contextuality in Knowing and Learning," *Intercultural Communications Review* 5 (2006): 36.

50. Quoted in Loce-Mandes, *Pascoli educatore*, 69.

51. For background on the graffito, I have relied on *Graffiti del Palatino*, ed. Veikko Väänäen, in *Acta Instituti Romani Finlandiae* (Helsinki: Tilgmann, 1966), 3:209–12. See also the opening pages of Aiello, Introduction, *Paedagogium*. When quoting from this poem, I provide parenthetical citations, with line numbers, rather than page numbers, given to refer to the text of Pascoli's poem, following the abbreviation *P* for *Paedagogium*. On the indexicality of graffiti, see Rosalind Krauss, "The Latin Class," in *Perpetual Inventory* (Cambridge, Mass.: MIT Press, 2010), 193–203. Although the Alexamenos graffito does not possess all of the "characteristics" of graffiti identified by Krauss, her understanding of graffiti is useful not only for its emphasis on indexicality, but also for the way in which it reads the temporality of the graffitist's gesture: "Graffiti is a medium of marking which has precise, and unmistakable, characteristics. First, it is perfor-

mative; it suspends representation in favor of action: I mark you, I cancel you, I dirty you. Second, it is violent; always an invasion of a space that is not the maker's own, it takes illegitimate advantage of the surface of inscription, violating it, mauling it, scarring it. Third, *it converts the present tense of the performative into the past tense of the index*; it is the trace of an event, torn away from the present of the maker.... Even as the graphic lash of the graffiti strikes in the present, it registers itself as past" (200–201; emphasis added).

52. Aiello, Introduction, *P* 21.
53. Quoted in Ibid.
54. Ibid., 22.
55. I cite from Charlton T. Lewis and Charles Short's *A Latin Dictionary,* http://www.perseus.tufts.edu/hopper/text?doc=Perseus%3Atext%3A1999.04.0059%3Aentry%3Dpaedagogium. The phrase *delicati pueri,* taken from another dictionary, appears in Aiello's note on *Paedagogium*'s first line (127). Intriguingly, an essay calling for the creation of an institution to be called a *Paedagogium* had appeared in the same issue of *La rassegna scolastica* in which Pascoli's "Pensieri scolastici" was first published. In this essay, "Scuole normali e riforme... impossibili!," Gino Toscano opposes the then-current configuration of higher education for women, arguing for a two-tiered alternative, in which the *Paedagogium* would be reserved for the best students. Defining this elite institution, Toscano writes, "The name and the aim say it all. Theoretical and practical Pedagogy should form the basis of all teaching: *the art of schooling* should be the aim kept constantly in view"; Toscano, "Scuole normali e riforme... impossibili!," *La rassegna scolastica* 2, no. 6 (December 16, 1896): 130; emphasis in original. I cite this moment in Toscano's text not to suggest that it influenced Pascoli directly (though it seems likely that the latter would have come across the proposed *Paedagogium*), but in order to highlight the contrast between Toscano's proposal and Pascoli's return to an earlier version of the *paedagogium*. That Pascoli's school is not, as its name might at first suggest, a college for the training of teachers perhaps prompts readers to stop to think.
56. Quoted in Aiello, Introduction, *P* 24.
57. Virgil, *The Aeneid,* VI.851–53; emphasis added; trans. Robert Fitzgerald (New York: Vintage Classics, 1990), 190.
58. Pascoli's pedantry colors all of *Paedagogium,* but it becomes particularly obvious when the poem's schoolboys argue not over this or that game or toy or bond of friendship or enmity, but over who has the best Greek. These boys are, it becomes clear, pedants in the making; see lines 46–51.
59. Empson, *Some Versions,* 260.
60. Ibid., 260–61.
61. Quoted in Loce-Mandes, *Pascoli educatore,* 66.
62. Aiello emphasizes the importance of this citation but does not note its proximity to the verses that Alexamenos recites earlier in the poem.
63. The epigraph beginning this section is taken from Pascoli, *Il fanciullino,* in *Prose,* 17.
64. Barbara Spackman, "Fascist Puerility," *Qui Parle* 13, no. 1 (2001): 13–28.
65. Gentile, *La riforma,* 168.
66. Pascoli, *Prose,* 138.
67. Ibid.
68. Ibid., 144.

69. Ibid., 641.

70. Marco Berlanda argues that this text by Gentile lays the foundation for the philosopher's "later and [more] famous polemics" as well as for the 1923 Reform, in Berlanda, *Gentile e l'ipoteca kantiana: Linee di formazione del primo attualismo (1893–1912)* (Milan: Vita e Pensiero, 2007), 132.

71. Orlando, "La riforma della scuola classica," 631.

72. Gentile, *La riforma*, 186.

73. Gentile, "L'unità della scuola," 23.

74. Ibid., 24–25.

75. Ibid., 28.

76. Pascoli, *Prose*, 148.

77. Here I would underscore the especially vexed status of the "national language" in the Italian context, where the *questione della lingua* would remain embattled until well after 1902. For a later dispatch from this front, see Pasolini's 1964 essay "Nuove questioni linguistiche," which begins by declaring a fact Pasolini takes to be "well known": "*In Italy a true and proper national language does not exist*"; Pasolini, *Empirismo eretico* (Milan: Garzanti, 1977), 5; emphasis in original.

78. A progress narrative is implicit throughout Gentile's essay "L'unità della scuola," and explicit at times as well, as when he defines "the life of man" as "a continual and progressive forming of the spirit" (22). For the relevant moment in Hegel's *Phenomenology of Spirit*, trans. A.V. Miller (New York: Oxford University Press, 1977), see Paragraphs 194 and 195 in "Independence and Dependence of Self-Consciousness: Lordship and Bondage." And for Hegel's more complex take on instruction in ancient languages, see his "On Classical Studies," trans. Richard Kroner, in *Early Theological Writings* (Philadelphia: University of Pennsylvania Press, 1971), 321–30.

79. In later and more openly political works, Pascoli advanced nationalist and even imperialist projects and produced progressive slogans to support these. See especially "La grande proletaria si è mossa," whose jingoistic progressivism might indeed seem to undermine my construction of Pascoli as a key figure in the counter-progressive pedagogical canon. But I would argue—returning to but also retooling Gentile's claim that the becoming being is not annulled in the being that it becomes—that there is no more need to take "La grande proletaria" as emblematic of Pascoli's poetics as a whole than there is to conclude on the basis of an anomalously progressive text like *The Future of an Illusion* that Freudian psychoanalysis is anti-counter-progressive; see Pascoli, "La grande proletaria si è mossa," in *Prose*, 557–68, and Sigmund Freud, *The Future of An Illusion*, in *The Standard Edition of the Complete Psychological Works of Sigmund Freud*, vol. 21, *1927–1931*, trans. and ed. James Strachey, with Anna Freud, Alix Strachey, and Alan Tyson (London: Hogarth, 1961), 5–56. Here again, I am distinguishing my version of Pascoli from Truglio's; for a reading of the poet's late essay "L'era nuova" alongside *The Future of an Illusion* that aligns the latter text with the former, and with Pascoli's project more generally, see Truglio, *Beyond the Family Romance*, Chapter 5, "Remembering the Golden Age," 135–58.

80. Pascoli, *Prose*, 144.

81. Ibid., 641.

82. Here D.W. Winnicott's distinction in "The Use of an Object and Relating

through Identifications," in *Playing and Reality* (New York: Routledge, 2005), 115–27, between relating and use, can help to clarify the difference between Gentile's vision of the school and Pascoli's. Gentile *relates* to Latin in Winnicott's sense, whereas Pascoli *uses* Latin. According to Winnicott, relating is primarily projective, whereas use can only take place after the object has become "real in the sense of being part of shared reality, not a bundle of projections" (118). Pascoli's Latin, to be sure, is not without projective elements. Commentators note, for instance, that the imperial *paedagogium* is unmistakably modeled on the poet's own boarding school (Aiello, Introduction, *P* 37). But Pascoli's insistence on the deadness of the ancient language also represents a way of staying in touch with what Winnicott calls "shared reality," a space that is not the subject's alone. Gentile's repeated assertions of Latin's aliveness, on the other hand, when read with Winnicott, start to sound a lot like attempts to avoid the "perception of the object as an external phenomenon, not as a projective entity" (Winnicott, "Use of an Object," 120). Inasmuch as Gentile takes Latin's survival to be already assured in and through Italian, he wards off the recognition of the fact that, in Winnicott's words, "there may or may not be survival" (121). Pascoli's account in "Pensieri scolastici," by contrast, takes this fact as its point of departure.

83. Walter Benjamin, "Paralipomena to 'On the Concept of History,'" trans. Edmund Jephcott and Howard Eiland, in *Selected Writings,* vol. 4, *1938–1940*, ed. Howard Eiland and Michael W. Jennings (Cambridge, Mass.: Harvard University Press, 2003), 401.

84. Ibid.

85. Rebecca Comay, "Benjamin's Endgame," in *Walter Benjamin's Philosophy*, ed. Andrew Benjamin and Peter Osborne (New York: Routledge, 1994), 266.

86. On the "tradition of the oppressed," see Walter Benjamin, "On the Concept of History," trans. Harry Zohn, in *Selected Writings*, vol. 4, *1938–1940*, ed. Howard Eiland and Michael W. Jennings (Cambridge, Mass.: Belknap, 2006), 392.

87. *Paedagogium* won the Amsterdam-based Certamen Hoefftianum in 1903.

88. Walter Benjamin, *The Arcades Project*, trans. Howard Eiland and Kevin McLaughlin (Cambridge, Mass.: Harvard University Press, 1999), 846; *Das Passagen-Werk*, in *Gesammelte Schriften*, ed. Rolf Tiedemann. (Frankfurt: Suhrkamp Verlag, 1982), 5:1015.

89. Giacomo Leopardi, *Pensieri* (Milan: Garzanti, 1985), 11.

90. Ibid., 11–12; emphasis added

91. "Obsessed" is W. S. Di Piero's translation of Leopardi's "studiosissimi"; see Leopardi, *Pensieri*, trans. W. S. Di Piero (Baton Rouge: Louisiana State University Press, 1981), 47.

92. Here I am referring back to my readings of two moments in the poem: (1) its conclusion, which has Kareius take Alexamenos by the hand, and which I also read as marking *the poem's own* approach to and alliance with Alexamenos, whose affinity for reciting verses has been apparent from the start; (2) *vv.* 104–5, where I earlier located the return of the past in and through Kaireus's doing tenses. (*Quidquid*, which I previously translated as "whatever," opens *v.* 104.) On the implications of *Paedagogium*'s landing on the fraternal bond between the two boys, see Aiello's Introduction, which charts a movement from *puer* to *frater* in the poem (*P* 35). Aiello also synthesizes other critical responses to *Paedagogium*'s figuration of fraternity, including Francesco Biondolillo's argument that fraternity has a specifically national valence for Pascoli, taking the

place of, and papering over, more partisan class struggle in the poet's scheme of values (*P* 33–34).

93. Pascoli, *Prose*, 636.
94. Cf. Aiello, Introduction, *P* 37.
95. Pascoli, *Prose*, 148.
96. Benjamin, "On the Concept of History," 391.
97. Franco Moretti, *The Way of the World: The* Bildungsroman *in European Culture*, trans. Alberto Sbragia (New York: Verso, 2000), 227; trans. modified, emphasis in original; *Il romanzo di formazione* (Turin: Einaudi, 1999), 254.
98. Moretti, *Way of the World*, 230.
99. Ibid., 233.

3. "Copied Out Big": Instruction in Joyce's *Ulysses*

1. James Joyce, "The Holy Office," in *The Poems in Verse and Prose*, ed. A. Norman Jeffares and Brendan Kennelly (London: Kyle Cathie, 1992), 44.
2. Oliver St. John Gogarty, *As I Was Going down Sackville Street* (New York: Reynal and Hitchcock, 1937), 295; quoted in Theodore Spencer's Introduction to Joyce, *Stephen Hero*, ed. Theodore Spencer (New York: New Directions, 1963), 16.
3. Jeri Johnson, Introduction to Joyce, *Dubliners*, ed. Jeri Johnson (New York: Oxford University Press, 2000), xiv.
4. "Nestor" and "Ithaca" are, according to the Linati Schema, catechisms personal and impersonal, respectively.
5. Richard Ellmann, *James Joyce* (Oxford: Oxford University Press, 1982), 521.
6. Virginia Woolf, *A Writer's Diary, Being Extracts from the Diary of Virginia Woolf*, ed. Leonard Woolf (New York: Harcourt, 1954), 48.
7. Daniel Mendelsohn, in Juliet Lapidos, "Overrated," *Slate (*August 11, 2011), http://www.slate.com/articles/arts/culturebox/2011/08/overrated.3.html. The quotations in my next paragraph are also taken from this source; the emphases in both quotations are in the original.
8. On *Ulysses*' desertion of its reader, see Hugh Kenner, *Joyce's Voices* (Berkeley: University of California Press, 1978), xii.
9. Here and throughout, I cite from Joyce, *Ulysses: The Corrected Text*, ed. Hans Walter Gabler, with Wolfhard Steppe and Claus Melchior (New York: Vintage, 1986), providing episode and line numbers after the abbreviation *U*.
10. For a counterargument that finds in Joyce confirmation of the value of being self-taught, see Patrick McGee, "Joyce's Pedagogy: *Ulysses* and *Finnegans Wake*," in *Coping with Joyce: Essays from the Copenhagen Symposium*, ed. Morris Beja and Shari Benstock (Athens: Ohio University Press, 1989), 206–19.
11. "The Reader Critic: The World Moves (from the *London Times*)," *Little Review* 7, no. 3 (1920): 93–94.
12. Ibid.
13. Harry Blamires, *The New Bloomsday Book: A Guide Through* Ulysses, 3rd ed. (New York: Routledge 1996), 146.
14. Ibid., 147.

15. Ellman, *James Joyce*, 475.

16. On the tradition that betrays itself by definition, see Giorgio Agamben, "Tradition of the Immemorial," in *Potentialities: Collected Essays in Philosophy*, ed. and trans. Daniel Heller-Roazen (Stanford, Calif.: Stanford University Press, 1999), especially 105.

17. On "*chrononormativity*, or the use of time to organize individual human bodies toward maximum productivity," see Elizabeth Freeman, *Time Binds: Queer Temporalities, Queer Histories* (Durham, N.C.: Duke University Press, 2010), 3 et passim; and on "reproductive futurism," see Lee Edelman's *No Future: Queer Theory and the Death Drive* (Durham, N.C.: Duke University Press, 2004).

18. For a different reading of the opening paragraphs of "Oxen," see Andrew Gibson, "An Irish Bull in an English China Shop: 'Oxen of the Sun,'" in *Joyce's Revenge: History, Politics, and Aesthetics in "Ulysses"* (New York: Oxford University Press, 2002), especially 150–62. Gibson reads the episode in light of English and Irish economic discourses and argues that in its first moments "Oxen" "proposes an increase in population as part of a drive away from the trauma of the Famine and its aftermath" (161), because against this backdrop, "in a famine-stricken or post-Famine Ireland, the central issue was a population decline presented as so drastic as to spell the end of a people" (158). This implies a differential handling of Irish and English claims to national "continuance," as well as a determination, on Joyce's part, to model "an Irish discourse [that has become] so self-confident that it can afford not to take itself very seriously at all" (162). I would claim instead that, as Joyce knew and "Oxen" illustrates, such an "Irish discourse" is no longer properly "itself." Likewise, whereas Gibson concludes that the episode "is far less concerned to traduce Irish than English traditions" (171), I would underscore its effort to make traduction into a general principle, one that crosses the traditions that it betrays.

19. Joyce, *A Portrait of the Artist as a Young Man*, ed. Jeri Johnson (New York: Oxford University Press, 1994), 194.

20. Joan Copjec, *Read My Desire: Lacan Against the Historicists* (Cambridge, Mass.: MIT Press, 1996), 58.

21. Joyce, *Portrait*, 75.

22. Barry McCrea, *In the Company of Strangers: Family and Narrative in Dickens, Conan Doyle, Joyce, and Proust* (New York: Columbia University Press, 2011), 113.

23. Ibid., 142.

24. *OED*, s. v. "catechism."

25. Elizabeth Switaj offers a reading of what she compellingly calls "The Pedagogical *Ulysses*" along these lines; see Switaj, *James Joyce's Teaching Life and Methods: Language and Pedagogy in "A Portrait of the Artist as a Young Man," "Ulysses," and "Finnegans Wake"* (New York: Palgrave, 2016), 75–113.

26. For a critique of queer repudiations of kinship, see Elizabeth Povinelli, *The Empire of Love: Toward a Theory of Intimacy, Genealogy, and Carnality* (Durham, N.C.: Duke University Press, 2006).

27. Ellmann, *James Joyce*, 475.

28. Leo Bersani, "Against *Ulysses*," in *The Culture of Redemption* (Cambridge, Mass.: Harvard University Press, 1990), 169.

29. Ibid., 172.

30. See, for instance, Leo Bersani and Ulysse Dutoit, *Arts of Impoverishment* (Cambridge, Mass.: Harvard University Press, 1993).

31. On the meaningless . . . *as meaningless"* in *Ulysses*, see Franco Moretti, "*Ulysses* and the Twentieth Century," in *Modern Epic: The World System from Goethe to García Márquez*, trans. Quintin Hoare (New York: Verso, 1996), 163 (emphasis in original).

32. Bersani, "Against *Ulysses*," 172.

33. Switaj notes that in his language teaching Joyce eschewed "the focus on grammar and translation" that characterized more traditional approaches, preferring "conversational" methods and privileging speech over writing; Switaj, *James Joyce's Teaching Life and Methods,* 16. "Joyce's rejection of grammar-translation methods," Switaj concludes, "suggests a judgment on the methods of most of his teachers that is borne out in the often unflattering depictions of learning and teaching in *A Portrait of the Artist as a Young Man*" (17). But "Oxen," whose first paragraphs require translation, compels us to recognize that Joyce's "judgment" on "the methods of his teachers" was considerably more dialectical than Switaj here suggests. Drawing admirably and exhaustively on the facts of Joyce's biography and the recollections of his students, Switaj nevertheless concedes, "There is more to be written about the erotics of pedagogy and about violence in education in Joyce's work" (156). This chapter seeks to address both of these sets of questions.

34. Philip Kerr, "Reverse Translation," in *Translation and Own-Language Activities* (Cambridge: Cambridge University Press, 2014), 75. In "Hermeneutics of Suspicion: Nativism, Nationalism, and the Language Question in 'Oxen of the Sun,'" *James Joyce Quarterly* 25, nos. 2/3 (1998): 349–71, Mary C. King cites a remarkable account of "how the repression of the Irish language and continuation of education through illegal hedge schools 'led to the curious situation where a landlord would address a tenant in English, only to be answered in Greek or Latin'" (369n9). King contends that Latin therefore "became . . . a substitute mediated or displaced 'mother' tongue" (353)—where the substitutions, mediations, displacements, and quotation marks seem to make a mother tongue into something else altogether. Indeed, Joyce's Latin is everywhere associated with church and school, marked as institutional rather than familial and therefore distinct from the mother tongue. "Oxen" at once heightens and undoes this distinction by reverting to Latin in the context of the maternity ward. On why such a distinction cannot be hard and fast, see Barbara Johnson's account of the mother as teacher and the mother tongue as "acquired speech" in *A Portrait*'s sense (159); Johnson, "The Poet's Mother," in *Mother Tongues: Sexuality, Trials, Motherhood, Translation* (Cambridge, Mass.: Harvard University Press, 2003), 65–93, especially 66.

35. William Peacock, Preface to *English Prose from Mandeville to Ruskin*, ed. William Peacock (London: Oxford University Press, 1912), v.

36. Andrew Lang, Preface to *An Anthology of English Prose (1332 to 1740)*, ed. Annie Barnett and Lucy Dale (London: Longmans, Green, 1912), vii.

37. Humbler, that is, but not without immodest pretentions. Robert Spoo notes that despite their apparent innocuousness, literary compilations like those on which Joyce relied were in fact technologies of progressive history; see Spoo, "'Oxen of the Sun,' 'Circe,' and Beyond," in *James Joyce and the Language of History: Dedalus's Nightmare* (New

York: Oxford University Press, 1994), 138. Andrew Gibson similarly calls Peacock's selections "nationalistic, militaristic, enthusiastically royalist, class-based, and antidemocratic"; Gibson, "Irish Bull," 175–76.

38. Ellman, *James Joyce*, 475.

39. Spoo, "'Oxen of the Sun,'" 146–47. See also, on "Oxen" as "anti-textbook," Christopher Ames, "The Modernist Canon Narrative: Woolf's *Between the Acts* and Joyce's 'Oxen of the Sun,'" *Twentieth Century Literature* 37, no. 4 (1991): 390–404; and as "anti-anthology," Gibson, "Irish Bull," 173, 182.

40. Ellman, *James Joyce*, 475.

41. See, on sexuality and reproduction, Richard Brown, "Copulation without Population," in *James Joyce and Sexuality* (Cambridge: Cambridge University Press, 1985), 63–78, and Mary Lowe-Evans, *Crimes against Fecundity: James Joyce and Population Control* (Syracuse, N.Y.: Syracuse University Press, 1989); on history, see Gibson and Spoo. More recent queer readings like McCrea's in *In the Company of Strangers* and David Kurnick's in "Joyce Unperformed," in *Empty Houses: Theatrical Failure and the Novel* (Princeton: Princeton University Press, 2012), 183–91, have tended to avoid the episode, perhaps on account of its apparent focus on reproductive, rather than queer, forms of sexuality. The essays collected in Joseph Valente, ed., *Quare Joyce* (Ann Arbor: University of Michigan Press, 2000), mention "Oxen" only in passing.

42. Kenner, *Joyce's Voices*, 91.

43. Ellman, *James Joyce*, 476.

44. Quoted in Maud Ellmann, "*Ulysses*: Changing into an Animal," *Field Day Review* 2 (2006): 79.

45. On "Circe" as utopian telos and place of polymorphous perversion, see Kurnick, "Joyce Unperformed."

46. The word "pensum" appears once in *Ulysses*, when, in "Circe," Bloom sees in passing "youthful scholars grappling with their pensums" (*U* 15.919). See also Samuel Beckett, *The Unnamable*, in *Samuel Beckett: The Grove Centenary Edition* (New York: Grove Press, 2006), 2:304–5, where "the remnants of a pensum one day got by heart and long forgotten" figure in the narrator's predicament.

47. But that the punishment is also a privilege is what Virginia Woolf suggests in *Jacob's Room* (1922). Here is "Miss Julia Hedge, the feminist," who looks at Jacob across the library table: "When her books came she applied herself to her gigantic labours, but perceived . . . how composedly, unconcernedly, and with every consideration the male readers applied themselves to theirs. That young man for example. What had he got to do except copy out poetry? And she must study statistics"; Woolf, *Jacob's Room*, ed. Kate Flint (New York: Oxford University Press, 1992), 144–45.

48. Chris Ackerley, *Demented Particulars: The Annotated "Murphy"* (Edinburgh: Edinburgh University Press, 2004), 114.

49. Gustave Flaubert, *Madame Bovary: Provincial Ways*, trans. Lydia Davis (New York: Viking, 2010), 5.

50. Joyce, *Portrait*, 39.

51. Gibson, "Irish Bull," 171.

52. McCrea, *In the Company of Strangers*, 113; *OED*, s.v. "frequentative."

53. The word "frequentative" also appears in *Ulysses* (17.382).

54. On the supplement, see Jacques Derrida, *Of Grammatology*, trans. Gayatri Chakravorty Spivak (Baltimore: Johns Hopkins University Press, 1997), 144–45. For a reading of the episode that instead affirms the reproductive and finds in "Oxen" "the triumph" of "paternal values" and a celebration of "successful fertilization," see John Gordon, "Obeying the Boss in 'Oxen of the Sun,'" *ELH* 58, no. 1 (1991): 244, 249.

55. Ellman, *James Joyce*, 475.

56. Gibson, "Irish Bull," 171.

57. J. E. Stone names Rousseau and Dewey as key proponents of developmentalism, which for Stone "refers to a broad doctrine that presumes 'natural' ontogenesis to be optimal"; Stone, "Developmentalism: An Obscure but Pervasive Restriction on Educational Improvement," *Education Policy Analysis Archives* 4, no. 8 (1996): 5. Stone's analysis lays out the assumptions that sustain Rousseauist and Deweyan views while attesting to the continuing afterlife of these canonical accounts. For another treatment of the relationship between Rousseau and Dewey, more attentive to the differences than to the similarities between the two, see William J. Reese, "The Origins of Progressive Education," *History of Education Quarterly* 41, no. 1 (2001): 1–24.

58. Ellman, *James Joyce*, 475.

59. Edelman, *No Future*.

60. Jean-Jacques Rousseau, *Émile, or On Education*, trans. Allan Bloom (New York: Basic, 1979), 46. Subsequent citations are given parenthetically in the text, using the abbreviation *E*.

61. Derrida, *Of Grammatology*, 198.

62. Incidentally, it also lands him in gender trouble (*E* 37). By contrast, Joyce lays stress on a certain "manfulness" required to give birth in the first place: "All that surgical skill could do was done and the brave woman had manfully helped" (*U* 14.1312–13). Here "manfully" undermines, even while it underscores, the woman's relegation to the status of helpmeet or afterthought. Compare the "modicum of man's work" mentioned elsewhere in the episode (14.1414).

63. For a study of the contradictions that this effort entails, see Diane Berrett Brown, "The Constraints of Liberty at the Scene of Instruction," in *Rousseau and Freedom*, ed. Christie McDonald and Stanley Hoffmann (Cambridge: Cambridge University Press, 2010), 159–73.

64. Gibson, "Irish Bull," 158. Joyce's Trieste library contained Rousseau's *Confessions* but not *Émile*. Still this does not rule out the possibility of a relationship between "Oxen" and the latter work.

65. On the processes by which reproduction was both "sexualized and biologized," see Alys Eve Weinbaum, *Wayward Reproductions: Genealogies of Race and Nation in Transatlantic Modern Thought* (Durham, N.C.: Duke University Press, 2004), 2.

66. John Dewey, *Democracy and Education: An Introduction to the Philosophy of Education* (1916; repr. New York: MacMillan, 1957), 84. Further citations are given parenthetically in the text, using the abbreviation *DE*. For Rousseau's critique of imitation and recall, see Book II in Jean-Jacques Rousseau, *Émile, or On Education*, trans. Allan Bloom (New York: Basic, 1979), especially 104–13.

67. Ackerley, *Demented Particulars*, 114.

68. But on the key place of "recapitulation theory" precisely in the formation of

progressive educational ideals, see Thomas D. Fallace, *Race and the Origins of Progressive Education, 1880–1929* (New York: Teachers College Press, 2015).

69. Bersani, "Against *Ulysses*," 172. On ritual in this sense, see Talal Asad, "Toward a Genealogy of the Concept of Ritual," in *Genealogies of Religion: Discipline and Reasons of Power in Christianity and Islam* (Baltimore: Johns Hopkins University Press, 1993), 55–79. In his differently inflected discussion of ritual in the episode, Gordon argues, "'Oxen of the Sun' persistently encourages us to reflect on the extent to which the heart has affinities with ancestral codes" and rituals "of which a reason of Bloom's bourgeois-progressive stamp would be mortified to know"; Gordon, "Obeying the Boss in 'Oxen of the Sun,'" 245.

70. Compare the title of the 1858 treatise *Kallipädie oder Erziehung zur Schönheit* written by Moritz Schreber, Daniel Paul Schreber's father. Henry Zvi Lothane translates the full title of the treatise as *Callipedia, or Education towards Beauty by Means of the Natural and Even Promotion of Normal Body Growth, Life-Sustaining Health and Spiritual Cultivation and in Particular through the Optimal Use of Special Educational Aids: For Parents, Educators, and Teachers*; quoted in Eric Santner, *My Own Private Germany: Daniel Paul Schreber's Secret History of Modernity* (Princeton: Princeton University Press, 1996), 175n40. The "educational aids" were, in fact, punishing devices. For Santner's description of Moritz Schreber's "medicopedagogical system" and its methods, see especially 90–91.

71. Edmund Wilson, "James Joyce," in *Axel's Castle: A Study in the Imaginative Literature of 1870–1930* (New York: Norton, 1931), 216–17.

72. Ames, "Modernist Canon Narrative," 391.

73. "Unquestionably, there is something onerous about so finished a system of dependencies, so many generations of authorial Anchiseses piling piggy-back onto a narrative base so obscurely rendered"; Gordon, "Obeying the Boss," 249.

74. Spoo, "'Oxen of the Sun,'" 147.

75. Ibid., 101, quoting Walter Skeat's *Etymological Dictionary*.

76. Karl Marx, *The Eighteenth Brumaire of Louis Bonaparte*, trans. Ben Fowkes, in *Surveys from Exile*, ed. David Fernbach (New York: Vintage, 1974), 146.

77. Gibson, "Irish Bull," 169.

78. On this nightmarishness, see, for instance, David Lloyd, "The Medieval Still: Postcolonial Temporalities in Joyce," in *Irish Times: Temporalities of Modernity* (Dublin: Field Day, 2008), 94, and Roberto Harari, *How James Joyce Made His Name*, trans. Luke Thurston (New York: Other Press, 2002), 276–77; and James Baldwin, "Stranger in the Village," *Notes of a Native Son* (Boston: Beacon Press, 1984), 162–63.

79. Blamires, *New Bloomsday Book*, 126; Gordon, "Obeying the Boss," 242.

80. Kenner, *Ulysses* (Boston: G Allen & Unwin, 1980), 79.

81. Walter Pater, *Studies in the History of the Renaissance*, ed. Matthew Beaumont (London: Oxford University Press, 2010), 121.

82. Pater, "Style," in *Appreciations, with an Essay on Style* (London: Macmillan, 1895), 1–36.

83. James Joyce, Trieste Notebook, James Joyce Collection, MS VIII.B.4v-7r, State University of New York, University at Buffalo Libraries. Further citations from these transcriptions are given parenthetically in the text, followed by page numbers in the source texts: Pater, *Imaginary Portraits* (London: Macmillan, 1910), abbreviated as *IP*, and

Marius the Epicurean, ed. Michael Levey (New York: Oxford University Press, 1985), abbreviated as *M*. To my knowledge, Joyce's transcriptions of Pater have not been analyzed in previous studies of the sources of "Oxen." For an overview of these sources, see Robert Janusko, *The Sources and Structures of James Joyce's "Oxen"* (Epping: Bowker, 1983). For recent studies, see Sarah Davison, "Joyce's Incorporation of Literary Sources in 'Oxen of the Sun,'" *Genetic Joyce Studies* 9 (2009); Gregory M. Dowling, "Joyce's 'Oxen of the Sun' Notesheets: A Transcription and Sourcing of the Stylistic Entries," *Genetic Joyce Studies* 2 (2002); and Chrissie van Mierlo, "'Oxen of the Sun' Notesheet 17: Commentary and Annotations with a New List of Sources, and Transcriptions; or Oxtail Soup: The Ingredients," *Genetic Joyce Studies* 14 (2014).

84. See Leela Gandhi, *The Common Cause: Postcolonial Ethics and the Practice of Democracy, 1900–1955* (Chicago: University of Chicago Press, 2014); especially Chapter 2, "On Descent."

85. On this subculture, see Linda Dowling, *Hellenism and Homosexuality in Victorian Oxford* (Ithaca, N.Y.: Cornell University Press, 1994); on Pater's place in it, see especially chapter 3. See also Colleen Lamos, "James Joyce and the English Vice," *Novel: A Forum on Fiction* 29, no. 1 (1995): 22.

86. The phrase "copied out big" appears in an especially dense passage late in "Oxen." Here one "lord Harry," hoping to learn Latin, "bought a grammar of the bull's language, . . . but he could never learn a word of it except the first personal pronoun which he copied out big and got off by heart" (*U* 14.632–35). Literally his majesty the ego, Harry is a hybrid formed from the English John Bull and Latin papal bulls, and he therefore represents the power of both colonial and church rule. Yet this power is no sooner asserted in "Oxen" than it is emptied out, erased, evacuated of all validity. For Harry lays claim to anything and everything by writing—or rather copying out—his imperial "I" in chalk, a medium that is as scholastic as it is water-soluble. Here, Joyce imagines—wishfully, to be sure—an "Imperator" whose mark is fleeting. But that he renders this wish in the style of Swift shows that he is still retraversing the past, after all. Throughout this chapter, I have focused on copying rather than "getting off by heart," but the latter technique—recitation—is also important to Joyce's ongoing engagement with instruction. Whereas Rousseau stipulates that Émile should "never learn anything by heart" (112), phrases learned by heart and lines recited recur in Joyce's work starting with *Dubliners* (e.g., 6, 16–17, 54, 103–5, 141). See also Stephen's listening in on adult conversations in *A Portrait*: "Words which he did not understand he said over and over to himself till he had learnt them by heart: and through them he had glimpses of the real world about him" (43).

87. Lee Edelman, "Learning Nothing: *Bad Education*," *differences* 28, no. 1 (2017): 129.

88. Ibid., 129, 165.

89. On identification in this sense, see Mikkel Borch-Jacobsen, *The Freudian Subject*, trans. Catherine Porter (Stanford, Calif.: Stanford University Press, 1988). Lacanian accounts might characterize Joyce's procedure as a matter of symbolic constraint rather than identification, which is more often associated with the imaginary. On symbolic constraint, see Tracy McNulty, *Wrestling with the Angel: Experiments in Symbolic Life* (New York: Columbia University Press, 2014).

90. Kurnick, "Joyce Unperformed," 187.

91. Woolf, *Writer's Diary*, 48.

92. Compare Jean-Michel Rabaté's claim that Joyce's pedagogy aims at the creation of a collective readership and an "expanding archive"; Rabaté, *James Joyce and the Politics of Egoism* (New York: Cambridge University Press, 2001), 196. For a counter-argument, see McGee, "Joyce's Pedagogy."

4. *Salò* and the School of Abuse

1. Gideon Bachmann, "Pasolini on de Sade: An Interview during the Filming of 'The 120 Days of Sodom,'" *Film Quarterly* 29, no. 2 (1975–76): 42.

2. Versions of this pathologizing response to *Salò* range from the early, phobic consensus distilled in Uberto Quintavalle's memoir *Giornate di Sodoma: Ritratto di Pasolini e del suo ultimo film* (Milan: Sugarco, 1976) to Georges Didi-Huberman's recent account of the apocalyptic turn and "death and disappearance of survivals" in Pasolini's last works, in *Come le lucciole: Una politica delle sopravvivenze*, trans. Chiara Tartarini (Milan: Bollati Bolinghieri, 2009). For more on Pasolini's pathologization, see Carla Benedetti, "Il 'capolavoro' di Pasolini," by Carla Benedetti and Giovanni Giovannetti, in *Frocio e basta* (Milan: Effigie, 2012), and for a cogent response to Didi-Huberman, see Alessia Ricciardi, "Pasolini for the Future," *California Italian Studies* 2, no. 1 (2011), http://escholarship.org/uc/item/8v81z3sg.

3. Marquis de Sade, *The 120 Days of Sodom*, in *The 120 Days of Sodom and Other Writings*, ed. and trans. Austryn Wainhouse and Richard Seaver (New York: Grove, 1966), 255.

4. Pasolini says that he wants *Salò* to be "a formally perfect film" and contrasts this perfectionist approach with his earlier, messy, "magmatic" procedure in Bachmann, "Pasolini on de Sade," 43.

5. See Leo Bersani and Ulysse Dutoit, "Merde Alors," *October* 13 (1980): 30. For them, "horror is almost constantly forestalled by a multiplication of aesthetic appeals" in the film, and the binoculars' framing in this sequence constitutes one such appeal, an appeal that is compatible with and even enhanced by estrangement; Bersani and Dutoit, "Merde Alors," 29. Ricciardi, by contrast, sees these backward binoculars as part of the film's effort to thwart both aesthetic and erotic enjoyment by ruling out "perverse proximity" in all its forms; see Ricciardi, "Rethinking *Salò* after Abu Ghraib," *Postmodern Culture* 21, no. 3 (2011); https://doi.org/10.1353/pmc.2011.002. For an account that differs from both Ricciardi's and Bersani and Dutoit's and instead emphasizes the sense of "suffocating nearness" produced by this shot, see Joan Copjec, "What Zapruder Saw," in *Imagine There's No Woman: Ethics and Sublimation* (Cambridge, Mass.: MIT Press, 2002), 203. And for a more recent reading of the same sequence that likewise lays stress on "identification" and complicity, see Gian Maria Annovi, *Pier Paolo Pasolini: Performing Authorship* (New York: Columbia University Press, 2017), 44.

6. To my mind, the best account of aestheticization in the film remains Bersani and Dutoit, "Merde Alors." But whereas Bersani and Dutoit associate aestheticization in *Salò* with "saving frivolity" and think that the film displays "Pasolini's refusal to be fixed—better, to be transfixed—by his subject" (29), I see no such saving and no such refusal in the film.

7. On *Salò* and bare life, see Ricciardi, "Rethinking *Salò*"; and on the film as fore-

casting the end of "the autonomy of the citizen-subject," see Copjec, "What Zapruder Saw," 229. Other recent readings that value *Salò* for its prophetic qualities include Massimo Recalcati, *Il complesso di Telemaco: Genitori e figli dopo il tramonto del padre* (Milan: Feltrinelli, 2013), 23–29, and Kriss Ravetto, "*Salò*: A Fatal Strategy," in *The Unmaking of Fascist Aesthetics* (Minneapolis: University of Minnesota Press, 2001), 97–147. For another instance, see the image by cartoonist Mathijs Hendrix showing Silvio Berlusconi on the libertines' throne from the courtyard massacre scene, wielding with a smile the binoculars that *Salò*'s libertines use to view the tortures taking place below: http://mathijshendrix.wordpress.com/tag/salo/.

8. For a notable exception, see John David Rhodes, "Watchable Bodies: *Salò*'s Young Non-Actors," *Screen* 5, no. 4 (2012): 453–58.

9. See Recalcati, *Il complesso di Telemaco*, 23–29; and on "the eclipse of desire" more generally Recalcati, "L'eclisse dei desideri," in *Forme contemporanee del totalitarismo*, ed. Recalcati (Turin: Bollati Boringhieri, 2007), 61–68. On "current methods of biopower" as they figure proleptically in the film, see, again, Ricciardi, "Rethinking *Salò*."

10. Pier Paolo Pasolini, "Il sesso come metafora del potere," in *Per il cinema*, ed. Walter Siti (Milan: Mondadori, 2000), 2:2063–67.

11. Ibid., 2065–66.

12. Ricciardi, "Rethinking *Salò*."

13. For a recent discussion of *Salò*'s pedagogy, see Roberto Chiesi, "Una nuova gioventù di spettatori e conniventi: Immagini della giovinezza nell'ultimo Pasolini," in *Fratello selvaggio: Pier Paolo Pasolini fra gioventù e nova gioventù*, ed. Annovi (Massa: Transeuropa, 2013), 132–35. On the pedagogical impulse in Pasolini more generally, see Andrea Zanzotto, "Per una pedagogia," *Nuovi argomenti* 49 (1976): 47–51, and Jennifer Stone, "Pasolini, Zanzotto, and the Question of Pedagogy," in *Pier Paolo Pasolini: Contemporary Perspectives,* ed. Patrick Rumble and Bart Testa (Toronto: University of Toronto Press, 1994), 40–55.

14. There is therefore some truth to the film's first spectators' sense that Pasolini must have been symptomatically "fixated" on both the Fascist and Sadean pasts. See, for instance, Quintavalle, *Giornate di Sodoma*, 14, 22. Indeed, Pasolini's Salò Republic bears more than a passing resemblance to the "province" to which Sigmund Freud alludes in an early letter discussing fixation: "In a certain province *fueros* [ancient laws or local sovereignties] are still in force, we are in the presence of 'survivals'"; Freud to Wilhelm Fliess, December 6, 1896, in *The Complete Letters of Sigmund Freud to Wilhelm Fliess, 1887–1904*, trans. and ed. Jeffrey Moussaieff Masson (Cambridge, Mass.: Harvard University Press, 1985), 208. Freud here maps the political onto the psychic, so that fixation becomes a matter of *fueros* within. I will be arguing, against Didi-Huberman's *Come le lucciole*, that we are still very much "in the presence of survivals" in *Salò*. To repeat this Freudian claim, though, is not to suggest that *Salò* is a mere record of its director's psychopathology, as his detractors contend.

15. Armando Maggi, *The Resurrection of the Body: Pier Paolo Pasolini from St. Paul to Sade* (Chicago: University of Chicago Press, 2009), 5.

16. Ibid.

17. I refer readers who may still be inclined to dismiss such a critique as "conservative" to recent left critiques of progress in fields ranging from Black studies to queer

theory and from visual studies to ecocriticism and beyond; see John Berger, *The Shape of a Pocket* (New York: Vintage, 2003); Colin Dayan, *The Law Is a White Dog: How Legal Rituals Make and Unmake Persons* (Princeton: Princeton University Press, 2013); Anne-Lise François, *Open Secrets: The Literature of Uncounted Experience* (Stanford, Calif.: Stanford University Press, 2008); Elizabeth Freeman, *Time Binds: Queer Temporalities, Queer Histories* (Durham, N.C.: Duke University Press, 2010); Heather Love, *Feeling Backward: Loss and the Politics of Queer History* (Cambridge, Mass.: Harvard University Press, 2007); Pankaj Mishra, *Age of Anger: A History of the Present* (New York: Farrar, Straus and Giroux, 2017); and Jared Sexton, *Amalgamation Schemes: Antiblackness and the Critique of Multiracialism* (Minneapolis: University of Minnesota Press, 2008). For an earlier instance, see Max Horkheimer and Theodor Adorno, *Dialectic of Enlightenment: Philosophical Fragments*, ed. Gunzelin Schmid Noerr, trans. Edmund Jephcott (Stanford, Calif.: Stanford University Press, 2002). And for a reading of *Salò* specifically that both considers and extends this critique, see Rei Terada, "Pasolini's Acceptance," in *Sovereignty in Ruins: A Politics of Crisis*, ed. Klaus Mladek and George Edmundson (Durham, N.C.: Duke University Press, 2017), 144–70.

18. *OED*, s. v. "backward."

19. On the movement from word to image as regression, see, for instance, Christopher Bollas, *Hysteria* (New York: Routledge, 2000), 111–12; and, in the art historical context, Aby Warburg, *Images from the Region of the Pueblo Indians of North America*, trans. Michael P. Steinberg (Ithaca, N.Y.: Cornell University Press, 1995), 8; and Didi-Huberman, *Confronting Images: Questioning the Ends of a Certain History of Art*, trans. John Goodman (University Park: Pennsylvania State University Press, 2005), 149.

20. This sentence reworks and adds to the litany of charges against "instruction" found in Giovanni Gentile, *La riforma dell'educazione: Discorsi ai maestri di Trieste* (Bari: Laterza, 1920), 186.

21. Pasolini, *Gennariello*, in *Lettere luterane* (Turin: Einaudi, 1976), 15.

22. Ibid., 33.

23. Gentile, *La riforma*, 176.

24. Giorigo Ruffolo, "The Italian Educational Crisis," *Review of the Economic Conditions in Italy* (1975): 30; Richard J. Wolff, "Italian Education during World War II: Remnants of Failed Fascist Education, Seeds of the New Schools," in *Education and the Second World War: Studies in Schooling and Social Change*, ed. Roy Lowe (Abingdon, UK: Routledge, 2012), 81–82; Eden K. McLean, *Mussolini's Children: Race and Elementary Education in Fascist Italy* (Lincoln, Neb.: University of Nebraska Press, 2018), 229; Luciana Bellatalia, "Da Gentile a Gelmini, quale identità per la scuola italiana?" *LaRivista* 2 (2015): 173. See also Claudio Fogu, who concludes, "Most of the administrative, judicial, and even police apparatus of the Fascist state and past was left untouched and effortlessly integrated into the new republican order"; Fogu, "*Italiani brava gente*: The Legacy of Fascist Historical Culture on Italian Politics of Memory," in *The Politics of Memory in Postwar Europe*, ed. Richard Ned Lebow, Wulf Kansteiner, and Claudio Fogu (Durham, N.C.: Duke University Press, 2006), 152.

25. See Suzanne Stewart-Steinberg, *The Pinocchio Effect: On Making Italians, 1860–1920* (Chicago: University of Chicago Press, 2007).

26. Paola Bonifazio, *Schooling in Modernity: The Politics of Sponsored Films in Postwar*

Italy (Toronto: University of Toronto Press, 2014). See also Ruffolo, "Italian Educational Crisis," e.g., 24–25.

27. See, for a historiographic instance, Alberto De Bernardi, *Una dittatura moderna: Il fascismo come problema storico* (Milan: Mondadori, 2001); and, for examples from film studies, Noa Steimatsky, "The Cinecittà Refugee Camp (1944–1950)," *October* 128 (2009): 23–50, and Lorenzo Fabbri, "Neorealism as Ideology: Bazin, Deleuze, and the Avoidance of Fascism," *Italianist* 35, no. 2 (2015): 182–201. For Croce's "parenthesis," see Benedetto Croce, "Chi è fascista?" *Il giornale di Napoli* (October 29, 1944): 3; and on the ongoing ideological work of this image, see Fogu, "*Italiani brava gente*," 149. Elsewhere Fogu notes that it was not until 1976, when "the famous televised debates between the historians Denis Mack Smith and Renzo De Felice" were broadcast, that "Fascism was suddenly brought out of the representational closet and in such a way that the Crocean image of a Fascist parenthesis in Italian history [began to be] thoroughly delegitimized" (158–59). It was therefore in the context of this closet—and, I am arguing, in an effort to counter its effects—that Pasolini made *Salò*.

28. This is one of many problems addressed in Franco Fortini, "The Writer's Mandate and the End of Antifascism," *Screen* 15, no. 1 (1974): 33–70. This text treats "the antifascist myth" mainly as a hindrance to revolution (53). Fortini also reminds readers, however, that such a reckoning would have made it possible to recognize Fascism's relation to capital rather than grant the "definition of fascism as 'enemy of civilisation'—including bourgeois civilisation" (45). Seeing Fascism as an extension or weapon of the latter would instead mean confronting continuities between the postwar period and the decades that preceded it—which need not entail minimizing the "ruin" to which Fascism leads (34).

29. Fogu, "*Italiani brava gente*," 156.

30. On the "historic compromise" that further consolidated this consensus during the years when the Italian left might have been best positioned to contest it, see Paul Ginsborg, "Crisis, Compromise, and the 'Anni di Piombo,'" in *A History of Contemporary Italy: Society and Politics, 1943–1988* (New York: St. Martin's, 2003), 348–405. Here I bracket the ultraleft movements associated with *operaismo*, or workerism, and Autonomia. But for a luminous recent discussion of these movements and their prefiguration in postwar culture, see Jaleh Mansoor, *Marshall Plan Modernism: Italian Postwar Abstraction and the Beginnings of Autonomia* (Durham, N.C.: Duke University Press, 2016).

31. Pasolini, "L'articolo delle lucciole," in *Scritti corsari* (Milan: Garzanti, 1975), 160–68.

32. Pasolini, "Fascista," ed. Massimo Fini, in *Scritti corsari*, 233.

33. Pasolini, "Abiura dalla *Trilogia della vita*," in *Lettere luterane* (Turin: Einaudi, 1976), 71.

34. Ibid., 72.

35. Ibid., 76; emphasis in original.

36. Roberto Esposito, *Living Thought: The Origins and Actuality of Italian Philosophy*, trans. Zakiya Hanafi (Stanford, Calif.: Stanford University Press, 2012), 208–9; Suzanne-Stewart-Steinberg, "*L'Abiura* di Pasolini: In margine all'*Italian Thought*," *Effetto Italian Thought* (Macerata: Quodlibet, 2017), 73–-84; Terada, "Pasolini's Acceptance."

37. *OED*, s. v. "detention."

38. Pasolini, *Trasumanar e organizzar* (1971; repr. Milan: Garzanti, 1976), 66.

39. François, "'The Feel of Not to Feel It,' or The Pleasures of Enduring Form," in *A Companion to Romantic Poetry*, ed. Charles Mahoney (Oxford: Wiley-Blackwell, 2010), 462.

40. Petrarch, *Petrarch's Lyric Poems: The "Rime Sparse" and Other Lyrics*, trans and ed. Robert M. Durling (Cambridge, Mass.: Harvard University Press, 1976), 290.

41. Compare Agamben's reflections on "revocation" and "re-evocation" in Pasolini's late work (though not in *Salò* specifically), in "From the Book to the Screen: The Before and the After of the Book," in *The Fire and the Tale*, translated by Lorenzo Chiesa (Palo Alto: Stanford University Press, 2017), 93–94.

42. On *Salò*'s response to these philosophical debates, see Ravetto, "*Salò*: A Fatal Strategy," 106.

43. James Steintrager, "Liberating Sade," *Yale Journal of Criticism* 18, no. 2 (2005): 357.

44. Ibid., 356.

45. Georges Bataille's writings on Sade include "The Use Value of D. A. F. de Sade," in *Visions of Excess: Selected Writings, 1927–1939*, ed. Allan Stoekl, trans. Allan Stoekl with Carl R. Lovitt and Donald M. Leslie Jr. (Minneapolis: University of Minnesota Press, 1985), 91–102, and "Sade," in *Literature and Evil*, trans. Alastair Hamilton (1957; repr. London: Marion Boyars, 1973), 105–25. Pasolini also refers to Bataille's *The Trial of Gilles de Rais* as a source of inspiration for *Salò*, but without naming Bataille's name; Pasolini, "Il sesso." 2063. Jacques Lacan's "Kant with Sade" (1963), trans. James B. Swenson, *October* 51 (1989): 55–71, is perhaps more Pasolinian than any of the texts listed in *Salò*. And conversely: there is already something Lacanian about the performance of aggressive erudition that is the "Essential Bibliography"; Max Horkheimer and Theodor Adorno's *Dialectic of Enlightenment* (first published in an Italian translation in 1966) also includes an "Excursus" on Sade that pairs his work with Kant's.

46. Annovi reads the bibliography as "a sort of *contrapasso* for the spectator of the *Trilogy*, an intellectual punishment," in *Pier Paolo Pasolini*, 139–40.

47. Roland Barthes, *S/Z*, trans. Richard Miller (New York: Hill and Wang, 1974), 156.

48. Ibid., 156.

49. Pasolini, "Abiura," 71.

50. On the place of the "project" in Pasolini's late work and for an account that makes *Petrolio*, rather than *Salò*, representative of the late Pasolini's legacy, see Carla Benedetti, *Pasolini contro Calvino: Per una letteratura impura* (Turin: Bollati Boringhieri, 1998).

51. Pasolini, *Petrolio* (Turin: Einaudi, 1992), 48.

52. Pierre Klossowski, *Sade My Neighbor*, trans. Alphonso Lingis (Evanston, Ill.: Northwestern University Press, 1991), 42. Further citations are given parenthetically in the text.

53. Ibid., 42.

54. Ibid., 40.

55. Ibid.; emphasis in original.

56. Pasolini, *Trasumanar e organizzar*, 121. I consider the problem of transgression, and the disobedience that is really deferred obedience, in connection with an earlier film in Ramsey McGlazer, "Learning by Hart: Gender, Image, and Ideology in Vittorio de Sica's *Maddalena, zero in condotta*," *Italianist* 36, no. 2 (2016): 187–213.

57. Klossowski, *Sade My Neighbor*, 41.

58. Ibid.

59. Ibid., 42.

60. The plot thickens when, midway through the film, it becomes apparent that Pasolini's libertines have in fact read their Klossowski. The Bishop drops the philosopher's

name, identifying the source of a phrase the Duke has quoted, having learned it by heart, at which point a guard exclaims, "Evviva, evviva!"; Pasolini, *Per il cinema*, 2:2042. The cheers are for someone else, who is just appearing on-screen, but still the sequence of lines is telling; the cheers might as well be for Klossowski. *Salò* repositions the postwar reception of Sade, backdating Klossowski's text so that it becomes diegetically available *during* the war.

61. Pasolini, "Fascista," 223.

62. See, again, Ginsborg, "Crisis, Compromise."

63. See Gentile, *La riforma*, e.g., 58–59; and his earlier "L'unità della scuola media e la libertà degli studi," in *La nuova scuola media*, ed. Hervé A. Cavallera, vol. 40, *Opere complete di Giovanni Gentile* (Florence: Casa Editrice Le Lettere, 1988), 1–39. To be sure, statements in favor of progressive-sounding educative freedom can be found in Pasolini's writings. See, for instance, "Le mie proposte su scuola e Tv," in *Lettere luterane* (Turin: Einaudi, 1976), 177. But such statements should be read alongside the others that insist that one must not accept progressive pieties but rather learn to "be progressive in another world; invent a new way of being free"; see Pasolini, "Due modeste proposte per eliminare la criminalità in Italia," in *Lettere luterane*, 168. See also Lorenzo Chiesa, "Wounds of Testimony and Martyrs of the Unconscious: Lacan and Pasolini contra the Discourse of Freedom," in *The Virtual Point of Freedom: Essays on Politics, Aesthetics, and Religion* (Evanston, Ill.: Northwestern University Press, 2016).

64. By contrast, John David Rhodes writes that "Pasolini's allegory is ... one in which there is no allegorical transparency: rather the bodies, buildings, and places that are posed as allegorical vehicles continue to assert their own irreducible specificity"; Rhodes, *Stupendous Miserable City: Pasolini's Rome* (Minneapolis: University of Minnesota Press, 2007), 137.

65. On forms of repetition inseparable from the resistance that they might seem to block, see Rebecca Comay, "Resistance and Repetition: Freud and Hegel," *Research in Phenomenology* 45, no. 2 (2015): 237–66. Pasolini considers ritual in his brief but suggestive review of a film to which *Salò* is heavily indebted: Marco Ferreri's *La grande abbuffata* [*Blow-Out*] (1973), "Le ambigue forme della ritualità narrativa," *Cinema nuovo* 231 (1974): 342–47.

66. Bachmann, "Pasolini on de Sade," 42.

67. Here again, I am relying on Talal Asad's account, according to which ritual privileges practice over signification; Asad, "Toward a Genealogy of the Concept of Ritual," in *Genealogies of Religion: Discipline and Reasons of Power in Christianity and Islam* (Baltimore: Johns Hopkins University Press, 1993), 55–79. Francesco Galluzzi eloquently describes *Salò*'s assault on signification in *Pasolini e la pittura* (Rome: Bulzoni, 1994), 143.

68. Mikkel Borch-Jacobsen, "Mimetic Efficacity," trans. Douglas Brick, in *The Emotional Tie: Psychoanalysis, Mimesis, and Affect* (Stanford, Calif.: Stanford University Press, 1992), 113.

69. Ernesto De Martino, *La terra del rimorso: Contributo a una storia religiosa del Sud* (Milan: Il Saggiatore, 1961), 13.

70. Ibid., 272–73.

71. This is already, then, the shift or "next stage" that Gayatri Chakravorty Spivak locates in the "trajectory of the subaltern": "Not to study the subaltern, but to learn";

see Spivak, "Scattered Speculations on the Subaltern and the Popular," *An Aesthetic Education in the Era of Globalization* (Cambridge, Mass.: Harvard University Press, 2012), 440.

72. My reading of *La terra del rimorso* differs from Simonetta Falasca-Zamponi's in her overview of De Martino's works, "Of Tears and Tarantulas: Folk Religiosity, de Martino's Ethnology, and the Italian South," *California Italian Studies* 5, no. 1 (2014): 57–60, http://escholarship.org/uc/item/7dw8v25r.

73. For an argument that associates modernity with a hypertrophy, rather than an impoverishment, of ritual in education, see Ivan Illich, *Deschooling Society* (New York: Harper & Row, 1971), especially chapter 3, "Ritualization of Progress."

74. For a further consideration of Pasolini's relationship to De Martino, though one that does not address *La terra del rimorso* specifically, see Tomaso Subini, *La necessità di morire: Il cinema di Pier Paolo Pasolini* (Rome: Ente dello Spettacolo, 2007), 26–34. Maggi also treats this relationship, but he sees Pasolini and De Martino as ultimately opposed; see Maggi, *Resurrection*, 7–8. According to Maggi, Pasolini reductively translates De Martino's complex, nondichotomous understanding of history into a neat and naïve division between past and present: De Martino's emphases are in this sense "at odds with Pasolini's belief in a sharp dichotomy between the 'then' of a premodern condition and the 'now' of post-history" (7). I am instead attempting to highlight how Pasolini's late work everywhere attests to the survival and the still-possible return of that which has been declared long gone. This is, in my view, a dynamic rather than dichotomous approach to history, one that does not declare any past over and done with definitively.

75. See, for instance, Maggi, *Resurrection*, 7–8, and Didi-Huberman, *Come le lucciole*.

76. I borrow this formulation from Joan Copjec, who insists that psychoanalysis is "not a regional discourse," in Jennifer Murray, "The Inheritance of Potentiality: An Interview with Joan Copjec," *E-rea* 12, no. 1 (2014), https://doi.org/10.4000/erea.4102.

77. For readings of this arresting rendition, see Maggi, *Resurrection*, 311, and especially Terada, "Pasolini's Acceptance," 150.

78. Galluzzi identifies this as an imitation of Raphael's *Madonna di Foligno in Pasolini e la pittura*, 144n164. For his part, Maggi emphasizes the Marian dimension of this image, so that Mary becomes one (absent) mother among many others in *Salò*; Maggi, *Resurrection*, 108–9.

79. Thus, according to Didi-Huberman, Fra Angelico "reenacts" "a *gesture of unction*" when he splashes paint onto a wall, punctuating figurative paintings with nonfigurative passages; Didi-Huberman, *Confronting Images*, 202–3; emphasis in original. And thus Donatello learns from the makers of *bòti*, or death masks for the still-living Florentine nobility, that sculpture is a matter of casting as much as of mimesis—of process, that is, as much as of appearance (226). Thus, finally, the maker of a painting honoring St. Veronica sets aside his brush, preferring to render the saint's cloth by painting with cloth, rather than realistically (197–98).

80. Ibid., 220.

81. Pasolini, "Il sesso," 2066.

82. I cannot engage with the *sacra rappresentazione* or with Didi-Huberman's account of the critical image in detail here. I note only that this engagement might complicate critical assertions that the film records the making of "bare life" in Ag-

amben's sense; see Giorgio Agamben, *Homo Sacer: Sovereign Power and Bare Life*, trans. Kevin Attell (Stanford, Calif.: Stanford University Press, 1998), 85.

83. Michel Foucault, "Sade: Sargeant of Sex," interview with G. Dupont, trans. John Johnston, in *Aesthetics, Method, and Epistemology*, ed. James D. Faubion (New York: New Press, 1998), 226–27. For another perspective on the rationality of Sadean eroticism, see Frances Ferguson, *Pornography, the Theory: What Utilitarianism Did to Action* (Chicago: University of Chicago Press, 2004).

84. Foucault, *Security, Territory, Population: Lectures at the Collège de France, 1977–1978*, ed. Michel Senellart, trans. Graham Burchell (New York: Palgrave Macmillan, 2007), e.g., 8, 107.

85. Bersani, "Is the Rectum a Grave?" in *Is the Rectum a Grave? and Other Essays* (Chicago: University of Chicago Press, 2010), 3–30. On complicity, see also Bersani, *Homos* (Cambridge, Mass.: Harvard University Press, 1995), 90; and for a later reassessment of the arguments advanced in "Is the Rectum a Grave?" including its arguments for the radical potential of masochism, see "Sociality and Sexuality," in *Is the Rectum a Grave?*, 102–19.

86. Bersani, "Is the Rectum," 22.

87. Ibid., 30.

88. Ibid., 27.

89. Ibid., 30.

90. Ibid., 29.

91. Ricciardi, "Rethinking *Salò*." For an opposed reading, see Chiesa, "Pasolini and the Ugliness of Bodies," in *The Virtual Point of Freedom*.

92. Gary Indiana memorably calls this "normal love," in Indiana, *Salò, or the 120 Days of Sodom* (London: BFI, 2000), 83.

93. Pasolini, "Abiura," 73.

94. Ricciardi, "Rethinking *Salò*."

95. Bersani, "Is the Rectum," 19.

96. Pasolini, "Fascista," 233.

97. That the old school had long since been a repository of ritual forms is shown in Walter Ong's classic, not to say old-school, essay "Latin Language Study as Renaissance Puberty Rite," *Studies in Philology* 56, no. 2 (1959): 103–24. Here Ong shows that "Renaissance educators did not, on the whole, abate the ferocity of medieval or ancient school punishment," undermining the teleology that associates modernity, early or otherwise, with tolerance (111), even if Ong appears uncritically to adopt this teleology elsewhere (122). Ong writes of the ritual practices in question: "Over all these presides the belief that ... youths must be made by their preceptors to assimilate their lessons the hard way" (106). In the early modern European context, according to Ong, this "belief" took hold with particular force in grammar schools, for vernacularization, Latin's "death" as a spoken language, meant that schools could seal themselves off, both linguistically and ritually, from the world of living languages (122).

98. Pasolini, "Fascista," 233.

99. Bachman, "Pasolini on Sade," 42. To be sure, the phrase "conceived as a rite" is, in a sense, a contradiction in terms, because a rite cannot, strictly speaking, be conceived, at least not if it is to be socially efficacious. On the contrary, traditionally, "for

ritual to function and operate it must first of all present itself and be perceived as legitimate, with ... [its] symbols serving ... to show that the agent does not act in his own name and on his own authority, but in his capacity as a delegate"; Pierre Bourdieu, "Authorized Language: The Social Conditions for the Effectiveness of Ritual Discourse," in *Language and Symbolic Power*, ed. John B. Thompson, trans. Gino Raymond and Matthew Adamson (Cambridge, Mass.: Harvard University Press, 1991), 115. There was, of course, no such delegation in Pasolini's case; or rather, the director himself did the delegating. In this sense, there is a qualitative difference between the rituals observed by De Martino and those imagined by Pasolini: whereas the *tarantate* studied by the anthropologist sought ritual cures in a communal context, even the most devoted cinephiles attended a film "conceived as a rite" by its director alone. For an analysis that runs counter to Bourdieu's and centers on an attempt to make images efficacious in the absence of social sanctioning, from within "the ruins of representation and culture," see Stefania Pandolfo, "*Ta'bīr*: Figuration and the Torment of Life," in *Knot of the Soul: Madness, Psychoanalysis, Islam* (Chicago: University of Chicago Press, 2018), 184–86.

100. De Martino, *La terra del rimorso*, 273.

101. Pasolini, *Per il cinema*, 2:2060.

102. The explicit reference in *Salò* is not to Eliot but to Ezra Pound, one of whose *Cantos* is quoted in translation on a radio program called "Poetry Corner" ("L'angolo della poesia"); see Pasolini, *Per il cinema*, 2:2060. Just after the lines from Pound are quoted, a movement from Carl Orff's *Carmina burana* begins: "Veris leta facies," in which a small choir welcomes the return of spring. The piece that plays after this and that ends the film is called "Son tanto triste"; it was composed by Franco Ansaldo and Alfredo Bracchi and arranged by Ennio Morricone.

103. On "the common association of flowers with ... commonness itself," see Anne-Lise François, "Flower Fisting," *Postmodern Culture* 22, no. 1 (2011).

104. Bersani and Dutoit, "Merde Alors," 29.

105. Maggi, *Resurrection*, 338.

106. Barbara Spackman, *Fascist Virilities: Rhetoric, Ideology, and Social Fantasy in Italy* (Minneapolis: University of Minnesota Press, 1996), 65. Here Spackman is paraphrasing Karl Marx.

107. Gentile, "L'unità della scuola media," 24.

5. Schooling in Ruins: Glauber Rocha's Rome

1. See Srinivas Aravamudan, "Theosophistries," in *Guru English: South Asian Religion in a Cosmopolitan Language* (Princeton: Princeton University Press, 2005), 115–26.

2. Dipesh Chakrabarty, "Introduction: The Idea of Provincializing Europe," and Chapter 1, "Postcoloniality and the Artifice of History," in *Provincializing Europe: Postcolonial Thought and Historical Difference* (Princeton: Princeton University Press, 2000), 3–46.

3. See Pier Paolo Pasolini, *Per il cinema*, ed. Walter Siti (Milan: Mondadori, 2000), 2:2057. The part of the "serva negra" is played by Ines Pellegrini, an Italian-born actress of Eritrean descent who had played Zemurrud in Pasolini's *Il fiore delle Mille e una notte* (1974). On Pellegrini's presence in *Salò*, see Shelleen Greene, *Equivocal Subjects: Between*

Italy and Africa—Constructions of Racial and National Identity in the Italian Cinema (New York: Continuum, 2012), 243–44.

4. Walter Pater, *Marius the Epicurean*, ed. Michael Levey (New York: Penguin, 1985), 185.

5. Antonio Gramsci, *Quaderni del carcere*, ed. Valentino Gerratana (Turin: Einaudi, 1975), 2:1317.

6. Gideon Bachmann, "Pasolini on de Sade: An Interview during the Filming of 'The 120 Days of Sodom,'" *Film Quarterly* 29, no. 2 (1975–76): 42.

7. Quoted in Bertrand Ficamos, "Glauber Rocha's *Claro*, or the Tragic Legibility of Chaos," in *Cinematic Rome*, ed. Richard Wigley (Leicester: Troubador, 2008), 137.

8. Monica Dall'Asta and Maria Rita Nepomuceno, "Glauber Rocha con e contra Pasolini," *Bianco e nero* 571 (2011): 21. Nepomuceno and Dall'Asta quote a letter from Rocha that, they write, characterizes *Claro* as "explicitly Pasolinian": "Christ arrives in Rome surrounded by workers.... Blind. Light that's blinding. Clearly." (28n4). Nepomuceno and Dall'Asta see both these remarks and *Claro* itself as referring back to *Il vangelo secondo Matteo* (*The Gospel According to Matthew* [1964]). I am not convinced by Rocha's framing of the film as allegory, though, and locate the "Pasolinian" element of *Claro* elsewhere. See also Glauber Rocha's short texts on Pasolini, "Un intellettuale europeo" and "Amor di maschio," trans. Nepomuceno, *Bianco e nero* 571 (2011): 30–35. In both of these texts, appreciation is laced with criticism of the tendencies in Pasolini's life and work that Rocha considers colonial. Compare Rocha's comments on the "cinema of men contaminated by phallocratic ideology" in his interview with Cinzia Bellumori, "Una intervista in Italia," in *Rocha: Glauber Rocha* (Florence: La Nuova Italia, 1975), 5. And for Pasolini's passing thoughts on Rocha, see his "Il 'cinema di poesia'" and "Il cinema impopolare," both in *Empirismo eretico* (Milan: Garzanti, 1972), 183, 278–97.

9. Rocha's exile was voluntary and preemptive. But in 2014, a Brazilian truth commission reportedly found that military officials had, in fact, identified the filmmaker as a target for assassination; see "Brazilian Dictatorship Wanted to Get Rid of Filmmaker Glauber Rocha," *Telesur* (August 18, 2014), http://www.telesurtv.net/english/news/Brazilian-dictatorship-wanted-to-get-rid-of-filmmaker-Glauber-Rocha-20140818-0009.html.

10. On *Salò*'s "pure interiority," see Gilles Deleuze, *Cinema 2: The Time Image*, trans. Hugh Tomlinson and Robert Galeta (Minneapolis: University of Minnesota Press, 2007), 175. And for another account of *Salò*'s closure, see Rei Terada, "Pasolini's Acceptance," in *Sovereignty in Ruins: A Politics of Crisis*, ed. Klaus Mladek and George Edmundson (Durham, N.C.: Duke University Press, 2017), 144–70.

11. See, for instance, Roberto Bolaño, *The Savage Detectives*, trans. Natasha Wimmer (New York: Farrar, Straus and Giroux, 2007), and Paul Beatty, *The Sellout* (New York: Farrar, Straus and Giroux, 2015). Bolaño's book begins and ends with poetry lessons, and Beatty's protagonist, who introduces backward reforms into local schools, also has a particular affinity for "rote" (106).

12. As in Chapter 3, I borrow the language of "retraversing" from John Dewey, *Democracy and Education: An Introduction to the Philosophy of Education* (New York: Macmillan, 1957), 85–86, where, to repeat, Dewey argues that "the business of education is rather to liberate the young from reviving and retraversing the past than to lead them to a recapitulation of it."

13. Deleuze, *Cinema 2*, 220. Joyce also approaches barbarism and cacophony in "Oxen": that episode's final paragraphs, for instance, open onto slang while also staging a release from the maternity ward in which "Oxen" has taken place. But this "afterbirth" in fact continues the adherence to stylistic sources that, throughout the episode, complicates Joyce's performance of defiance. *Claro*'s brand of barbarism differs from Joyce's in this sense, then: for all its insistence on the inescapability of Rome and empire, Rocha's film keeps inviting spectators to imagine the "decomposition" of both, or what Berto calls their "total, definitive destruction." Another difference follows from the different mediums in which Joyce and Rocha work. Film affords possibilities for cacophony (deliberately unrealized or at least understated in the "legible" *Salò*) that, with their simultaneity of sight and multiple sounds, far exceed what even Joyce could deliver. In another context, Roland Barthes distinguishes between true cacophony and what he calls "cacography": "the writing of noise, of impure communication; but this noise is not confused, massive, unnamable; it is a clear noise made up of connections, not superpositions"; Barthes, *S/Z*, trans. Richard Miller (New York: Hill and Wang, 1974), 132. *Claro*, by contrast, uses superpositions to produce noise that is indeed confused.

14. For a reading of the film that emphasizes exile, see Hudson Moura, "Glauber Rocha et l'image-exil dans *Claro*," *Cinémas* 15, no. 1 (2004).

15. These are also the languages used in *Le vent d'est* [*Wind from the East*] (1970), a film made by the Dziga Vertov Group, whose members included Jean-Luc Godard and Jean-Pierre Gorin. Rocha himself appears briefly in the film as himself, or rather as a Third World filmmaker who can literally point the way to politically engaged cinema. But his directions are ignored. *Le vent d'est* anticipates *Claro* in several other respects, including its reliance on repetitive voiceover. Although voiceover had already played a key role in Rocha's films at least since *Terra em transe*, and frequent repetition already characterizes the diegetic chants in *Der Leone Have Sept Cabeças* [*The Seven-Headed Lion*] (1970), *Claro* combines these elements, voiceover and repetition, in ways that recall *Le vent d'est*. Rocha, for his part, saw in *Le vent d'est* "a bourgeois anarchism, a destructive moralism," and even "the corpse of Godard"; see Glauber Rocha, "Godard's Latest Scandal," trans. Stoffel Debuysere, with Mari Shields, *Diagonal Thoughts*, December 21, 2013, http://www.diagonalthoughts.com/?p=2020; originally published as "O último escândalo de Godard," *Manchete* 928 (January 31, 1970). For more general reflections on the often-ambivalent relationship between Rocha and Godard, see Mateus Araújo, "Jean-Luc Godard e Glauber Rocha: Um diálogo a meio caminho," in *Godard inteiro ou o mundo em pedaços*, ed. Mateus Araújo and Eugenio Puppo (São Paulo: Heco Produções, 2015), 29–44.

16. *OED*, s. v. "barbarism." "The use of words or expressions not in accordance with the classical standard of a language, especially such as are of foreign origin; [*originally*] the mixing of foreign words or phrases in Latin or Greek; *hence*, rudeness or unpolished condition of language."

17. See, for instance, Humberto Pereira da Silva, *Glauber Rocha: Cinema, estética e revolução* (Jundiaí: Paco Editorial, 2016), loc. 1037, Kindle. *Claro* is mentioned only once in Ismail Xavier's *Allegories of Underdevelopment: Aesthetics and Politics in Modern Brazilian Cinema* (Minneapolis: University of Minnesota Press, 1997), 256, in which Rocha's work occupies a central place.

18. These were previously excerpted at http://www.tempoglauber.com.br/b_07.html.
19. No DVD of *Claro* currently exists. This fact points to one important difference between Rocha and Pasolini, one that I hope readers will keep in mind even while I emphasize the continuities between the two directors' projects: their different standings within world cinema. Whereas an entire critical industry guarantees the global circulation and institutional survival of Pasolini's corpus, parts of Rocha's remain quite literally difficult to see. *Claro*, for instance, is very seldom screened, and so (at least until it recently became available on YouTube, though still only intermittently) the film has been more often cited than seen, more often gestured toward than critically analyzed. To borrow one of Rocha's own formulations, this marks one way in which colonialism still perdures. Thanks to Althea Wasow for our conversation about this.
20. Leo Bersani and Ulysse Dutoit, in "Merde Alors," *October* 13 (1980): 29.
21. James Joyce, *A Portrait of the Artist as a Young Man*, ed. Jeri Johnson (New York: Oxford University Press, 1994), 178–79.
22. Carlos Drummond de Andrade, *Claro enigma: Poesia* (Rio de Janeiro: José Olympio, 1951).
23. I cite from a Portuguese translation of the interview with Rocha originally published in *Paese sera* (July 23, 1975), excerpted at http://www.tempoglauber.com.br/f_claro.html.
24. On the pedagogical dimension in Godard's films from this period, including *La chinoise* and *Le gai savoir*, see Michael Cramer, "Idées vagues/images claires: Image, Pedagogy, and Politics in the Films of Jean-Luc Godard, 1966–1969," *October* 157 (2016): 90–106.
25. See, for instance, Sigmund Freud, *Civilization and Its Discontents*, in *The Standard Edition of the Complete Psychological Works of Sigmund Freud, vol. 21, 1927–1931: The Future of an Illusion, Civilization and Its Discontents, and Other Works*, ed. and trans. James Strachey with Anna Freud, Alix Strachey, and Alan Tyson (London: Hogarth and Institute of Psycho-Analysis, 1961), 69–71. Marco d'Eramo recalls and updates Freud's reflections in "The Not So Eternal City," trans. Oonagh Stransky, *New Left Review* 106 (2017): 77–103.
26. Rocha, "Uma estética da fome," *Revista Civilização Brasileira* 3 (1965): 170; "The [sic] Aesthetics of Hunger," trans. Burnes Hollyman and Randal Johnson, in *Twenty-Five Years of the New Latin American Cinema*, ed. Michael Chanan (London: BFI, 1983), 13. I note that the English translation is abridged and otherwise inaccurate. Compare this "germe vivo" to the "living word" emphasized in Moura's account of the movement in "Glauber Rocha et l'image-exil dans *Claro*," 86.
27. Rocha, "Uma estética da fome," 170; "Aesthetics of Hunger," 14.
28. Ibid.; emphasis in original, translation modified.
29. Deleuze, *Cinema 2*, 218.
30. On *conscientização* defined as "the deepening of the attitude of awareness characteristic of all emergence," see Paulo Freire, *Pedagogy of the Oppressed*, trans. Myra Bergman Ramos (New York: Continuum, 2005), 109; *Pedagogia do oprimido* (Rio de Janeiro: Paz e Terra, 2014), 142. Hereafter, citations of Freire are given parenthetically in the text, with the abbreviation *Pedagogy* used for the English and *Pedagogia* for the Portuguese. For Denise Ferreira da Silva, Freire's call for the "humanization" of the oppressed

would follow from a belief in "the promise of historicity." See Ferreira da Silva, *Toward a Global Idea of Race* (Minneapolis: University of Minnesota Press, 2007).

31. Rocha, "Uma estética da fome," 166; "Aesthetics of Hunger," 13; translation modified.

32. Pier Paolo Pasolini, "Fascista," ed. Massimo Fini, in *Scritti corsari* (Milan: Garzanti, 1975), 233.

33. I am thinking in particular of the work of Jared Sexton; see especially *Amalgamation Schemes: Antiblackness and the Critique of Multiracialism* (Minneapolis: University of Minnesota Press, 2008), which centers on "a figure of blackness supposed to stand in the way of future progress" (252). For a distillation and more recent reformulation of this book's argument, see Jared Sexton, "Don't Call It a Comeback: Slavery Is Not Yet Abolished," *Open Democracy* (June 17, 2015), https://www.opendemocracy.net/beyond slavery/jared-sexton/don%E2%80%99t-call-it-comeback-racial-slavery-is-not-yet -abolished. And for a key study informing Sexton's project, see Guyora Binder, "The Slavery of Emancipation," *Cardozo Law Review* 16 (1996): 2063–2102.

34. Rocha, "Uma estética da fome," 165; "Aesthetics of Hunger," 13; emphasis in original.

35. Rocha, "Uma estética da fome," 166; "Aesthetics of Hunger," 13; emphasis in original.

36. Frantz Fanon, *Black Skin, White Masks*, trans. Richard Philcox (New York: Grove, 2008), 130, 128. Fanon quotes the phrase "mnemonic residues" from Freud on page 111 of the same text. The phrase is taken from the first of Freud's *Five Lectures*; see Freud, *Standard Edition of the Complete Psychological Works of Sigmund Freud*, vol. 11, *1910*, ed. and trans. James Strachey, with Anna Freud, Alix Strachey, and Alan Tyson (London: Hogarth Press and Institute of Psycho-Analysis, 1957), 14, but Fanon's translator renders the German "Gedächtnisreste" differently than does Strachey. For the German, see Freud, *Gesammelte Werke, vol. 8, 1909–1913*, ed. Marie Bonaparte et al. (London: Imago, 1943), 9. For Rocha's tribute to "father Fanon," see Rocha, "Amor di maschio," 33.

37. Here and in the rest of this chapter, I transcribe the film's monologues, marking both grammatical errors and the mixing of languages by indicating the wording in the original after my English translation.

38. For an account of Rocha's time in Cuba, where he lived before settling in Europe, see Eryk Rocha's documentary *Rocha que voa* (2002).

39. For more on the Italian context during this period, as well as the place of Chile in the imaginary of the Italian left, see Paul Ginsborg, "Crisis, Compromise, and the 'Anni di Piombo,'" in *A History of Contemporary Italy: Society and Politics, 1943–1988* (New York: St. Martin's, 2003), 348–405.

40. See also Xavier, *Allegories of Underdevelopment*, e.g., 124, which locates the decisive shift away from "an allegory of hope, or the teleological view of history," in Rocha's work in *Terra em transe* (89).

41. James Phillips, "Glauber Rocha: Hunger and Garbage," in *Cinematic Thinking: Philosophical Approaches to the New Cinema*, ed. James Phillips (Stanford, Calif.: Stanford University Press, 2008), 93, 92.

42. Pereira da Silva, *Glauber Rocha*, loc. 1037, Kindle.

43. But on Rome's ongoing disintegration, see d'Eramo, "Not So Eternal City."

44. Rocha, "The Tricontinental Filmmaker: That Is Called the Dawn," trans. Burnes Hollyman and Robert Stam, in *Brazilian Cinema*, expanded edition, ed. Randal Johnson and Robert Stam (New York: Columbia University Press, 1995), 77. On "guerrilla cinema," see also Octavio Getino and Fernando Solanas, "Toward a Third Cinema," *Tricontinental* 14 (1969): 107–132.

45. "For the Third World filmmaker, commitment begins with the first light, because the camera opens onto the Third World, an occupied land"; ibid., trans. modified.

46. Imperial Rome is, however, already apostrophized in the clearly "tricontinental" *Der Leone Have Sept Cabeças*, when a would-be postcolonial African dictator, backed by the European powers only apparently gone, quotes Corneille in a vivid and strangely beautiful sequence that anticipates the brilliant, satirical opening of Ousmane Sembène's *Xala* (1975). "Roma," he recites, "o único objeto do meu ressentimento!"

47. Phillips, "Glauber Rocha: Hunger and Garbage," 108.

48. Ibid., 102, 108.

49. For another argument against such a decision, see Edward Said, *Freud and the Non-European* (New York: Verso, 2003).

50. *OED*, s. v. "barbarous."

51. Phillips, "Glauber Rocha: Hunger and Garbage," 90.

52. Ibid.

53. Ibid.

54. Ibid., 92.

55. Ibid., 100.

56. Ibid., 108.

57. See Walter D. Mignolo, *The Idea of Latin America* (London: Blackwell, 2005), 75–76.

58. And when her interlocutor names "maestro Rossellini," she makes the sign of the cross, as if some directors were not only despotic but also divine.

59. For an account of *Claro* as autobiography and a reading of the film that emphasizes Rocha's "vulnerable politics," see José Gatti, "Impersonations of Glauber Rocha by Glauber Rocha," in *The Cinema of Me: The Self and Subjectivity in First-Person Documentary*, ed. Alisa Lebow (London: Wallflower, 2012).

60. Moura, too, misidentifies the statue, claiming that it is of Augustus Octavian, the emperor Rocha will go on to name in the voiceover that captions this shot; Moura, "Glauber Rocha et l'image-exil dans *Claro*," 92. This slip perhaps illustrates the surprising power of Rocha's monologue; for all its apparent incoherence, the repetitive voiceover prompts the critic to repeat, rather than interrogate, its phrases.

61. For more recent reflections on the Roman Empire's endlessness, see Ika Willis, "The Empire Never Ended," in *Classics in Post-Colonial Worlds*, ed. Lorna Hardwick and Carol Gillespie (Oxford: Oxford University Press, 2007), 329–48. For a contrasting argument that warns against "our present moment's obsessive returns to Rome" on grounds that these lead to accounts of empire as "a vague, transhistorical, deterritorialized" and wishfully "postnational mode of existence," see Vilashini Cooppan, "The Ruins of Empire: The National and Global Politics of America's Return to Rome," in *Postcolonial Studies and Beyond*, ed. Ania Loomba, Jed Esty, Antoinette Burton, Matti Bunzi, and Suvir Kaul (Durham: Duke University Press, 2005), 83–84.

62. Thus whereas Gatti argues that *Claro* points up "the uselessness of a certain political cinema based on the repetition of empty directives," I would counter that the film in fact engages (whether "uselessly" or otherwise) in this repetition precisely. What else but an "empty directive" is it when Rocha instructs spectators to behold "the last image of the West" in a frame that neither ends his film nor effects the decline and fall of what *Claro* calls "democratic imperialism"? See Gatti, "Impersonations of Glauber Rocha by Glauber Rocha."

63. For an introduction to the role of Romanness in the discourse of the Fascist regime, see Marla Stone, "A Flexible Rome: Fascism and the Cult of *romanità*," in *Roman Presences: Receptions of Rome in European Culture, 1789–1945*, ed. Catherine Edwards (Cambridge: Cambridge University Press, 1999), 205–20. On "the cult of the *Duce*" in particular, see 208. See also Simonetta Falasca-Zamponi, "The Myth of Rome," in *Fascist Spectacle: The Aesthetics of Power in Mussolini's Italy* (Berkeley: University of California Press, 1997), 90–99.

64. As in Jean-Marie Straub and Danièle Huillet's adaptation of Brecht, *Geschichtsunterricht* [*History Lessons*], 1972.

65. On the films that Rossellini made for television between 1962 and 1976, during the final phase of his career, see Michael Cramer, "Television as Enlightenment: Roberto Rossellini's History Lessons," in *Utopian Television: Rossellini, Watkins, and Godard Beyond Cinema* (Minneapolis: University of Minnesota Press, 2017), 41–80. On the avowedly progressive as well as the pedagogical nature of this project, see, e.g., 48.

66. See, again, Dall'Asta and Nepomuceno, "Glauber Rocha con e contra Pasolini," 21.

67. Gramsci, *Quaderni del carcere*, 3:1544; *Selections from Prison Notebooks*, ed. and trans. Quinton Hoare and Geoffrey Nowell Smith (New York: International, 1971), 37.

68. J. Laplanche and J.-B. Pontalis, *The Language of Psychoanalysis*, trans. Donald Nicholson-Smith (New York: Norton, 1973), 365; quoted in Joan Copjec, "*India Song/Son nom de Venise dans Calcutta désert*: The Compulsion to Repeat," *October* 17 (1981): 49.

69. Jacques Derrida, *Of Grammatology*, trans. Gayatri Chakravorty Spivak (Baltimore: Johns Hopkins University Press, 1997), 168. For a historical account of liberal freedom's inseparability from various forms of bondage, see Domenico Losurdo, *Liberalism: A Counter-History*, trans. Gregory Elliott (New York: Verso, 2011).

70. Phillips, "Glauber Rocha: Hunger and Garbage," 108.

71. Indeed, circular movements recur frequently and strikingly in Rocha's other films. Consider the scene that shows Rosa grinding manioc early in *Deus e o diablo*, or the remarkable, repetitive shot showing soldiers as they march in circles for what feels like forever in *Der Leone Have Sept Cabeças*.

72. For a reading that emphasizes the role of spontaneity in Rocha's work, see Phillips, "Glauber Rocha: Hunger and Garbage," 102, 106, 108. Again, the phrase "priority of the other" is used several times in Jean Laplanche, *Essays on Otherness*, ed. John Fletcher (New York: Routledge, 1999), e.g., 74.

73. Jean Laplanche sees "the site of culture" as "reopening ... the dimension of alterity" and thus, like analysis, reactivating the subject's (non-)relationship to the enigma; Laplanche, *Essays on Otherness*, 229–30. I am suggesting that education belongs on this same continuum, together with the "culture" that *Claro* instantiates. See also Barbara Johnson, "The Poet's Mother," in *Mother Tongues: Sexuality, Trials, Motherhood, Translation*

(Cambridge, Mass.: Harvard University Press, 2003), 66. Remarkably, Gramsci makes a comparable suggestion when he notes that in a sense the study of grammar begins with the infant's babbling "under the guidance of its parents" and continues "always," throughout adult life as well as youth. Such study therefore cuts across the divide between home and school; see Antonio Gramsci, *Quaderni del carcere,* ed. Valentino Gerratana (Turin: Einaudi, 2007), 1543, 2349.

74. Walter Pater, *Plato and Platonism* (London: Macmillan, 1901), 221.

75. Deleuze, *Cinema 2*, 220.

76. Ibid., 216. Interestingly, Deleuze adapts this phrase from Bene. See Deleuze, *Cinema 2*, 320n41. In "Pasolini's Acceptance," in *Sovereignty in Ruins: A Politics of Crisis*, ed. Klaus Mladek and George Edmundson (Durham, N.C.: Duke University Press, 2017), Rei Terada argues persuasively that both *Salò* and Pasolini's "Abiura" haunt Deleuze's pages on modern political cinema. Returning to these same pages in the context of Rocha's films, which Deleuze addresses explicitly, can lead to another account of their significance and Third World specificity.

77. Deleuze, *Cinema 2*, 217.

78. Ibid., 218.

79. Ibid., 217.

80. Ibid., 218.

81. Ibid., 220.

82. Compare the moment when, earlier in *Cinema 2*, Deleuze writes that the "purely optical and sound situation" in postwar film "makes us grasp, it is supposed to make us grasp, something intolerable and unbearable"; *Cinema 2,* 18. I noticed this "stutter" thanks to Terada, who offers an appreciative but ultimately critical take on Deleuze's account of the time-image in her extraordinary essay "Looking at the Stars Forever," *Studies in Romanticism* 50, no. 2 (2011): 285.

83. Deleuze, *Cinema 2*, 222.

84. Gilles Deleuze and Claire Parnet, "Dead Psychoanalysis: Analyse," in *Dialogues*, trans. Hugh Tomlinson and Barbara Habberjam (New York: Columbia University Press, 1987), 78. But on Freud's own identification with Hannibal, see Ellen Oliensis, "Freud's Rome," in *Freud's Rome: Psychoanalysis and Latin Poetry* (Cambridge: Cambridge University Press, 2009), 128–29. Following Laplanche, I have been calling the insight that I refer to here an insight into "the priority of the other." It might also be called an insight into "constitutive alienation." On why, in addition to being Freudian and Lacanian, this understanding of alienation is also Marxist, see Samo Tomšič's magisterial *The Capitalist Unconscious: Marx and Lacan* (New York: Verso, 2015).

85. Recall these lines delivered by Berto in voiceover in Godard's *Le gai savoir*: "I'm listening. In films, we always see people talking, never listening." It is as though Berto's capacity for listening carries over, then, into *Claro*.

86. Deleuze, *Cinema 2*, 2.

87. In another context, Judith Butler distinguishes between the idea "that violence can be understood to bring the human into being" and the claim "that colonization is a precondition for humanization." The latter claim characterizes apologies for colonialism, Butler observes, whereas the former underwrites Fanon's anticolonial stance; see Butler, "Violence, Nonviolence: Sartre on Fanon," in *Senses of the Subject* (New

York: Fordham University Press, 2015), 184. I am suggesting that *Claro* makes the former, not the latter, kind of claim. On Rocha's controversial late-career praise for leading figures in the Brazilian military government, see Serge Daney, "Glauber Rocha's Death," in Costantini, Goldman, and Cangi, *Glauber Rocha*, 332–34, and Carlos Lopes, "Glauber Rocha e a ditadura," *O Martelo* 22, http://omartelo.com/omartelo22/materia1.html.

88. Alenka Zupančič writes, "Contradiction is not simply something that we have to accept and 'make due with'; it can become, and be 'used' as, the source of emancipation from the very logic dictated by this contradiction. This is what [psycho]analysis ideally leads to: contradiction does not simply disappear, but the way it functions in the discourse structuring our reality changes radically. And this happens as a result of our fully and actively *engaging in the contradiction,* taking our place in it"; Zupančič, *What Is Sex?* (Cambridge, Mass.: MIT Press, 2017), 72; emphasis in original.

89. Glauber Rocha, "Uma estética da fome," *Revista Civilização Brasileira* 3 (1965): 166; "The Aesthetics of Hunger," trans. Burnes Hollyman and Randal Johnson, in *Twenty-Five Years of the New Latin American Cinema*, ed. Michael Chanan (London: BFI, 1983), 13. This is also how Getino and Solanas, for instance, distinguish neocolonialism from colonialism; see Getino and Solanas, "Toward a Third Cinema," e.g., 117; see also their film *La hora de los hornos* [*The Hour of the Furnaces*] (1968). And here is Rocha in a later interview, again recalling Fanon indirectly: "The American cinema has to take a lot of the blame for Third World colonisation. That is to say the American cinema created the framework for the national inferiority complexes of the peoples of the Third World"; Simon Hartog, "There's Nothing More International than A Pack of Pimps: A Conversation between Pierre Clémenti, Miklos Jansco, Glauber Rocha, and Jean-Marie Straub," trans. John Matthews, *Rouge* 3 (2004), http://www.rouge.com.au/3/international.html; originally published in *Cinematics* 4 (1970). Compare the claim made in *Der Leone Have Sept Cabeças*: "the principal problem of the struggle against colonialism is the destruction of the national inferiority complex."

90. Joyce, *Ulysses*, 17.703–4.

91. Some readers may be thinking that the problem is surely not that we have learned too much from Freire, but rather that we have learned too little. *Pedagogy of the Oppressed* was, for instance, among the so-called "ethnic studies" books banned in Arizona public schools until August 2017. And this fact attests to the text's lasting power—or rather to the still-real threat it is perceived to pose to those in power. In Brazil, Freire remains the target and the most visible representative of the kind of "indoctrinating" education that the far-right Programa Escola sem Partido (or Program for School without Party) seeks to outlaw. And yet here we come full circle, back to Gentile, because the Programa Escola sem Partido's discourse, like the discourse of Mussolini's minister of education, relies on constant appeals to students' freedom from impingement, from imposition, from outmoded instruction. This discourse distorts, in other words, almost but not quite beyond recognition, Freire's own vocabulary in order to recast him as the Latin teacher from whose coercive class we need to graduate. I have tried to show, following Gramsci, why the amenability of progressive education to co-optation by reactionary forces, forces opposed to real freedom but claiming to defend it, is worth taking seriously, and why this co-optation is worth reading symptomatically—that is, as a symptom of a disavowal in the progressive tradition itself. Again, to say this is not to say

that we can do without this tradition. But it is to call for analysis of countertraditions and to try to account for the critical force of the particular countertradition that I call counter-progressive.

92. See Rocha, "Aesthetic of Dream," in Costantini, Goldman, and Cangi, *Glauber Rocha*, 289–290; for the Portuguese, see "Eztetyka do sonho," 47–49. Note that I have modified the translation of the manifesto's title. On *Claro*'s close relation to this manifesto, see Rubens Machado Jr., "The Resonant Times of Hélio Oiticica's Quasi-Film," in *Ism, ism, ism / Ismo, ismo, ismo: Experimental Cinema in Latin America*, ed. Jesse Lerner and Luciano Piazza (Oakland: University of California Press, 2017), 358.

93. In another context, I argue for the necessity of non sequitur in Ramsey McGlazer, "The Fortress Deserted: Bersani's Pastorals," *Qui Parle* 24, no. 1 (2015): 147–59.

94. I note that Freire's translator omits the final phrase, which anticipates the end of Pasolini's "Abiura," at a distance: "in the face of which the obvious is adaptation." *Esmagadora*, rendered by Freire's translator as "overwhelming," can also mean "crushing."

95. Nancy Scheper-Hughes, *Death Without Weeping: The Violence of Everyday Life in Brazil* (Berkeley: University of California Press, 1992), 531. Scheper-Hughes is relying on the critique of Freire found in Roger Lancaster, *Thanks to God and the Revolution: Popular Religion and Class Consciousness in the New Nicaragua* (New York: Columbia University Press, 1988), 199. Here, too, we come full circle, returning to Gramsci's response to the Riforma Gentile. For Gramsci argued inter alia that the reformers' efforts to "liberate the school from mechanism" led them to imagine a student who was in fact more passive and mechanical, not less, than the student in the old school: "The more the new curricula nominally affirm and theorise the pupil's activity ... the more they are actually designed as if the pupil were purely passive [una mera passività]"; Gramsci, *Quaderni del carcere*, 1543; *Selections from Prison Notebooks*, 37.

96. For a critique of the Freirean discourse of dialogue as it entered educational theory in the United States, see Elizabeth Ellsworth, "Why Doesn't This Feel Empowering?: Working through the Repressive Myths of Critical Pedagogy," *Harvard Educational Review* 59, no. 3 (1989): 297–324. For a broader overview of Freire's reception and a response to some of the most influential critiques of his work, see Kelvin Stewart Beckett, "Paulo Freire and the Concept of Education," *Educational Philosophy and Theory* 45, no. 1 (2013): 49–62. And for a moving recent defense of Freire, see Nivedita Menon, "The University as Utopia: Critical Thinking and the Work of Social Transformation," *Critical Times* 2, no. 1 (2019).

97. Rocha, "Aesthetic of Dream," in Costantini, Goldman, and Cangi, *Glauber Rocha*, 290, translation slightly modified; for the Portuguese, see "Eztetyka do sonho," 49.

98. Adam Phillips reminds us that dreaming is "something we are not taught to do"; "we can be taught to interpret dreams but not to dream them"; Phillips, "Learning to Live: Psychoanalysis as Education," in *Side Effects* (New York: Harper Perennial, 2006), 143.

99. "Top down" is Freire's translator's way of rendering Freire's "veritcalidade" idiomatically (*Pedagogia* 117).

100. Pater, *Marius the Epicurean*, ed. Michael Levey (New York: Penguin, 1985), 137.

101. Joyce, *Ulysses*, 14.1591.

Index

"Abiura dalla *Trilogia della vita*" (Pasolini), 20, 120–22, 124, 125, 129, 133, 144, 174n82, 215n76, 217n94
actualism (in Gentile), 84, 191n70
Adorno, Theodor, 10; *Dialectic of Enlightenment*, 123, 204n45; "Education for Autonomy," 8
Aeneid (Virgil), 77, 80, 184n115
aestheticism, 33, 93, 108, 110, 149, 182n82, 183n83
aesthetics, 6, 30, 33, 36–9, 41, 52–3, 57, 115–16, 169n53, 181nn51,57, 200nn5–6
"Aesthetics of Hunger" (Rocha), 141–42, 144–45, 149, 157, 159
"Aesthetics of the Dream" (Rocha), 159
Aetius, 152–53
Agamben, Giorgio, 173n79, 187n22, 204n41, 206–7n82; "Pascoli and the Thought of the Voice," 62, 64–67, 71, 72, 75
Alexamenos graffito, 75–78, 83, 185–86n9, 189n51
alienation, 2, 48, 145, 151, 215n84
allegory, 97, 117, 126, 205n64, 209n8, 212n40
Althusser, Louis, 12
Amiran, Eyal, 183n87
ancient languages. *See* dead language
Angelico, Fra, 206n79
anthologies, 97, 102
anticolonialism, 102, 138, 141, 148, 149, 159, 215n87, 216n89
anti-democratic education, 5, 136, 169n54, 195–96n37
anti-fascism, 119, 203n28
Antonines, 152, 155
Aquinas, Thomas, Saint, 89

Aravamudan, Srinivas, 208n1
Arcades Project (Benjamin), 85–86
Arendt, Hannah, 148
Asad, Talal, 173n79, 183–84n96, 205n67
Ascham, Roger, *The Scholemaster*, 97
Asquith, Anthony, *The Browning Version*, 14–16, 17
assemblies, 54, 105, 129, 158
Atilla, 152
Auden, W. H., "In Memory of Sigmund Freud," 22
Aurelius, Marcus, 46, 47, 48, 151
auteurs, 149, 172n71, 213n58
Autobiography (Mill), 28, 35, 38, 43

backwardness, 4, 10, 22, 23, 48, 72–74, 83, 91, 98, 100, 106, 114–18, 128, 136, 139, 175n95
bad education, 101, 112, 167n29
Baer, Benjamin Conisbee, 11, 12
Baldwin, James, 198n78
banking concept of education, 6
"barbarism," 64, 139, 149, 210nn13,16
Barravento (Rocha), 148
Barthes, Roland, 31, 52; *How to Live Together*, 53–55, 57; *S/Z*, 123, 124, 125, 210n13
Bataille, Georges, 123, 204n45
Beatty, Paul, *The Sellout*, 209n11
Beckett, Samuel, *The Unnamable*, 196n46
belatedness (national), 23, 67–8, 75, 119
Bellini, Vincenzo, *Norma*, 153
Bene, Carmelo, 151–53, 155, 215n76; *S.A.D.E.*, 151
Benedetti, Carla, 204n50
Benjamin, Walter, 20, 84, 88; *Arcades Project*, 85–86

Berardi, Franco "Bifo," 171n67
Berger, John, 201–2n17
Berlanda, Marco, 191n70
Berlusconi, Silvio, 200–1n7
Bersani, Leo, 21, 89, 96–98, 104, 132, 134, 200nn5–6
Berto, Juliet, 141, 149–50, 152–53, 155–59, 210n13, 215n85
Bettini, Maurizio, 170n63, 189n41
Bildung, 35, 47, 63, 68, 84
Bildungsromane, 88
Biscuso, Massimo, 11, 12
Blake, William, 40
Blanchot, Maurice, 123, 187n20
Bolaño, Roberto, *The Savage Detectives*, 209n11
Bollas, Christopher, 202n19
Bologna Process, 171n68
Bonetta, Gaetano, 69, 70, 189n41
Bonifazio, Paula, 119
boredom, 13, 14, 108, 167n29
Borch-Jacobsen, Mikkel, 199n89
Bourdieu, Pierre, 12, 207–8n99
Brazil, 216n91; military dictatorship (1964–1985), 144, 146, 209n9, 215–16n87
Browning Version, The (Asquith), 14–16, 17, 18
Butler, Judith, 12, 215n87

cacophony, 139, 148, 158, 210n13
capitalism, 11, 13, 23, 146, 169n58, 170n57, 175–76n103; Pasolini's account of, 117, 119–22, 125, 126; Rocha's account of, 141. *See also* modernization
Cannes, 140
canon, 59, 61, 97, 108, 186n12, 211n19
Cantos (Pound), 208n102
Carlyle, Thomas, *Sartor Resartus*, 42–43, 52
Carson, Anne, 189n47
casting (in film), 115, 127, 141, 149, 208–9n3, 215n85
catechism, 2, 89, 95, 193n4
Catholicism, 19, 31, 36, 110, 199n86

Certamen Hoefftianium, 192n87
Chakrabarty, Dipesh, 208n2
Chaldea, 78, 137
Chiesa, Lorenzo, 205n63, 207n91
Chiesi, Roberto, 201n13
Chile, 144, 212n39
child-centered education, 165n8, 171–72n68
"Child in the House, The" (Pater), 34–35, 37, 39–40
chinoise, La (Godard), 141, 211n24
chrononormativity, 92, 194n17
cinema. *See* film
Cinema 2 (Deleuze), 141–42, 145, 157, 158, 209n10, 210n13, 215nn76,82
Cinema Novo, 10, 141–44, 146
citizenship, 6, 92, 116, 148, 149, 156, 200–1n7; as abstraction, 183n87; education as training for, 7, 29, 43, 68, 71, 75
civilizational hierarchy, 6, 30, 52
Clark, T. J., 172n71
Claro (Rocha), 13, 17, 23, 138–60, 167n29, 211n19, 215n85
Claro enigma (de Andrade), 140
class (struggle), 5, 6, 11, 69, 158, 169n54, 180n45, 192–93n92, 195–96n37
classical political cinema, 141–42
classicism, 6, 31, 70, 74–75, 82, 84, 106, 108, 112, 169n54, 189nn40–41
cliché, 18, 25, 61, 73, 189n47
commonplacing, 173n76
common sense, 17, 18, 41, 44, 70
communism, 119, 143, 158
colonialism, 50, 138, 209n8, 211n19, 215n87; English, 102, 182n64, 199n86; Italian, 137, 191n79; Latin American, 138, 141–43, 149, 216n89. *See also* anticolonialism; neo-colonialism; postcoloniality
Comay, Rebecca, 84–87, 174n89, 205n65
comparativism, 20, 173n80
compulsoriness, 2, 6, 7, 13, 17, 112, 119, 122, 155
compulsory Greek, 79

compulsory Latin, 5, 119. *See also* educational reform; Riforma Gentile
Confusions of Young Törless (Musil), 88
conscientização, 142, 211n30
constraint, 2, 7, 8, 10, 17, 28, 40, 49, 93, 102, 114–15, 126, 138, 156, 157, 158, 168n36, 172n69, 199n89
contradiction, 5, 7, 8, 74, 126, 141, 145, 159, 173n79, 216n88
convention, 8, 125, 133, 166n14; in Pater, 10, 28, 31, 39, 47, 48, 50–51, 55, 138
Contini, Gianfranco, 65, 185n4
Cooppan, Vilashini, 213n61
Copjec, Joan, 200n5, 200–1n7, 206n76
copying, 19, 98; in Flaubert, 14, 99; Joyce's passages from Pater, 109–11; in Joyce's *Portrait*, 99; in Joyce's *Ulysses*, 17, 94–95, 101, 104, 112, 138, 160, 199n86; in Spark, 18, 173n76; in Woolf, 196n47. *See also* pensums
Cramer, Michael, 211n24
Crary, Jonathan, 175–76n103
critique, immanent, 7; of aesthetic autonomy, 149; of cram, 18, 43, 182n64; in Derrida, 188nn25,28; of the "family romance" in Pascoli criticism, 185n8; of Freire, 159, 217nn95–96; of modernist studies, 165–66n10; of the old school, 7, 68, 82, 118, 197n66; old school as unlikely resource for, 4, 32, 41; of pedagogy, 174n86; of progress, 11, 20, 30, 32, 118, 201–2n17; queer, 92, 194n26; of Rancière, 175n97; Rocha's of Pasolini, 155; of violence, 150
Croce, Benedetto, 119, 121, 184–85n1, 185n2, 203n27
counter-progressive pedagogy, 1–23, 27, 51, 93, 112, 114, 126, 137–39, 145, 150, 156, 158–60
Cuba, 212n38

Daney, Serge, 215–16n87
Dante, 39, 185n7. *See also* Dolce Stil Novo

Darwin, Charles, 106, 107
da Silva, Denise Ferreira, 210n17
Dayan, Colin, 201–2n17
de Andrade, Carlos Drummond, *Claro enigma*, 140
de Beauvoir, Simone, 123
dead language, 5–6, 17, 23, 42–43, 168–69n45; in Gentile, 21, 23, 82–83; in Joyce, 94, 100, 102; in Pascoli, 21, 64, 70–75, 78, 82, 83–84, 137; in Pater, 34, 41, 44. *See also* Latin (language)
deconstruction, 41
Deleuze, Gilles, 158, 203n27; *Cinema 2*, 141–42, 145, 157, 158, 209n10, 210n13, 215nn76,82
De Man, Paul, 181nn51,57
De Martino, Ernesto, *La terra del rimorso*, 127–29, 130, 134, 206n74, 207–8n99
democracy, 5, 6, 7, 69, 119, 136, 151, 177n11, 180n45, 182n79, 184n106, 214n62
Democracy and Education (Dewey), 102–4, 105–7, 111, 112, 146, 209n12
dependency, 156, 57, 113; in Rocha, 142–43, 149; in Rousseau, 7, 29
d'Eramo, Marco, 211n25
Derrida, Jacques, 156, 181n57, 188n25; on analysis, 175n95; on literacy, 66, 188n28; on ritual, 179n41; on the supplement, 100
de Sanctis, Francesco, 67
detention, 98, 99, 103, 122
Deus e o diablo na terra do sol (Rocha), 148
Deutscher, Penelope, 2
developmentalism (in educational theory), 101, 197n57
De Vos, Betsy, 171n68
Dewey, John, 3, 16, 99, 101, 145, 155, 166n11, 197n57; *Democracy and Education*, 102–4, 105–7, 111, 112, 146, 209n12
dialectic, 7, 125, 130, 138, 140, 160, 167n29, 195n33; Hegelian, 83

Dialectic of Enlightenment (Adorno and Horkheimer), 123, 201–2n17
Díaz, Porfirio, 144
dictation, 46, 51, 64, 66, 188n28
dictatorship, 18, 144, 146, 175–76n103, 209n9, 213n46
dictionaries, 18; Pater and, 34, 41–42, 44, 57
diegetic music, 135, 153
Didi-Huberman, Georges, 130, 182n71, 200n2, 201n14, 202n19, 206n79
disavowal, 130; of fascism, 115, 130; in progressive educational theory, 8, 22, 156, 159, 216n91
discipline, 7, 16; in Gramsci, 5, 6, 7; in Foucault, 130–31; in Pater, 30, 38, 42
Divina Commedia (Dante), 39
docility, 13, 23, 109
Dolce Stil Novo, 60, 61
Donatello, 206n79
doodling, 155
Dowling, Linda, 41–42, 177n11
drag, 151, 153, 155
dreaming, 7, 23, 160; in Joyce, 105, 112; in Pater, 37, 47, 54–55; in Rocha, 23, 159–60
Dubliners (Joyce), 10, 89, 199n86
Dutoit, Ulysse, 200nn5–6
Dziga Vertov Group, 210n15

Edelman, Lee, 2, 101, 112, 175n92, 187n20
educational reform, 7, 13, 18, 99, 101–3, 112; in liberal Italy, 68–70, 74–75, 78, 82, 84–85, 189n40; neoliberal, 16, 171n68; in Victorian England, 17, 28, 29, 32, 38, 43, 52, 180nn45,47, 183n89. *See also* liberalism; progressive education; Riforma Gentile
educational theory. *See* pedagogy
Egyptians, 148, 149, 157–58
Eisenstein, Sergei, 149
Eliot, T. S., 6, 91, 112, 135, 208n102
Émile, or On Education (Rousseau), 3, 7, 16, 28–30, 35, 99, 101–5, 110, 112, 113, 118, 127, 146, 155–56, 166n11, 167n28, 197n66
empire, 6, 77, 78, 136, 148, 150–51, 182n79, 199n86, 210n13, 213n61, 214n62. *See also* Rome; United States
Empson, William, *Some Versions of Pastoral*, 62–63, 79
English (language): in Joyce, 92, 95–97, 100, 104, 137, 195n34; in Pater, 26, 42, 43, 51, 57, 179n35
Enlightenment, 28, 168n36. *See also* Kant, Immanuel; Rousseau, Jean-Jacques
Escola sem Partido, 216n91
Esposito, Roberto, 121
Ethiopia, 120
etymology, 22, 28, 43, 98, 108, 136, 172n75; in Pater, 41, 44, 46; in Spark, 18, 19
Every Student Succeeds Act, 171n68
examinations, 38, 166n14, 180nn45,47

Fabbri, Lorenzo, 203n27
Falasca-Zamponi, Simonetta, 206n72
Fallace, Thomas, 171n68, 197–98n68
fanciullino, Il (Pascoli), 10, 59–63, 67, 80, 87, 185n7, 187n20
Fanon, Frantz, 146, 215n87, 216n89; *Black Skin, White Masks*, 212n36; *The Wretched of the Earth*, 149
Fascism (Italian), 18, 19, 80–81, 115, 118–20, 126, 130, 134–35, 142, 151, 157, 202n24, 203nn27–28; and ancient Rome, 6, 82–84, 152–153, 214n63. *See also* neo-Fascism; Republic of Salò; Riforma Gentile
feminism, 196n47
Ferguson, Frances, 166n11
Ferreri, Marco, *La grande abbuffata*, 205n65
film: as medium, 160; studies, 172n71, 203n27, 211n19
fiore dei Mille e una notte, Il (Pasolini), 120, 208n3

fixation, 201n14
Flaubert, Gustave, 184n115; *Madame Bovary*, 14, 98–99
Fogu, Claudio, 202n24, 203n27
forgetting, 1, 2, 8, 121–22, 130, 138; of Fascism in Italy, 127, 138, 203n27
Fortini, Franco, 203n28
Foucault, Michel, 130–32, 135
Franco, Jean, 11
François, Anne-Lise, 11, 12, 122, 201–2n17, 208n103
freedom: counter-progressive, 40, 156, 205n63; in education (fantasy of), 5, 17, 105, 216n91; in Gentile's educational theory, 7, 119, 126, 167n28; liberal, 8, 28, 54, 55, 90, 119, 156, 172n69, 214n69; in Marinetti, 165n10; in Pasolini, 10, 205n63; in Pater, 40, 49, 50, 180n48; in Rocha, 141, 148, 149; in Rousseau's *Émile*, 7, 167n28. *See also* liberation
Freeman, Elizabeth, 175n92, 194n17, 201–2n17
Freire, Paulo, 146, 166n11; *Pedagogy of the Oppressed*, 14, 142, 145–46, 151, 153, 155, 159, 211n30, 216n91, 217n96
frequentative, 100, 196n53
Freud, Sigmund, 21, 22, 213n49, 215n84; *Civilization and its Discontents*, 141; *The Future of An Illusion*, 191n79; letters to Wilhelm Fliess, 201n14; on psychoanalysis as education, 21, 177n86; "Remembering, Repeating, and Working Through," 22, 174n87; as Roman, 158; on Rome, 215n84; on survivals, 20, 21, 201n14; "Thoughts for the Times on War and Death," 22; on trauma, 142, 212n36. *See also* psychoanalysis
Futurism (Italian), 3, 165–66n10

gai savoir, Le (Godard), 141, 211n24
Gallo, Franco, 11, 12
Gallop, Jane, 174–75n90
Galluzzi, Francesco, 205n67, 206n78

Gandhi, Leela, 182n79
Gautier, Théophile, 15
gay marriage, 132, 149
gender, 97, 155, 172n75, 173n76, 180n45, 185n2; trouble, 197n62
generations, 7, 16, 21, 71–72, 73, 94–95, 103, 108, 125, 133, 166n11, 175n92
Genoa, 141
Gennariello (Pasolini), 23, 118
Gentile, Giovanni: "La libertà della scuola media," 67–68, 82–85, 87, 126, 136, 191nn70,78; *La riforma dell'educazione*, 2–9, 12, 16, 18, 19, 21, 22, 23, 81, 97, 99, 104, 112, 118–19, 126, 127, 155, 166nn11–12, 191n79, 191–92n82. *See also* Riforma Gentile
Getino, Octavio: *La hora de los hornos*, 216n89; "Toward a Third Cinema," 213n44, 216n89
Giansiracusa, G., 189n40
Gibson, Andrew, 99, 101, 64, 108, 194n18, 195–96n37
Godard, Jean-Luc: *La chinoise*, 141, 211n24; *Le gai savoir*, 141, 211n24, 215n85; *Le vent d'est*, 210n15; and Rocha, 210n15
Gorin, Jean-Pierre, *Le vent d'est*, 210n15
Goulart, João, 144
grades, 38
graffiti, 189–90n51. *See also* Alexamenos graffito
Grafton, Anthony, 169n54
grammar drills, 17, 78, 81
Gramsci, Antonio, *Prison Notebooks*, 3–9, 12, 16, 17, 18, 19, 20, 22–23, 30, 68, 119, 121, 167n28, 170n63, 214–15n73, 216–17n90, 217n95
grande abbuffata, La (Ferreri), 205n65
Greek (language, ancient), 28, 36, 42, 69, 72–74, 78, 79, 81–83, 89, 95, 149, 168–69n45, 170n63, 177n15, 189n41
Greeks (ancient), 148–49, 158
Greene, Shelleen, 208–9n3
Guillory, John, 186n12
gym class, 56

habit, 6, 25, 31, 33, 36, 45, 48–49, 92, 108, 177n11
Hanson, Ellis, 50
Harari, Roberto, 198n78
Harney, Stefano, 13, 170n62, 171n66
Harootunian, Harry, 174n81, 175–76n103
Hegel, G. W. F., 84; "On Classical Studies," 170n63, 191n78; *Phenomenology of Spirit*, 83, 191n78
hegemony, 12, 17, 68–69
Heidegger, Martin, 66
Heraclitus, 73
higher education. *See* universities
historicism, 20, 84
Hollywood, 148
Homer, 37; and Joyce, 90, 96, 112
home schooling, 29, 35, 43
homosexuality: in Joyce, 106–8, 110–11; in Pasolini, 10, 120, 132–14; in Pater, 32, 55–56, 111, 177n18, 178n27
hora de los hornos, La (Getino and Solanas), 216n89
Horace, 26, 27, 32, 58
Horkheimer, Max, *Dialectic of Enlightenment*, 123, 204n45
Hornby, Louise, 165–66n10
Hugh of St. Victor, 25
Huillet, Danièle, *Geschichtsunterricht*, 153, 214n64
Huxley, Thomas Henry, 106

identification, 112–13, 191–92n82, 199n89, 200n5. *See also* psychoanalysis
identity, 6, 13, 93, 112–13, 170n63
ideology, 11, 12, 27–28, 71, 101, 138, 209n8
Ignorant Schoolmaster, The (Rancière), 21, 175n97
Illich, Ivan, 172n75, 206n73
imperialism. *See* empire
indexicality, 41, 63, 66, 75–76, 189n51
infancy, 34, 59–61, 63, 65, 67, 103, 156, 185n5, 185–86n9, 187n20, 214–15n73

In Memoriam (Tennyson), 36–38
institutionality, 4, 12–13, 31, 62, 66, 79, 88, 89, 93, 112, 114, 168–69n45, 195n34, 211n19
instruction (as opposed to education), 1–4, 7, 10, 12, 13, 17, 19, 23, 68–69, 151, 156, 158, 160, 173n76, 199n86, 216n91; in Gentile, 2–4, 5, 18, 19, 21, 22, 68, 81, 82, 119; in Gramsci, 4–7, 8–9, 10, 18, 22, 166n14; in Joyce, 89, 93, 95–100, 105, 112–15; in Pascoli, 72–73, 78–79; in Pasolini, 118–19, 126, 127, 134, 136; in Pater, 27, 31, 32, 38, 43, 48; in Rocha, 139–40, 145, 153, 156
intellectuals, 69; in Gramsci, 4, 7, 8
interiority, 3, 27, 35, 36, 43, 45, 50, 84–85, 86, 118, 181n51, 183n89, 209n10
internalization, 7, 52, 120, 145, 159, 172n69
inwardness. *See* interiority
Iran, 120
Ireland, 4, 10, 102, 106, 166n12, 168–69n45, 194n18, 195n34
Irish (language), 95, 195n34
Italian (language), 60, 82–83, 139, 143, 191n77
Italy, 4, 11, 23, 67–70, 75, 81, 83, 87, 115, 118–20, 137, 153, 168–69n45, 170n63, 174n82, 191n77, 202n24, 203nn27,30. *See also* belatedness (national); Fascism (Italian); nation

Jacob's Room (Woolf), 196n47
Jackson, Virginia, 186n12
Jameson, Fredric, 169n48, 175–76n103
Jardine, Lisa, 169n54
Johnson, Barbara, 195n34
Joyce, James: reception, 89–90, 93, 96, 113; as teacher, 4, 166n12; Trieste Notebooks, 109–11, 198n83; works: "Drama and Life," 165n2; *Dubliners*, 10, 89, 199n86; "Epiphanies," 89; *Finnegans Wake*, 89; "The Holy Office," 89; *A Portrait of the Artist as*

a Young Man, 10, 89, 94, 99, 103, 140, 195n34, 199n86; *Ulysses* ("Circe," 98, 112, 196nn45–46; "Ithaca," 1–4, 22, 94–95, 193n4; "Lestrygonians," 107; "Nausicaa," 91, 107; "Nestor," 93–95, 97, 193n4; "Oxen of the Sun," 13, 17, 91–113, 114; "Penelope," 95; "Proteus," 107; "Wandering Rocks," 107)
Juvenal, 26

Kant, Immanuel, 6, 38, 168n36, 204n45
Kaufman, Robert, 12, 169n53
Kay-Shuttleworth, James, 43, 44, 52, 183n89
Keane, Webb, 50
Kenner, Hugh, 98, 109, 181n53, 193n8
Khalip, Jacques, 178n27, 181n51
Klossowski, Pierre, 104n60; *Sade My Neighbor*, 123, 125–26, 104n60
Kovács, András Balint, 172n71
Krauss, Rosalind, 189–90n51
Kurnick, David, 112, 196n45

labor, 5, 34, 37, 96–98, 104–5, 107, 140, 167n28, 170n62, 171n66, 196n47
laboriousness, 6, 26, 49, 93, 104, 105, 112, 146, 160
Lacan, Jacques, 158, 199n89, 214n84; "Kant with Sade," 123, 204n45; "The Signification of the Phallus," 61, 185n5; *The Sinthome*, 173n76
Laplanche, Jean, 20–21, 57, 155, 156, 174n88, 214–15n73, 215n84
late style, 9, 12, 23, 137, 170n55
Latin (language), 2, 5–8, 10, 12, 14, 17, 18, 20, 28, 42, 43, 45–46, 49, 57, 61, 62, 65, 68–69, 70, 73–75, 77, 78–79, 81–83, 85, 89, 91–92, 94, 96–97, 98–100, 101, 109, 118–19, 135–36, 139, 149, 167n30, 168–69n45, 169n54, 170n63, 173n79, 177n15, 185–86n9, 189n41, 191n82, 195n34, 199n86, 207n97, 216n91
Latin America, 141–43, 144, 149, 168–69n45

learning by heart. *See* memorization
lectures (in teaching), 17, 48, 151, 155
Leone Have Sept Cabeças, Der (Rocha), 148, 213n46, 216n89
Leopardi, Giacomo, 11, 12; "La ginestra," 23, 87; "L'infinito," 60; *Pensieri*, 85–88; *Zibaldone*, 61, 185n4
Lewis, Wyndham, *Time and Western Man*, 62, 186n13
liberalism, 8, 12, 13, 17, 27–30, 32, 40, 55, 138, 146, 166n11, 167n28, 176n9, 178n21, 182n79, 214n69; and individualism, 58, 177n11
liberation, 142–45, 146; alternative forms of, 145, 156, 205n63; progressive education as, 5, 6, 102–4, 112, 119, 209n12, 217n95; sexual, 117, 120
libertarianism, 4, 82, 171n67
liturgy, 31, 36, 39, 45, 50, 52, 166n14
Lloyd, David, 198n78
locations (in film), 141
Losurdo, Domenico, 214n69
love, 10, 35, 44, 49, 56, 64, 94, 102, 120–22, 134, 151, 184n115, 207n92; poetry, 122, 184n7
Love, Heather, 175n92, 178n27, 181n51, 201–2n17
Lycidas (Milton), 94
lyric poetry, 10, 12, 45, 59–61, 122, 184n7, 186n12

Madame Bovary (Flaubert), 14, 98–99
Maggi, Armando, 118, 135, 206nn74, 77–78
Mallock, W. H., *The New Republic*, 180n47
Mansoor, Jaleh, 203n30
Mao, Douglas, 180n48
Marcuse, Herbert, 125
Marinetti, F. T., 3, 165–66n10
Marius the Epicurean (Pater), 9, 13, 29–31, 33, 35, 37–38, 41, 44–52, 58, 110–11, 138, 139, 156, 179n42, 179–80n43

Marx, Karl, 146; *Capital, Volume 1*, 40; *Eighteenth Brumaire of Louis Bonaparte*, 108; *Grundrisse*, 136
maternity, 91, 96, 97, 99, 100, 101–2, 104–5, 111, 185n5, 195n34
McCrea, Barry, 11, 12, 94–95, 99, 169n54, 172n71
McGee, Patrick, 193n10
McGlazer, Ramsey, 113, 204n56, 217n93
McNulty, Tracy, 168n36, 172n69, 199n89
memorization, 3, 5, 7, 19, 25–27, 29, 31, 35, 39–40, 60, 68, 77–78, 80, 81, 86–87, 95, 145, 181n51, 185n4, 196n46, 199n86, 204–5n60
Mendelsohn, Daniel, 89–90, 91, 93
metaphor, 72, 74, 117, 126–27, 132
Mill, John Stuart, 177n11; *Autobiography*, 28–3, 35, 43, 48, 50, 51, 155
Miller, D. A., 175n92
Milton, *Lycidas*, 94
minorities, 157
Mishra, Pankaj, 201–2n17
modernism, 3, 11–12, 91, 112, 169n53, 175–76n103, 183n87, 186n13; Brazilian, 140; cinematic, 157, 172n71, 215n76; defined, 172n71; Italian, peculiarity of, 172n71; limit cases of, 172n71; Pascoli and, 88; Pasolini and, 129, 172n71; Pater and, 51, 183n87; Rocha and, 157, 215n76
modernist studies, 8, 11–12, 165–66n10, 169n52
modernity, 4, 8, 9, 11, 12, 13, 14, 21, 27–28, 32, 42, 50, 62, 69–70, 75, 87–88, 106, 118–20, 128, 134, 137, 158, 168n36, 173n79, 206n73, 207n97
modernization, 4, 8, 16, 17, 20, 23, 32, 67, 82, 119–20, 166n11, 169n52, 172n71, 189n40
Montessori, Maria, 67
Moretti, Franco, 88, 195n31
Morgan, Benjamin, 177n11
Morley, John, 178–79n29
Moten, Fred, 13, 170n62

mother tongue, 91, 195n34, 214n73
Muzak, 107
Musil, Robert, *Confusions of Young Törless*, 88
mure di Sana'a (Pasolini), 120
Mussolini, Benito, 2, 5, 18, 119, 153, 167n30, 216n91

Nacherziehung, 21
nation: in Fascism, 80–81; formation, 67–71, 74–75, 79, 87; in Gentile, 3, 82–83; in Gramsci, 6; in Joyce, 91–92, 100, 102, 107; in Pascoli, 79, 81, 83, 84, 87, 191n79, 192–93n92, 195–96n37; in Pasolini, 20, 119, 135, 174n82; persistence of, 213n61; in Rocha, 216n89; as school, 74–75. *See also* Italy
national language, 191n77
Nealon, Christopher, 175n92
negative capability, 60
negativity, 9–10, 83, 112, 125–26, 156, 169n53, 170n63
neo-colonialism, 142, 159, 216n89
neo-Fascism, 120, 125, 126, 136, 151–53
neoliberalism, 16, 144, 171n67, 175n103
neorealism, 203n27
Nesbit, Molly, 168n34
Ngai, Sianne, 173n76, 175–76n103
non sequitur, 135, 154, 159, 217n93
normativity, 12, 34, 114, 125, 134, 172n69, 173n79, 175n92, 198n70, 207n92. *See also* chrononormativity
nuova gioventù, La (Pasolini), 10

obsolescence, 5, 45, 68, 85, 101, 105, 11, 166n11
Ong, Walter, 207n97
Orff, Carl, 208n102
Orlando, V. E., 69, 82
Oxford, 32, 38, 43, 110, 177–78n18; as Oxenford, 111, 112
outcomes, 1, 58, 160
Ovid, 45

Paedagogium (Pascoli), 9, 17, 62, 63, 74–88, 137, 138, 139, 156, 190n58, 192n87, 192–93n92
paedagogium (Roman institution), 190n55
painting, 115, 129–30, 206nn78–79
palinodes, 122
Pandolfo, Stefania, 12–13, 21, 208n99
Pascoli, Giovanni: reception, 10, 59, 61–62; works: *Il fanciullino*, 10, 59–63, 67, 80, 87, 185n7, 187n20; *Paedagogium*, 9, 17, 62, 63, 74–88, 137, 138, 139, 156, 190n58, 192n87, 192–93n92; "La scuola classica," 81–83; "Pensieri scolastici," 62, 64, 66, 70–75, 79, 81–83, 85, 189n40, 190n55, 192n82; *Primi poemetti*, 61
"Pascoli and the Thought of the Voice" (Agamben), 62, 64–67, 71, 72, 75
Pasolini, Pier Paolo: reception, 10, 115–18, 126–27, 132–33, 136, 200nn2,5–6, 200–1n7, 201nn8–9,13, 206–7n82; works: "Abiura dalla *Trilogia della vita*," 20, 120–22, 124, 125, 129, 133, 144, 174n82, 215n76, 217n94; *Gennariello*, 23, 118; *Il fiore dei Mille e una notte*, 120, 208n3; *Il vangelo secondo Matteo*, 136, 209n8; *Le mure di Sana'a*, 120; *La nuova gioventù*, 10; *La rabbia*, 117; other essays, 187n19, 191n77, 203n31, 205n63, 209n8; *Petrolio*, 124–25, 204n50; *Salò*, 10–11, 13, 17, 21, 23, 114–36, 137, 138, 139, 140, 142, 149, 151, 152, 153, 156, 167n29, 172n71, 200n4, 204n45, 204–5n60, 205nn65,67, 206n78, 208n102, 208–9n3, 209n10, 210n13; *Teorema*, 117; *Trasumanar e organizzar*, 122, 125
Passeron, Jean-Claude, 12
pastiche, 96, 99, 101, 108–10
Pater, Walter: reception, 10, 25, 29, 31–32; as teacher, 38–39; works: "The Child in the House," 34–35, 37, 39–40; "Emerald Uthwart," 26–30, 32, 33, 40, 42, 44, 58, 177n15; *Marius the Epicurean*, 9, 13, 29–31, 33, 35, 37–38, 41, 44–52, 58, 110–11, 138, 139, 156, 179n42, 179–80n43; *Plato and Platonism*, 33, 38–39, 53, 55–58, 184n113; *Studies in the History of the Renaissance*, 10, 25, 28, 29, 31–32, 35–38, 42, 48, 50, 52, 54–55, 58, 179n42, 179–80n43
paternalism, 138, 155
paternity, 94,
Paul, Saint, 64
pedagogy, 3, 5, 7, 18, 19, 29, 51, 67, 102–4, 126, 127, 159, 165n8, 166n11, 217n96. See also counter-progressive pedagogy
Pedagogy of the Oppressed (Freire), 14, 142, 145–46, 151, 153, 155, 159, 211n30, 216n91, 217n96
pedantry, 30, 31–33, 38, 42, 61, 70, 71, 77, 79, 84, 87, 124, 190n58
pederasty, 56, 111
Pellegrini, Ines, 208n
Pensieri (Leopardi), 85–88
"Pensieri scolastici" (Pascoli), 62, 64, 66, 70–75, 79, 81–83, 85, 189n40, 190n55, 192n82
pensums, 14, 17, 98–99, 102, 104, 124, 126, 135, 196nn46–47
Persians, 148, 149, 156
Pertinax, 152, 153
Petrarch, 122
Petrolio (Pasolini), 124–25, 204n50
Phenomenology of Spirit (Hegel), 83, 191n78
Phillips, Adam, 173n76, 217n98
Phillips, James, 144, 146–49, 156
Plato, 48, 53, 54, 55, 56
Plato and Platonism (Pater), 33, 38–39, 53, 55–58, 184n113
poetry, 27, 45, 59–67, 71–80, 87–88, 98, 132, 181n53, 186n12, 196n47, 208n102; lessons, 22, 209n11. See also lyric poetry

policing, 54, 144, 152, 202n24
Pope, Alexander, 34, 40, 181n53
Portrait of the Artist as a Young Man, A (Joyce), 10, 89, 94, 99, 103, 140, 195n34, 199n86
Postone, Moishe, 175–76n103
postcoloniality, 143, 182n79, 198n78, 213n46
postwar period (after World War II), 23, 117, 118–21, 123, 135, 202n24, 203nn28,30, 204–5n60, 215n82
Pound, Ezra, *Cantos*, 208n102
Povinelli, Elizabeth, 194n26
pragmatics (language in use), 41–42, 66, 74
presentism, 23, 84, 126, 175–76n103
Prime of Miss Jean Brodie, The (Spark), 18–19, 173n76
Primi poemetti (Pascoli), 61
Prins, Yopie, 186n12
prison abolition, 79
Prison Notebooks (Gramsci), 3–9, 12, 16, 17, 18, 19, 20, 22–23, 30, 68, 119, 121, 167n28, 170n63, 214–15n73, 216–17n90, 217n95
progress, 3, 7, 9–10, 11, 12, 13, 14, 16, 20, 22–23, 27, 30, 31, 32, 68–71, 79, 83–84, 85–86, 91–92, 106, 107, 108, 113, 115, 118–20, 122, 126, 127, 130–32, 134, 137, 138, 139, 140, 142–43, 165–66n10, 169n54, 175n92, 180n47, 191nn78–79, 195–96n37, 201–2n17, 205n63, 206n73, 212n33
progressive education, 4–5, 7–8, 17, 18–19, 22, 28, 29, 40, 70–71, 93, 101–4, 110–13, 118–19, 126, 127, 146, 156, 159, 165n8, 169n53, 172n68, 197n57, 197–98n68, 216–17n91; defined, 166n11
Protestantism, 50, 183–84n76
psychoanalysis, 20–22, 142. *See also* Freud, Sigmund; Lacan, Jacques; Laplanche, Jean; repetition; transference
Puglia, 127–29

punishment, 10, 14, 17, 19, 39, 56, 77, 79–80, 90, 98–99, 107, 114–15, 135, 138, 156, 196n47, 198n70, 204n46, 207n97
Purgatorio (Dante), 39

queerness, 94–95, 106, 112, 114, 135
queer theory, 21, 22, 132, 175n92, 187n20, 194n17
Quintavalle, Uberto, 201n14

rabbia, La (Pasolini), 117
Rabaté, Jean-Michel, 200n92
Rancière, Jacques, *The Ignorant Schoolmaster*, 21, 175n97
Raphael, 206n78
reaction, 4, 10, 12, 27, 29, 71, 82, 85, 96, 216–17n91
Recalcati, Massimo, 174n88, 174–75n90, 200–1n7, 201n9
recanting, 122
recitation, 19, 22, 26, 31, 36, 37, 39, 40, 52, 58, 77–78, 94, 138, 173n76, 192n92, 199n86, 213n46
Redgrave, Michael, 14–16
regression, 9, 22, 47, 91, 92, 98, 127, 146, 202n19
religion, 27–29, 31, 35–36, 38, 39, 42, 45–46, 49, 77, 106, 140, 168–69n45, 178–79n29, 179n42, 183–84n96 *See also* secularism
repetition, 84, 86, 94; in education, 1–3, 4, 5, 7, 12, 14, 17, 19, 22, 27, 31–33, 36, 39–40, 44, 58, 101–6, 118, 127, 132, 139, 140, 166n11, 171n67, 184n113; in film, 17, 19, 114, 144, 146, 148, 151, 156, 210n15, 213n60, 214nn62,71; in literary form, 4, 14, 23, 91, 95, 98, 100, 112, 173n76; in psychoanalysis, 21–23, 174n89
reproduction, 2, 92, 94, 95, 99–107, 112, 197n65
reproductive futurism, 92, 95, 101, 106
Republic of Salò (1943–1945), 115, 133–34, 201n14

reverse translation, 96–97, 102
revolution, 11, 12, 67, 84, 141–44, 157–58, 203n28
Rhodes, John David, 201n8, 205n64
Ricciardi, Alessia, 116–17, 132, 200nn2,5, 200–1n7
riforma dell'educazione, La (Gentile), 2–9, 12, 16, 18, 19, 21, 22, 23, 81, 97, 99, 104, 112, 118–19, 126, 127, 155, 166nn11–12, 191n79, 191–92n82
Riforma Gentile, 5, 8–9, 16, 82, 119, 165n8, 217n95
ritual, 10, 9, 21, 87–88, 183n96, 179n41, 206n73, 207n97, 207–8n99; in Joyce, 100, 104, 110, 198n69; in Pasolini, 114, 117, 118, 127–30, 134, 135, 137, 138, 205n65, 207–8n99; in Pater, 37, 31, 32, 36, 38, 39, 41, 44, 45, 47, 49–50, 52, 58, 179nn41,42; in Rocha, 138
Rocha, Eryk, *Rocha que voa*, 212n38
Rocha, Glauber: exile, 138, 139–40, 144, 209n9; reception, 140, 211n19; works: "Aesthetics of Hunger," 141–42, 144–45, 149, 157, 159; "Aesthetics of the Dream," 159; *Barravento*, 148; *Claro*, 13, 17, 23, 138–60, 167n29, 211n19, 215n85; *Der Leone Have Sept Cabeças*, 148, 213n46, 216n89; *Deus e o diablo na terra do sol*, 148; *Terra em transe*, 144, 148, 210n15, 212n40, 214n71; "The Tricontinental Filmmaker," 213nn44–45
Romanticism, 11, 12
Rome: ancient, 19–20, 23, 23, 46–47, 50, 51, 52, 80, 81, 85, 111, 137, 140, 141, 144, 146–48, 151–53, 155, 156, 158–60, 210n13; modern, 120, 138, 141, 146, 151–53, 155, 158–60, 209n8, 212n43
Rossellini, Roberto, 153, 213nn46,58,61, 214n65
rote learning, 12, 17, 22, 23, 43, 86, 87, 94, 95, 118, 141, 153, 156, 166n11, 183n89, 209n11
Rousseau, Jean-Jacques, 197nn57,64; *Émile*, 3, 7, 16, 28–30, 35, 99, 101–5, 110, 112, 113, 118, 127, 146, 155–56, 166n11, 167n28, 197n66
ruins, 23, 87, 141, 160, 203n28, 207–8n99
rules, 53, 56, 114, 115, 172n69

Sade, Marquis de, *The 120 Days of Sodom*, 115, 200n3
Sade My Neighbor (Klossowski), 123, 125–26, 104n60
Said, Edward: *Freud and the Non-European*, 213n49; *On Late Style*, 9–10, 12, 213n49
Sallust, 96, 97
Salò (Pasolini), 10–11, 13, 17, 21, 23, 114–36, 137, 138, 139, 140, 142, 149, 151, 152, 153, 156, 167n29, 172n71, 200n4, 204n45, 204–5n60, 205nn65,67, 206n78, 208n102, 208–9n3, 209n10, 210n13
Sanskrit, 81, 83, 137, 168n45
Santner, Eric, 198n70
Sarap, Madan, 165n8
Sartor Resartus (Carlyle), 42–42, 52
Scappettone, Jennifer, 169n52, 172n71
Schreber, Daniel Paul, 198n70
Schreber, Moritz, *Kallipädie*, 198n70
secularism, 32, 168–69n45
self-interest, 1, 3, 17, 22, 113
Sellout, The (Beatty), 209n11
Sembène, Ousmane, *Xala*, 213n64
Septimus Severus, 152–53
Seth, Sanjay, 52, 182n64
sex, 10, 32, 105; in *Salò*, 115–18, 120, 126, 130–35, 140. *See also* homosexuality
Sexton, Jared, 201–2n17, 212n33
Shakespeare, William, 40
Shuman, Cathy, 180n45
Shuter, William F., 32, 177n15
Solanas, Fernando: *La hora de los hornos*, 216n89; "Toward a Third Cinema," 213n44, 216n89
Sontag, Susan, 41
Spackman, Barbara, 80, 136
Spark, Muriel, 173n76; *The Prime of Miss Jean Brodie*, 18–19, 173n76

Sparta, 33, 39, 53–58, 156
Spivak, Gayatri Chakravorty, 8, 167n30, 173n80, 205–6n71
Spoo, Robert, 97, 108, 195n37
stagnation, 7, 12, 101, 140, 146
Steimatsky, Noa, 203n27
Steintrager, James, 123
Stewart-Steinberg, Suzanne, 67–68, 70, 75, 121
Stiegler, Bernard, 174n88
Stockton, Kathryn Bond, 287n20
Stone, J. E., 197n57
Stone, Jennifer, 201n13
Straub, Jean-Marie, *Geschichtsunterricht*, 153, 214n64
Studies in the History of the Renaissance (Pater), 10, 25, 28, 29, 31–32, 35–38, 42, 48, 50, 52, 54–55, 58, 179n42, 179–80n43
study, 5, 6, 9, 26, 69, 81, 86, 87, 93, 94, 109, 136, 170n62, 196n47, 205–6n71, 214–15n73
subalternity, 6, 205–6n71
superstition, 44, 46, 52, 127, 168–69n45
survivals, doctrine of, 20, 21, 42, 44–47, 52, 137, 168–69n45, 183n96, 200n2; in Freud, 201n14
Swift, Jonathan, 40, 181n53, 199n86
Swinburne, Algernon Charles, 25, 176n2, 186n12
Switaj, Elizabeth, 194n25, 195n33

Taormina, 140
tarantismo, 127–29
Tennyson, Alfred, Lord, *In Memoriam*, 36–38
Teorema (Pasolini), 117
Terada, Rei, 121, 201–2n17, 206n77, 209n10, 215nn76,82
terra del rimorso, La (De Martino), 127–29, 130, 134, 206n74, 207–8n99
Terra em transe (Rocha), 144, 148, 210n15, 212n40
Third Cinema. *See* "Toward a Third Cinema"

Third World, 148, 151, 157, 210n15, 213n45, 215n76, 216n89
Third Worldism, 148
Thomas, Edward, 34, 44
Tibullus, 45
Tomšič, Samo, 215n84
Toscano, Gino, 189n40, 190n55
"Toward a Third Cinema" (Getino and Solanas), 213n44, 216n89
tradition, 6–7, 17, 19, 20, 21, 28, 30, 41–42, 47, 56, 61, 68–71, 84–87, 92, 108, 173n79, 175n92, 177n11, 187n19, 194nn16,18
transference (in psychoanalysis), 21, 47, 174n87
translation. *See* reverse translation
Trasumanar e organizzar (Pasolini), 122, 125
Traverso, Enzo, 175–76n103
"Tricontinental Filmmaker" (Rocha), 213nn44–45
Trieste, 2, 3, 109, 166n12, 197n64
Truglio, Maria, 185–86n9, 191n79
Tylor, Edward Burnett, 44–46, 52

Ulysses (Joyce): "Circe," 98, 112, 196nn45–46; "Ithaca," 1–4, 22, 94–95, 193n4; "Lestrygonians," 107; "Nausicaa," 91, 107; "Nestor," 93–95, 97, 193n4; "Oxen of the Sun," 13, 17, 91–113, 114; "Penelope," 95; "Proteus," 107; "Wandering Rocks," 107
United States, 141, 144, 148, 171–72n68, 216–17n91, 217n96
universities, 32, 38, 43, 110, 111, 112, 170n62, 177–78n18
The Unnamable (Beckett), 196n46
Uruguay, 144

Valesio, Paolo, 172n71
Vallejo, César, 11
Il vangelo secondo Matteo (Pasolini), 136, 209n8
vent d'est, Le (Dziga Vertov Group), 210n15

Vergegenwärtigung, 84, 86
Veronica, Saint, 206n79
Vico, Giambattista, 23
Vietnam, 151, 158
Virgil, *Aeneid*, 77, 80, 184n115
voiceover, 144, 155, 210n15, 215n85

Waquet, Françoise, 169n54
Warburg, Aby, 202n19
Warner, Michael, 8
Washington, D.C., 148
waste, 4, 73, 103, 108, 118
Weaver, Harriet Shaw, 98
Weil, Simone, 25, 27
Weinbaum, Alys Eve, 197n65
Wilde, Oscar, 44
Williams, Raymond, 11, 34, 40, 168n45, 182n62
Wilson, Edmund, 108
Winnicott, D. W., 20, 191–92n82
Woolf, Virginia: *Jacob's Room*, 196n47; on *Ulysses*, 89, 93

Wordsworth, William: "Intimations" Ode, 63; "My heart leaps up when I behold," 63; "Nuns fret not," 23, 138; "Preface" to *Lyrical Ballads*, 40; *Prelude*, 62, 63
Wright, Thomas, 34

Xala (Sembène), 213n64
Xavier, Ismail, 210n17, 212n40

Yeats, W. B., 25, 32–33, 34, 40, 166n12, 178n29
Yemen, 120

Zanzotto, Andrea, 201n13
Ziarek, Ewa Płonowska, 183n87
Zibaldone (Leopardi), 61, 185n4
Zupančič, Alenka, 216n88
Zurich, 2

Ramsey McGlazer is Lecturer in Italian and Comparative Literature at the University of St Andrews.

Sara Guyer and Brian McGrath, series editors

Sara Guyer, *Reading with John Clare: Biopoetics, Sovereignty, Romanticism.*

Philippe Lacoue-Labarthe, *Ending and Unending Agony: On Maurice Blanchot.* Translated by Hannes Opelz.

Emily Rohrbach, *Modernity's Mist: British Romanticism and the Poetics of Anticipation.*

Marc Redfield, *Theory at Yale: The Strange Case of Deconstruction in America.*

Jacques Khalip and Forest Pyle (eds.), *Constellations of a Contemporary Romanticism.*

Daniel M. Stout, *Corporate Romanticism: Liberalism, Justice, and the Novel.*

Kristina Mendicino, *Prophecies of Language: The Confusion of Tongues in German Romanticism.*

Jaime Rodríguez Matos, *Writing of the Formless: José Lezama Lima and the End of Time.*

Geoffrey Bennington, *Kant on the Frontier: Philosophy, Politics, and the Ends of the Earth.*

Frédéric Neyrat, *Atopias: Manifesto for a Radical Existentialism.* Translated by Walt Hunter and Lindsay Turner, Foreword by Steven Shaviro.

Jacques Khalip, *Last Things: Disastrous Form from Kant to Hujar.*

Jacques Lezra, *On the Nature of Marx's Things: Translation as Necrophilology.* Foreword by Vittorio Morfino.

Jean-Luc Nancy, *Portrait.* Translated by Sarah Clift and Simon Sparks, Foreword by Jeffrey S. Librett.

Karen Swann, *Lives of the Dead Poets: Keats, Shelley, Coleridge.*

Ramsey McGlazer, *Old Schools: Modernism, Education, and the Critique of Progress.*

www.ingramcontent.com/pod-product-compliance
Lightning Source LLC
Chambersburg PA
CBHW020107020526
44112CB00033B/1078